The Spain of the Catholic Mor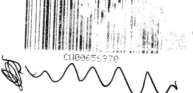

History of Spain

Published

Forthcoming

The Spain of the Catholic Monarchs 1474–1520

John Edwards

First published 2000

2 4 6 8 10 9 7 5 3 1

Blackwell Publishers Ltd
108 Cowley Road
Oxford OX4 1JF
UK

Blackwell Publishers Inc.
350 Main Street
Malden, Massachusetts 02148
USA

British Library Cataloguing in Publication Data

A CIP catalogue record for this book is available from the British Library.

Library of Congress Cataloging-in-Publication Data

Edwards, John, 1949-
    The Spain of the Catholic Monarchs, 1474–1520 / John Edwards.
        p. cm. — (A history of Spain)
    Includes bibliographical references and index.
    ISBN 0–631–16165-1 (hardcover : alk. paper) — ISBN 0–631–22143–3 (pbk. : alk. paper)
    1. Spain – Civilization – 711–1516. 2. Spain — History — Ferdinand and Isabella,
1479–1516. I. Title. II. Series.
    DP164 .E39 2000
    946'.03 – dc21   00-009574

Typeset in 10.5 on 12pt Sabon
by Kolam Information Services Pvt Ltd
Printed in Great Britain by Biddles, Guildford
This book is printed on acid-free paper

Contents

For Roger Highfield

Maps and Plates

Preface

On 22 April 1451, in Madrigal de las Altas Torres, a daughter was born to Isabella of Portugal, queen of Castile, and to her husband John II. Nearly a year later, on 10 March 1452, Princess Isabella's husband-to-be, Ferdinand, was born in Sos, an Aragonese town near the border with Navarre, the son of a Castilian noblewoman, Juana Enríquez, and her husband John II of Aragon and Catalonia. After many twists of fortune, the couple were married, at the ages of eighteen and seventeen, respectively, and after even more troubles and manoeuvres, they became rulers of both Castile and Aragon. The era of Ferdinand and Isabella, who were labelled 'Catholic Kings' (*Reyes Católicos*) on 19 December 1496, by Pope Alexander VI, had some genuinely remarkable features, and many more have been identified or imagined by subsequent scholars, and admirers of Spain, as well as some Spaniards. During the civil war of 1936–9, General Francisco Franco not only described his forces' rebellion against the Second Republic as a 'crusade', but claimed to model his crushing of Basque and Catalan nationalism on the 'unifying' efforts of Ferdinand and Isabella. After the war, he adopted their personal emblems, the yoke and arrow, for his new 'Movement' (*Movimiento*), which was the sole legal political organization in Spain between then and his death, in 1975, and placed their coat of arms on the national flag.[1] Closely connected with Franco's use of the 'Catholic Monarchs' as a model was the support for this view of many circles in the Catholic Church, which focused particularly on the devotional life of Isabella. A cause for her canonization as a saint of the Roman Church is still pursued by some. Yet against this positive story is set another, which is blacker and less salubrious. In Spain itself, after Franco's death and the subsequent restoration of democracy, the study of the reign of Ferdinand and Isabella, which had previously attracted some of the country's finest historians, whose work is reflected in the pages which follow, fell under something of a cloud. Another crisis for the Catholic Monarchs' reputation arrived in 1992, when some of their more questionable achievements were elaborately, and exhaustingly, commemorated. Five hundred years before, on 2 January 1492, Isabella and Ferdinand had marched into Granada as conquerors, thus ending nearly eight hundred years of Muslim rule in the Iberian peninsula. On 31 March of that year, they had issued edicts for the forced expulsion or conversion of the Jews of Castile and Aragon. On 12 October, Christopher Columbus, under the patronage of the Spanish sovereigns, sighted land in the Caribbean, and began Spain's long and often tortured relationship with the American continent. While some celebrated in 1992, Muslims, Jews and native Americans did not. The present king, Don Juan Carlos, made public apology for the failings of Christian Spaniards at that time and subsequently. Whatever their failings, among which the two rulers' revival of the Inquisition must be counted, Ferdinand and Isabella undoubtedly took Spain a long way towards status as not only a European but a world power. Yet there is still a marked reluctance, in the English-speaking world, to investigate and attempt to understand the internal history and character of the country which, under Habsburg rule, was to intervene so forcefully, and sometimes disastrously, in the affairs of others. Given the extent to which the history of Spain, at least since the Middle Ages, has been interlocked with that of other European countries, including England, such a failing is hard to excuse, despite the continuing power of the 'Black Legend'. Research done, by Spaniards and others, in recent decades, is serving to fill this lacuna.

Situated on the frontier between the 'medieval' and the 'modern', in terms of the history of Europe and its outposts in other continents, the reign of the Catholic Monarchs has its own peculiar fascination. This particular author, who was already drawn to the fifteenth and sixteenth centuries in general, and to Spain in particular, was inducted in the study of Ferdinand and Isabella by the teaching and supervision of Roger Highfield, to whom this work is dedicated with gratitude. Historians of Spain tend, perhaps by the very neglect of their subject both within academic precincts and outside them, to be an individualistic bunch, in whom the normal virtues and vices of researchers and teachers are writ large. Roger is not of that ilk, and this writer is profoundly appreciative of that. Another feature of those who venture into what is still seen by some, with false perspective, as a 'small' subject is a mixture of excitement, warmth and generosity, which is duly acknowledged here. Many people have been companions and guides on the way, and it is hoped that those who are not individually named will nonetheless be assured that their help and friendship is fully appreciated. In Britain, a special debt is owed to Angus MacKay, as a scholar and companion. In Spain, the writer of this treatment of the reign of

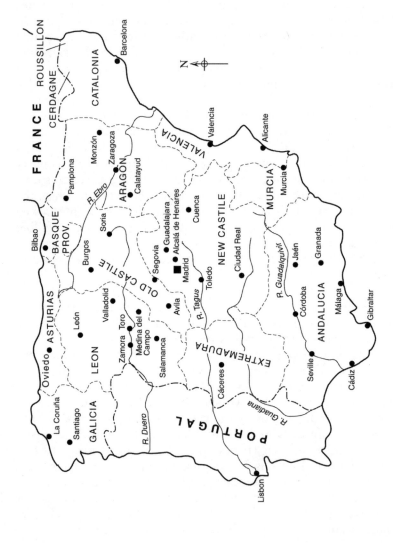

Map 1 Spain 1469–1714, based on John Edwards, *The monarchies of Ferdinand and Isabella* (Historical Association pamphlet), p. 4.

Ferdinand and Isabella owes a huge debt to another who has published on this subject, Miguel Angel Ladero Quesada, for his learning, his support, his humour and his friendship over many years. Some may notice, in the following pages, a certain tendency to linger on the affairs of Andalusia in general, and Córdoba in particular. Apart from the significance of the city of the Caliphs in the events of the reign, this emphasis also acknowledges personal debts, to Manuel Nieto Cumplido, and above all to Emilio Cabrera Muñoz, a companion and friend of many years' standing, who, with his family, provides a home from home. Thanks are also offered, for companionship, debate and resources, to past and present members of The Queen's College, Oxford, the former School of History of the University of Birmingham, and the Casa de Velázquez in Madrid. The production of this work has been greatly assisted by the patience, as well as the advice and support, of John Lynch, who as editor of the series gave encouragement at a crucial stage, and Tessa Harvey, for Blackwell. Finally, it is customary, at this stage, to thank one's production editor. In the case of Louise Spencely, these thanks are no device of rhetoric, but heartfelt.

Oxford, May 2000

1

The War of the Castilian Succession

The war fought between Castile and Portugal, from the spring of 1475 until peace was finally made in 1479, has been variously described by historians of differing periods and national perspectives. For William Prescott, it was an evidently foolish war, from the Portuguese point of view, and was to be ascribed to Prince John of Portugal's 'impetuosity and the ambition or avarice of his father', Afonso V. Peter Russell has characterized it as 'perhaps the most frivolous of all the wars ever waged by the Portuguese Crown'. There is, in any case, no doubt that the Portuguese threat was a real one to Castile and its new queen, and that it had significance for the rest of Spain too. As John Elliott has observed, 'the war was much more than a dispute over the debatable legal claims of two rival princesses to the crown of Castile. Its outcome was likely to determine the whole future political orientation of Spain.' Because of external involvement, particularly from Louis XI's France, it also had implications for the balance of power in the west of the continent. Henry Kamen, while observing a rapid return, in 1475, to the 'anarchy' of the preceding reigns of John II and Henry IV of Castile, says nothing about Portuguese motives in the conflict, while Joseph Perez rightly points out that 'the Catholic Monarchs needed five years definitively to assure themselves of power'. Tarsicio de Azcona goes so far as to suggest that the political and constitutional upheavals in Castile would have led to civil war even if Afonso V had never claimed the kingdom's throne. How and why, then, did the Portuguese invasion of Castile in 1475 pose such a threat to Ferdinand and Isabella's brand-new regime, and in whose interest did it take place?[1]

The kingdom of Portugal was the first to settle its boundaries definitively, in and shortly after 1238, during the rapid advance of the Christian 'Reconquest' which brought the authority of Castile into western Andalusia (the later provinces of Jaén, Córdoba, Seville and Cádiz), and that of the king of Aragon and count of Barcelona into Valencia. In the mid-fifteenth century, the kings of Castile ruled over about two-thirds of Iberian land and its population, while their Portuguese equivalents had only a quarter of these resources. In addition, the very success of the thirteenth-century conquest of the Portuguese Algarve, which brought Christian rule to the southern coast, had forced the kingdom's rulers to look elsewhere for further expansion. This reaction famously took the form of overseas exploration, and a battle for independence from neighbouring Castile. These activities, together with a search for a continuing alliance with England from the later fourteenth century onwards, could and did not prevent further and close dynastic involvement with the other main royal houses of the Peninsula. Thus, not only were Ferdinand and Isabella descendants of the same Trastamaran house, but Isabella had a Portuguese mother, also named Isabella, who was the daughter of Constable John of Portugal, while her brother Henry's second wife, Joanna, was Portuguese as well, and the daughter of the late King Edward (Duarte). The ensuing conflict, which was to occupy much of the first five years of Ferdinand and Isabella's joint reign in Castile, partook both of the peculiar venom and of the potential for sudden reconciliation which are characteristic of family quarrels. While no doubt has ever been shed on the legitimacy of the birth of Isabella, or that of her younger brother Alfonso, the same could not be said of her older half-brother Henry, or of his proclaimed daughter Joanna. In the very first chapter of his history of the lives and reigns of Henry IV, Isabella and Ferdinand, written in Latin on the model of Livy's history of Rome and given the same title of *Decades* (see chapter 8), Alfonso de Palencia (1424–92) claimed that a rumour was circulating to the effect that Prince Henry was not in fact the son of his supposed father. This appears not to have directly affected the prince's subsequent career, but the case of princess Joanna was to prove much more grave and portentous.[2]

While most significant events associated with the Castilian monarchy were surrounded by ceremony, the same did not unfortunately apply to the conception of Joanna, which seems to have taken place in or about April 1461. In almost all historical works, whether specialized or general, the name of the princess has attached to it the sobriquet 'La Beltraneja'. The message contained in this nickname, which was freely used by opponents both of Henry and of Joanna, was that the girl's mother may indeed have been Queen Joanna of Portugal, but that her father was not the king, but rather a scion of the Castilian nobility, Beltrán de la Cueva. Unusually, in the case of royal children, even the exact date of Joanna's birth is not known. The writer, diplomat, and bishop of Oviedo, Rodrigo Sánchez de Arévalo, still made no mention of the event in a letter written from Rome on 15 February 1462, but on 9 April of that year, he preached a sermon in St Peter's 'in action of grace for the birth of the first-born of Henry IV'. At home, the Castilian cortes met in Madrid and, on 9 May 1462, swore allegiance to Joanna as her father's heir. In the following month, the king instructed the cities of the kingdom to follow suit. The prime suspect as Joanna's father, in the eyes of the opposition to Henry's regime, Beltrán de la Cueva, undoubtedly had circumstantial opportunity to commit the act. He had been in the king's service since 1456, being rapidly promoted, in the following year, to the politically important post of royal steward (*mayordomo*), and by 1462 was definitely a member of the inner circle at court. Whatever the truth concerning the infant Joanna's parentage, immediately after the cortes of Madrid of that year, where the leading churchmen and secular magnates swore allegiance to the princess, a campaign began to replace Henry with Alfonso as king of Castile. Important parts of this effort were to be the discrediting of Henry's second marriage and accusations that he was either homosexual, or impotent, or both.[3]

Long before the military conflict which followed Isabella's occupation of the Castilian throne, Henry had already been involved, in marital matters, with Afonso V of Portugal. On 15 September 1440, the then prince of Asturias had been married to Blanche (Blanca) of Navarre, an alliance which lasted more than twelve years. The couple failed to produce offspring and, on 11 May 1453, sitting in his episcopal court, Bishop Luis Vázquez de Acuña of Segovia annulled the marriage and decreed a separation. For the first time, sexual impotence was associated with Henry, but this was attributed to black magic (*maleficio*). Even before he was freed from his ties to his Navarrese/ Aragonese bride and close relative, Blanche, Henry had gone to Evora, in Portugal, in March 1453, to visit king Afonso, and ask for the hand of his sister Joanna. Once again, as with virtually all Trastamaran marriages, there was consanguinity, within the third and second degrees, but the Portuguese king blessed the match, and, on 1 December 1453, Pope Nicholas V issued the bull *Romanus pontifex*, in which he gave the necessary dispensation for Henry's second marriage and also accepted the finding of the bishop of Segovia's court, that the infertility of the prince's first marriage, to Blanche of Navarre, was caused by witchcraft. After this, the accusation of sexual impotence against Henry refused to go away, even though it was officially ascribed to external factors. Not only was this charge to blight the life of the unfortunate Princess Joanna, but it was also to exacerbate the problem of consanguinity, which was common at the time to royal marriages throughout Europe. The supporters of princess Isabella were not interested in the pope's legal distinctions, and after the Segovia 'coup' of December 1474, Henry's supposed inadequacies were used to provide a moral and legal basis for the new regime. A fine example of the genre is the *converso* chronicler Fernando del Pulgar's 'portrait' of the king in his collection entitled *Claros varones de Castilla* ('Famous men of Castile').

> While a prince, he married the lady Blanche, to whom he was married for the space of ten years, and in the end they were divorced for childlessness, which he blamed on her and she on him...While his first wife, from whom he was separated, was still living, he married someone else, a daughter of the king of Portugal, and in this second marriage, his impotence was made manifest. Because although he was married to her for fifteen years, and had communication with other women, he never succeeded in any manly function *(allegamiento de varón)*.[4]

Nevertheless, it was Pulgar's predecessor as official royal chronicler of Castile, Alfonso de Palencia, who provided the most vivid and hostile account of Henry's physique and character. For him, the king's supposed personal and moral decline was directly linked to the history of his kingdom. It began, in this account, with his corruption, as a child and youth, by various courtiers, and in particular Juan Pacheco, marquis of Villena, who infected him with the 'vice of the vicious'.[5] Even before the birth of Joanna, in 1462, tension had been rising, both within the ranks of the Castilian upper nobility and between certain magnates and the king. In particular, there was already a conflict between the royal favourite, Beltrán de la Cueva, and Juan Pacheco. One issue in question was the place of residence and custody of Henry IV's half-brother and sister, Alfonso and Isabella. This matter assumed pressing importance because of supposed doubts in some ambitious political circles about the king's governmental competence, the main centre of opposition being Pacheco, who saw the prince and princess as pawns in his private power game. Henry's subsequent reputation for pusillanimity appears to gain substance from the fact that he failed to nip the potential Pacheco rebellion in the bud. On 11 December 1464, a joint committee of two royal and two rebel representatives, under the presidency of the general of the Jeronymite order of friars, Alonso de Oropesa, began its deliberations on the future governance of the kingdom. The result of the arbitrators' work was a 'sentence', which was issued at Medina del Campo, on 16 January 1465. In over a hundred clauses, the so-called 'sentence of arbitration' effectively conceded all the rebels' demands and placed severe restrictions on the monarch's role in government. The Medina del Campo 'sentence' meant that Henry had virtually surrendered to Pacheco's 'League' but, with the treacherous encouragement of Archbishop Carrillo of Toledo, he rejected the judgement of the 'arbitrators' and attempted to fight back. The reaction of Pacheco and his allies was forceful, to say the least. Its first public manifestation was a spectacular and macabre ceremony, the so-called 'Farce of Avila', which took place outside the eastern wall of Avila, on 5 June 1465, and consisted of the 'deposition' of Henry IV in effigy, and the crowning of Prince Alfonso in person. Alfonso 'XII', as he was known to his supporters, 'reigned', as 'the ghost of a sovereign' in the eyes of his enemies, for just over three years, until he was taken ill on 2 July 1468, at Cardeñosa, near Avila, and died three days later. His death was said to be due either to a fever or to an infected fish pie or a trout, which some said had been deliberately poisoned by agents of the marquis of Villena.[6]

When civil war broke out in Castile in 1465, Isabella had duly received from Henry, in accordance with the arbitration of Medina del Campo, a small household, with Gonzalo Chacón as its steward, and the support of *juros* from the steadily depleting royal exchequer. She was also granted seigneurial jurisdiction over Trujillo and Casarrubios del Monte. Faced with growing, and potentially overwhelming, opposition within his own kingdom, Henry sought the aid of Portugal. No doubt with the benefit of hindsight conferred by the consequences of Isabella's subsequent marriage with Ferdinand of Aragon, the authors of general histories and biographies tend to gloss over the significance of Henry's difficulties between 1465 and 1468 for future relations between Castile and its western neighbour. Yet until the knot was secretly tied between the future Catholic Kings in 1469, Afonso V of Portugal was a serious suitor for Isabella's hand. The failure of his attempts was to give the Portuguese king a reason for personal rancour towards Queen Isabella, long before her disputed accession to the Castilian throne. In the Portuguese town of Guarda on 12 September 1465, King Afonso agreed to marry Isabella, and to assist Henry in his struggle with dissident members of the Castilian aristocracy. The king's half-sister succeeded in avoiding this marriage, but was then faced, in April 1466, with an equally unacceptable suitor, Juan Pacheco's brother Pedro Girón, who was then a forty-three-year-old widower. With the marquis's support, Pedro offered Henry 3000 cavalry and 60,000 gold *doblas* to assist him against their supposed protégé, Alfonso. Later believers in the beneficence of Divine Providence and in the manifest destiny of Castile to rule both Spain and the world saw evidence for their faith in these articles, and of the efficacy of Isabella's own prayers, in Girón's sudden death, which was ascribed at the time to a throat infection and took place while he was travelling to meet his potential bride in Madrid. Despite this setback, in 1467 the fortunes of Juan Pacheco and his allies were at their height. In that year, John II of Navarre and Aragon proposed to the marquis that his son and heir, Prince Ferdinand, should marry Pacheco's daughter Beatriz and, in

Plate 1   Portarait of Isabella, Queen of Castile (1451–1504), artist unknown.
Courtesy of the Royal Collection Picture Library, © HM Queen Elizabeth II

Plate 2 Portrait of Ferdinand II, King of Aragon (1452–1516), artist unknown
Courtesy of the Royal Collection Picture Library, © HM Queen Elizabeth II

Hillgarth's phrase, 'Villena and his family were almost kings.' Alfonso 'XII''s sudden death, on 5 July 1468, was to change the situation once again, and demand new thought and action from Isabella. To begin with, the seventeen-year-old princess took Archbishop Carrillo's advice and attempted to succeed Alfonso in pursuing a claim to the Castilian throne, but it soon became apparent that her half-brother Henry would not easily be defeated. He had the continuing support of the Papacy as well as that of the new general of the prestigious Jeronymite order, Alonso de Oropesa; the symbolic 'capital of Castile' (*cabeza de Castilla*) of Burgos returned to him, as did increasing numbers of the nobility; and other towns remained neutral, awaiting the outcome. Significantly, from 17 July 1468, he also had the official support of an institution which was later to be a bastion of Isabella and Ferdinand's regime, the *Hermandad* (brotherhood). The city of Seville actually proclaimed Isabella queen at this time, and, with Avila and other towns still in her possession, she had the power to mount a plausible claim to the throne, but by September 1468 this had been abandoned. Yet while Isabella was now willing to accept Henry as king, she appeared to have accepted rebel propaganda by refusing to acknowledge the six-year-old Joanna as his legitimate daughter, and hence his heir. She also began to style herself as heir to the throne in written documents. Henry assured his wife, Joanna of Portugal, on 25 August of that year, that he would do nothing to prejudice either the queen herself or the young Princess Joanna's right to succeed him. By this time, Isabella was seeking a compromise and, on 18 September 1468, she and the king began a week-long meeting at the roadside inn (*venta*) of Los Toros de Guisando, near Avila, in an open field outside a nearby Jeronymite friary, and close to the eponymous ancient carved bulls.

It was evident to all bystanders and commentators that Isabella was engaged in establishing a claim to rule, but first, the rebels had to receive forgiveness from Henry for their disloyalty before and during the 'reign' of Alfonso 'XII'. Yet once again the two main noble leaders disagreed. Archbishop Carrillo did not wish Isabella to make an agreement with her half-brother, while Pacheco was eager to do so, and hence regain all the benefits of royal patronage which he had lost, and in particular effective possession of the mastership of Santiago. In the event, the marquis of Villena's view prevailed, and Archbishop Carrillo led Isabella to the meeting at Guisando, walking beside her mule and leading it, in a conspicuous demonstration of her regal status. The surviving accounts of the meeting were written later and with evident hindsight, but there is no real doubt concerning the two main items of business which were transacted. First, Isabella and her supporters submitted to Henry as their sovereign, and secondly, the king recognized Isabella as his legitimate heir. While not admitting the claim of the former rebels that he was not in fact the father of Princess Joanna, Henry did accept the specious argument that his own marriage to her mother, Joanna of Portugal, had taken place without the necessary papal bull of dispensation for consanguinity, with the result that his daughter was not legitimate in terms of canon law, and therefore could not inherit the Crown. As well as giving orders that Isabella should be sworn in as heir to the throne, Henry granted her the lordship of the economically crucial town of Medina del Campo, which had, ironically, been the scene of his humiliation in the 'arbitration' of 1465. She also received the jurisdiction over Avila, Alcaraz, Escalona, Molina and the principate of Asturias, which was normally granted in such circumstances. Crucially, it was also agreed that Isabella's marriage would not take place without the agreement of the king, as well as leading members of the nobility. Unsurprisingly, the pact of the Toros de Guisando did not lead to peace in the kingdom. The deep division between the old noble sparring-partners was demonstrated at once, with Pacheco joining Henry at Court while Carrillo stayed with Isabella, working to distance her from the king, and at the same time steering her in the direction of his Aragonese friends, including John II himself. In the long run, the archbishop was to gain the most from this situation. After the meeting at Los Toros de Guisando, Isabella spent some time with her half-brother, at Ocaña, but she soon found the atmosphere at Court stifling, and withdrew to Madrigal de las Altas Torres, under the protection of Carrillo. Marriage was now at the top of her agenda.

The circumstances in which Isabella came to marry Ferdinand of Aragon have constituted another temptation to those with an inclination to see Providence at work in history. The story has many of the ingredients of a romance, including apparently overwhelming political and personal obstacles, a secret journey, by night and in disguise, and a narrow escape from death for the bridegroom. Afonso of Portugal had already thrown his cap into the ring in 1465, but the eligibility of Isabella in the European matrimonial stakes was greatly enhanced when Henry recognized her as his legal heir under the gaze of the stone bulls of Guisando. In a fairly desperate situation in the previous year, John II of Aragon had effectively offered his son to all comers, and first to the marquis of Villena's daughter, but Isabella became his target as soon as 'King' Alfonso died. England produced a potential suitor in the form of a brother of Edward IV, probably Richard, duke of Gloucester, the future Richard III, while Louis XI's brother, Charles, duke of Berry, who was to become duke of Guyenne in 1469 and was at the time heir to the French throne, was also a candidate. Juan Pacheco and

Carrillo took opposing views, in this as in other matters, with the marquis proposing first the Portuguese king and then the French heir, either of whom would, as he evidently intended, have taken Isabella out of Castilian politics. The archbishop, on the other hand, resolutely pursued the Aragonese marriage with the potential bridegroom's father. King Henry himself favoured the French or the Portuguese alliance, either of which appeared to assist his own political interests. He was to prove particularly reluctant to abandon the Portuguese option, which also involved the marriage of young Joanna to the Portuguese king's son John. While she was still at his Court in Ocaña, Isabella, on the other hand, expressed her absolute determination not to marry Afonso of Portugal, despite threats from the king that she would be imprisoned in the Alcázar of Madrid if she did not do so. Once she reached Madrigal, and was under the tutelage of Archbishop Carrillo, she also rejected the blandishments of the cardinal of Albi, Jean Jouffroy, on behalf of Charles of France, although this was done with such finesse that the seasoned ecclesiastical diplomat seems to have gone home with the delusion that he had been successful. With the French candidature effectively over, and since the English suit seems not to have been effectively pursued, the only remaining candidate was Ferdinand of Aragon. The 'hereditary princess', to use her contemporary style, seems to have made her definite choice in January 1469. In their evident anxiety to see the betrothal go through, John II and his son signed a preliminary marriage agreement on 7 January. John and Ferdinand's speed and anticipation in drawing up this document seem to have been due to Carrillo's urging. In the event, however, the next few months placed Isabella in the midst of two opposing campaigns, one successfully orchestrated by the archbishop, with the aim of marrying her to the Aragonese heir, who was then king of Sicily, and the other undertaken by Henry, at Pacheco's urging, to tie her to Afonso of Portugal.

All available evidence suggests that the Portuguese monarch's suit had no chance of success at the personal level. He was too old, already had a grown-up son, and was thought unlikely to be able to produce an heir in a new marriage. The main problem, however, was that the Castilian and the Portuguese Courts both intended that Prince John of Portugal should marry Isabella's rival Joanna, which would have consigned the older princess to political outer darkness. It is evident that Henry's half-sister was by this time absolutely determined to gain the Castilian crown for herself, and saw marriage to Ferdinand as the best, if not the only, way of achieving this. The Aragonese king, John II, threatened from within by both urban and rural rebellion in Catalonia and from without by the ambitions of Louis XI of France and Henry IV of Castile, was equally anxious that the couple should tie the knot. He was greatly encouraged in this by his queen, Juana Enríquez, and her Castilian noble family, which at this time dominated the Castilian royal administrative centre of Valladolid, and was also in close alliance with Archbishop Carrillo. Despite his apparent desirability, both personally and politically, there was, however, fear in the minds of Isabella and her advisers that Ferdinand would seek to wield excessive power in Castile. The marriage agreement, signed in Cervera on 5 March 1469, addressed this potential problem. Among other things, the Aragonese prince thereby agreed to observe the *fueros*, uses and customs of Castile, and to reside permanently in the kingdom with his wife, the fear being that he would otherwise continue to concentrate on the multifarious duties and complications which had up to then come his way in the far-flung territories of the crown of Aragon. In the Cervera agreement, Ferdinand also swore to take no political or military action in Castile without Isabella's consent, and not to give any office or power in the kingdom to 'foreigners', by which was evidently meant Aragonese or Catalans. Ominously for the couple's future freedom of action, if realistically in view of the current political balance in Castile, Ferdinand was further constrained to undertake that he would at all times submit to the judgement of the nobility in political matters. The prince obliged himself to surrender to his future spouse, as a marriage portion (*arras*), various possessions of the Aragonese crown, including Borja, Magallón, Tarrasa, Sabadell, Elche, Crevillente, and the queen's chamber in Syracuse in Sicily. The Aragonese were to make an immediate payment of 20,000 gold florins as well as handing over a necklace of rubies, which had been pawned by Queen Juana Enriquez to the councillors (*jurats*) of Valencia in return for a loan to her husband. In addition, 100,000 gold florins were to be paid to Castile within four months of the consummation of the marriage, and despite their inability to meet their existing commitments, the Aragonese undertook to provide 4000 lances to serve in the neighbouring kingdom in time of need. In this way, Ferdinand effectively undertook to become a mercenary (*condottiere*) in the service of Henry's aristocratic enemies in Castile, as well as that of his future wife. All depended, of course, on Isabella's ability to put her decision into effect, but once this had become evident, a canonical impediment had once again to be overcome before the couple could marry. The prospective partners were related within the forbidden degrees, in this case the third, and therefore required a papal dispensation. The reigning pope, Pius II, was however a supporter of the legitimate sovereign, Henry, and no friend to the Aragonese crown, so that there was little prospect of the issue of the appropriate bull. Isabella's supporters counteracted this by winning over the papal legate to Spain, who would in due course provide a solution.

In the meantime, though, king Henry and his adviser Pacheco continued to pursue their aim of marrying Isabella to Afonso of Portugal and Joanna to his son John. Negotiations reached the stage of a formal agreement between Henry and Afonso, dated 30 April 1469, for the Portuguese king's marriage to Isabella, which was to take place within two months of his arrival in Castile for the purpose. If Isabella did not agree to this, she and her supporters were to be declared outlaws, and war was to be undertaken against them. Afonso was to be allowed to enter the kingdom with 2000 cavalry and 3000 infantry, which were to be paid their wages by Henry for three months. Once they had been married through representatives (*por palabras de presente*), Afonso was to be styled 'prince of Castile and León', and 'prince of Asturias', and might retain these titles for life, even if children were born to the couple. Any such children were to be brought up entirely in Castile, and all the officers of the couple's household were to be Castilians. After Henry's death, the couple would reign in Castile, and, if Isabella died first, Afonso would continue as ruler alone, until any children of the marriage inherited the throne. Realistically in the circumstances, though perhaps remarkably in the context of such a document, Henry's draft marriage agreement with Afonso also contained a reserve plan, in case the latter's marriage with Isabella did not go ahead within two months, presumably because it had been thwarted by the machinations of Carrillo and the Aragonese. In this event, Joanna was to be substituted as Afonso's queen, the Portuguese king thereby acquiring the title of 'prince of Castile' as in plan 'A'. If Afonso did marry Joanna by 30 July 1469, according to plan 'B', Henry would hand over to him, as pledges, the strategically important border towns of Badajoz and Ciudad Rodrigo, and the two kings would join together in a war against Isabella and her supporters. It is evident that Henry, caught between the commitments to Isabella into which he had entered at Guisando, and his natural desire (for so it appears) to secure the interests of his daughter Joanna, was prepared to enter, whichever marriage took place, into an arrangement which was grossly disadvantageous to Castile. The Portuguese king was to be allowed to march into the kingdom with a significant military force, he was to be handed on a plate two important frontier towns, he was to receive a dowry of 30,000 Castilian *doblas* with his wife, whether it were Isabella or Joanna, and even the required papal dispensation in either case was to be obtained at Henry's expense.

It is also worth noting, in view of subsequent events, that at this stage the Castilian king evidently still treated Joanna as a possible and legitimate heir to the throne, despite her apparent marginalization at Guisando. One of the more remarkable features of the draft marriage agreement of 30 April 1469 was that, if Afonso and Isabella had been married under plan 'A' for five years, and had produced a son, the child was to be married to Joanna. Although this document became hypothetical, as a result of subsequent events, it nonetheless illustrates the alternative strategies which Henry was pursuing in the months before Isabella ended such discussion by marrying her prince, Ferdinand of Aragon. The king and Pacheco were probably well aware of her intentions by the time they went to Andalusia in May 1469, even though the princess seems to have given a self-evidently false undertaking at this time that she would not marry without Henry's permission.[7]

While the Castilian monarch was vainly pursuing the Portuguese option, the Aragonese appeared to accept, with an alacrity born of desperation, the demanding and in some cases wholly unrealistic conditions of the Cervera agreement of earlier in the year. Two obstacles remained: a dispensation for the marriage had to be obtained from the pope, and Ferdinand and Isabella had somehow to meet. Henry's opposition meant that the latter aim could not be achieved openly, while the pope's continuing support for the Castilian king made the issuing of the required document highly unlikely. In the event, both problems were solved by subterfuge. In the case of the dispensation, the then papal legate in Spain, Antonio Veneris, was persuaded to forge a bull which purported to have been issued by Pope Pius II on 18 May 1464, allowing Ferdinand to marry an unnamed woman who was within the third degree of relationship to him. This just happened to be the nature of his relationship with Isabella, and the marriage went ahead on this entirely false legal basis. The problem of bringing the couple face to face was solved somewhat melodramatically, and soon gave rise to legend. In mid-May 1469, Isabella left Ocaña semi-secretly, ostensibly to visit relatives. Under the protection of Archbishop Carrillo's troops, she went to Valladolid, a town under the effective control of Fadrique Enríquez, admiral of Castile, who was Ferdinand's maternal grandfather. The princess stayed in the house of Juan de Vivero, whose wife was also an Enríquez. At this point, John II of Aragon confirmed the marriage agreement and, as tokens of his good faith, delivered to her a pearl necklace worth 40,000 ducats and 20,000 gold florins. Nevertheless, during the summer, Isabella's situation still seemed so precarious and uncertain that even her close friend and attendant Beatriz de Bobadilla abandoned her. On 8 September 1469, she wrote a letter to Henry, in which she affected to justify her actions but effectively broke her relations with him. It was at this point that the Aragonese marriage plan went ahead. Isabella sent two agents secretly to the neighbouring kingdom, to meet Ferdinand and bring him to her, preferably before Henry and Pacheco returned from the south. One of these agents was the chronicler Alfonso de Palencia and the other was her retainer Gutierre de Cárdenas, and they quickly discovered that Beatriz de Bobadilla was not the only one among Isabella's supporters to have changed sides during the summer. In particular, the Mendoza family had returned to Henry's allegiance, thus placing between Ferdinand and his prospective spouse a formidable line of frontier castles and forts stretching from Almazán to Guadalajara. At the end of September, Palencia and Cárdenas reached Zaragoza, where they met the Aragonese heir, and king of Sicily, in a Franciscan convent. John II hesitated up to the last moment, but agreed at the beginning of October to risk his son and heir in a surreptitious expedition to Castile. On the fifth of the month, Ferdinand set out very publicly from Zaragoza in an easterly direction, but soon doubled back. For once, a major historian was not only an eye witness but a participant in an important event. Palencia reports that the party, which had no military protection, masqueraded as a group of merchants with their servants. The prince, who had taken six of his own men with him, acted as one of the servants, serving meals and looking after the mules. At nightfall on 7 October, the group arrived in the Castilian border town of Burgo de Osma, where the subsequent history both of Spain and of the rest of Europe was nearly drastically and unexpectedly altered. Although the town was friendly, it had not been warned of the Aragonese prince's imminent arrival. The party's disguise was so effective that it was taken for a band of intruders and subjected to a volley of stones, one of which nearly cracked Ferdinand's skull. The true identity of the visitors was recognized in time, however, and Gómez Manrique, who was subsequently to be a faithful supporter of Isabella and Ferdinand's regime, provided them with a military escort. Two days later, they arrived at Dueñas, a town which was held from the Crown by one of the princess's backers, Pedro de Acuña, count of Buendía. Ferdinand stayed there, while Palencia and Cárdenas rode ahead to Valladolid to inform Isabella of his safe arrival. Thus emboldened, the princess wrote to Henry, on 12 October, expressing her determination to go ahead with the marriage, and two days later, at midnight, the couple set eyes on each other for the first time in Juan de Vivero's house, in the presence of Archbishop Carrillo of Toledo.[8]

It is sometimes difficult to discern the actual events of this time through the mist of the legends which were concocted when the 'Catholic Monarchs' were safely on their respective thrones. Two stories are particularly associated with the couple's marriage, in the autumn of 1469. In one, Ferdinand's arrival in Castile was greeted with popular acclaim, including chants of *'Flores de Aragón dentro en Castilla son'*, ('Flowers of Aragon are in Castile') and children crying, while playing in the streets,' *¡Pendón de Aragón! ¡Pendón de Aragón!'*, ('The Aragonese flag! The Aragonese flag!'). A second, and long-standing legend is that, when the young prince was ushered into the presence of his intended, the courtier Gutierre de Cárdenas cried out *'Ese es'* ('This is the one'), for which his was later allowed to display a double 'S' on his coat of arms. Less romantically, it has to be borne in mind that the couple had not seen each other before, and were to be married against the will of the king of Castile, without a proper canonical dispensation, and at very short notice. In these circumstances, it is unlikely that the people of Valladolid could have mounted any great demonstration of public joy. The wedding itself was celebrated privately on 19 October 1469 by the archbishop of Toledo, in the presence of a small group of intimate supporters who were to be prominent in the subsequent regime, including Gómez Manrique, Gonzalo Chacón and Gutierre de Cárdenas, as well as the admiral of Castile, Fadrique Enríquez, who was the sole representative of the upper nobility. Other circumstances were no more auspicious. Not only was a forged bull read out, to overcome the impediment of the couple's common descent from John I of Castile, but the seventeen-year-old bridegroom came to the sacrament of holy matrimony with two illegitimate children, Alfonso de Aragón, who was later to be archbishop of Zaragoza, and Juana de Aragón, who would later marry the constable of Castile, Bernardino Fernández de Velasco. During the winter of 1469–70, Isabella and Ferdinand were to plumb some of their lowest political depths. They had effectively mortgaged their future to archbishop Carrillo and the Enríquez, the kings of Portugal and France were likely to seek revenge for the clandestine Aragonese marriage, the Castilian king and Juan Pacheco were sure to retaliate, and the reaction of the nobles and major towns of the kingdom was uncertain in the extreme. The teenage newly-weds, whose far-off kingdom of Sicily was of little use in the circumstances, could only count on the support of Valladolid itself and of Tordesillas, Olmedo and Sepúlveda, while Henry bided his time. The king first showed his displeasure by depriving Isabella's mother, Isabella of Portugal, of the lordship of Arévalo, which was transferred to the count of Plasencia. In February 1470, having received no direct communication from him since their marriage, the king and queen of Sicily wrote to Henry, demanding that he accept the *fait accompli*, and, when they received no reply, they began to circulate their letters both within Castile and abroad, in order to put pressure on the king to give formal recognition to their succession rights. As 1470 progressed, Isabella and Ferdinand's situation deteriorated further. In March, military action by another of the king's supporters, the count of Benavente, deprived them of their base in Valladolid, since Ferdinand could not field sufficient forces to recapture the town. All that was now left to the couple was the support of the faithful Chacón family, Gonzalo, the father, holding Medina del Campo for them, while his son Juan assured them of the revenues of Avila. The prince and princess themselves meanwhile took refuge in Carrillo's town of Dueñas, where, on 2 October 1470, Isabella gave birth not to the hoped-for son but to a daughter, who was named after her mother. Not only was Ferdinand so disappointed at the gender of his child that he succumbed for a while to illness, but the news gave great consolation to Henry and his supporters. In that same month, Henry entered Valladolid, and entrusted the town to the count of Benavente, while the wealthy mercantile centre of Medina del Campo abandoned Isabella, and support in Avila also wavered. The princess and mother, meanwhile, moved from Dueñas to Medina de Rioseco, a town under the jurisdiction of Admiral Fadrique Enríquez.[9]

Even the Aragonese, including the wily and cautious John II, appeared to hesitate in their support of the king and queen of Sicily. A request for 1000 Aragonese troops, to counteract possible military action by Henry and his supporters, was refused. In September 1470, before the birth of Isabella's daughter, an agent of Ferdinand's father, Pedro Vaca, was negotiating with the couple's arch-enemy, the marquis of Villena. His proposition was that, if Isabella had a son, he should marry Joanna ('La Beltraneja') and be declared heir to the Castilian throne. In these circumstances, the king and queen of Sicily would leave the kingdom. Having heard about this intrigue, Isabella immediately had her newborn daughter declared *infanta* of Castile and Aragon. Not only did this Aragonese manoeuvre fail, but it served to annoy Isabella and delight king Henry. Adversity not only made the royal couple ever more intransigent, but led to dissension between them and their mentor, Archbishop Carrillo. The conflict between the senior cleric and Ferdinand seems to have been particularly acute, and John II had to intervene to calm things down, inviting the prince and princess to Aragon, where they eventually went in 1472. Relations between them and Carrillo were never to be the same again, but, in the meantime, it was essential that they should widen the basis of their support in Castile. Their prime target at this time was the powerful Mendoza family, which remained obstinately loyal to princess Joanna. The charm offensive of 1470 was, however, spectacularly unsuccessful. In October of that year, Henry finally declared himself on the questions of Isabella's marriage and the succession to the throne. On the 26th of that month, at Valdelozoya, the king announced that, by marrying Ferdinand, Isabella had broken the agreement of the Toros de Guisando. He therefore revoked her title as princess and heir to the kingdom, and gave it back to Joanna, who was thus proclaimed as his legitimate daughter. The major cities were instructed to swear allegiance to her, and the princess was returned by the Mendoza to the care of the king at Segovia. Henry's plan at this stage was to marry Joanna to Charles of France, duke of Guyenne, and thus isolate the Aragonese party, which included for this purpose Isabella, and once again he received a lavish embassy led by the duke of Boulogne and Cardinal Jouffroy of Albi. By October 1470, after some months of diplomatic work, a new set of marriage terms had been drawn up, which closely resembled those which had earlier been agreed with Afonso V of Portugal. Thus it was in the context of the burgeoning alliance with France that the events on the plain of Valdelozoya took place. Indeed, after Joanna had been declared heir to the Castilian throne, the preliminary agreement for her French marriage was formally made with the duke of Boulogne and the cardinal of Albi. Although the marriage scheme was to founder, when Charles of Guyenne was killed, on 24 May 1472, as a result of a joust to celebrate the forthcoming marriage, the French alliance continued to receive considerable support among the great and the good of Castile until Henry's own death in December 1474. During this period, the king's allies included the marquis of Villena, the counts of Plasencia, Miranda and Benavente, the archbishop of Seville, and the Mendoza, as well as seven of the major towns of Castile, Burgos, Salamanca, Avila, Segovia, Guadalajara, Valladolid and Soria.

In the meantime, on 1 March 1471, Isabella issued her countermanifesto to her half-brother's recent actions. The document contained the accusation that Henry and Joanna of Portugal had not been canonically married, so that their daughter was illegitimate and could not inherit the kingdom. There was no suggestion, however, that the king was not the young Joanna's father. The March manifesto was evidently an appeal to public opinion, and particularly to Isabella's enemies among the nobility and to the leaders of the major towns. The 'princess' compared her sufferings to those of the legendary third-century Roman martyr Susanna, and excused her earlier refusal to marry Afonso of Portugal on the grounds that she could not have thus passed up the great inheritance of the Castilian throne. Isabella also confronted the delicate question of the canonical validity of her marriage to Ferdinand, which was much and rightly questioned by her opponents. Having no firm legal defence, she fell back on her virginal honesty and her royal blood, as well as the much older Afonso's unsuitability as her marriage partner. This dark moment in the queen of Sicily's life did, however, presage at least a glimmer of a future dawn. In May 1471, she and Ferdinand had a much-needed stroke of good fortune, when the counts of Treviño and Haro defeated the supporters of Henry in the Basque country, and brought the area over to their side. The royal couple also began to patch up their quarrel with Archbishop Carrillo, who received them in Torrelaguna, within his diocese. Early in 1472, Henry made what turned out to be a political misjudgement, when he made over the royal town of Sepúlveda to his ally Juan Pacheco. The local inhabitants rebelled against this move, Ferdinand astutely moved in to exploit the situation, and the town came over to Isabella's side. Thus, even in Henry of Castile's reign, the princely couple were posing as defenders of the royal patrimony and of municipal freedoms against seigneurial abuse and exploitation. During 1471, their external standing was also improving. In November of that year they signed a treaty with Charles the Bold of Burgundy, as part of an effort by John II of Aragon to counterbalance Henry's alliance with France. Earlier, and much more significantly in the long run, Pope Paul II, who like his predecessors had uniformly favoured Henry, died at the end of July, and was replaced on 9 August by the Franciscan Francesco della Rovere, as Sixtus IV. The new pope named as his legate to Spain Rodrigo Borja (Borgia), the future Pope Alexander VI, who, as a Valencian, was a subject of John II of Aragon. Ferdinand's father went into action immediately, alerting the legate against Henry of Castile and engineering, probably through Rodrigo Borja's mediation, a reconciliation between Ferdinand and Isabella and the powerful Mendoza family. One inducement was the possibility of a cardinal's hat for the then bishop of Sigüenza, and later archbishop of Seville, Pedro González de Mendoza. The crucial political realignment in Castile took place towards the end of 1472. Isabella and Ferdinand thereby acquired as allies the three sons of the poet Iñigo López de Mendoza, the first marquis of Santillana. These were his namesake, the count of Tendilla, the bishop of Sigüenza, and the second marquis, Diego Hurtado de Mendoza, together with their numerous allies and supporters. Having previously been stout supporters of Joanna's claims, and aloof from the faction conflicts of previous years, the family appears to have come to the conclusion that these aims were more likely to be achieved by Isabella and her husband. The rapprochement was gradual, at least in public. When the couple travelled to Alcalá de Henares, in February 1473, to meet the papal legate, the marquis of Santillana invited them to visit him in nearby Guadalajara, but Carrillo, who cared little for the Mendoza clan, persuaded them not to accept. Nevertheless, during the last two years of Henry's reign, a number of the king's supporters left him in favour of Isabella and Ferdinand. After the princess's former confidante Beatriz de Bobadilla, with her husband Andrés Cabrera, had been reconciled with her, a plot was hatched in which she was to meet Henry in a last attempt at reconciliation, while Ferdinand was away, providing military assistance to his father against the French at Perpignan. It was eventually decided that the opportune moment would occur in December 1473, when Henry was in the Alcázar of Segovia, where Andrés Cabrera was governor. Cabrera tipped Isabella off that her half-brother was temporarily without his normal counsellors, and the princess hurried to meet him. With that spontaneous friendliness which often baffled both his allies and his enemies, the king welcomed her warmly, and even led her mule when they went on a tour of the city, but there was no substantive reconciliation between them. Having returned from the Perpignan front, Ferdinand reached Segovia on 1 January 1474, armed with instructions in how to conciliate Henry, and, five days later, he and his wife celebrated the Epiphany with him and the Cabreras in the Alcázar.[10] It seems probable that attempts were being made behind the scenes to resolve the succession problem, but Henry, who was already suffering from the intestinal problems which were probably the cause of his death later in the year, seems to have allowed matters to drift. Ferdinand left Segovia in the second half of January, without an agreement, while the king himself departed a few weeks later. Yet Isabella and Ferdinand's position was now very much stronger over all. In Andrés Cabrera and his wife Beatriz they had strong allies, and also friends in charge of the royal treasury, which was kept in the Alcázar of Segovia. Although no other city overtly supported them at the time, they were now popular there, and Segovia was to be the base of Isabella's initial seizure of the Castilian throne. In addition, the support of the Mendoza clan was becoming ever more explicit. In May, the marquis of Santillana received Ferdinand and pledged his allegiance, while the now Cardinal Archbishop Pedro González de Mendoza proposed an alliance of his own family, the Enríquez and the duke of Alba, to support Isabella and her husband against the opposing grouping of the Pacheco, the Zúñiga and Archbishop Carrillo. In June, Ferdinand and the duke of Alba seized Tordesillas by force. During the summer and autumn of 1474, Carrillo withdrew to his episcopal town of Alcalá de Henares, leaving the Mendoza in possession of the field, but Juan Pacheco was still to be reckoned with. Soon death was to strike, drastically altering the political landscape of Castile.

First, on 4 October, the marquis of Villena died, then in mid-December, it was the turn of the king himself. Henry's health had been deteriorating throughout the year, and he had retired to the Alcázar of Madrid to nurse it. On 11 December, he returned to the castle from a hunting expedition in the forest of El Pardo. He felt particularly poorly, and retired to bed, where his condition became steadily worse. The marquis of Villena, the constable of Castile, Cardinal Mendoza and the count of Benavente were summoned to his bedside, and having realized the gravity of the situation, they in turn called Juan Mazuelo, prior of the Jeronymite house of San Jerónimo del Paso in Madrid, to administer the last rites. Before departing this life, at the age of fifty, Henry made his confession and asked to be buried in the Jeronymite order's house at Guadalupe, in Extremadura, next to his mother, María de Aragon. This wish was eventually carried out, though the king was initially interred, with little ceremony, in the church of Santa María in Madrid. The news of Henry's death seems to have reached Isabella in Segovia by the evening of 12 December. Ferdinand was in the neighbouring kingdom at the time, but the princess immediately went into court mourning, donning garments of white serge. On the following day, the feast of St Lucy, in accordance with the advice of her trusted counsellors Andrés Cabrera and Gutierre de Cárdenas, she went to the church of San Miguel in Segovia, where the royal and municipal standards were draped in black. After a requiem mass and office for the dead in memory of the dead king, she reappeared in jewels and gold raiment, on a platform outside the church, overlooking the city's main square (Plaza Mayor). To the sound of trumpets, clarinets and drums, heralds proclaimed Isabella queen of Castile, with her husband named second as her 'legitimate husband'. Apart from this, much comment seems to have been occasioned by one aspect of the subsequent procession through the streets of Segovia. According to the royal chronicler, Alfonso de Palencia, the newly-proclaimed queen was preceded by Gutierre de Cárdenas, who carried a sword of state by its point with the pommel raised, 'after the use of Spain, so that it could be seen by everyone, even the most distant, and so that they should know that she who had the power to punish the guilty with royal authority was approaching'.

On 16 December, the Castilian chancery issued documents to all the cities represented in the Cortes, ordering them to send delegates to Segovia to swear allegiance to the new queen. The Castilian political classes were amazed by Isabella's pre-emptive strike, which was evidently intended to prevent any general negotiation concerning the succession. The upper nobility, as well as the leading towns, were to be required to make an instant and definite decision. Some magnates' viewpoints were entirely predictable. Isabella's accession was bound to be opposed by the new marquis of Villena, Diego López Pacheco, who had Joanna in his care, and also by his relatives, Rodrigo Téllez Girón, master of Calatrava, Juan Téllez Girón, count of Urueña, and his main allies, Álvaro de Zúñiga, duke of Arévalo, and Rodrigo Ponce de León, marquis of Cádiz. The question was what would be the course of action of those who had been quietly shifting their allegiance to Isabella and Ferdinand during the former king's last months. Although no doubt shocked by the speed and vigour of Isabella's actions, the admiral,

Fadrique Enríquez, and the duke of Alba, the duke of Alburquerque, the constable of Castile and the count of Benavente declared for her. Last of the group and with evident reluctance, Archbishop Carrillo did so too, all of them coming to Segovia to swear allegiance. Much more ready in his support was the cardinal of Spain, Pedro González de Mendoza, who had been present at Henry's death and who, before himself coming to Segovia, had accompanied his former sovereign's remains to Guadalupe for burial, in accordance with the terms of the will. This gesture, which asserted the dignity of monarchy in general, was much appreciated by Isabella, and, from 27 December 1474, the cardinal was wholly at her service. Reactions throughout the kingdom were equally various. Isabella's proclamation as queen was generally well received in Old Castile, not only in Segovia but also in Avila, Sepúlveda, Valladolid and Tordesillas. In the Basque country, the notables swore allegiance to Ferdinand and Isabella as 'lords of Vizcaya', amid great celebrations, under the famous oak of Guernica. Thus the northern half of the kingdom at least seemed willing to acquiesce in Isabella's accession, except for areas closer to the Portuguese border, such as Zamora. Things were more complicated south of the Sierra de Guadarrama, with Toledo and Murcia accepting the new queen, while there were considerable doubts in Andalusia and Extremadura. In the north-west, Galicia appeared to be a likely centre of resistance. Of most immediate interest, though, was the reaction of Ferdinand himself to his wife's Segovia 'coup'.

Ferdinand received the news of King Henry's death in Zaragoza, on 14 December, not from his wife but from Archbishop Carrillo, who urged him to come to Castile at once. The archbishop of Toledo's letter was accompanied in the post of that day by another from his brother of Seville, Pedro González de Mendoza, which informed Ferdinand of Henry's severe illness, and also urged him to cross the Castilian border as soon as possible. Only two days later did Isabella's own letter arrive. Unlike the ambitious prelates, she did not appear particularly anxious that her husband should join her, leaving it to him to decide according to the current situation on the Aragonese frontier with France. Whether or not Ferdinand was aware at this stage of the possibility of future strife in the marriage, from 16 December the Castilian chancery routinely referred to Isabella as 'queen and natural lady' of Castile, but to Ferdinand only as her 'lord' and 'legitimate husband'. The Aragonese heir was informed of developments on 19 December, and immediately set out for Segovia. It appears that it was only two days later at Calatayud, while he was en route, that Ferdinand was told how Gutierre de Cárdenas had carried the naked sword of state by its point in front of his wife. Clearly, there was some negotiating to do, in order to establish the respective roles of the new king and queen, and despite the courtly ceremonial in the Alcázar of Segovia, the couple's initial meeting on 2 January 1475 seems to have been fairly stormy. When theory became reality, Ferdinand and his Aragonese advisers, perhaps influenced by the Salic law of his father's kingdom, which debarred women from direct rule, evidently felt the need to renegotiate the terms of the 1469 agreement of Cervera, under which Isabella had been proclaimed queen, and which indeed gave Ferdinand no more than the role of 'prince consort'. The result was the concordat of Segovia, which was drafted by the archbishops of Seville and Toledo, was agreed on 15 January, and did at least something to smooth the Aragonese heir's ruffled feathers, though in essence it changed little. Under its terms, Isabella remained 'proprietary queen' of the domains of the crown of Castile, with the clear implication that her descendants, and not Ferdinand, would inherit the Crown on her death. Her spouse continued to be referred to as her 'legitimate husband', but he was now offered at least some of the trappings of kingly dignity. The Segovia concordat ordained that on letters patent, proclamations, coins and seals, the names of both rulers would appear as king and queen of Castile, with Ferdinand's placed first because of his gender. In heraldry, however, the arms of Castile and León would have precedence over those of Sicily and of the crown of Aragon. The fundamental point in the Segovia agreement was that sovereignty in the crown of Castile, including the appointment of accountants and treasurers and the disposal of the entire royal patronage, would reside in the queen alone.[11]

This attempt to hammer out the rules of government which were to be observed by Isabella and her husband seems to have calmed the fears of at least some of those who anticipated another upsurge of Aragonese meddling in Castilian affairs, such as had blighted the kingdom for much of the century, not least because of the activities of Ferdinand's father, John II. A month of negotiations, running through the Christmas and Epiphany seasons, had settled most doubts, and others were to be laid to rest in April 1475, when Ferdinand received various royal powers *de facto*, even though not *de jure*. Sheer necessity, rather than abstract political skill, had concentrated minds wonderfully, and the indivisible external face of the joint rule of Ferdinand and Isabella was already in the making. It was evident, though, that the settlement in Castile would have immediate international consequences. The new royal couple's political worries primarily concerned the threat of a Portuguese invasion on behalf of Joanna and her Castilian supporters. As soon as Henry died, and before Ferdinand's arrival in Castile, Isabella had summoned Afonso's ambassador, Pedro de Sousa, from Madrid to Segovia, to receive a message for his master which urged the Portuguese king to accept her accession and not intervene in Castilian affairs. Though Afonso's true intentions were still unknown to Ferdinand and Isabella at this stage, the reality of the threat he posed had already been made manifest on 27 December 1474, in letters sent from Estremoz to the marquis of Cádiz, Don Rodrigo Ponce de León, and to other Castilian nobles and major towns, urging them to obey the terms of Henry's will, and accept Joanna as his heir, with Afonso himself, her cousin, as her protector during her minority. Damião de Góis later claimed that Henry's will, of which the executors were the marquis of Villena, Cardinal Mendoza, the duke of Arévalo and the count of Benavente, was in fact smuggled to Portugal by the parish priest of Santa Cruz, in Madrid, and was finally seen by Isabella just before she died in 1504. Whatever the truth or otherwise of this, Portuguese sources indicate that, while celebrating Christmas at Estremoz, Afonso consulted his counsellors, notably the bishop of Evora, the prior of Crato, and Lopo de Albuquerque. In this council, a plan was discussed for the defence of the whole Portuguese frontier, and recipients were even named for grants which were to be made by the Cortes of the kingdom, when they assembled on 15 January 1475. A hundred artillery pieces were demanded immediately for the frontier castles, and a further hundred for the invading army, as well as small arms. Within Portugal, Afonso's subsequent measures made it amply obvious that an invasion was being planned in order to secure for him the Castilian throne, yet the picture of his intentions was not as clearly seen across the border.

Troubled both by dissidence within Castile and by threats from France, Isabella and Ferdinand made every effort to persuade Afonso to stay his hand. Suárez Fernández emphasizes the importance placed by Isabella, even in such difficult circumstances, on good relations with Portugal. In his view, the queen had no personal animosity towards Portugal, and always regarded the succession war as a necessary evil, to be ended as soon as possible, but of course with herself firmly in place as ruler of Castile. In these circumstances, it was inevitable that the Portuguese king would offer marriage to Joanna, despite their consanguinity and her tender age, and that he would join forces with her main Castilian supporters. At this time, under the influence of the agents of the marquis of Villena, Afonso apparently believed that many other nobles wanted to declare for Joanna, but feared the retribution of Ferdinand and Isabella. Thus the conflict between the royal spouses over their respective roles in government in Castile was exacerbated by the fear that further magnates, as well as important towns, might be tempted by the offers of the Portuguese, which were backed by growing colonial wealth. All the weakness was not on the side of Isabella and her husband, however. Isabella's 'coup' in Segovia had surprised not only Ferdinand but also her rival's supporters, who had only belatedly begun to organize themselves under the leadership of the marquis of Villena. Thus, while pro-Joanna factions in important towns such as Zamora, Burgos, Salamanca, Ciudad Real, Jaén, Carmona and Seville still had hopes of swinging their municipal governments in favour of Afonso's future wife, the situation, as 1475 began, remained fluid. The only certainty seemed to be that the massive resources of the new marquis of Villena, together with those of his Pacheco and Girón relatives, would be at the service of Henry IV's daughter. The marquis had effective control over most of the modern province of Albacete, together with parts of Murcia, Valencia and Cuenca, as well as considerable influence in Madrid, Trujillo, Plasencia and Jaén. A significant part of this control was exercised through his network of castles, which included not only the original lordship of Villena (Alicante), but also Alcalá de Júcar, Almansa and Chinchilla de Montearagón (Albacete), Jumilla, Mazarrón and Xiquena (Murcia), Requena (Valencia) and Belmonte, La Cañada del Hoyo, Castillo de Garci Muñoz and Moya (Cuenca). He also had castles in the areas surrounding the royal towns of Madrid, Jaén, Jerez de la Frontera, Zamora, Valladolid and Soria. It is thus hardly surprising that, according to the chronicler Alonso de Palencia, the marquis adopted at this time the dual policy of acting as a particularly tender guardian of Princess Joanna, and ensuring, as far as possible, that his castles were in good military shape. In addition to his own seigneurial resources, Villena also had supporters, or at least potential allies, in strategic places, such as Alfonso de Valencia, governor of Zamora castle, and Don Juan de Acuña, duke of Valencia, who were both, as Palencia remarks, of Portuguese origin. The marquis evidently regarded Joanna as a potentially docile queen, who would allow him and his supporters to act freely. Isabella, on the other hand, could at this juncture only count with some certainty on most of Old Castile, including Segovia itself, Avila, Sepúlveda, Valladolid and Tordesillas, as well as the Basque country.

By the nature of things, the initiative at this stage was with Afonso. According to the Castilian royal chronicler Palencia, the Portuguese king believed the account given by the marquis of Villena of the current level of support for him and Joanna in Castile, and urged his counsellors to follow him in an invasion. In Palencia's view, which was always strongly favourable to Isabella and hostile to her deceased brother Henry, Afonso's previous, and justified, scepticism concerning the reliability of assurances given by Castilian grandees evaporated when he became enthused with the prospects of marrying Joanna and peacefully annexing the vastly larger and richer neighbouring kingdom. The king's flourishing of letters from Castile did not immediately convince some of his advisers, but enthusiasts for the scheme, notably the prior of Crato, estimated that he would be able to assemble an army of 7000 men-at-arms, and that there was ample gold in Portugal to support them. The main opponent of the invasion plan, the elderly duke of Bragança, was discounted, as he was a relative of Queen Isabella, and the project continued, with an agreement between Afonso and Louis XI of France, under which the French would intervene militarily and acquire either the Basque provinces, if the Portuguese were victorious, or financial compensation if they were not. Damião de Góis's later version of these deliberations, at Estremoz and after, gives the impression of a more open consultation than is provided by contemporary sources, but also offers further details of the opposition to the invasion of Castile. While the heir to the throne, Prince John, was strongly in favour, others, including Jorge da Costa, archbishop of Lisbon, Rui Gomes de Alvarenga, Chancellor of Portugal, and the duke of Guimarães, were against it. With what Castilian writers regarded as uncharacteristic foolishness and impetuosity, Afonso accepted the more militant counsel, but Isabella and Ferdinand, who according to Palencia's account were alarmed by the Portuguese threat, made efforts to secure peace. They engaged in international correspondence, protesting at the 'unholy' alliance which was building up between the Portuguese, some of their own Castilian aristocracy, and Louis XI's France. In order to make more effective military preparations, the king and queen moved from Segovia to the more northerly strategic and military centre of Valladolid. The move had the added advantage of confronting the influence in that part of Old Castile of Joanna's supporter, the count of Benavente, who had achieved considerable influence in the town during the reign of Henry IV. Having begun, with their arrival in Valladolid, the policy of reducing aristocratic power in the major towns which they were to continue during the rest of the 1470s, Ferdinand and Isabella despatched, in February 1475, an embassy to the Portuguese king, consisting of a military man, Vasco de Vivero, and the Salamanca law professor and high-court judge (*oidor*), Dr Andrés de Villalón. The ambassadors' task was to persuade Afonso both to keep the peace and to undermine the position of Villena and the other Castilian dissidents by marrying Ferdinand's sister Joanna of Aragon, instead of her namesake of Castile, whose legitimacy they denied, and to whom he was already betrothed. When the first pair of envoys failed, they were replaced by two friars, the Franciscan Pedro de Marchena and the Dominican Alfonso de San Cipriano, who were preceded by Diego García de Hinestrosa. Further letters were written by Cardinal Pedro González de Mendoza and the royal secretary and chronicler, Fernando del Pulgar, begging Afonso to abandon his invasion plans. It appeared at this time that Isabella's natural supporters in Portugal, including her aunt Beatrice, were not willing to commit themselves against Afonso's new militant policy towards Castile. The king himself rejected the allegation of the Isabel-line side that Henry IV was not the father of his young prospective wife, and insisted that it was his destiny to become king of Castile. The friars withdrew defeated, although, as military fervour increased in Portugal, the duke of Bragança, in his refuge in the monastery of Villaviciosa, feared the worst for the expedition, and in particular for his five sons who were serving the king.

On the south-eastern front, as a further precaution while these last efforts were being made to prevent war with Portugal, Ferdinand had sent the count of Cabra, a Cordoban magnate, to arrange a truce with the emir of Granada, Abu'l Hasan Ali. Negotiations were lengthy, and a treaty of neutrality was not signed until 17 November 1475, under which Granadan help was offered to Isabella's supporters in the Cór-doba area. Such a possibility seemed remote, however, when the Casti-lian diplomats returned from Portugal without success. Having first attempted to secure the support of leading Castilian magnates, includ-ing the archbishop of Toledo, the marquis of Villena, the marquis of Santillana, the duke of Arévalo and his mother, the dowager duchess Leonor Pimentel, by means of messages carried by Lopo de Albuquer-que, Afonso attempted a final diplomatic assault on his rivals in Castile. He chose as his ambassador Rui de Sousa, who is described by Góis as 'a person who, apart from his ancient nobility, was very wise and a good courtier'. Sousa travelled from Evora to Valladolid, where, in early April, he found himself in the midst of chivalric pursuits, organ-ized by the duke of Alba, in which Ferdinand was taking a leading part. The arguments over the legitimacy or otherwise of Joanna, and hence her new husband's claim to rule over Castile, were rehearsed once again, in Palencia's view in the form of an ultimatum rather than negotiation, but to no avail. Sousa returned to Evora with the message that Ferdinand and Isabella would resist any invasion with military force, and with the protection of God and the apostle St James. Such defiance seems justified from the Castilian rulers' point of view, seeing that the Portuguese king had another envoy, Rodrigo de Melo, in Castile at that very time, negotiating with dissident members of the aristocracy, including the archbishop of Toledo, the marquis of Villena and the duke of Arévalo, with a view to invading in May. Ferdinand and Isabella were sufficiently worried at the prospect of Portuguese military action to offer a general pardon to all nobles and knights who had been disloyal to them during the preceding months. Those who had been banished or had fled to Portugal would be allowed to return, and, in their anxiety to gain as much support as possible for themselves, and this with the utmost rapidity, the king and queen over-rode existing laws of Henry IV which required that such pardons should be issued individually rather than *en masse*. How, though, had Afonso's young wife, Joanna, conducted herself during the months which followed Henry's death?

Like her main noble supporters in Castile, Joanna seems to have reacted much more slowly than Isabella to the news of the king's demise. She did, however, write to Afonso of Portugal, the first recorded letter being dated 27 December 1474, while her mother, Joanna of Portugal, made largely unsuccessful efforts to rally political and military support. Afonso was happy to portray his wooing of his thirteen-year-old niece, and perhaps not only for public consumption, in chivalric terms, as a knight's rescue of a damsel in distress. It was evident, however, that the Portuguese could not help her without at least making visible and serious moves towards his kingdom's border with Castile, and the steps towards marriage would prove to be short. On 10 March 1475, Enrique de Figueredo wrote to his Portuguese master, recommending the marquis of Villena as a likely organizer of his entry into Castile. On 29 March, Afonso duly signed at Evora a letter to Pacheco in which he referred to his agreement and contract to marry Joanna, and, as putative sovereign of Castile, promised to protect the estates of the marquis, to confirm all grants which he had received from his previous master, Henry IV, and to place him in charge of the royal administration as his favourite (*privado*). Afonso similarly attempted to bribe Villena's allies with the prospect of reward. The bishop of Burgos, for example, was offered the first vacancy of the archbishoprics of Toledo and Seville. Finally, he promised to marry his nephew, the duke of Viseu, to Pacheco's sister Juana.

War was now imminent. Having received Rui de Sousa's report from the Castilian court, Afonso at once summoned his army to Arronches, north-west of Badajoz, assuming that his nobles would agree to an invasion, on the grounds of their sovereign's inflated estimate of the support which awaited him in Castile, as well as the supposed legitimacy of his claim to the Castilian throne. The Portuguese invasion in effect took place twice. On 10 April, Afonso brought the main part of his army across the border into Extremadura, through the pass of Codiceira (in Spanish La Codosera), in the direction of Carmovillas and Mirabel. He changed his mind, however, and by 12 April was back in Arronches, to sign a document which declared what the succession to the Portuguese crown would be, if he entered Castile and married Princess Joanna. Perhaps ironically, Afonso's purpose was to avoid in his own kingdom precisely the kind of succession dispute which he was in the process of exploiting in Castile. His heir in Portugal, regardless of what happened as the result of his current military adventure, was to be his son John, in the case of whose death his grandson Afonso was to succeed. On the advice of the Castilian count of Feria, the Portuguese then invaded for a second time, in greater force though still with only part of the army, via Alcántara rather than Badajoz, as had been his original intention. According to Ferdinand's estimate, in a letter at the time to his father, John II of Aragon, Afonso's forces consisted of about 5000 lances of cavalry and 10,000 infantry (Portuguese sources estimate 15,000 infantry), together with artillery, siege engines, and material to set up semi-permanent camps. Princess Joanna was taken from Madrid to Trujillo, and then to Plasencia to meet her new husband, who had arrived through Zúñiga territory, and been welcomed there by Álvaro de Zúñiga, himself. The couple were legally betrothed at Trujillo, through representatives, on 12 May. The surviving manifesto, containing the conditions of the marriage, indicates that Joanna's noble supporters in Castile agreed to Afonso's entry into the kingdom as her husband. The marriage contract was agreed in Trujillo castle, where Joanna was then residing, after which Afonso finally put his invasion plans into effect.

Afonso arrived at Plasencia and the marriage was ratified in person on 29 May, in secular and religious ceremonies, which appear to have taken place under a general dispensation from Pius II to Afonso, which allowed him to marry any free noblewoman who had not previously been subjected to rape. On 30 May, letters were despatched to the bishops, nobles and larger towns of Castile, setting out Joanna's, and hence her new husband's, claim to the throne, this propaganda offensive being accompanied by the publishing of prophecies which identified Afonso with the 'Hooded King' (*El Rey Encubierto*), who would come into the kingdom to free it from tyranny. It is doubtful how much circulation was achieved by Joanna's manifesto, which represented the pro-aristocratic theories of government which were espoused by its 'authors', the marquis of Villena, the duke of Arévalo, Comendador Gonzalo de Saavedra, Licenciado de Ciudad Rodrigo and the royal secretary Juan de Oviedo, who were all in Plasencia at the time. Isabella and Ferdinand's reaction to the actuality, as opposed to the threat, of invasion was to abandon all notion of pardoning dissidents and condemn Afonso and Joanna's supporters as traitors, just five days before the couple were married. In the meantime, on 12 May, Ferdinand had taken the precaution of making his will, which was drawn up by the Jeronymite friar and royal confessor, Hernando de Talavera, while his wife, fearing that Juan de Ulloa would hand over the town of Toro and its fortress, of which his brother Rodrigo was governor, to the invaders, took up her position in nearby Tordesillas. Authors from Prescott to

Perez have agreed with the contemporary chronicler Palencia that, at this point, Afonso made a crucial error, which probably cost him the campaign and the kingdom, when, after the wedding celebrations, he headed towards Arévalo, rather than southwards into Andalusia. Although the potential support for Joanna's cause in Seville, Carmona, Ecija and Córdoba had been considerable earlier in the year, by the time that his agents met the duke of Medina Sidonia in Seville in May, this Andalusian magnate was posing as the keeper of the peace in the region. As a result, the possibility of active co-operation between Afonso and Medina Sidonia's arch-rival, the marquis of Cádiz, had effectively disappeared.

Had the Portuguese army gone south, an alliance with the marquis of Villena might well have given Joanna and her husband control over the southern half of the crown of Castile. Instead, hoping for a French invasion through the Basque country and a rendezvous in Burgos, where the governor of the castle was favourable, the main Portuguese army headed for Salamanca and Zamora. Ferdinand, who knew by 28 May that Afonso was in the vicinity of Plasencia, moved to try and prevent these latter towns from falling into Portuguese hands, also writing to the authorities in his father's kingdom of Valencia, to ask them to attack the neighbouring lands of the marquis of Villena. Isabella, meanwhile, made a last desperate appeal to the archbishop of Toledo to come out on her side, but she failed and, having suffered a miscarriage at Cebreros on 31 May, withdrew to Avila to spend the month of June recovering. Afonso then captured Toro, but Ferdinand, who had made full use of the Portuguese king's two-month dalliance in Arévalo to turn his paltry force of an estimated five hundred cavalry into a significant army, succeeded in blocking the way to Burgos. The French made no move and a front was formed between Ferdinand and Afonso's forces in the region of Zamora, while a diversion was attempted in the form of a proposed invasion of Portugal by Alonso de Cárdenas, who was recognized by Isabella's side as the master of the military order of Santiago. During June and July 1475, Ferdinand and Isabella cheerfully granted to their supporters governorships, towns and lands in Portugal which were yet to be captured. After considerable exertion, she and her husband succeeded, by the beginning of July, in assembling at Tordesillas what was, at least on paper, an impressive army of about 2000 men-at-arms, 6000 cavalry and 20,000 infantry, consisting of seigneurial and municipal forces. Having moved off on 15 July, Ferdinand and his army arrived within a league of the walls of Toro four days later. In a chivalrous manner, which corresponded to the traditional and variegated nature of his army of seigneurial contingents and municipal levies, each under it own independent command,

Ferdinand sent Gómez Manrique to challenge Afonso to single combat, in order to settle their quarrel, but refused to accept the latter's condition, which was that they should fight for possession of Joanna and Isabella themselves. In the haste of their muster, Ferdinand's troops had come unprepared for siege warfare, and when Afonso refused them a pitched battle outside the walls, news having already arrived, by 20 July, that Zamora had surrendered to Joanna, the 'loyal' seigneurial contingents began to disperse, and the municipal levies, particularly the Basques, declared themselves to have been betrayed and became mutinous, so that retreat seemed inevitable. At this stage, things could hardly have looked more bleak for Isabella's cause, as the citadel of Toro fell to Afonso, Ferdinand's army disintegrated, and the archbishop of Toledo declared himself openly for Joanna's cause. According to the anonymous *Crónica incompleta*, Isabella and her ladies rode out from Tordesillas to give Ferdinand a dusty welcome on his return.

It is true that, by the end of the Toro débâcle, the Castilian monarchs' situation did not seem healthy. They had been able to do nothing to prevent Zamora and Toro being handed over to Afonso, there was a real danger that the Portuguese king's army might link up with the Burgos garrison and perhaps with French troops, which could invade through Navarre and/or Guipúzcoa, and, to cap it all, the royal exchequer, in Segovia castle, was virtually empty. Isabella and Ferdinand responded by calling a council at Medina del Campo, on 27 July, at which it was decided that the Castilian Church should be asked to loan half its precious vessels, the value of which was estimated at thirty million *maravedíes*. The plate, which was voted by the clergy to the Crown, apparently without reluctance, in August, was to be redeemed within three years. At this time, the royal strategy was firstly to besiege Burgos castle, with the help of artillery commanded by Ferdinand's half-brother Alfonso, the bastard son of John II, who was to be summoned from Aragon, and secondly to prevent any northward advance by the Portuguese. While Ferdinand devoted himself, for the rest of the year, to the siege of Burgos, Zamora castle was to be infiltrated and recaptured. Isabella based herself in Valladolid, to organize forces in order to prevent Afonso's army linking up either with Burgos or with the French. In the meantime, on 31 July, Isabella and Ferdinand told the towns of Coria, Badajoz, Trujillo, Cáceres and Alburquerque, all close to the Portuguese border, to prepare their resources to support an invasion of the neighbouring kingdom by Francisco de Solís, whom they had designated master of the order of Alcántara, who was himself to become governor of the Portuguese town of Uguela, if the expedition was successful. Such raids, from Extremadura and Andalusia, caused increasing devastation in Portugal as the year went on. The most notable early example was the capture of Nodar, by forces from Seville, on 6 June. In the meantime, Alfonso's army, effectively confined to Toro, became frustrated at its inability either to advance in Castile or to defend its homeland. While Ferdinand concentrated on Burgos castle, an important symbol of resistance to his and his wife's regime, Isabella's efforts succeeded in preventing the Portuguese from reaching there. Instead, they went to the massive Peñafiel castle, and also acquired the reinforcement of 500 lances from the archbishop of Toledo. They captured Baltanás, near the town of Palencia, and secured the count of Benavente, Rodrigo Alfonso de Pimentel, who was to prove a useful counter for bargaining with Ferdinand and Isabella. On 18 September, Isabella arrived in Palencia with a contingent of carefully chosen troops, in order to rectify this situation, and achieved success, in that Afonso withdrew to the reigning queen's childhood home, Arévalo.

While the Portuguese king's other Castilian allies, such as the duke of Arévalo and the marquis of Villena, were finding it increasingly difficult to raise forces, the latter being hampered in addition by a rebellion in his town of Alcaraz, Isabella and Ferdinand were concerned at the now daily violence and deaths in the streets of the 'capital' (*cabeza*) of Castile. The chronicler Palencia presents a picture of a patriotic and popular rising against the governor of the castle, Iñigo de Zúñiga, the bishop of Burgos, Luis de Acuña, and the *adelantado* of Castile, who were of the Alfonsine party. As so frequently in this war, for example in Zamora, and as a kind of forestate of the fate of the Alcázar of Toledo at the beginning of the 1936–9 Civil War, a situation had developed in which the garrison supported one party to the conflict and the bulk of the population supported the other. Ferdinand hastened to bolster the authority of the *corregidor* of Burgos, Alfonso de Cuevas, and bring military forces, with Sancho de Rojas as captain, but Rojas proved unsatisfactory, and further reinforcements had to be sent from Valladolid, whither the king had departed. The pattern for the rest of 1475 was set, with the Portuguese army cooped up in Toro, while Ferdinand and Isabella, with the help of finance from the Church, restored their military and political situation. To begin with, Afonso attempted to bargain by means of his prisoner, the count of Benavente, offering to release him if the siege of Burgos were abandoned within thirty days. He persuaded the count to appoint new, pro-Portuguese governors to his castles, but, as the countess remained loyal to Isabella, these measures had no effect. Ferdinand and Isabella held a further council of war at Dueñas, between 5 and 10 November, which considered the fate of Zamora, and more particularly of its castle, which was even more crucial than that of Burgos, in terms of its closeness to Portugal. Ferdinand put his hope in supporters infiltrating the city, while he awaited the arrival from Aragon of his half-brother Alfonso to help him recapture Burgos castle. The Dueñas council also discussed the possibility of a treaty with France, to secure that country's neutrality in the conflict, and further efforts to secure Valencian intervention in the lands of the marquis of Villena. The fate of the pro-Portuguese garrison in Burgos castle was sealed when Alfonso of Aragon arrived in the city on 22 November, accompanied by siege specialists. An agreement for the surrender of the castle by its governor, Juan de Zúñiga, was signed ten days later, though the queen did not take possession of it until 19 January 1476. The reason for this delay was that strategic attention had shifted to Zamora, since, if Afonso and his army could be shifted from there, they would have little alternative but to abandon their venture and return to Portugal. At the end of November, Isabella moved from Dueñas to Valladolid, thinking that she was about to sign a treaty for the surrender of Zamora, but the conspiracy was discovered by Joanna's supporters, on 3 December, and Ferdinand secretly left the siege of Burgos castle, in order to supervise operations in Zamora personally. The town was conquered in a very short time, but the castle held out, awaiting reinforcements, so that Ferdinand and Isabella's Christmas celebrations were overshadowed by the pressing need to bring the garrison's resistance to an end.

Afonso, being well aware that if he lost Zamora his own communications with Portugal would be severely disrupted, duly summoned Prince John, with an army of 2000 lances of cavalry and 8000 infantry which eventually joined his forces outside Toro, having travelled through San Felices de los Gallegos and Ledesma, on 9 February 1476. By this time, though, Ferdinand and Isabella's troops had been strengthened by forces released after the surrender of Burgos castle, and it became increasingly apparent that a final reckoning between the rival claimants to the Castilian throne would not be long delayed, despite the expressed concern of Ferdinand's father, John II of Aragon, that the matter should be resolved peacefully. In addition, the count of Benavente was released, and returned to Isabella's side. On 13 February, the Portuguese army left its base in Toro, but no military action followed, so Alfonso and his son John transferred their attention to Zamora, where their forces arrived between 16 and 18 February. According to some accounts, Afonso at this time made a last desperate bid to salvage something from his ill-fated expedition by agreeing to abandon his claim to the Castilian throne if he received the towns and territory of Toro and Zamora, and the kingdom of Galicia, in compensation. Now that Ferdinand had been joined by his highly experienced half-brother Alfonso, however, the stage was set for the long-awaited conclusive field battle, which took place on 1 March 1476 at Peleagonzalo, near the town of Toro, after which it is commonly named. This time, the result was conclusive. An estimated 2000 Portuguese prisoners were taken, and Afonso initially took refuge in the nearby stronghold of Castronuño, held by Pedro de Avendaño, which Ferdinand was forced to besiege for eleven months, and then demolished. Isabella, who was informed of the result in nearby Tordesillas on the following day, immediately issued proclamations of the victory to all the authorities of the kingdom. On 5 March, she joined Ferdinand in Zamora, where the fortress was finally reduced to obedience, after negotiations with the governor. Centres of dissidence in Madrid, Baeza, and Toro itself, quickly followed suit. Just over two weeks later, on 22 March, the royal couple felt able to order general celebrations in the kingdom, and vowed to begin work on the Franciscan church of San Juan de los Reyes in Toledo, which was to serve as a perpetual memorial of their triumph, and was planned as their place of burial.

At this point there seems to have been some disagreement between Isabella and Ferdinand over future strategy. The queen wished the last pockets of resistance to be removed from her kingdom, while her husband was more concerned with the continuing French threat. Although a large French army had been driven back more than once from Hendaye, the border castle of Fuenterrabía was still under siege in May. In the meantime, Alfonso had retreated to Portugal with his young bride, taken back the royal authority from his son John, and decided on a last, desperate appeal for help to his supposed ally, Louis XI of France. The Portuguese king arrived in France in September 1476, with a retinue of 200, and was received with public honour, but Louis made it plain that he would receive no more concrete assistance until Charles the Bold, duke of Burgundy, had been defeated, and Afonso had obtained a papal dispensation for his marriage with Joanna. After some months of this empty welcome, and apparently with a genuine desire (a 'chimerical purpose', as Prescott expressed it) to reconcile Louis with Charles, the Portuguese king visited the duke in midwinter, but could not prevent the final battle, in which the prospect of Burgundian independence was extinguished with its ruler. After spending much of the following year in the vain hope of help from Louis, who had in the meantime decided that Isabella and Ferdinand had won the contest for the Castilian throne and was acting accordingly, Afonso retired, with a few servants, to rural Normandy.

Expecting ridicule if he returned to Portugal as a failed ruler, he informed his son John, who had effectively become king during his absence, that he intended to withdraw from the world, go on a pilgrimage to the Holy Land, and then live out his life in a monastery. In the event, Afonso returned to Portugal, with French help, on 20 November

1478, just five days after John had been crowned king. Not only had he abdicated from the Portuguese throne and failed to gain that of Castile, but he was also denied the solace of his young bride, Joanna, thanks to the reversal of the dispensation for them to be married, which was obtained from Pope Sixtus IV, at the instigation of Isabella and Ferdinand. The unfortunate princess eked out her days in a monastery, surviving until 1530. In the spirit of early nineteenth-century enlightened liberalism, William Prescott had little sympathy with Afonso's reaction to his predicament, asserting that the Portuguese king's 'character always had a spice of Quixotism in it', and that he 'seems to have completely lost his wits at this last misfortune'. Thus, by this account, it was fortunate that his 'retreat was detected before he had time to put his extravagant project into execution'. The contemporary French chronicler Philippe de Commynes, who had served the dukes of Burgundy for many years, gave a fuller and more sympathetic version of Afonso's visit to France.

According to Commynes, the Portuguese king came to France, going to Tours and making a solemn entry into Paris on 23 November 1476, with the aim of obtaining a large army from Louis to help him invade Castile through Vizcaya or Navarre. It soon became clear, though, that Louis's troops were required for his campaign in Lorraine against Afonso's cousin, Charles the Bold of Burgundy. 'This poor king of Portugal', in Commynes' phrase, 'who was very good and just', decided that the only way in which he could obtain French military aid, and thus avoid humiliation in his own country and in Castile, was to negotiate a peace between Louis and Charles. Thwarted in this ambition, and in his subsequent aim of going on pilgrimage and becoming a religious, Alfonso died, marginalized and disillusioned, in 1481.[12] In the view of Alfonso de Palencia, who was, of course, no friend of the Portuguese cause in Castile, Afonso's failed policy towards France was due to his excessive trust in the notoriously slippery Louis. According to Palencia, the intention was to carve up both Castile and Aragon between Portugal and France, but Afonso should have realized, as soon as he met Louis in Tours, that there was no real prospect that such a scheme would be implemented. The Castilian chronicler confirms that the French king had indeed, by the autumn of 1476, accepted Isabella and her husband as legitimate rulers of Castile, and was negotiating with them behind Afonso's back. According to Damião de Góis, Afonso was not out of touch with the government of his kingdom during his stay of over twelve months in France. His son John, who acted as regent, consulted him regularly and reported on the affairs of Portugal, but the disillusioned king, convinced that Louis was about to hand him over to Isabella and Ferdinand, decided to go to Jerusalem, and withdraw from the world. Once he had come to this resolution, he gave instructions to his son to have himself declared king, as 'his intention was to exchange the things of this world for those of God, and to go and serve in the city of Jerusalem, something which he had been preoccupied by for many days, and had decided in himself ever since the death of the queen, his mother'. Although Afonso was prevented from conducting his spiritual pilgrimage as he intended, his abdication brought to a temporary end the violent conflict between Castile and Portugal.[13]

Much of the conflict between the two kingdoms in 1475–6 took place on their territory, but, throughout the period of this peninsular war, another battle was being fought out in the seas off Andalusia, in the eastern Atlantic, and on the west coast of Africa. When Isabella acceded to the Castilian throne in December 1474, Portugal was well ahead in exploration of these areas. The Canary Islands, on the other hand, had been a source of conflict between Castile and Portugal ever since Prince Henry of Portugal set his sights on them in the 1420s. After Henry's death, the *infante* Fernando inherited the eventually abortive Portuguese claim, but it seems that the attractions of the West African coast became stronger when the Canaries failed to produce commercial quantities of gold. It is perhaps ironic that the major advances in the Portuguese search for gold and slaves in West Africa took place after the 'Navigator's' death. In 1469, Fernão Gomes, a Lisbon merchant, was granted a monopoly of trade and exploration in the region which he held until 1475, profiting greatly from ivory and malaguetta pepper, as well as gold in both its metallic and its human form. After earlier attempts, which seem to have been more theoretical than actual, in June and July 1439, seeds and perhaps some settlers were sent to Madeira and one or more of the Azores, and serious efforts began to be made to develop the islands economically. 'Lords' were appointed by the Portuguese princes to supervise the settlers, the most famous of them being a knight from Henry's household who became known, in Arthurian style, as 'Tristão da Ilha' ('Tristan of the Isle'). The result was an often violent blend of European feudalism and customs which were later to become typical of the early American West, and these conditions were to last into Alfonso V's reign. In their methods of settlement and exploration, the Portuguese seem to have been copying the Castilian example in the Canary Islands. In order to counteract the reluctance of Iberians to settle permanently in the islands, both crowns granted extensive jurisdictional concessions to the 'lords', including such traditional privileges as control of flour mills, bread ovens and the sale of salt, as well as taxes on water sources for irrigation and on mining. Straightforward financial inducements, on the model which had been long established on the frontiers of continental Europe, for example in Spain and eastern Germany, were offered to ordinary settlers. Each island was exempt from duty on its exports to Portugal. In Madeira, by the time of Alfonso V, the majority of the settled population consisted of Portuguese peasant farmers, but indigenous slaves from the Canary Islands were also employed in specialized tasks, such as stockherding and sugar-milling. In the Azores, development was slow, but the islands gradually became staging-posts for traffic returning from West Africa. Madeira, on the other hand, became, like the Canaries, an industrial producer of sugar, which in this period replaced honey as Europe's main sweetener. Partly as a result of the efforts of its other 'lord', João Gonsalves, the wood which had originally given the island its Portuguese name came, after 1450, to be largely replaced by a destructive monoculture of sugar cane. The development of this industry, which required heavy capital invest-ment in the planting of canes, and the building of mills and furnaces to refine the cane into sugar, could not have been achieved without foreign capital, which was mainly provided by the Genoese, who had been producing sugar in the Algarve, in southern Portugal, since early in the fifteenth century. The Genoese investors, who dominated the eco-nomy of Madeira just as the Flemish, mainly from the mercantile centre of Bruges, came to control that of the Azores, were not, however, committed to the interests of any particular kingdom or dynasty. They were equally keen to invest in the Castilian Canary Islands, and thus inevitably became embroiled in the conflict surrounding the succession of Isabella to the Castilian throne.

Before Afonso returned to Portugal from France, he claimed to Louis XI that he had support in Castile for a new attempt to secure the throne on his own and his wife's behalf. In the event, however, only the ever-fickle Archbishop Carrillo rose on his behalf. During 1477 and 1478, Isabella and Ferdinand were able to establish their authority in Extre-madura and Andalusia. They also made peace with France, confining their alliances with England and Burgundy to economic matters. Their priority was now to secure their government within Castile and, after John II's death on 19 January 1479, negotiations for peace with Portu-gal lasted from February to September of that year. The first phase was conducted personally, with great toughness, between Isabella and Afonso V's aunt, Beatrice of Lancaster. The initial Portuguese proposals were that there should be marriages between members of the Castilian and Portuguese royal houses, that the frontier between the two king-doms should be examined and redrawn, that Castile should pay the expenses of the recent war, and that all Castilian subjects who had supported Afonso and Joanna should be pardoned. Unsurprisingly, the two royal negotiators soon reached deadlock, and a second phase became necessary, this time conducted by diplomats. Thereafter, not only was there a surer legal basis for the negotiations, but other issues were included, not least the question of discovery and colonial expansion. As a result, peace treaties were signed at Alcaçovas on 4 September 1479. In the process, Joanna effectively sacrificed her claim to the Castilian throne, when she agreed to enter a convent of the Clares in Portugal.[14]

2

The Consolidation of a Regime

It has been argued that Isabella and Ferdinand's reign in Castile only began effectively in 1479, at the same time as the latter inherited the crown of Aragon from his father. Having already made peace with Louis XI of France on 9 October 1478, the Castilian rulers legally achieved the same result with Aragon, when King John II died on 19 January 1479. Despite this, and Sixtus IV's revocation, in December 1478, of his dispensation to Afonso to marry Joanna 'la Beltraneja', the Portuguese king attempted to renew his military struggle for the Castilian throne. Apart from his own pride, Afonso was also fighting to preserve the Portuguese monopoly over trade with Guinea, which was under increasing threat from Andalusian seafarers. In February, he invaded Castile once again, but his son, soon to be King John II, refused to support the expedition, and it was quickly defeated. There now seemed to be no alternative to peace, and on 4 September 1479, four separate treaties were signed at Alcaçovas. Portugal thereby abandoned all claims to Castile, and the Castilians in turn renounced their claims to the newly-conquered territories in Africa and the Atlantic, retaining only the Canary Islands. As a measure of healing after the political conflict of the previous decade, a general pardon was granted to all Castilians who had supported Afonso's and Joanna's claim, and the two kingdoms once again affirmed their previous alliance. Thus it was in 1479 that the civil war in Castile was legally ended, and the dynastic unification of the two Crowns of Castile and Aragon became effective. Contrary to the widely-held notion that Ferdinand and Isabella 'united' Spain, it must again be stressed that, under the terms of the marriage contract of 1469 and the Segovia concordat of 1475, Isabella was the sole legitimate ruler of Castile, while her husband had similar status in Aragon. The royal couple, both scions of the House of Trastámara, thus presided over two amalgams of territory which were quite distinct from each other in terms of institutions, social and economic organization, currency and language. Under the revised agreement of 1475, documents issued by the monarchs in both Castile and Aragon were headed with alternating titles, or groups of titles, from their respective 'Crowns', as kings of Castile and León, Aragon and Sicily, Toledo, Valencia, Galicia, Majorca, Seville, Sardinia, Córdoba, Corsica, Murcia, Jaén, the Algarves, Algeciras, Gibraltar, Guipúzcoa, and counts of Barcelona, lords of Vizcaya and Molina, dukes of Athens and Neopatria, and counts of Roussillon and Cerdagne. Some of these titles were by this time theoretical, for example those in Greece, which reflected ancestral Aragonese claims, rather like English kings' use, over many centuries, of the style 'king of France'. Also largely theoretical were the titles of queen (and nominally king) of the separate 'kingdoms' of Castile, León, Toledo, Galicia, Seville, Córdoba, Murcia, Jaén, the Algarves, Algeciras and Gibraltar, which had all long since lost their individual identities within the 'Crown' of Castile. Isabella and her husband thus inherited, in Castile, a territory in which only the Basque province of Vizcaya (Biscay) retained a small degree of autonomy, while the rest of the Crown had the same royal institutions, laws and parliament (Cortes) and, with minor variations, the same taxation system. The situation of Ferdinand's inheritance in the Crown of Aragon was very different. In 1479, the 'Crown' still consisted of several distinct legal and political entities, the kingdoms of Aragon and Valencia, the counties of Barcelona (Catalonia) and the Balearic Islands, Sardinia, Sicily and, later, the kingdom of Naples. Each of these units had its own laws and legislature and its own taxation, so that the king was constrained to demand taxation separately from each, and had virtually no centralized power, whether legislative or political. If a 'stronger' state was to be built under the new regime, it thus seemed inevitable that its basis would be Castilian rather than Aragonese.[1]

Although it is commonly assumed, with hindsight, that Ferdinand and Isabella must have aimed to transform their respective domains into a 'modern' unitary state, such as their Habsburg successors attempted, it is in fact by no means clear that this was their intention. At the time of Isabella's disputed accession to the Castilian throne, and in the succeeding years, there was an extraordinary weight of expectation on her and her husband's shoulders. The two main sources of this eager and anxious anticipation were the thinking on monarchy which had developed in Castile during the preceding decades, and explicit prophesy concerning the immanent future role of Spain and its rulers, which originated on both sides of the Castilian – Aragonese border. Messianic belief was prevalent in the Iberian peninsula throughout the period of civil conflict which preceded Isabella and Ferdinand's victory in the war of the Castilian succession, though it did not always work to their advantage, as when Afonso of Portugal invaded Castile in 1475, on behalf of his young wife Joanna, his Castilian supporters apparently supposing that he was the much-prophesied 'hidden king' (*rey encubierto*), who was about to be revealed. Ferdinand, too, was the subject of extensive and fervent prophetic expectation. His marriage with Isabella in 1469 had led to expectations of a union between the 'flowers of Aragon' and the Castilian Crown, which would bring an end to conflict between the two main branches of the Trastamaran dynasty and hence to violence within the two kingdoms. An anonymous poet wrote of Ferdinand, in 1472, that Spain desired 'a God in heaven and a king on earth', while the poet Gómez Manrique expressed what he saw as the people's desire for the country's wounds to be healed. Once Isabella had obtained the Castilian throne, the Franciscan Iñigo de Mendoza compared her to the Virgin Mary, who according to tradition came into the world to restore fallen humanity, the queen's role being to perform this service for the people of her own kingdom. The writer and military man Diego de Valera, on the other hand, placed his hopes in Ferdinand at least from 1476, during the dangerous phase of the war against Afonso of Portugal. Not unnaturally, the new king and queen took such support seriously, even in its more prophetic vein, during the difficult early years of their reign in Castile. Isabella's reaction to her half-brother's death had demonstrated her determination all too clearly, and when a revolt broke out in Segovia, where she had first been proclaimed queen, at the end of July 1476, she reacted with speed and severity. She went at once to the town to support her steward (*mayordomo*) Andrés Cabrera, and told the delegation from the city which came to meet her that she would brook no questioning of her authority as queen of Castile. For Isabella and her husband, 1474 was 'Year Zero', before which there had been chaos and misrule, and after which there was a strong and divinely-inspired monarchy in Castile, and then in Aragon and Granada.[2]

The temptation of later historians to regard Ferdinand and Isabella's regime as 'absolutist' may at least in part be justified not only by the couple's political actions but also by the political thinking with which they had both been brought up. During the fifteenth century, a 'high' doctrine of monarchy had been developed in Spain, and especially in Castile, by political theorists, many of whom took an active part in government. The theory owed much of its inspiration to notions of government in the biblical Jewish monarchy, in the Roman Imperial period, and in the Visigothic monarchy in Spain. Rodrigo Sánchez de Arévalo, for instance, set out for Henry IV of Castile, in his *Garden of princes* (*Vergel de los príncipes*), a programme for government which was only to be attempted by his successors.

We hope that, through your immense virtues and magnificent deeds, your royal dignity and your commonwealth [*república*] will increase so much

THE CONSOLIDATION OF A REGIME

that between your kingdoms and the infidel barbarian peoples, you will place as walls the great [Atlantic] Ocean and the Mediterranean, as deep seas. Nor will your strength [*virtud*] tire in this, until in the wild parts of Africa your name and power spread, your money is minted, and you recover those wide provinces which are due to your royal person, just as they were possessed peacefully by the famous king Theodoric and your progenitors in the great monarchy of Spain. (Sánchez de Arévalo BAE 116: 312)

In the late fifteenth century, the Visigothic period in Spain was seen as an exemplary time of unitary Christian rule. As early as the thirteenth century, chroniclers such as Lucas de Tuy and Rodrigo Jiménez de Rada had begun to identify the Christian Spaniards of their own day, who were making spectacular gains on the Andalusian and Valencian fronts, with their Visigothic predecessors. In the mid-fifteenth century, the 'Gothic' myth of Christian Spanish identity received further support from the Old Christian Sánchez de Arévalo and the *converso* Alonso de Cartagena, the latter in his *Anacephaleosis*, or 'Recapitulation', which was explicitly based on the work of Jiménez de Rada. Yet although the Visigothic kingdom was seen by fifteenth-century Castilian commentators as the ideal combination of the Judeo-Christian and Classical Roman traditions of monarchy, it was not regarded as the only model for the exercise of rule in Spain. Another important influence was the then current notion of 'feudal' monarchy, and in particular the relationship between the king and his subjects, which had so tormented the reigns of Isabella's two predecessors on the throne of Castile. None of the main Castilian political treatises of the period between 1420 and 1480 use the explicit vocabulary of 'textbook' feudalism, as it was to be understood from the seventeenth century onwards. These writers make no reference to vassals (*vasallos*) or benefices (*beneficios*), but only to such general concepts as 'monarchy' (*monarquía*), lordship (*señorío*) and power (*poder*). Yet the 'feudal' notion of monarchy, as it later became known, as a compact, or contract, between a ruler, who was first among equals, and his leading subjects was not the only theory available to monarchs in late medieval Europe. The late Roman Empire, of East and West, had bequeathed an idea of monarchy in which the ruler was qualitatively distinct from his subjects, and this notion naturally appealed to many a medieval ruler. The Trastamaran theorists' talk of the king's 'certain knowledge' (*çierta çiençia*) and 'absolute power' (*poder absoluto*) did not, however, preclude recognition, both in theoretical treatises and in Cortes legislation, of the realistic need for monarchy to work with subjects as well as against them. It remained to be seen whether Isabella and her husband would remain faithful to the 'imperialistic' approach to monarchy, which was clearly congenial to them, or make compromises with the vested political interests which predated their accession.[3]

Historians have rightly regarded the cortes of Toledo in 1480, which quickly followed the signing of the treaties of Alcaçovas, as the main legal foundation of the regime of the future 'Catholic Monarchs' in Castile. Even during the civil war, though, a start on the new pro-gramme had been made at the cortes of Madrigal, in 1476. On the face of it, and as was natural in time of war, the apparent main preoccupation of this parliament was law and order. The most noted achievement at Madrigal was the establishment of a new organization for the whole of Castile, called the *Santa Hermandad* (Holy Brother-hood). As with so many of their policies and measures, Ferdinand and Isabella, in adopting this approach, built on earlier experience. In the later medieval period, the expression *hermandad* had been used to describe brotherhoods which were formed on local initiative, often by groups of towns, to secure law and order and trade by patrolling the roads and countryside and arresting and punishing malefactors. In the thirteenth and early fourteenth centuries, Hermandades had sprouted to keep local order during unstable royal minorities. During the reign of Alfonso XI, for example, a Hermandad of this kind had been formed in Burgos, in 1315, to deal with the problem of highwaymen in that part of Old Castile. When Alfonso assumed the powers of government personally, in 1325, he suppressed local Hermandades. The civil conflict of the 1350s and 1360s led to their reappearance, but the first two rulers of the new Trastamaran dynasty ensured that the revived Her-mandades were under royal control. A specific prototype of Isabella and Ferdinand's institution was the 'Old Brotherhood of shepherds and honey-producers of Toledo, Talavera and Ciudad Real', in New Castile and La Mancha, which was also set up in the fourteenth century, to keep law and order particularly in mountainous areas. Its squadrons (*cuadrillas*) administered summary justice to robbers and other offen-ders. Despite the determination of the Trastamarans to keep the Her-mandades under their control, local initiative continued to surface in the form of petitions to the Crown from the Cortes. For instance, the cortes of Segovia in 1386 produced a plan for what would be effectively a national 'civil guard' for Castile, consisting of Hermandad *cuadrillas*, which was to be financed by the major towns, but in the turbulent political circumstances of the period, with a weak dynasty and major conflict in progress with Portugal, the plan advanced no further. In 1456, however, Henry IV followed this precedent in providing some initiative for the establishment of a Hermandad under royal authority to keep the peace during the period of his campaigning in Granada.

During the civil disturbances in Castile in the mid-fifteenth century, such Hermandades on occasions, for example at Fuensalida in 1464 and Medina del Campo in 1467, offered their services to Henry IV in bringing recalcitrant nobles to heel. Local councils were the main organizing agents, but sometimes bishops took the lead, as in the case of Fray Lope de Barrientos in Cuenca, and diocesans sometimes, as in the case of Palencia, became *alcalde mayor* (chief magistrate) of the Hermandad in their jurisdiction. During this period, the organization had some success in restraining aristocratic excesses, and it remained neutral in the dispute between the king and his rival Prince Alfonso in the 1460s. At the height of the conflict, between 1465 and Alfonso's death three years later, the network constructed by the juntas of Fuensalida and Medina del Campo covered most of the Crown of Castile. After the junta of Palencia, in 1468, as the political situation in Castile declined, the power and effectiveness of the Hermandad diminished accordingly, and the organization seems to have become almost totally inactive. A further attempt was made to revive it in 1473, at the junta of Villalón, but by this time the king had neither the will nor the ability to take up the offer of support by a group of representatives, including numerous churchmen, who were eager to assist the Crown in the restoration of law and order. Things were to be different in the new reign. The two representatives (*procuradores*) of Burgos, at Madrigal in 1476, brought a proposal from their city council which was clearly intended to improve the security of the lucrative export trade in merino wool which was carried on by local merchants, a number of whom were city councillors (*regidores*) as well. The king and queen, with a much more general preoccupation with law and order in the kingdom, took up the proposal with alacrity and transformed it into something much greater in scope. Nevertheless, the notion that Ferdinand and Isabella's Hermandad was an entirely new creation was carefully fostered by their propagandists. The 'Incomplete chronicle' (*Crónica incompleta de los Reyes Católicos*) ignores Henry IV's Hermandad, and states that, in 1476, the queen established a new institution, which immediately became a glittering success. If it was influenced by any precedent, this was the companies of royal lancers which had recently been created by Louis XI of France, rather than any native Spanish institution. This account has been accepted by many modern historians, including Lunenfeld, but, in reality, the Santa Hermandad was not an original concept, and its authority was built up only gradually in Ferdinand and Isabella's reign. Given the evident insecurity of the times, it was not difficult for the king and queen to convince the *procuradores* of the need for such an institution. Not only was there an invading army in the kingdom, but the justice system in large parts of the country was effectively under the control of dissident members of the nobility rather than royal officials.

The Crown's rhetoric at Madrigal stressed the traditional character of the new Hermandad as well as the current crisis of public order. The initiative, however, was now to come from the government and not from the localities. The Cortes duly approved the establishment of the new Santa Hermandad for an initial period of three years, though, in the event, they were not to be asked to give an opinion on the subject again. The new national body significantly covered lands under seigneurial jurisdiction, as well as those directly subject to the crown. Local committees (juntas) were set up between May and July 1476, for example, in Madrigal itself and Cigales. A general junta was held in Dueñas, between 25 July and 5 August of that year, which established a national structure for the various local Hermandades. The early meetings were chaired by reliable officials and supporters of the king and queen, in particular Alfonso de Quintanilla and Juan de Ortega, then one of Ferdinand's chaplains and subsequently the first bishop of Almería, and the Dueñas junta laid down that the presidency of the new organization should be held by Fray Alonso de Burgos, bishop of Córdoba, and Lope de Rivas, bishop of Cartagena, who were both close collaborators with Isabella and Ferdinand. The close involvement of the Church with the Hermandad continued under the new arrangements, and, for example, the 1477 junta of Burgos met in the chapter house of the cathedral. Every six months, each centre of population with more than thirty households (hogares, or hearths) was to elect two magistrates, one from among the knights (caballeros) and the other from the common people (villanos), and recruit at its own expense a cuadrilla, which was to be responsible for pursuing offenders within a radius of five leagues, after summons by the ringing of a bell. The new Hermandad had jurisdiction over violent incidents on roads and highways, robberies and kidnappings outside centres of population, arson of houses and crops, and robbery within settlements with fewer than fifty inhabitants. The squads of brothers were also empowered to pursue offenders in these categories who had fled from larger towns into the countryside. Once captured, supposed offenders were subjected to summary justice, which contrasted with the safeguards, and the delays, which were a part of the conventional justice system. Those who had committed a theft with a monetary value of more than 500 maravedíes were to have a foot cut off, while those convicted of murder were summarily executed in open country, by means of the arrows which became the emblem of the organization. The institution, which was to endure into the seventeenth century, soon acquired some popularity because of its 'vigilante' effectiveness in providing quick, but rough, justice, if not its respect for what would in later centuries become known as 'human rights'.

From June 1476 onwards, Isabella and Ferdinand expanded the scope of the new 'Holy' Hermandad by requiring participating towns to make special efforts to finance the recruitment of one cavalry soldier for every hundred households and one man-at-arms for every 150 hearths. Eight autonomous provinces of the organization were set up, in Burgos, Palencia, Segovia, Avila, Valladolid, Zamora, León and Salamanca, each with its own captain (*capitán*), secretary, and military forces. The Council of the Hermandad consisted of delegates from each province, under the presidency of the bishop of Cartagena and former councillor of Henry IV, Lope de Rivas, with Alfonso de Quintanilla as treasurer, and as general-in-chief Ferdinand's bastard brother Alfonso de Aragón, duke of Villahermosa. An annual assembly of provincial representatives (*diputación provincial*) was also set up. Under the pretext of tackling crime, Ferdinand and Isabella thus succeeded in establishing what was effectively a national Castilian army, which overrode the fragmentation of local jurisdiction in the kingdom. The 1476 cortes of Madrigal did not establish the Hermandad on a permanent basis, but the extension of its remit, for example for three years from 1478 to 1481, became a matter for the royal prerogative. The renewal of the organization's remit in 1478 was in fact opposed by the body which had first suggested it, Burgos city council, which rightly feared a consequent loss of local autonomy and parallel growth of royal power. Isabella and Ferdinand had to threaten the citizens of Burgos, the traditional 'capital of Castile' (*cabeza de Castilla*), before the consent of its municipal fathers could be obtained. There had also been unsuccessful opposition to the new organization in Toledo and Andalusia. 'Provinces' of the Hermandad were duly set up in the rest of the Crown of Castile, partly anticipating the Spanish system of government in nineteenth and twentieth centuries. In Córdoba, for instance, the city council elected one of its members to serve in the *diputación provincial*, and the provincial Hermandad was administered by two *alcaldes* (magistrates), one representing the minor nobility (*hidalgos*) and the other the taxpaying citizenry (*pecheros* or *peones*). The receiver (*receptor*) of goods confiscated by the local Hermandad in the course of its operations was a full councillor (*veinticuatro*) of Córdoba, chosen by his colleagues, and the organization, here as elsewhere, had its own prison. In addition to the two *alcaldes*, the local squadrons were supervised by a constable (*alguacil*). Although its primary purpose was explicitly to preserve law and order in the Castilian countryside, during the Granada war it also became a means of raising revenue for the Crown without recourse to the Cortes (see chapter 5). To begin with, the Crown's aim seems to have been to use the Hermandad as a means of recruiting elite military units which would be under its own direct control, and the organization's troops were used against supporters of Alfonso and Joanna. In 1480, the junta in Madrid asked the monarchs to recruit a permanent force of 200 men-at-arms, who were to be independent of local influence, because troops of this type would be more effective in the event of war. This was the origin of the royal army which continued to serve in the Granada war. There was also an unsuccessful project to form a royal navy under the auspices of the Hermandad, with contributions from Galicia, Asturias and the Basque country, in the north, and Moguer and Palos in the south-west, but the scheme was abandoned, probably as a result of the general lack of preoccupation with naval matters which appeared to be characteristic of royal advisers at that time. The successive demands of civil conflict before 1480 and the Granada campaigns thereafter encouraged the Crown to see the Hermandad as an instrument of financial extraction as well as law enforcement. As a price for the acceptance of the national organization, Ferdinand and Isabella had had to lower the contributions which were to be made by seigneurial jurisdictions, which served only to increase the burden on the royal towns and their populations. In Burgos, for instance, council revenues had to be assigned as annuities (*juros*) in order to meet the Crown's demands.[4]

The establishment of the Hermandad affected both central and local government in Castile, and was part of the ambitious programme for the reform of government at both levels, which the king and queen began to implement as soon as Isabella gained the Castilian throne. It has already been noted that she and her husband both inherited a 'high' doctrine of monarchical power, but it remained to be seen how, if at all, this would be implemented. One of the achievements of the cortes of Toledo in 1480 was to establish in its definitive form the Castilian royal council (*consejo real*, known in the Habsburg period and thereafter as the *consejo de Castilla*). Traditionally, there had been two distinct yet overlapping categories of royal councillor. One formed a coherent group which had both administrative and judicial responsibilities, and by 1385 the basic elements of this body had been established. It consisted of some bishops, some nobles, and an increasingly important element of lesser- or non-noble professional administrators with legal training, known as *letrados*. By Ferdinand and Isabella's reign, these officials were also to be found in parallel councils, which supervised the Inquisition, the Hermandad (until 1498), the military orders of Santiago, Calatrava and Alcántara, and later the Indies. The Castilian royal council was chaired by a bishop, and its administrative core consisted of three leading nobles and eight or nine *letrados*. The second traditional category of royal councillor had a less formal role, which depended on individuals' political experience, and their personal influence with the ruler. The role of councillors of this kind, who included both nobles and senior churchmen, was diminished under the new regime, with the result that after 1480 they were only allowed to attend the council of Castile as observers. At the beginning of their reign, the king and queen perhaps inevitably relied to a great extent on councillors who had served Henry IV. These included Bishop Lope de Rivas and Cardinal Pedro González de Mendoza, as well as Iñigo Manrique de Lara, bishop of Coria, who was rewarded for his earlier support of Princess Isabella with the presidency of the council. In general, the royal couple were keen to reward those who had supported them in previous years, and leading churchmen, including both bishops and *letrado* clerics, benefited from this preference. The cortes of Toledo made a distinction between prelates, masters of military orders and titled nobles, who were given the right to take part in all business, and *letrados* and knights (*caballeros*), who were henceforth entitled to attend meetings only when business with which they had been personally entrusted was being transacted. A conservative view was thus taken by the new monarchs of who should be involved in the inner workings of the political process, though pragmatism often dictated the adoption of a different outlook, in effect if not in theory.[5] Increasingly, the highest court of appeal in legal cases in Castile was effectively no longer the royal council but the *audiencia real* at Valladolid. This too had been set up by Henry II in 1371, at the cortes of Toro. It was then ordained that seven judges (*oidores*) should be set up as a high court, to hear such appeals in the residence of the king and queen. In the monarchs' absence, they were to operate as part of the chancellor's department (*chancillería*), which had traditionally had overall responsibility for legal matters, as well as guardianship of the great seal of the kingdom. On 15 April 1475, Isabella and Ferdinand confirmed the existing royal privileges of the *oidores* of the high court, and named as the tribunal's president a clerical member of the Mendoza clan, Diego Hurtado de Mendoza, bishop of Palencia. At the same time, the bishop was given powers to carry out any reforms which he thought necessary in the functioning of the court, and was also made appeal judge (*juez mayor de las suplicaciones*) for Vizcaya. Both prelates and secular lawyers served the Catholic Monarchs as *oidores* and, on 9 January 1478, Bishop Mendoza became president of the royal council, and was replaced as president of the court by Juan de Meneses, bishop of Zamora. At this stage, the monarchs transferred the resolution of certain legal disputes from the *consejo real* to the *chancillería*. During Ferdinand and Isabella's joint reign, the *audiencia* in Valladolid heard appeals in civil cases. The aggrieved party would, through his legal representative (*procurador*), ask the higher tribunal to issue a summons in the name of the Crown (*real provisión de emplazamiento*) for all the documents of the case to be handed over. A hearing (*prueba*) would then take place, after which the judges concerned would give a preliminary sentence (*sentencia de vista*), bearing a minimum of three signatures. If an appeal was lodged immediately against this, the case would be reviewed, and a further sentence (*sentencia de revista*) issued. If the case was fully concluded, which often did not occur, a letter of execution (*carta ejecutoria*) would be issued, containing the definitive sentence, and orders with full royal authority for its implementation. Criminal appeals were heard not by *oidores* but by a committee of three magistrates (*alcaldes*). In 1494, the Valladolid court gave up its jurisdiction over the southern half of the Crown of Castile to a new tribunal in Ciudad Real (from 1505 in Granada), and each was henceforth officially styled a *chancillería*, a term which had been in habitual use since the beginning of Isabella and Ferdinand's reign.[6]

The royal council of Castile, as it evolved during the late fourteenth and fifteenth centuries, was thus more a political and administrative than a judicial body. Traditionally, it had had a deliberative role in home and foreign policy, and was responsible for the creation of seigneurial jurisdictions and the granting of public offices, annuities (*juros*) and military commands, such as the governorship of fortresses (*alcaidías*). A conspicuous casualty of Ferdinand and Isabella's reforms was, however, the Castilian parliament, or Cortes. Even before the arrival on the throne of Henry II of Trastámara, kings had attempted to limit the role of the assembly, but the position of the representatives (*procuradores*) of the towns was strengthened by the political and economic difficulties which assailed John I of Castile during the 1380s. In 1386, a year of crisis in relations with Portugal, the king made the crucial concession of allowing the Cortes to inspect the royal accounts. In the normal way of parliamentary history in western Europe, such a sign of weakness proved hard to recoup, and in the following year the *procuradores* once again demanded to see the books, this time as of right. In 1388, they voted only a third of the subsidy (*servicio*) which the king had requested, and nominated their own commission, consisting of a bishop, a nobleman and four representatives of towns, to collect and administer the money. In 1391, the year of the violent attacks on the Spanish Jewish communities (see chapter 3), no fewer than forty-nine towns sent representatives to the Cortes, but this proved to be the peak of the parliament's power. The king succeeded in exploiting divisions between noble (*hidalgo*) *procuradores* of the towns, who did not have to pay the direct taxes voted by the Cortes, and the non-noble tax payers (*pecheros*) who did. Between 1390 and 1395, the largely urban 'third estate' failed to break the noble's control of the boy king, Henry III, and in the period of his personal rule, between then and 1406, the political and economic influence of the Cortes declined steadily. As the Trastamarans steadily gave away urban lord-ships to members of the upper nobility, the representation of towns in the Cortes declined accordingly, so that only twelve sent *procuradores* in 1425. By the time of Isabella's accession in 1474, the number of towns represented had settled at seventeen, with Granada being added after 1492. Many of the cities concerned were the capitals of the notional 'kingdoms' which made up the crown of Castile, but whole regions, notably Galicia, Asturias and the Basque country in the north, and Extremadura in the south-west, were left without even notional repre-sentation. The other two 'estates' (a term not normally used in Castile in the sense of an order of society), that is, the clergy and the nobility, ceased during the fifteenth century to function as 'houses of parliament'. In addition, the Crown exerted increasing control over the representa-tives of the towns, providing them with salaries from the royal treasury, and after 1432 requiring that they should all be noble *hidalgos* and not common *pecheros*. Increasingly, the Cortes came under the thumb of the king, obeying his will in everything and in any case representing no more than a small group of rich and powerful citizens in the home towns. The Castilian cortes had never succeeded in reaching a situation in which *procuradores* might receive a royal response to their petitions before granting financial supply to the Crown.

Even before Isabella and Ferdinand moved further in the direction of non-parliamentary government, the Cortes had become an almost wholly passive advisory body, giving automatic assent to legislation which had been drafted by the royal administration. As a result of these developments, the towns with the privilege of representation in the Cortes after 1474 were Burgos, Soria, Segovia, Avila, Valladolid, León, Salamanca, Zamora, Toro, Toledo, Cuenca, Guadalajara, Madrid, Seville, Códoba, Jaén and Murcia. Some of the excluded regions of the kingdom were notionally represented by the nearest cortes town so that, for example, Salamanca claimed to speak for Ciudad Rodrigo, and Zamora for the whole of Galicia, though Santiago de Compostela was excluded with the agreement of all the existing members of the assembly. An indication of the practical workings of the Cortes is the register for the period 1445–74, which reveals that the *procuradores* had succeeded on occasions in exploiting the difficulties of the monarchy under Isabella's two predecessors. In 1445, for ex-ample, they had gained control over the nomination of those in charge of the collection of the royal revenues, the *recaudadores mayores*, a measure which was only revoked ten years later by Henry IV. Never again, after the death of the constable of Castile, Alvaro de Luna, in 1453, were the cortes towns given the opportunity to join the Crown in a combined force to counterbalance the overweening power of the upper nobility. Throughout their joint reign, Isabella and her husband appear to have regarded the Cortes as a broken reed, and during his regency in the early sixteenth century, Ferdinand continued with the policy of summoning the assembly only for short periods, and allowing it almost no political influence. After the cortes of Madrigal in 1476 and Toledo in 1480, the *procuradores* of the towns were not summoned again until 1498, their revenue-granting functions being entrusted in the meantime, which included the whole of the Granada war, to the juntas of the Hermandad. The frequency of summons for the Cortes increased thereafter, during the turbulent beginning of the sixteenth century, with meetings occurring in 1502, 1505, 1506, 1512 and 1515, but the assembly never succeeded in securing the role in government which had been briefly offered to it in the latter years of John II's reign. The participants in the Madrigal and Toledo meetings had simply been required to 'rubber-stamp' the Crown's plans for establishing the new and strong monarchical regime, and their value to the royal adminis-tration largely evaporated thereafter. After 1480, the Crown legislated by means of ordinances and other administrative measures (*pragmáticas* and *cédulas*) which were held to have the authority of laws passed by the Cortes but which were not referred to that assembly. The royal court was now explicitly the main, if not the only source of political legitimacy.

Documents issued by the administrations of the Trastamaran mon-archs in the fifteenth century, as well as political treatises of the period, continued to proclaim Castilian rulers' 'natural lordship' (*señorío nat-ural*) over their kingdom, as well as their 'absolute power' (*poder absoluto*) within it. Yet the period since Henry of Trastámara's violent seizure of the throne in 1369 had seen a steady erosion of the Crown's resources, in terms of jurisdiction, lands and vassals. Some of these lordships (*señoríos*) had traditionally been in the hands of the Church (*abadengo*) or the military orders (see chapter 6), but the great bulk of these jurisdictions, which might include quite large towns as well as extensive tracts of land, were placed in the hands of the military aristocracy, and in particular those of the small number of noble families which benefited particularly from the Trastamaran takeover. Yet even under the feeble regimes of John II and Henry IV, the most important Castilian towns had not been alienated to noble jurisdiction, or *señorío*. Until the introduction by Alfonso XI of councillors, known generally as *regidores*, to the main towns under direct royal jurisdiction (*realengo*), the constitutional relationship between the Crown and its urban subjects seems to have been quite straightforward. Particularly in New Castile, Andalusia and Extremadura, though also further north, the king appointed to each town chief magistrates (*alcaldes mayores*) and a chief constable (*alguacil mayor*), who would rule in conjunction with elected representatives of individual parishes, who were often elected, and were generally known as *jurados* (those who had been sworn in). In northern towns, such as Burgos, the *alcaldes* were accompanied by another privileged magistrate, known as a *merino*, and, there and elsewhere, the officials who were responsible for law and order became known collectively as the *justicia*. Ever since the early stages of the 'reconquest' of lands from Muslim rule, Christian urban settlements had been legally underpinned by charters, known as *fueros*. By the late Middle Ages, a mythology had developed, in which the traditional Castilian method for the government of towns had been a council (*concejo*) which supposedly consisted of all male inhabitants, or 'good men' (*omes* or *hombres buenos*) who qualified as citizens by means of permanent residence and the payment of taxes, and was hence known as an 'open council' (*concejo abierto*).

Whether or not open councils ever existed, and recent studies suggest that this is doubtful, they were clearly not a part of late medieval government in Castile. After councils of *regidores* were introduced to the major towns – in some places they were known after their number as *veinticuatros* ('twenty-fours') or *doces* ('twelves') – they took over from the Crown the appointment of the magistrates and constable, though *jurados* continued to be elected by the parishes. In reality, though, this change did not weaken royal control over the cities because the Crown in any case appointed the *regidores*, and normally for life. The attractions of power and influence for individuals in their localities, and the anxiety of Trastamaran kings to placate and neutralize likely enemies, had led by the time of Isabella's accession to a proliferation of office-holders in the royal towns. As early as 1428, John II had proclaimed to the Cortes his desire to reduce the urban *regidores* to their former number (*antiguo número*) by not making further grants of the superfluous offices (*oficios acrecentados*) when their holders resigned or died. In practice, though, John continued with the previous policy, so that the number of *regimientos*, and of other urban offices in the Crown's gift, such as the post of public scribe (*escribano público*), continued to proliferate. Henry IV's reaffirmation, at the cortes of Ocaña in 1469, of the policy of returning to the 'ancient number' of office-holders was no more effective than his father's proclamation to the same effect. Isabella and Ferdinand tackled the problem once again at the cortes of Toledo in 1480, and when they did so, they concentrated on offices which had been added to urban establishments after 1440, thus implicitly blaming John II for the problem. Those who had received the surplus offices (*oficios acrecentados*) after that date would not be permitted to resign them to any other individual, and the Crown would make no further provision to individuals in such cases. The seriousness of the situation was illustrated by the case of Córdoba, a town which had become well known to the king and queen during their attempts to restore order in the kingdom and secure their own regime. By the time that the small group of cortes deputies from the towns assembled in Toledo in 1480, Córdoba's notional council of twenty-four had expanded to about a hundred, no doubt at least in part as a result of the conflict in the area between rival noble factions in the previous two reigns. Although the council in this particular city had been reduced by 1515 to thirty-four, the demand for offices in royal towns remained as insistent as ever. Apart from the obvious attractions of status, local power and influence for the councillors themselves, there was also the beguiling possibility of handing the office on to a designated heir, by means of a resignation which was ratified as a matter of routine by the royal administration. In 1465, for example, Henry IV had explicitly admitted the hereditary principle when establishing a council of *veinticuatros* in Jerez de la Frontera. Evidently Ferdinand and Isabella had quickly realized the importance of gaining control over the office-holding system in the towns. The relevant legislation at the cortes of Toledo proclaimed that 'It would be a great error in thought to suppose that the gift or grace of governing well is derived from the father by the son or by one person from another'. If public office was open to all suitable candidates, 'all will exert themselves to practise goodness and virtues, to win the prize of honour'. As so often in their programme of 'reform', the king and queen justified their efforts to claw back royal powers which had been lost in previous reigns by appealing to a mythical previous age of Castilian purity, virtue and freedom, that of the largely illusory 'open councils', in which election to urban office had been annual. In reality, the Crown's intention was to achieve nothing of the kind, and the actual terms of the relevant legislation were much simpler and more mundane than its high-flown preamble. All individuals who were in possession of offices by royal appointment, and had already received a licence from the Crown to resign them to named recipients, were to be given a period of ninety days' grace in which to make use of that privilege. If they failed to do so within that interval, they were to lose not only the office concerned but also their property. In reality, the practice of licensed resignations to named individuals continued after 1480, and the existing elites in the major towns were thus reinforced for future generations.

Indeed, even the laws (*cuadernos*) of Toledo themselves implied that such planned resignations to relatives would continue. The new code stated that such *renunciaciones* would be regarded as valid if the office-holders concerned died within three weeks of using them. Although royal anxiety to control the major towns focused mainly on full members of city councils, that is, the *regidores* or *veinticuatros*, the Crown also exercised influence over appointments to other urban offices. The representatives of the parishes (*jurados*) in the fifteenth century were also part of the system of crown appointments and planned resignations, though even in Isabella and Ferdinand's reign it was still possible on occasions for the citizens in parishes to elect their own representatives, usually at a meeting in the parish church. The crown tried to control the appointment of *jurados* in the same way as that of *regidores*, but with equally limited success. In some towns, for example in Córdoba, the *jurados* had their own *cabildo*, or council, meeting separately from the main council of *veinticuatros*, which they also attended, with limited rights to speak and vote. By the late fifteenth century, the appointment of other municipal officials was mainly in the hands of the councils of *regidores*, and in some cases with the *jurados* as a body, but the Crown continued to intervene spasmodically in certain appointments, for example those of public scribes (*escribanos públicos*), who were the backbone of the Castilian notarial system.[7]

One of the notable features of Castilian society in the latter part of Henry IV's reign, and during and after the Portuguese invasion of 1475, was disorder in the major towns of the kingdom. The establishment of firmer royal control was evidently a priority for the new sovereigns and there were many bad old ways in the towns to be changed, from the Crown's point of view. The problem of urban violence, much of it sponsored and sometimes led by prominent citizens, had been rife throughout the fifteenth century. In the large Andalusian port of Seville, for example, violence and misgovernment had been rife since before 1400. Complaints about crime and gangsterism occurred regularly beween then and the early sixteenth century. At the end of John II's reign, for example, in 1454, the city's *jurados* issued a formal statement (*requerimiento*) to the council of *veinticuatros*, in which they protested against a wide range of political, economic and social abuses. Among them was the question of law and order. According to the Seville *jurados*, unemployed males were terrorizing the population. The matter had been discussed by the council of *veinticuatros* early in 1453, and the result had been an order whereby such 'vagabonds' (*vagamundos*) were to leave the city within a few days and not return for at least six months. The measure had clearly been unsuccessful, however, since the *requerimiento* returned to the subject, stating that it is contained in the aforesaid

> ordinance that there should be no ruffians [*rufianes*] nor should they have prostitutes in the [public] brothel. And not only is this [provision] not kept, but the said ruffians walk publicly with the said women in the main streets of the city, and among the good women. And many inhabitants abandon their houses and go to live in other parts for this reason, and they do not even dare to complain, saying that they will be killed if they complain.

Lack of local action led to the matter's being referred to the king, who despatched three letters to Seville, expressing horror at the fact that vagabonds and ruffians were apparently allowed to carry on their activities there with impunity, and ordering their permanent expulsion from the city, on pain of loss of office for the councillors and their officials. The political and social turmoil of Henry IV's reign was hardly conducive to the solution of such problems, and complaints continued to be made by the *jurados*, for example in 1460 and 1472. Troubles with the unemployed, gangsterism and prostitution were also endemic in other Andalusian towns, such as Córdoba, and were a major worry for Isabella and Ferdinand, particularly in the early years of their joint reign.[8]

Perhaps inevitably, Alfonso XI's reorganization of the government of the Castilian royal towns, by magistrates and life councillors, with the assistance of parish representatives and public scribes, did not prove to be permanent. As was commonly the case with medieval government, new tiers of administration did not replace existing ones but were simply added to them. The most significant change of this kind was the introduction to the government of the major royal towns of a new supreme official called a *corregidor* ('co-ruler' or 'corrector'). As Bermúdez Aznar has noted, such offices had existed in western Europe since Roman times, under names which included *corrector* and *reformador*. Thus the Castilian *corregidor* formed part of a continuing dispute between medieval kings and their subjects over the origins and exercise of sovereignty. Such officials should not, however, be seen simply as agents of monarchical authority. As in the case of the Hermandad, initiative for the appointment of a *corregidor* was at least as likely to arise locally as in the central government. Despite the concept of such a *corrector*, to act as a check on local faction-fighting and misrule, as in the case of its earliest explicit appearance in Castile during the reign of Alfonso XI, the proliferation of such officials under Henry II of Trastámara largely arose from regional worries about disorder. On the other hand, his successor, Henry III, sent out numerous *corregidores* with the explicit intention of re-establishing royal authority and curbing local abuses. In 1406, at the very end of his reign, this ruler was the first to state an intention to sent a *corregidor* to every part of his kingdom which was under direct royal jurisdiction. Royal officials attempted to apply this policy during the lengthy reign of John II, and as early 1419, the cortes of Madrid attempted to return to the former situation, in which the Crown appointed *corregidores* at the request and on the initiative of local councils. During the instability of the following two decades, towns often overcame their fear of royal authoritarianism and asked for the appointment of officials, including *corregidores*, to keep the peace. On occasions though, as in Murcia in 1452, a *corregidor* might be expelled by local councillors and their henchmen. Henry IV continued with his father's policy, launching a campaign in 1455 to send *corregidores* to 'correct' abuses throughout Castile. Contemporary commentators, such as Diego de Valera and Alfonso de Palencia, attacked this move, on the grounds first that it was contrary to the laws and liberties of the kingdom, and secondly that such officials were in any case far too prone to greed and the abuse of their considerable power. In 1459, during a local rebellion, the people of Burgos expelled their *corregidor*, Fernando de Fonseca, without resistance from the *regidores*, and in 1464 the council refused to accept the renewal of the appointment of another such official. From 1459, here and in Murcia, the king responded by downgrading the office of *corregidor* to that of *asistente* (assistant), with fewer powers to override the wishes of local politicians. This approach soon backfired in Seville, where a revolt broke out in September 1463 against the city's *asistente*, Pedro Manrique, who had attempted to impose taxes (*sisas*) on meat and fish, which were not normally taxed. For the rest of his troubled reign, Henry pursued the policy of appointing *asistentes* rather than *corregidores* to some of the main royal towns, including tenures in Seville and Toledo which in each case totalled eleven years. The king appeared to accede to the demand of the cortes of Toledo, in 1462, and of the noble 'reformers' of 1465, that *asistentes* should be appointed for only one year at a time, but the former practice continued up to his death in 1474. In the early years of her reign, Isabella named *asistentes* to several towns, but made their powers effectively equivalent to those of a *corregidor*. She also toyed with the novel title of *gobernador* (governor), which was conferred, during the civil war between 1475 and 1477, on her main representatives in Galicia, in Ciudad Rodrigo and in the marquisate of Villena, while Pacheco himself was in rebellion against her.[9]

The spread of *corregidores*, and the strengthening of their authority, was to be a major part of Isabella and her husband's plans to subdue their opponents and secure their regime. The cortes of Madrigal in 1476 had demonstrated the monarchs' problems at that time, since not all towns were in a position to send representatives. Toro, for example, was in Afonso and Joanna's camp, while Madrid, Cuenca, Guadalajara, Córdoba and Murcia were divided and uncertain in their allegiance. Even towns which proclaimed their support for Isabella were reluctant to see her extend royal control over the government of urban communities and the outlying lands, small towns and villages (the *'tierra'*) over which local councils had jurisdiction on behalf of the Crown. In February 1475, for example, Salamanca told the queen that it would not accept a *corregidor* appointed by her, except at the request of the *regidores*, and in that same year Alcaraz politely refused to accept Diego de Madrid as *corregidor*, on account of the lack of need and the expense. Having accepted this veto, at the cortes of Madrigal, Isabella accepted a petition from the *procuradores* that no town would be forced to receive a *corregidor*. She also agreed at this time that such officials should be appointed for no more than one year, in the first instance, renewable subject to the approval of the local authorities in the town and *tierra* concerned. Under these stringent conditions, the queen and her husband appointed twenty-five *corregidores* in 1475, ten more in 1476 and a further five in 1477. By the time that the treaties of Alcaçovas had been signed, a total of forty-four such officials were in post. As far as their areas of jurisdiction were concerned, Isabella made almost no change to the arrangements which had prevailed under her predecessor. *Corregidores* were particularly concentrated in Old Castile, the traditional heart of her domains, with sixteen such jurisdictions to be found within a radius of fifty kilometres from Valladolid. In contrast, there was only one *corregidor* in La Mancha and there were just seven in Extremadura. The new rulers clearly intended to change this situation, however, and they began in the north, establishing *corregidores* in Oviedo to supervise the principality of Asturias, and in Bilbao and Vitoria to control the Basque provinces of Biscay (Vizcaya) and Guipúzcoa, respectively. Galicia was placed under the dual authority of a governor (*gobernador*) and of a *corregidor* in La Coruña. The 'kingdom' of Murcia, in the south-east of Castilian territory, had traditionally been semi-independent, under the control of an *adelantado* (chief man or governor). The area also contained the extensive marquisate of Villena, which Isabella broke up as a punishment for Pacheco's rebellion. A new *corregimiento* was established in Murcia itself, and another, between 1483 and 1493, in Villena itself. In some cases, nearby towns were grouped under the control of a *corregidor*, examples being

Logroño, Calahorra and Alfaro on the Ebro in the north-east, Murcia, Lorca and Cartagena in the south-east, from 1477 Baeza and Úbeda in Andalusia, from 1478 Carrión and Sahagún in the kingdom of León and from 1480 Sepúlveda and Aranda in Old Castile. By the early sixteenth century, nearly a third of the *corregimientos* in the crown of Castile, forty-five in all, had been grouped in this way.[10]

The basis on which *corregidores* were to operate had largely been laid down earlier in the century. The cortes of Zamora had prescribed, in 1433, that a *corregidor* should hold his appointment for no more than two years, renewal being required after one. In theory, this continued to be the case in Ferdinand and Isabella's reign, but there were notable exceptions to the rule, for example in Andalusia, where Juan de Robles kept his office in Jerez de la Frontera for two spells of fourteen years, interrupted by his captivity in Moorish hands, which followed the disaster in the Ajarquía of Málaga in 1483 (see chapter 4), while there were only three *asistentes* in Seville between 1478 and 1510. In Córdoba, on the other hand, it was the normal practice in this period for the term of a *corregidor* to be renewed no more than once. One of the main concerns of the cortes *procuradores* in John II's reign had been that effective legal checks should be in place to prevent abuses of power by *corregidores*. At the cortes of Toledo in 1436, the *procuradores* obtained agreement from the king that holders of the office of *corregidor* should in future be subject to the requirement of Alfonso X's thirteenth-century *Siete Partidas* that holders of public offices on behalf of the Crown must provide financial guarantees, before taking up their appointments. The intention was that such officials should be able to compensate any whom they treated unjustly. It was further agreed that, when a *corregidor* reached the end of his term of office, he should have to remain available in his former jurisdiction for fifty days, in order to give satisfaction to any who had just claims against him. This procedure, which was known in Ferdinand and Isabella's reign as a *toma de residencia*, was carried out out by a royal official of equal rank to the *corregidor* himself, who was described either as a *juez de residencia* ('judge of residence') or as a *pesquisidor* (investigator). A *toma de residencia* was supposed to occur at the end of each two-year term served by a *corregidor*, but this pattern was not strictly adhered to. In Córdoba, for example, '*residencias*', as they became known, are documented irregularly, in 1480, 1490, 1494, 1495, 1499, 1500 and 1514.[11]

What Ferdinand and Isabella required of their *corregidores* is best summed up in a pragmatic which they issued in Seville in July 1500. This incorporated earlier legislation on the subject, including the Seville ordinances of 1485, and set out what was effectively the role of a viceroy, in the context of a particular town. A *corregidor* was to be fully devoted to the royal interest, and not to that of his own family or the locality in which he was sent to serve. His salary was to be limited to the sum specified in his letter of appointment and his assisting officials were to adhere rigidly to the official scale of charges for their legal and judicial services. When a *corregidor* was appointed, local chief magistrates (*alcaldes mayores*) and chief constables (*alguaciles mayores*), often local magnates in this period, were suspended during his term of office, and replaced by equivalent officials who were brought in from outside and paid out of the *corregidor*'s salary. Isabella and Ferdinand's *corregidores* were not to acquire any personal or financial interests in the district which they served and were not, of course, to accept any form of bribe. They were not to bring any property of their own (livestock is mentioned) into their town or its *tierra*, or engage in trade there without specific permission from the Crown. Their officials were to be natives and inhabitants of another place, and should not be close relatives. Specific royal permission would be required for the appointment of such officials if they were related within the fourth degree to the *corregidor* concerned. To ensure that the legal and judicial duties attached to the post were properly carried out, the Crown required that either the *corregidor* himself or his *alcalde mayor* should be qualified in civil and criminal law. There was thus still a possibility for military men (*caballeros*) to fulfil this important office. When a *corregidor* was appointed, he had to make a formal visitation of his whole territory within sixty days, and report annually to the Crown on its state, detailing any problems which he had encountered and the measures which he had taken to deal with them. He was required to avoid any form of corruption in his own and his officials' administration, and to investigate any matter which hindered the good government of the district in his charge. He had the power to change municipal laws, though with the important proviso that this might not be done without the consent of the town's *regidores*. In principle, all matters concerning urban government and the local councils' administration of the towns and villages of their *tierra* were the responsibility of the *corregidor*. His tasks ranged from curbing the activities of seigneurial retinues to ensuring that the streets were kept clean. *Corregidores* were also to play a part in ensuring that municipal archives were properly kept, and that the prerogatives and privileges of the Crown and its agents were preserved from the encroachment of both seigneurial and ecclesiastical jurisdictions. The 1500 pragmatic also laid down that the investigators who carried out the *toma de residencia* should have the same powers as the *corregidor* himself. They were to be free to call witnesses but, in contrast with the agents of the Inquisition (see chapter 3), they were to act only on specific charges and not on vague accusations.

During their period in government, *corregidores* were responsible not only for appointing their own teams of officials, but also, in most cases, for supervising existing magistrates in smaller towns which were included in their districts. In addition, *corregidores* also appointed their own deputies (*lugartenientes*), to act as magistrates (*alcaldes de la justicia*) or constables. As, for example, in the case of Seville, the *asistente*, who was equivalent to a *corregidor* elsewhere, chaired a committee the members of which were known as *fieles ejecutores* (literally, 'faithful executors'). Apart from its chairman, this group consisted of the senior lieutenant of the *asistente*, two *veinticuatros* and two citizens. It was also customary for the *corregidor* or his deputy to preside over meetings of the council of *regidores* or *veinticuatros*. He would communicate royal legislation and administrative measures to its members, and organize subcommittees, in some cases including parish councillors (*jurados*), to formulate the council's response. Legal advice was frequently sought, in addition to whatever experience and qualifications may have been possessed by the *corregidor* and his own team. This constant need led many councils to retain permanent legal counsel (*letrados del cabildo*), who sometimes, controversially as in the case of Córdoba, sat in on the deliberations of the *regidores*. Delay was a frequent response to the steady stream of laws and orders which emanated from Isabella and Ferdinand's administration. A ritual commonly took place in which, when such a document was communicated to them by the *corregidor*, the *regidores* would receive it with due reverence as the command of their 'natural lord and lady', the king and queen, but then add, in the words of the town clerk (*escribano del concejo*) who took the minutes, the ominous phrase '*pero en lo del cumplimiento*' ('but when it comes to compliance'). Legal advice would then be taken, and in very many cases an appeal would be lodged against the document concerned, thus putting off the evil day when it would have to be put into effect.[12]

It was evident to Isabella and her husband, from the turbulent beginning of their reign, that in order to secure their regime they would have not only to defeat the Portuguese king and end his young wife's claim to the throne, but also curb the power of the Castilian upper nobility. Apart from their own lordships and possessions, these magnates and their supporters had, by the end of Henry IV's reign, also gained control over the major towns. One of the main factors in Ferdinand and Isabella's success against Afonso and Joanna was the firm grip which they were able to achieve over various rebel or neutral towns. In January 1476, military action removed the town of Villena from

Pacheco control, while in July of that year Isabella secured the strategic border town of Ciudad Rodrigo by appointing the governor (*alcaide*) of its castle, Diego del Aguilar, as her own *gobernador*. The greatest need for action was, however, in Andalusia, where the king and queen were to achieve spectacular successes, particularly in Seville and Córdoba. In this region, as well as in other parts of the crown of Castile, the royal towns had inevitably been sucked into the combination of national and local conflicts which had plagued the reigns of John II and Henry IV. Typically, political life in the major towns, as well as in the surrounding countryside, had polarized into two rival groups, which fought for control of the power and rewards of municipal government. Modern historical study has tended to complicate the use of English terms to describe such groupings, in particular the word 'faction', but too much should probably not be hung on definitions in such cases. In late fifteenth-century Castile, the normal term used to describe the retinue and other supporters of a nobleman was a *bando*, though the blood ties which commonly linked some, but certainly not all, of its members with their leaders sometimes led to the use in this context of the term 'lineage' (*linaje*). Groups of this kind were also sometimes known as *parcialidades*, or 'affinities'. It is thus evident that *bandos* were complex and often amorphous alliances, which partook of the characteristics of clan groups, feudal retinues and political parties. In the circumstances of the late 1460s and early 1470s, it was very difficult for any ordinary inhabitant of a town, whether a full citizen (*vecino*) or not, to avoid links with one or other of these *bandos*. Control over the office-holding system was a crucial part of the nobles' dominance of important towns in this and other regions. Not only did magnates pay retainers (*acostamientos*) to members of the lesser nobility, and others, who held office as councillors or in other capacities, but they effectively decided whom the Crown appointed to such posts. As early as 1476, Isabella sent Diego de Merlo to Córdoba as *corregidor*, with a mandate to end the debilitating dispute in that city and its *tierra* between the two main branches of the Fernández de Córdoba family, led by Alonso de Aguilar and the count of Cabra, respectively. The queen's authority was insufficient at this time to guarantee her official's safety, and Merlo had to take refuge in a church from the wrath of Don Alonso, who had been chief magistrate of the city for some years. When Isabella and Ferdinand came to Andalusia in 1477, they symbolically reinstated the *corregidor* in order to save face, but soon transferred him to the post of *asistente* in Seville. The two aristocratic rivals were, however, forced out of the town, on royal insistence. In the two succeeding decades, slowly and painfully, the systematic governance of Córdoba by royally-appointed *corregidores* became established, though it was to fall into decline after 1500. Even greater was the task of restoring effective royal authority in Seville, which was in practice governed by Enrique de Guzmán, duke of Medina Sidonia, who was known unofficially as the 'duke of Seville'. Here, too, there was longstanding rivalry between two aristocratic families, the Guzmán and the Ponce de León, lords of Arcos de la Frontera and marquises of Cádiz. The duke of Medina Sidonia appeared to be inclined towards the claim of Joanna to the Castilian throne, and as early as December 1474, Isabella sent a courtier, her *maestresala* Pedro de Silva, to persuade the city's *veinticuatros* to support her instead. After she had agreed to confirm all Seville's privileges, she and her husband were permitted to make a ceremonial entry on 25 July 1476, though the Crown did not gain a full grip on the municipal government until 1478, when Diego de Merlo became *asistente*. Other towns, in which Isabella and her husband took forceful measures aimed at bringing conflict between *bandos* to an end, were Cáceres in Extremadura, where the quarrelling families had constructed tower houses on the northern Italian model, and Toledo, where rival aristocratic families, in particular the Ayala and Silva, had been fighting for control of the municipal government for many decades.[13]

In the past, some historians have been tempted, driven by hindsight, to assume the existence of an inexorable progress, under Isabella and Ferdinand's rule, towards Castilian centralization and dominance in the Peninsula. The obstacles to their regime, which existed within the crown of Castile itself, are evident, but they almost paled into insignificance compared with the complexities of ruling Ferdinand's inheritance, the crown of Aragon. It should be borne in mind that Aragon and the Catalan territories had themselves been under the rule of the Castilian Trastamaran royal house since 1410, and that Ferdinand's immediate predecessors, Alfonso V and John II, had certainly not lacked absolutist tendencies of their own. Nevertheless, the crown of Aragon was still, in 1479, a complex of diverse and independently-minded territories, which was, and was to remain for many more decades, inimical to centralizing tendencies in the royal government. One permanent feature of Ferdinand's reign as king of Aragon was his large-scale absence from his own patrimony. Although he was not, in the event, kept to the terms of his 1469 marriage agreement with Isabella, whereby he might not leave Castile without the permission of the Castilian royal council, or take his wife and any children out of her kingdom without her consent, during his reign of thirty-seven years, he spent less than seven of them in the crown of Aragon, consisting of less than three in the kingdom of Aragon, three in Catalonia, and no more than six months in Valencia. Nevertheless, the documentation of the period shows that, even while he might have been distracted by events in Granada, for example, Ferdinand paid regular and detailed attention to Aragonese and Catalan affairs. Problems of communication, with letters taking several weeks, for example, to pass between Seville, or the war-base in Córdoba, and Barcelona, did however make it difficult to achieve a rapid and effective response if a crisis occurred. In the kingdom of Aragon itself, there was a strong tradition in the late Middle Ages of '*pactismo*', in which traditional estates and corporations, such as the Church, the upper and lower nobility and the towns, jealously guarded their rights and privileges and negotiated with the monarch as with a 'first among equals'. It is evident that Ferdinand, no doubt in part inspired by his wife's apparent early victories against vested interests in Castile, did not like this situation, and wished to shift the balance in favour of central monarchical power. There were many similarities, in terms of both problems and their remedies, between Aragon and Castile. The new king evidently regarded it as a priority to gain greater control over the towns. Urban government in the kingdom of Aragon in the fifteenth century was very much more participative, at least theoretically, than it was in Castile. In Teruel, for instance, which admittedly still claimed for itself a special degree of autonomy as a result of a period of effective independence during its 'reconquest' from the Muslims, which was enshrined in its *fuero* of 1177, a large proportion of the citizen body played a direct part in municipal government. Teruel exercised jurisdiction over a group of outlying villages known as its *comunidad*. The town's inner council, or *consejo*, which was elected annually, consisted of a judge (*juez*), two *alcaldes*, five *regidores*, seven councillors (*jurados*) and two legal assessors (*letrados*), who were in this case recognised by the *fuero* as full members of the council. The *consejo* met in a purpose-built chamber, to which the citizens were summoned by a bell for meetings, although they were allowed only to attend and not vote. There was also a much larger 'full' council, similar to the 'traditional' Castilian open council, which might be summoned in times of great emergency such as the introduction of Ferdinand's Inquisition in 1484–5. In this assembly, each secular 'estate' or order of society had its own *procurador*, or representative, one for the knights (*de a caballo*) and the other for the middling and lesser people (*mediana y menor*). Like the other muncipal officials, these *procuradores* were elected annually. While not all Aragonese towns were necessarily as independently-minded as Teruel, Ferdinand felt it necessary to try to gain the same degree of control of the office-holding system in his ancestral kingdom as he and his wife were attempting at that time to achieve, against lesser odds, in Castile. His aim was to replace annual elections of municipal officials, such as those which caused him such irritation in Teruel, with elections by lots, in which names were chosen from a pre-selected list. The new system was successfully imposed in the Aragonese capital, Zaragoza, in 1487, and spread to other cities. Ferdinand was also able to adopt and adapt, on the Castilian model, a pre-existing tradition of Hermandades in Aragon. As in the neighbouring kingdom, private warfare, largely instigated by nobles, was endemic, and the suggestion for a Hermandad to curb it seems to have originated not with the king, as royal propagandists liked to assert, but with the authorities in the Pyrenean town of Huesca. Although the institution was revived under royal authority in 1487, the Aragonese nobility rebelled against it as soon as it acted against one of their number. This Hermandad effectively disappeared in 1488 and was officially abolished by the Cortes in 1495. The Aragonese cortes, which was summoned six times during Ferdinand's reign, consisted of four estates (*brazos*, or arms), clergy, the towns, and a noble estate divided into upper and lower houses. Although the Salic law, which excluded women from succession to the throne, was supposedly in force in Aragon, Isabella presided over the cortes of Zaragoza in June 1481, while her husband was in Barcelona. She found the deputies far more jealous of their constitutional rights than their Castilian colleagues, and could not avoid the conclusion that monarchical power in Aragon was a shadow of its equivalent in Castile. The Aragonese nobility was to remain defiant of royal authority for many years to come.[14]

Within the crown of Aragon, the country of Barcelona and principate of Catalonia presented the king and his wife with their most severe difficulties. The rebellion and civil war between 1462 and 1472, in which the youthful Ferdinand had acquired his first political experience, continued to influence events. There were unsolved economic problems both inland and in the coastal towns, especially Barcelona, and maritime trade was plagued by piracy. Inland, there were continuing disputes over the ownership of lands which had been confiscated from former rebels who had since received amnesties from the Crown. The standing committee of the Catalan corts, the *diputació del general de Catalunya*, commonly known as the *generalitat*, along with other public bodies, refused to pay interest on its loans to the city council of Barcelona. Both institutions were financially weak, while the disputes which had led to the peasant revolts known as the *remensas* (see chapter 5) had still not been fully resolved. Although, during a brief visit to Catalonia in 1479, he had begun restoring alienated goods to former rebels, Ferdinand's plan to govern the principality through a council of thirteen, the *tretzena*, quickly collapsed, and it was not until the corts of 1480–1 that he made a systematic effort to settle the troubles of the principate. To begin with, the new ruler gained little satisfaction from the Catalan deputies, and in March 1481 he left the principality in a vain attempt, which lasted until June of that year, to gain more satisfaction over the border in Aragon, at Zaragoza and Calatayud. On his return, and with the active assistance of his wife, who was paying her first visit to Catalan soil, he had greater success. Although the views of subsequent historians have differed, it is evident that in the decree known as the *constitució de l'observança*, which was promulgated at the Corts, Ferdinand recognised the force of all Catalonia's privileges. Under the terms of this document, he confirmed the powers of the *generalitat*, and ordained that the supreme court of Catalonia, the *reial audiencia*, had to settle within ten days cases which were brought before it of infringement of the *generalitat*'s liberties, or *contrafueros*, as such offences were known in both Catalonia and Aragon. In 1479, the king-count had also appointed a deputy (*llochtinent*) who was effectively his governor, or viceroy, in Catalonia, like a Castilian *corregidor* on a much larger scale. This office, which was held until 1493 by Ferdinand's first cousin prince Enrique, continued to be filled until 1506. More urgent in the early 1480s, however, was the restoration of a good relationship between the Crown and the leading citizens of Catalonia's largest city, Barcelona. Ferdinand's attempts to resolve the disputes between the principality's 'feudal' aristocracy and the peasants had created a suspicion in the minds of the bourgeoisie of Barcelona that he was on the side of the rebel commoners. To begin with, the city's councillors worked to persuade the new king to reform the *diputació/ generalitat*, and reduce what they saw as its overweening power. Ferdinand's response was only gradual, as in 1488 he suspended triennial elections to the *generalitat*, and in 1493, he introduced a system for the selection of its members by lot.

The troubles and abuses in the city's government proved to be a harder nut to crack. In 1455, Alfonso V had attempted to reform its institutions which, in their conservatism and social snobbery, represented all that he abhorred. At that time, power in Barcelona lay with a small group of bourgeois rentier families, the *ciutadans honrats*, who were interrelated with the Catalan lesser nobility, and also had close links with the ruling families of other towns in the region. Seven or nine of the *ciutadans honrats* formed the executive council which governed the city on a daily basis. There was also a supposedly more representative assembly, the 'council of a hundred' (*consell de cent*), which in reality had about 250 members. The *ciutadans honrats* and the *consell de cent* together constituted the dominant faction, which was known as the 'Biga', or rooftree. Ranged against this ruling group were the three estates of citizen-merchants, members of the professions, and artisans (*artistes*), who were called the 'Busca', that is, the 'mote' or shavings. Alfonso's attempts to reform Barcelona's municipal government began in 1453, and in November of the following year, after some experimentation, he ordered that the system which had existed in 1274 should be restored. As no one knew what that was, the measure provided ample scope both for royal initiative and for local 'constitutional' resistance. Even those sticklers for precedent, the Biga, had only the vaguest notion of how the city had been run in the late thirteenth century. Alfonso's agent Galceran de Requesens, bailiff-general (*batle general*) of Barcelona and, from 1443, governor of Catalonia, seems to have regarded the reform of the city's government as a personal crusade. Faced, at the end of 1454, with utter confusion over what form the new electoral system should take, Requesens applied to Alfonso's government in Naples for guidance. The reply, which arrived in February of the following year, was that all four estates, that is, the *ciudatans honrats* who formed the Biga and the three branches of the Busca, citizen merchants, professional men and artisans, should have an equal say in affairs. For the first time, the lower estates were to be represented at the highest level of government, with the executive council consisting of two leading citizens, a merchant, a representative of the professions and an artisan, while *ciutadans honrats* and merchants were henceforth to have equal status in the council of a hundred. In the event, the latter assembly effectively fell under the control of the Busca, as the members of the Biga boycotted it in protest at the diminution of their powers. The 1455 reform achieved only a partial success, as the Busca merchants generally worked together with the Biga *ciutadans*, and continued to exclude the professionals and artisans. The 'citizens' and merchants generally held, between them, three out of the five senior posts of *conseller* (councillor), who were elected annually by the inner council (*consell*). The *consellers* had the sole right to propose agenda items to the *consell* and its subcommittees, and also chose the members of that body on an annual basis. In practice, these important posts were largely restricted to citizens and merchants of the old ruling families, and this situation continued during the first decade of Ferdinand's reign in the crown of Aragon. In that period, only ten 'new men' were admitted as members of the inner council or as *consellers*. On average, a *ciutadan* or merchant was accepted into the *consell* only every few years, and would serve a two-year term. Such people might be elected in rotation to the senior posts in the city government, such as that of *conseller*. Effectively, an oligarchy of sixteen families ran the city, and accusations of corruption and financial mismanagement were rife. Eventually, in 1490, Ferdinand stepped in, suspending the election of *consellers* and appointing new ones on his own authority, though he had no choice but to choose them from among the 'bad' old political class, which continued to make itself indispensable. Thus when a new constitution was introduced in Barcelona in 1493, under the terms of an agreement (*pacto municipal*) for the city's government, it bore a marked resemblance to the previous system. Far from increasing the influence of the less privileged Busca estates, Ferdinand gave the *ciutadans* three posts as *conseller* instead of the former two, and forty-eight places, over one-third of the total, instead of the previous quarter (thirty-two places). After further strife, the king finally imposed on Barcelona, in 1498, the system of selecting office-holders by lots, which he had previously introduced in Aragon. Although the new arrangements left the balance between the respective estates unchanged, it was no longer possible, at least in theory, for individuals to accumulate multiple offices, and the citizen body was expanded to include knights who were resident in the city.[15]

The port of Valencia appeared to contradict the picture of economic decline in the other territories of the crown of Aragon, especially after the beginning of the Catalan rebellion in 1462 (see chapter 5). It is true that foreign visitors in the latter part of the fifteenth century were often impressed with the capital of the kingdom of Valencia, which had been captured from the Muslims in 1238, but the city's problems did not remain below the surface. During the frequent, and for long periods total, absence of the ruler, Valencia had traditionally been governed by a king's lieutenant, who was assisted by a bailiff-general with charge over financial affairs. After 1419, the kingdom was independent of Barcelona, for accountancy purposes, with its own chief accountant (*mestre racional*). The Valencian corts consisted of the traditional three estates of medieval Europe, clergy, nobility, and 'third estate' or representatives of the Crown, and met every three years. In 1418, Valencia acquired its own standing committee of the corts, or *generalitat*, which consisted of two delegates from each of the three estates, with a support staff of three treasurers, several secretaries, a syndic and a permanent advocate in the law courts, who were responsible for administering the institution's finances. The city and the surrounding lands which fell under its jurisdiction were primarily administered by a council consisting of the leading citizens, which was divided into three branches, or 'hands', which reflected the conventional divisions of urban society. The *ma major* consisted of the members of the leading families, while the 'middle hand' (*ma mitjana*) contained the merchants, notaries, and other honourable professions, the *ma minor* being formed by master craftsmen and artisans. On Quinquagesima, the Sunday before Ash Wednesday, four 'good men' were elected to represent each of the city's twelve parishes, but a much larger proportion of the inhabitants was represented by the four men who were elected every Whitsun from each trade or guild, whose number grew steadily after 1300.

By the end of the fifteenth century, the *consell* had no fewer than 116 members. In addition, four lawyers were members of the council, as were eight knights, six representing the city itself and two the lands over which it had jurisdiction. The city magistracy was in the hands of four *jurats*, who were appointed by the king. In the thirteenth century, the nobility had been excluded from the government of Valencia, but in 1329, Alfonso IV had added two extra *jurats* from their number. From then on, two lists were drawn up, one of knights and the other of burgesses, from which the king chose the executive of *jurats*. Early in the fifteenth century, selection of office-holders by means of lots was introduced, but the candidates were still carefully screened to exclude the less privileged. The artisans never succeeded in obtaining their two *jurats*, who had supposedly been allowed to them in 1278. The council, which met in a designated town hall, was assisted by a municipal accountant or *racional*, who was appointed by the king from a list of three candidates which it presented to him. By the time of Ferdinand's accession as king of Valencia in 1479, after which he paid a whirlwind visit to swear allegiance to its charters (*fors*) and liberties, the city and the rest of the kingdom had been plagued for many years by noble feuding. Two years previously, the *jurats* had petitioned Ferdinand's father, John II, for help, saying that the whole kingdom was up in arms. In addition, in the new reign, large loans to the Crown seriously damaged the municipal finances, preventing the building of a new port (see chapter 5). The 1480s saw continuing violence and economic dislocation, some of it, as in Barcelona, being caused by the arrival of Ferdinand and Isabella's new Inquisition. Although the *mestre racional*, Gullem Zaera, provided some continuity in government by remaining in office after John II's death, the council of a hundred (*consell de cent*) became increasingly militant during that decade. In 1492, Ferdinand appointed to the city a new *llochtinent* (lieutenant), who was already justiciar of Aragon, and was later to be *llochtinent* of Catalonia and viceroy of Sicily. Lanuza was not a Valencian, so that his appointment was against the charters (*fors*) of the kingdom, and he proceeded at once to override traditional jurisprudence by reserving the right to modify the traditional judicial penalties at will. Although Lanuza did not stay long, his royal master seems to have had little difficulty in controlling the city and kingdom by appointing his chosen candidates, or rather those recommended by his agents, as magistrates. In the Balearic Islands, which had been in the hands of the kings of Aragon since their thirteenth-century 'reconquest', a *llochtinent* was imposed in Palma (then known as Majorca City), on the model of Lanuza in Valencia, but with little success. The feuding aristocracy largely retained its somewhat anarchic control, at least in the perception of the rulers and their agents, in the Mediterranean islands.[16]

3

The New Inquisition

When Ferdinand and Isabella visited Andalusia in 1477 and 1478, with the intention of establishing firm control over its main cities and the countryside, they were faced not only with independently-minded noblemen and councillors, and violent and disorderly *bandos* and 'ruffians', but also with what was believed to be a problem of religion. At first, there was little sign of any such dimension to their quest. The queen had left Madrid on 20 April 1477 in the direction of Extremadura. First, she visited the Jeronymite convent of Guadalupe for the final burial of her half-brother Henry, and then she proceeded to the town of Trujillo where, after some negotation, she received the surrender of the castle from its governor (*alcaide*), who was a supporter of her enemy, the marquis of Villena. In July, she moved on to Cáceres, where she brought about a truce between the two warring factions, but then she carried out one of the audacious manoeuvres by which she was coming to be known. This was to attempt, without her husband, to take on the Andalusian magnates and the cities of Seville and Córdoba. When she arrived in the great port on the Guadalquivir on 24 July 1477, and set about restoring the Crown's authority in the city, an estimated 4000 Sevillanos fled, apparently concerned that their ill deeds of the previous decade would be exposed and punished. By the time that Ferdinand came to join her, on 13 September, Isabella had already secured the reluctant surrender by the duke of Medina Sidonia, whom she had suspended as *alcalde mayor*, of the castle (*alcázar*), the royal dockyards (*atarazanas*) and the Triana castle, as well as an undertaking that the duke would subsequently give up the royal castles which he had seized in Seville's *tierra*. When the king arrived, there was an increase in the speed with which the magnates and towns submitted to his and Isabella's authority. The duke of Medina Sidonia's main rival in the region, Rodrigo Ponce de León, marquis of Cádiz, travelled in secret from Jerez de la Frontera, a royal town which he effectively controlled, to meet Ferdinand and make his submission. As a result, the king and queen visited Jerez at the end of September 1477, and then proceeded, on their voyage of reconciliation, to the duke of Medina Sidonia's stronghold at Sanlúcar de Barrameda, for further celebrations of supposed peace and harmony. During the winter of 1477–8, military resistance in Andalusia to Isabella and Ferdinand's regime came to an end when Fernán Arias, marshal (*mariscal*) of Castile and a supporter of the marquis of Cádiz, surrendered the governorship of Utrera. The king and queen stayed in Seville until 29 September 1478, when they moved the Court to Córdoba, by way of Carmona and Ecija. By the time that they left Andalusia, in December 1478, the royal couple had largely restored the authority of the Crown, at least on the surface, in all the main towns of the region, from Seville as far as Ubeda and Baeza (Jaén). They had suspended leading magnates, such as the duke of Medina Sidonia in Seville and Don Alonso de Aguilar in Córdoba, from their offices as magistrates, and had put in their own appointees as *corregidores* of the towns and governors (*alcaides*) of the royal castles and fortresses.[1]

During their time in Seville, first Isabella and then she and her husband together heard preaching which went beyond conventional exhortation to Catholic piety. In particular, the prior of the Dominican convent of San Pablo, Fray Alonso de Hojeda, urged them to consider that the defiance of their royal authority, which had until recently been a notable feature both of Seville and of the rest of Christian Andalusia, was caused not only by rebellious magnates, and towns jealous of their civic liberties, but by religious dissidence. Specifically, the friar asserted that large numbers of converts from Judaism, or the descendants of such converts, had reverted to the Jewish faith, and were threatening not only Isabella and Ferdinand's regime but the very fabric of Castilian society. Soon, what has become known to history as 'the Spanish Inquisition' was to come into being. In 1914, a minor civil servant and historian, Julián Juderías, coined the term 'black legend' (*leyenda negra*) to describe a complex of attitudes towards Spain and the Spanish, which was and sometimes still is to be found particularly in Northern Europe and North America, and especially in what is known on the continent of Europe as the 'Anglo-Saxon' world. According to Juderías this 'legend' may be characterized as 'the climate created by the fantastic stories about our native land which have seen the light of day in all countries'.[2] An intrinsic part of this 'black legend' has always been the new Inquisition which was introduced, first to Castile and then to the crown of Aragon, by Isabella and Ferdinand, with the overt purpose of testing the Christian orthodoxy of converts from Judaism.

Ever since the beginning of the Christian Church, there had been difficulties in the relationship between the Jewish and non-Jewish followers of Jesus of Nazareth, and some of these are recorded in the New Testament. The apostle Paul came to believe that Gentile Christians, those who were not of Jewish origin, should not be made to conform to Jewish practice by keeping the precepts of the Torah (the 'Law'), and by being circumcized if male. Other early Christian leaders, such as James the brother of Jesus, felt that the teachings of Judaism should be fully observed within the new Church, but Paul's views prevailed. With hindsight, it is evident that a split between Judaism and Christianity became unavoidable at this point. Yet Paul himself seems to have believed, according to his account in his epistle to the Romans, that the Jews were still, despite their rejection of the claim that Jesus was the Messiah, the 'chosen people' of God, just as they were held to be in the Hebrew scriptures which formed the Christian 'Old Testament'. During the first and second centuries of the Christian era, the books which were to constitute the 'New Testament' record increasingly acrimonious conflicts between the youthful and growing Church and the synagogues in which Jewish life was nurtured after the destruction by the Romans of the Temple at Jerusalem, in AD 70. As a result of this dissension within the Church, it became increasingly difficult for followers of Christ who had formerly been Jews to achieve recognition, at the same time, of their Christian faith and life and of their Jewish heritage. The history of Jewish–Christian relations in the late Middle Ages, and in particular of the arrival and work of the new Inquisition in Spain, was to be dominated by this early Christian polemic. It appears that Jews had settled in Spain before the lifetime of Jesus, and it is possible that Christianity first arrived in the Iberian peninsula by means of its Jewish communities. By the beginning of the fourth century (c.300–3), just before the persecution of the Church which took place under the emperor Diocletian, when clergy representing thirty-seven Hispanic churches assembled in council at Illiberris, near modern Granada, the issue of Christian–Jewish relations was clearly a pressing one. Jews, like the remaining pagans, were regarded as a serious danger to the Christian community. Thus the assembled bishops, priests and deacons ordained that if Christian parents arranged for their daughters to be married to Jews, they themselves should be excommunicated for a period of five years. This provision also applied in the case of heretics from the Christian faith, and both rules appear to have been based on the assumption, which was to be prevalent in Spain in later centuries, that the greatest danger to the Church came from those who had either once been part of it or else were spiritually close to it, but hostile. Again, as in later centuries in western Europe, social contact between Christians and Jews was to be severely restricted under the canons (decrees) of Illiberris. Clergy and lay Christians who ate with Jews were to abstain from communion afterwards, and Christian landlords were not to have their crops blessed by Jews.[3]

Plate 3 The Departure of the Jews from Egypt, from a fourteenth-century Sephardic *Haggadah* (Passover service book). *Courtesy of the John Rylands Library, Manchester*

The anti-Jewish measures which were taken at the Council of Illiberris reflected a growing tradition of Christian teaching and practice. During the third century, a new genre of polemics against Jews and their religion had begun to emerge, but its most influential exponent in the Western Church was to be Augustine, bishop of Hippo in North Africa (354–430). His views became authoritative throughout the

medieval period, and influenced both ecclesiastical and secular treatment of Jews, in Spain as elsewhere, up to and beyond Isabella and
Ferdinand's reign. Augustine had come to the Catholic Christian faith as
a convert from the dualist Donatist version of the religion, and he saw
the battle against heresy within the Church as an essential priority.
Judaism remained the 'old enemy', however, so that the protection
and development of the Church, for him and for his medieval successors, was to include measures to avoid its 'corruption' by Jewish belief
and practice. Nevertheless, Jews were not to be persecuted to death, but
retained in a subservient state, as a warning to Christians of the consequences of failure to believe in Jesus, until they eventually converted
in the last days of the world, which would arrive in God's good time.
This preoccupation with the combined danger to the Church of external
attack by its traditional enemies, the Jews, and infiltration and destruction from within by heretics, was to resurface with a vengeance in
Andalusia in 1478. Over the thousand years which separated Augustine
from Ferdinand and Isabella, the teaching of contempt for Judaism had
survived the vicissitudes of Spanish history. The Visigoths, who dominated the Iberian peninsula between the end of the fifth century and the
Muslim invasion in 711, produced increasingly severe, though see-
mingly largely ineffective, legislation against the Jewish population.
During the sixth and seventh centuries, a series of measures ordered
by councils of the Spanish Church, which were held at Toledo with full
royal authority, appeared to threaten the very possibility of leading a
Jewish life in the kingdom. The onslaught began after King Reccared
converted, in 587, from Arian to Catholic Christianity. Two years later,
the Third Council of Toledo forbade Jews to have Christian wives or
mistresses, to own Christian slaves, or to hold public office. In the reign
of Sisebut, between 612 and 621, an apparently unsuccessful attempt
was made to force all Spain's Jews to be baptised at once, while the
Sixth Council of Toledo, in 638, decreed that the then ruler, Chintila,
intended to expel from the kingdom all those who were not Catholic
Christians. In his general law code of 654, King Recceswinth outlawed
a set of essential Jewish practices, including circumcision of males,
dietary laws (*kashrut*), marriage laws and ceremonies, and the celebration of Passover. In 694, Egica enslaved all the Jews in his kingdom,
apart from those in the province of Narbonne (Narbonnensis), on the
north-eastern border with France. Although the general feebleness of
the Visigothic state seems to have rendered these laws largely ineffective, they provided unfortunate precedents for those who wished to
attack Jews and Judaism in the fifteenth century. In addition, while it
was hardly unnatural that the Jews of Spain should have been relieved
to see the defeat and destruction of the Christian state at the hands of

Muslim invaders, between 711 and 713, the accusation was still current, in the reign of Ferdinand and Isabella, that it was the Jews who handed Spain over to the Muslims. The continued existence, up to 1492, of the Nasrid kingdom of Granada, served to keep this issue very much alive.[4]

In the meantime, both Jews and Christians in Muslim-controlled areas became subject to the eighth-century Syrian 'pact of Umar', which regulated Muslim relations with the two other 'peoples of the Book', who shared with them the Hebrew Scriptures. By its provisions, Jews and Christians were allowed, as 'protected peoples', or *dhimmis*, to worship freely, under the authority of their own rabbinical or episcopal leadership. The intention was that Judaism and Christianity should survive but not expand, so that the building of new synagogues and churches was not permitted, though existing ones might be repaired, on condition that they did not rise above neighbouring mosques. In Islamic states, including Spain, Christians and Jews were also required to pay a special poll tax, or *jizya*, in addition to the financial burden which fell on their Muslim neighbours. During the eleventh, twelfth and thirteenth centuries, the balance of power in the Peninsula shifted, by a series of stages, in favour of the Christian kingdoms of the north. In the territory under Christian rule, religious freedom was guaranteed for Jews and Muslims, again subject to restrictions, which were included both in royal laws and in local charters, or *fueros*. In Castile, Alfonso X's *Siete Partidas* (Seven Parts) laid down severe penalties for those who engaged in sexual relations across the boundaries between religious communities. As in earlier Christian and Muslim practice, in Spain as elsewhere, religious minorities were allowed freedom of worship and self-government in internal matters. The building of new synagogues and mosques was forbidden, however, and all cases involving Christians, as well as Jews or Muslims, were reserved to the Christian courts. These rules reflected the provisions of church, or canon, law, which applied in the other Christian states of the Iberian peninsula as well as elsewhere in Catholic Europe. Alfonso 'the Wise' of Castile's law-code, although it was not fully embodied in the kingdom's law until 1348, made other provisions which were to have unfortunate consequences for Jews and, later, Muslims. Following Augustinian principles, Castilian Jews were to be treated as a 'remnant', the former chosen people of God, who were to be tolerated by Christian rulers, while Islam was referred to in the *Partidas* as 'an insult to God'. Not only were Jews and Muslims forbidden to seek converts, but they were even forbidden to possess books from their own traditions which attacked Christianity, and were liable to severe penalties if they blasphemed against Christ and his religion, even in the stressed (and common) circumstances of games and gambling. As in earlier centuries, this preoccupation with the dangers to Christian society of Jewish and Muslim 'error' was accompanied by a fear of 'heresy' within the Church itself.[5]

The Greek word for heresy, *hairesis*, appears in the Christian Scriptures which are known as the New Testament. In the epistle to Titus [3: 10], which has traditionally been ascribed to St Paul, the term *hairetikos* is used to refer to a man who is 'factious', but elsewhere it means 'a separatist'. In the Acts of the Apostles, the noun *hairesis* is used to describe a religious grouping or party, for example the Sadducees and Pharisees in the Jewish Temple at Jerusalem [Acts 5: 17, 15. 5] and the early Christians themselves [Acts 24: 5]. Both Paul and the author of the Acts, who in the Middle Ages was believed to be the gospel-writer Luke, apparently thought of heresy as the belief and activity of partisan groups who produced that great dread of church leaders from the earliest days, division or 'schism'. The direct link between disagreement in religious matters and physical violence and wickedness was thus established in the early centuries of the history of the Church. In the late twelfth and early thirteenth centuries, it was to be institutionalized in the form of systematic investigations, or 'inquisitions', first by diocesan bishops or their appointed representatives and, after 1230, by specialized tribunals of canon lawyers and theologians, many of them members of the Dominican and Franciscan orders of friars. It is still necessary to insist that the ecclesiastical 'inquisition' was not Spanish in origin, and that its main and ostensible aim was to root out heresy from the body of Christians, rather than to make a direct assault on the supposed threat posed by Jews and Muslims to the Church. The first tribunals of the Inquisition, which were set up under the authority of Pope Gregory IX, fought to expose and defeat two kinds of heresy which had become prominent in northern Italy and southern France after about 1170. The first was what became known as Waldensianism, its name and existence being derived from a merchant of Lyons called Peter Waldo, or Valdes, who appears to have heard the call, in 1170 or soon thereafter, to an apostolic life of poverty. Recent research suggests that he may have been a pawn in a dispute within the Church in Lyons between a reforming bishop and a traditionalist and socially exclusive cathedral chapter, but his lay preaching and encouragement of the participation of women in church leadership soon brought a reaction which condemned Waldo and his followers as heretics. There is little sign, in this early period, that the group who became known, to the authorities of the Catholic Church and increasingly to themselves, as 'Waldensians', differed greatly in doctrine from the Catholic Church, though Waldensians were to become linked to the Protestant Reformation in the sixteenth century. Their initial offences in Catholic eyes were disciplinary rather than theological, though rejection by the mainstream Church made them increasingly anticlerical. The other main 'heretical' movement of the period, which is known to historians as Catharism, was a very different case. The groups of Cathars, or 'perfect ones', which became particularly active in southern France and northern Italy in the years around 1200, seem to have been offshoots of the Bogomil movement which began in Bulgaria in the tenth century. Their theology, like that of Augustine's Donatist opponents, was 'dualist', which meant that they did not believe in a single, all-powerful creator God, to whom all other human and spiritual forces, whether good or evil, are subordinated, but in two opposing forces, one of good and the other of evil, which fought for control over the earth.

The first major assault of the Catholic Church on Catharism was spearheaded by the reformed Benedictine order of monks known as the Cistercians, under the leadership of the abbot of their mother house at Cîteaux. In alliance with a papal legate, Peter of Castelnau, they undertook preaching missions in the south of France, but with only limited success. The effort to combat Cathar and Waldensian heresy in France and Italy by spiritual means was subsequently taken up by the Spaniard Domingo de Guzmán's Dominican order of friars, which pioneered a new combination of monastic discipline and ministry in the everyday world. The Dominicans made theological study a priority, and took time away from choir services and their own community business to assemble their arguments to confute the 'heretics'. The Church's offensive was paralleled by military action, particularly against the counts of Toulouse, in whose territory many Cathars and Waldensians lived, and who were accused of giving them support. The Church declared a crusade, the first against Christians within its own direct jurisdiction, and gained the support of the French crown, which was interested in curbing the power of feudal magnates such as the counts of Toulouse. In 1229, a treaty was signed in Paris which brought a temporary halt to military hostilities, but although the count thereby agreed to give his full backing to the repression of heresy, the war for souls went on. In that same year, Pope Gregory IX authorized the setting up, in parishes where Catharism and Waldensianism were rife, of commissions which each consisted of a priest and two or more laymen, to investigate heresy. The scheme failed, however, because the amateur inquisitors proved to be unwilling to denounce their neighbours to the authorities. More drastic measures were evidently required, and in 1233 the pope instructed the provincial of the Dominicans in Toulouse to appoint members of his order, who were sufficiently qualified in theology, to act as inquisitors in France, from Narbonne in the south to Bourges in the north. Thus was born the papal Inquisition, a specialized form of investigation which adapted techniques which were already commonly applied to secular matters, such as property and inheritance, to questions of religious belief and practice. The new Inquisition, which only slowly adopted regular and legal procedures and frequently acted in an arbitrary and violent manner, quickly spread to the neighbouring crown of Aragon. The Aragonese royal house had perforce been involved in events in Languedoc in previous decades. The rulers of Aragon and Catalonia had dynastic lands in Montpellier, and the French crusaders, led by Simon de Montfort, had as one of their war aims the removal of Aragonese influence from what they saw as an integral part of the French royal domain. In this they succeeded, when they defeated Peter I of Aragon in the battle of Muret in 1213. Meanwhile, given the close cultural, linguistic, political and economic links which existed between Languedoc and the Catalan lands, it was perhaps inevitable that Cathar and Waldensian ideas should spread south across the border. In October 1194, Alfonso I of Aragon–Catalonia had declared, at a royal council held in Lleida (Lérida), that heresy was henceforward to be treated as *lèse majesté*, and thus a direct and treasonable offence against the Crown. His successor, Peter I, sponsored the investigation and punishment of heresy, while James I invited Gregory IX's new specialized Inquisition into his realm. Such a development did not, however, take place in the neighbouring crown of Castile.[6]

During the 'long' fourteenth century from about 1280 to 1410, which has commonly been regarded as a period of economic, social and political crisis in Western Europe, Spain was not immune from such troubles. The Castilians struggled to digest the extensive conquests of Muslim territory in Andalusia, which they made in the period between their victory in the battle of Las Navas de Tolosa in 1212 and the capture of Seville in 1248, while the Aragonese, and more particularly the Catalans, not only added the kingdom of Valencia to their domain, but also built up a maritime and trading empire in the western and central Mediterranean, including the 'reconquered' Balearic Islands, Sardinia and Sicily (see chapter 7). The Iberian peninsula was affected by a series of bad harvests and epidemics in the 1330s and 1340s, and particularly by the European plague epidemic known as the 'Black Death', which reached Spain and Portugal in 1351. It is from this period that may be dated the increase of tension between Jews and Christians in Castile and Aragon. After 1350, the whole peninsula became embroiled in military conflict on three levels. On the international stage, Iberian forces became involved in the Hundred Years War between England and France. In terms of peninsular politics, Castile and Aragon fought diplomatically, and sometimes militarily, for hegemony, while Portugal struggled successfully to retain its independence from Castile. It was, however, the civil war in Castile, between the legitimate king, Peter or 'Pedro the Cruel', and his illegitimate half-brother Henry of Trastámara who founded the dynasty from which both Isabella and Ferdinand were descended, which first produced physical, as opposed to verbal, violence against Spanish Jews. In May 1355, the forces of the future Henry II attacked the Alcaná, a Jewish quarter in Toledo. In this case there is little doubt that the Jews were the specific and premeditated target and throughout the war, which lasted until Henry himself murdered the king while supposedly negotiating with him in a tent at Montiel on 13 March 1369, the rebels used Peter's supposed 'Judeophilia', as evidenced by his patronage of Samuel ha-Levi's new synagogue in Toledo (1357), as grounds for declaring him unfit to rule. The arrival of the house of Trastámara on the Castilian throne ushered in a period of widespread social and economic disruption, but it was not until the summer of 1391 that anti-Jewish feeling in Spain spilled over into large-scale violence. At that time, Ferrán Martínez, who was archdeacon of Ecija, and administrator of the large and wealthy archdiocese of Seville, brought his regular anti-Jewish preaching to fever pitch, not merely seeking the conversion of the Jews to Christianity but inciting physical attacks upon them.

Between 6 June and mid-August 1391, urban Jewish communities were subjected to attacks in a swathe from Andalusia in the south-west to Barcelona in the north-east, including Seville, Córdoba, Ciudad Real, Toledo and Logroño in Castile, and Orihuela, Alicante, Valencia, Barcelona and Jaca in the crown of Aragon. It may be argued that the 'prehistory' of Isabella and Ferdinand's Inquisition began with these attacks, which involved robbery, arson, violence and murder. Apart from a large amount of damage and some loss of life, the main consequence of the 1391 attacks was the dispersal, or diaspora, of the great historic Jewish communities of the Spanish cities. This was achieved partly by the flight of many Jews from the larger towns to the comparative safety of smaller urban settlements and villages, many of them under seigneurial jurisdiction rather than that of royally-appointed municipal councils, and partly by large-scale conversion to Christianity. The two decades or so which followed the 1391 attacks saw a phenomenon which was unique in late medieval Europe. For the first time since the missions of the Catholic Church to northern Europe in the early Middle Ages, thousands of individuals sought baptism within a short interval. After 1391, the Castilian and Aragonese royal administrations mounted a campaign of legal, economic and social restrictions on those who remained as Jews, while the Church tried to convert them by means of preaching, as in the missions of the Valencian Dominican

Vincent Ferrer (canonized in 1458), and theological disputation, as in the controlled and more than somewhat one-sided discussions held between Christian and Jewish representatives at Tortosa, in 1413–14, under the auspices of the anti-pope Benedict XIII. Given the social structure of the period, it is unsurprising that conversions commonly took place in household units, with women, children and servants following the lead of the patriarchal head. This pattern of religious change was to have important implications later in the century, when the 'new' Spanish Inquisition began to function after 1478, but in the meantime the Church was presented with a unique and demanding pastoral opportunity, to bring fully into the Body of Christ thousands, some estimates suggest up to two-thirds, of the former Jewish population. The skills for such a task simply did not exist in the experience of fifteenth-century churchmen, so that it is hardly surprising that problems subsequently arose. Nonetheless, whatever the weaknesses which were to be revealed, or supposed, in later decades, the initial period of entry by thousands of former Jews into positions in Church and State which had previously been closed to them seems to have given rise to remarkably little conflict. Whether or not this true, it is certainly the case that the situation changed drastically, especially in Castile, after 1449, when riots in Toledo, during a virtual rebellion there against the government of John II and his Constable, Alvaro de Luna, targeted not Jews, as in 1355, but rather converts from Judaism and their families, the 'converts' (*conversos*) or 'New Christians' (*cristianos nuevos*). The *conversos* were accused not only of crimes against society, such as unjust tax collection on behalf of the Crown, but also of returning to their Jewish ways. The leader of the rebellion, Pero Sarmiento, promulgated a document, known as a 'sentence-statute' (*sentencia-estatuto*), which had been drafted by his legal adviser, Bachiller Marcos García de Mora or Mazarambrós, nicknamed 'Marquillos', which forbade any *converso* to hold public office in the town thereafter. This was the first statute of 'purity of blood' (*limpieza de sangre*). Paradoxically, one consequence of this measure was that Jews replaced New Christians in farming the cathedral's rents. Already, in 1440, an attempt had been made to enact such a measure in Toledo, and Pope Eugenius IV responded with a bull, *Super gregem dominicam* ('Over the Lord's flock'), dated 8 August 1442 and addressed to John II of Castile. This document restated traditional Catholic teaching on the subservient but secure status of Jews in Christian society, but it also stressed the need to protect the rights of *conversos*, because they were just as much Christians as those who were increasingly becoming known in Spain as 'Old Christians' (*cristianos viejos*). It is easy to suppose that the conspicuous success of some *conversos* in their new careers in the Church and the public service, both nationally and locally, may have incited the envy and malice of those who might, in other circumstances, have expected to secure those posts. At least as significant, at least from 1450 onwards, was the apparent perception, among clergy and laity of various social ranks, that the genuineness of many of the New Christians was suspect. Popes from Eugenius IV onwards, and in particular Nicholas V, reaffirmed the scriptural teaching, to be found in various passages of the epistles of Paul [for example Galatians 3: 27–9], that converted Jews should be fully accepted as members of the Church, with all appropriate rights and privileges. Yet the accusation continued to be made in Spain that many *conversos* were false Christians, who had accepted baptism for personal gain but who in their hearts, and often in their religious practice, remained Jews. This was the accusation which Prior Hojeda was to put into Isabella and Ferdinand's minds in Seville in 1477–8.

Anti-*converso* agitation in Castilian towns did not cease with the suppression of the Toledan rebellion in 1451, and neither was the accusation of 'Judaizing' laid to rest. The idea of introducing an Inquisition to Castile for the purpose of identifying false converts had already surfaced in Eugenius IV's bull of 1442. In this document, the pope stated that if the Spanish *conversos* did indeed return to the 'law of Moses', they should be investigated, and if necessary punished, by the normal inquisitorial procedures, which at that time involved the action of diocesan bishops in Castile and specialized tribunals in Aragon and Catalonia. In his bull dated 20 November 1451, Nicholas V followed this up with a stipulation that while, contrary to the Toledan 'sentence-statute' of 1449, sincere *conversos* were entitled to full participation in ecclesiastical and secular structures, the bishop of Osma and the vicar-general of the diocese of Salamanca were to be granted inquisitorial powers to act against those who were 'suspect in the faith'. This was the traditional method of identifying and punishing heretics in the Catholic Church, before the development of specialized tribunals of inquisitors in the thirteenth century, and still applied in dioceses where such Inquisitions did not exist. In the event, the provisions of Nicholas V's 1451 bull were never put into effect, but the polemical climate in Castile was increasingly bringing into question the Christian orthodoxy of the *conversos*. In 1461, a group of observant Franciscans (see chapter 7) including Fray Alonso de Espina, who was the author of a vitriolic compendium of anti-heretical, anti-Muslim and especially anti-Jewish polemic entitled *Fortalitium Fidei* ('Fortress of the Faith'), met and put pressure on the general of the Jeronymite order of friars (see chapter 7), Fray Alonso de Oropesa, to help them persuade King Henry IV to set up a new Inquisition in Castile to investigate the *conversos*. As a result,

Archbishop Carrillo of Toledo asked Oropesa to carry out an investigation (*pesquisa*) into the matter, while the king petitioned Pope Pius II to
appoint four new inquisitors to work in the crown of Castile, two in
New Castile and two in Andalusia. Evidently, these were the areas in
which 'Judaizing' by *conversos* was believed to be most prevalent, and
they were later to be the first to attract the attention, in this connection,
of Ferdinand and Isabella. As another sign of things to come, it is clear
that, even at this early stage, Henry's determination was that the new
tribunal should not simply be papally controlled, like its predecessors
elsewhere in Europe, including Aragon and Catalonia, but that it should
be explicitly subordinated to the Crown. Thus the king asked Pius II to
delegate his power to appoint inquisitors for Castile to a committee
consisting of himself, Lope de Rivas, bishop of Cartagena, who was one
of his councillors, and the papal nuncio to Castile, Antonio Giacomo
Venier (De Veneris). Pius, although no doubt anxious to curb any
'Judaizing' among the New Christians in Spain, was evidently even
more anxious to retain papal control over any new Castilian Inquisition, and thus appointed Venier as its first inquisitor-general. The pope
informed Henry of his decision by means of a bull dated 1 December
1461 which was followed, on 15 March of the following year, by
another naming Venier to the post. The new institution remained largely a dead letter, but public anxiety about the religious beliefs and
practices of the *conversos* remained strong. Later in 1462, there was a
further attack on New Christians in Carmona, which was repressed by
troops from the neighbouring royal towns of Seville, Ecija and Córdoba. According to the chronicler, and supporter of Henry IV, Diego
Enríquez del Castillo, Alonso de Espina and a group of his fellow
Observant Franciscans came to the king in Madrid, in December
1463, in the hope of persuading him to address the problem of the
conversos who, they claimed, were even having their male children
circumcized as Jews. One of the delegation, Fernando de la Plaza,
announced that he had access to a hundred foreskins from such boys,
but was unable to produce them when requested to do so by the king.

The 'remonstrance' to King Henry which was drawn up on behalf of
the nobility in January 1465 (see chapter 1) contained no fewer than
twenty-nine sections on the subject of Jews. Although *conversos* are not
explicitly mentioned in the document, it is evident that they were the
main concern from the fact that it contained a request for an Inquisition
to be introduced to Castile, under papal supervision, to detect those
who were 'bad Christians and suspicious in the faith'. It is very likely
that the Jeronymite General Oropesa was involved in drafting at least
this section of the 'memorandum', which asked that, until such a
tribunal was established, diocesan bishops or their suffragans should

use their existing powers to identify false 'New Christians' and root out their 'heresy'. The period of instability in Castile during the 'reign' of Prince Alfonso was not helpful to the physical safety of the *conversos*. In 1467, there was further violence in Toledo, which apparently arose when the city's cathedral chapter demanded its rents from the town of Maqueda. This time, the aggression seems to have come from New rather than Old Christians. According to the slightly later account of one of the canons, Pedro de Mesa, on Sunday 19 July a group of *conversos* invaded the cathedral during the high mass, shouting such things as 'Die, die, this is not a church but a congregation of the wicked and vile.' Open violence broke out in four places in the city on the following Tuesday afternoon, and lasted for about twenty-four hours. Several people were killed and some houses were burned down, but the *conversos* were eventually defeated by Old Christians, apparently under the leadership of scandalized clergy. Prince Alfonso sent two letters to the city, which was supposedly under his lordship at the time, with representatives who had instructions to restore order there on his behalf. One result of this new outbreak of violence was the reintroduction in Toledo of a purity of blood statute, which went further than the 1449 measure in that it barred *conversos* not only from secular offices but also from clerical benefices. According to the chronicler Alfonso de Palencia, as well as another anonymous contemporary source, there was by this time a deep-seated enmity between Old and New Christians in the city, which was reflected in their respective approaches to national politics. He claims that the *conversos* in Toledo favoured Henry, while the Old Christians supported Alfonso. Whatever the rights and wrongs of the various contemporary accounts of events in Toledo in 1467, it is clear that a considerable amount of looting and burning took place, and that numerous *conversos*, who on this occasion appeared as the aggressors, were killed or wounded, though by no means all Toledans took part in or condoned the violence. Although a tense peace appeared to follow the 1467 outbreak in Toledo, what turned out to be a more ominous incident took place four years later in Segovia. In 1471, an ecclesiastical court under the presidency of the diocesan bishop, the *converso* Juan Arias Dávila, son of Henry IV's chief accountant (*contador mayor*) Diego Arias, condemned to death some Jews from Sepúlveda who had supposedly committed the 'ritual murder' of a child in the town. According to contemporary accounts, between eight and seventeen men were either hanged or burned on this charge. This violence, whatever its full extent, seems to have been part of a more general campaign by the Observant Franciscans to end Jewish moneylending and convert the Jews, which had begun in Italy under the influence of the general of the order, John of Capistrano (canonized in 1724). In Spanish circumstances, this became an attack on supposedly 'false' *conversos*, as well as the country's remaining Jews, and included the charge that Jews habitually committed 'ritual murder' on young Christian children, almost always boys. The Sepúlveda case, which was tried by Bishop Arias, seems to have been the first such trial in Spain, though such things were quite common elsewhere in fifteenth-century Europe.

As Henry IV's reign progressed into its final years, the *conversos* of the larger cities continued to be targeted by Old Christian violence. One of the most notorious events of the kind took place in Córdoba, in March 1473. By this time, the city and its surrounding countryside were divided between two warring branches of the Fernández de Córdoba family. By 1470, a perception had developed that the prevailing *bando*, led by the *alcalde mayor* Don Alonso de Aguilar, was excessively favourable to the *conversos*, so that the main opposing faction, headed by the count of Cabra, found it expedient to present itself as the champion of the Old Christians. In this it was supported by the then bishop of the city, Don Pedro Solier, who despite his name was also a member of the Fernández de Córdoba family, and joined the opposition to Don Alonso and his supporters outside the city (see chapter 2). Within Córdoba itself, Old Christians had established a religious confraternity, known as the Brotherhood of Charity (*Cofradía de la Caridad*). At the beginning of March 1473, the brotherhood held a procession, carrying a statue of the Virgin Mary, supposedly to raise the Christian fervour of the citizens. The procession passed along the main trading street of the city, the Calle de la Feria (Fair Street), which still crosses the centre of the city from north to south. The street itself, and those surrounding it, were heavily populated with the *converso* descendants of those who had moved from the Jewish quarter on the west side of the city after 1391. At the junction on the Calle de la Feria known as La Cruz del Rastro, an incident occurred which was to have fateful consequences for New Christians not only in Córdoba but throughout Spain. A young girl, eight or ten years old according to contemporary sources, spilt some fluid on to the canopy over the statue. A blacksmith in the procession, named as Alonso Rodríguez, immediately cried out that the liquid was urine and that it was a deliberate insult to the Virgin by New Christians. He declared that he personally would take revenge on the *conversos*, and was supported by enough of the crowd to enable him to lead attacks on some neighbouring houses. At this stage a Cordoban squire (*escudero*), Pedro de Torreblanca, attempted to block the path of the rioters, but he was wounded and trampled on by members of the 'charitable' brotherhood. Torreblanca's supporters responded by attacking the looters, and the fighting spread to the surrounding streets. The blacksmith and his henchmen then took refuge in the Franciscan church of San Pedro de Real (known locally as San Francisco), on the Calle de la Feria, but by this time Alonso de Aguilar had arrived on the scene. By offering negotiations, he inveigled Rodríguez out of his sanctuary, and, after an ensuing altercation, stabbed the blacksmith with a lance. The dying man was taken to his own house by his supporters and, as *conversos* attempted to protect their property by hiding away their valuables, a crowd gathered around the Rodríguez household, and was told that he had died, had been resurrected, and was once again demanding action against the New Christians. This macabre re-enaction of the Christian story of salvation led to further looting, which Don Alonso attempted to stop by arriving outside the blacksmith's house with a squadron of mounted retainers. In view of the failure of the *alcalde mayor* to impose his authority, a member of one of Córdoba's lesser noble families, the *veinticuatro* Pedro de Aguayo, attempted to organize armed resistance by the *conversos*. At this stage, Alonso de Aguilar and his supporters, who had controlled the city for several years, were driven out of its eastern sector, the Ajerquía. They retired, under a hail of missiles, to their headquarters in the royal castle (Alcázar), leaving the *conversos* open to attack not only from urban rioters, including those who crossed the Roman bridge (Puente Romano) over the Guadalquivir from the suburb on the Campo de la Verdad, but also from day-labourers (*jornaleros*) and other rural workers who came into the city with the hope of supplementing their wages with loot. Don Alonso offered the *conversos* protection in the Old Castle (Castillo Viejo), a walled enclosure which adjoined his headquarters, and there followed a two-day stand-off, during which the opponents of the New Christians armed themselves but took no overt action. On 16 March, the main attack on the *conversos* began, after Don Alonso de Aguilar, together with his brother Gonzalo Fernández de Córdoba, the 'Great Captain' (see chapter 7), in one of his less auspicious early military exploits, decided to abandon to their fate all those who had failed to reach the protection of the Castillo Viejo. As a result, numbers of *conversos* were killed or wounded, and houses and shops were looted and burned.

According to the chronicler Alfonso de Palencia, the violence then spread to various towns under the jurisdiction of Córdoba, and many New Christians from the area fled towards Seville, where further riots took place in the following year, leading some to take refuge in Gibraltar, under the protection of the duke of Medina Sidonia, while others left for Italy or Flanders. Meanwhile, in Córdoba, an immediate result of the violence was the issue, under the authority of the supposedly pro-*converso* Alonso de Aguilar, of a law of *limpieza de sangre*, which forbade New Christians to hold any public office in the city or its outlying territories in future. The departure, through death or exile, of victims of the 1473 riots is indicated by the subsequent large-scale letting of property belonging to the Cathedral, in the parish of St Mary adjoining the Calle de Feria, and similar changes no doubt occurred in the neighbouring parishes of the Ajerquía. This supposed settlement, to the great disadvantage of the *conversos*, did not end social tensions in the city concerned with the real or imagined presence of 'Judaizing' Christians within it. On 11 December 1474, just before Henry IV's death in Madrid and Isabella's proclamation at Segovia, the Cordoban notary Gonzalo González records a second 'robbery of the *conversos*', thus suggesting that the scattering of the previous year was either less complete than the contemporary chronicles of Alonso de Palencia and Diego de Valera suggest, or else, and more probably, had been at least partially reversed. On this occasion, Don Alonso, possibly sensing an imminent reduction of the freedom of action which he had enjoyed under Henry IV, acted in his royal office of *alcalde mayor*, and repressed the outbreak with exemplary punishment, having three men hanged, three flogged, and another three banished. It was in Seville that the *converso* question next surfaced, in a particularly dramatic form.[7]

During their first visit to Seville as monarchs, Isabella and Ferdinand summoned a national council of the Castilian Church, which met in the city from 8 July to 1 August 1478. The primary aim of this assembly was to draw up a programme for the complete reform of the Church in that kingdom (see chapter 7), but the discussions took place against a background of fear, and accusations of secret 'Judaizing' and conspiracy by New Christians, in Seville itself and elsewhere. At this time, the archbishop of Seville, Cardinal Pedro González de Mendoza, published a pastoral letter, which was intended to help the *conversos* to a greater knowledge of the Christian faith, and thus draw them away from Judaism. He was joined in this enterprise of denouncing Judaism and supposed crypto-Jews by his assistant, the bishop of Cádiz, the *asistente* of Seville, Diego de Merlo (see chapter 2), and the Dominicans of St Paul's priory in Seville. While Cardinal Mendoza's pastoral programme was supposedly being put into place, further lurid accusations were made, especially in Seville, of *converso* treachery. The Dominicans seem to have led a propaganda campaign to convince the sovereigns that Seville was full of secret, or not so secret, Jewish practice, which was threatening not only the integrity of the Church but also the political and social order of the city. In this the friars were supported by Cardinal Mendoza who, in addition to issuing his pastoral letter, which was apparently aimed at peacefully bringing errant New Christians back into the fold, also began to exercise his traditional rights as diocesan bishop, either directly or through his deputy (*gobernador*), the bishop of Cádiz and the royal *asistente* Diego de Merlo, to investigate the orthodoxy of *conversos*. The seventeenth-century annalist of Seville, Diego Ortiz de Zúñiga, not unreasonably described this activity as a trial run (*bosquejo*) for the new Castilian Inquisition.[8] Tradition in Seville maintained that pressure on the New Christians was increased by an incident which supposedly took place on 18 March 1478. A young Gentile knight, who had supposedly entered the city's Jewish quarter (*judería*) at night to see his Jewish girlfriend, claimed to have surprised a gathering of both Jews and New Christians, who were engaged in what was to him a mysterious celebration, which if it happened at all was very probably the observance of the eve of the Passover, which in that year coincided with Holy Week. The matter was reported to the Dominican prior, Alonso de Hojeda, who immediately confronted the king and queen with the news, and it was afterwards said that the incident finally persuaded them to petition Pope Sixtus IV for a new Inquisition, which was to begin its work in Seville.

On 1 November 1478, Sixtus duly issued a bull (*Exigit sincere devotionis*) which allowed the appointment of two or three priests, who should be over forty years of age, to act as inquisitors in the archdiocese of Seville, with the possibility of further posts in other parts of the crown of Castile. It may seem surprising that Isabella and Ferdinand did not immediately put the provisions of the bull into effect, but the likely reason is that they first wished to give Cardinal Mendoza's pastoral campaign, which itself contained an inquisitorial element, an opportunity to succeed. According to the chronicler Fernando del Pulgar, the archbishop's 'constitution' for the Church outlined the proper behaviour of a Catholic Christian from birth to death (see chapter 6). The document was to be displayed on noticeboards in the parishes, and the parish clergy were to teach it to the adult laity, who were in turn to instruct their children. During this lengthy period of catechetical instruction in the archdiocese of Seville, some *conversos* seem to have been lulled into a false sense of security, but this was to end in 1480, after the cortes of Toledo (see chapter 2). On 27 September of that year, the Crown issued letters of commission, under the terms of Sixtus's bull, to two Dominicans, Juan de San Martín and Miguel de Morillo, to act as inquisitors in Seville. Both had already achieved distinction in their order. San Martín, who at the time was prior of St Paul's in Burgos, had previously been vicar of the reformed, or Observant, houses in the Dominican province of Castile, while in the previous year Morillo had become provincial of the order in Aragon, with the evident approval of King Ferdinand. The assessor for the new inquisitorial tribunal, Dr Juan Ruiz de Medina, was both a secular cleric and a member of the Castilian royal council and, as he had previously assisted

Cardinal Mendoza with his pastoral offensive, the *asistente* of Seville, Diego de Merlo, also worked with the new tribunal. On New Year's Day 1481, the inquisitors sent a letter to all the nobles with jurisdiction (*señores de vasallos*) in Andalusia, asking for their assistance. It appears that the appointment of San Martín and Morillo had caused a mass flight of *conversos*, in November and December 1480, from Seville to the smaller *seigneurial* towns, where they expected to receive effective protection, as some Cordoban New Christians had done in 1473. At the same time, stories of *converso* plots developed, which served the purpose of discrediting all resistance to the inquisitors, who enjoyed the much-publicized support of both the ecclesiastical and the secular authorities. Perhaps the most lurid tale which arose in this period concerned a wealthy *converso* called Diego de Susán, who was said to be the focus of resistance to the new tribunal, and to have attempted to organize a military rebellion, with the help of New Christians from the neighbouring towns of Utrera and Carmona. While there may have been some truth in the accusation that political resistance was attempted by the *conversos*, there was none at all in the legend which subsequently developed concerning his daughter Susana, the *fermosa fembra* ('beautiful girl'). The demonstrably apocryphal story was that the fair *conversa*, afraid that her Old Christian lover would suffer, betrayed the conspiracy to the authorities. The imagined consequences of this act of treachery were, according to legend, that she first withdrew to a convent, and later resorted to the streets to beg for food. A further elaboration was that when she died, she supposedly ordered that her skull should be placed above the door of the family house, as a warning to others. In reality, there is no reliable evidence of the *converso* plot, and Diego de Susán had in any case died in the previous year. The notion that Jewish belief and practice among New Christians was a direct threat to the social fabric was, however, to remain a prevailing belief of churchmen and politicians throughout Isabella and Ferdinand's reigns and beyond.

Seville's new inquisitors, San Martín and Morillo, established themselves in the Dominican convent of St Paul but, during 1481, shortage of space induced them to accept the offer of the *asistente* Diego de Merlo, and move across the river to the castle of Saint George in Triana, of which he was the governor (*alcaide*). It was at this stage that San Martín and Morillo began to parade convicted 'Judaizers' in ceremonies known as 'acts of faith' (*autos de fe*), after which relapsed heretics were handed over to the secular authorities to be burned (see below). Almost immediately, concerns surfaced that abuses were being committed by the new tribunal. On 29 January 1482, Pope Sixtus IV wrote to Ferdinand and Isabella, praising their Catholic devotion and zeal, and making the remarkable admission that the institution which had been set up as a result of his 1478 bull went against the traditional practice of the Church in that it was directed not against heresy in general but specifically against 'Judaizing' Christians. The error was blamed on the confused presentation of the issues by the Castilian envoys, rather than the papacy itself. Sixtus recognized that there had been 'many quarrels and lamentations' against him and the Castilian rulers, as a result of the initial actions of the inquisitors in Seville, and appeared to accept that the two Dominicans had illegally and unjustly imprisoned large numbers of people, falsely accusing them of heresy, robbing them of their goods and sending some of them to the stake. The pope had called the cardinals together in conclave to discuss the complaints of the Spanish *conversos*, and, according to this account, some suggested that San Martín and Morillo should be removed from their posts, although the majority agreed that they should continue. Sixtus blamed any errors committed by the inquisitors on the excessive influence on them of the Castilian crown, and intimated that any future appointees to such a post in that kingdom who behaved in a similar manner would be removed by authority of the Holy See. If other members of the Dominican order were appointed as inquisitors in future, this would be done by their own superiors, who were ultimately under papal control. Sixtus decreed that the Seville inquisitors should in future act in conjunction with the archbishop and his agents, thus preserving papal prerogatives without necessarily hindering the quest for *converso* 'Judaizers', which was just as much the concern of Cardinal Mendoza.

The original 1478 bull, under the terms of which San Martín and Morillo were appointed to Seville, had stated that inquisitors were to be more than forty years of age, of good knowledge and life, to be bachelors or masters of theology or else doctors of canon law, or, failing that, at least 'God-fearing' licentiates (graduates) by examination. It seems that, having seen Ferdinand and Isabella exploit to the full the powers which they were given in the bull of 1 November 1478, the pope now wished to regain some lost ground, and was happy to use *converso* complaints for this purpose. The following year saw a controversy in Seville which gave him a further opportunity to do so. On 23 May 1483, Sixtus wrote to Iñigo Manrique, who by now was archbishop of Seville, after the translation of Cardinal Mendoza to the primatial see of Toledo. The pope appointed Manrique as his judge-delegate, to hear appeals against the sentences of the Inquisition in his diocese, and also took the opportunity to regularize the position of the Seville tribunal in terms of canon law. He withdrew privileges which had been granted by the inquisitors to certain *conversos*, as individuals or in groups, who had received the lesser penalty of being 'reconciled' to the Church after conviction for 'Judaizing'. Sixtus's action was, by his own account in Manrique's letter of appointment, prompted by the report of an investigatory commission of senior churchmen, chaired by Cardinal Rodrigo Borja (later pope Alexander VI). The pope accompanied his appointment of Archbishop Manrique as judge-delegate for heresy in Seville with the nomination, on 2 August 1483, of further judges in the Roman Curia to hear the appeals which had been lodged by *conversos* against the activities of the inquisitors San Martín and Morillo. The relevant document refers to burnings in effigy of those who had fled from Seville, as well as burnings in person, and declared all wrongful convictions would be annulled. Soon afterwards, though, Sixtus appeared to withdraw from this militant position, revoking Manrique's nomination as judge-delegate and declaring that he might have been misinformed about the goings-on in Seville. Nevertheless, Sixtus did not totally abandon at this stage his concern for papal prerogatives or his desire to root out inquisitorial injustice. On 25 November 1483, he ordered San Martín and Morillo to 'rehabilitate' a *converso* couple who had previously been burned in effigy after evading interrogation in Triana castle. The husband in question, Juan Fernández de Sevilla, was chief accountant (*contador*) to Enrique, duke of Medina Sidonia, whose political dominance over Seville and its region was at that time under threat from the Crown. Juan and his wife, although in dire straits as fugitives from the Inquisition, had declared their penitence and appealed to the pope. Not for the first or last time, the Roman Curia was the recipient of skilled and contradictory lobbying from supporters and opponents of the New Christians and of the Inquisition. In the last months of his reign, Sixtus appears to have favoured the enemies of the new tribunal, and by June 1484 he was quashing convictions and annulling sentences of the Seville inquisitors without even consulting them. For example, his papal auditor in Rome, Antonio de Grasso, intervened to annul sentences of burning, for being relapsed heretics, which had been given locally against a parish councillor (*jurado*) of Seville, Pedro Fernández and his wife Francisca de Herrera.[9]

Meanwhile, the tentacles of the new Castilian Inquisition were spreading. On 11 February 1482, the pope issued a brief whereby he appointed seven further inquisitors to the kingdom, including the Dominican prior of Holy Cross (Santa Cruz), Segovia, Fray Tomás de Torquemada. On 4 September of that year, the chapter of the Mosque-Cathedral of Córdoba gave permission to Pedro Martínez del Barrio, Bachiller Alvar García de Capillas and Bachiller Antón Ruiz de Morales, who had recently been appointed by the Crown and the pope as inquisitors in the city and diocese, to absent themselves from services in choir when carrying out their duties in the pursuit and punishment of 'heretical depravity'. Like its counterpart further down the Guadalquivir, in Seville, the new Cordoban tribunal established itself in a castle, in this case the royal Alcázar, which had previously been the headquarters of Don Alonso de Aguilar and was now occupied by Isabella and Ferdinand's *corregidor*, Francisco de Valdés. The 'reconciliation' of penitent 'Judaizers' was soon taking place in *autos de fe*, and the burning of the relapsed began, in the Campo de los Santos Mártires, the ground in front of the Cistercian monastery of the Holy Martyrs. The early records of the Cordoban tribunal have largely disappeared, probably having been lost or destroyed in 1809 or 1810, during the Napoleonic occupation of the city, but the first person to be burned for heresy, in 1483, appears to have been the mistress of the Cathedral treasurer, Don Pedro Fernández de Alcaudete, who was himself burnt as a 'Judaizer' in the following year. There were subsequent *autos de fe* in Córdoba in 1485, 1486 and 1492, in all of which various individuals were burned in effigy, while in the last of this series no fewer than twenty-four men and seven women were burned as 'Judaizers'. In 1483, the Inquisition established itself in the upper Andalusian cathedral city of Jaén, probably first in the house of the late Constable (*Condestable*) Miguel Lucas de Iranzo, but soon in the Dominican priory of St Catherine. The first inquisitors in the city were Juan García de Cañas, who had taught law in Calahorra, and Fray Juan de Yarza, who had been prior of the Dominican house of St Peter Martyr (dedicated to the first martyr of the Inquisition, killed by 'heretics' in Lombardy in 1252), in Toledo, where it was to become the headquarters of another inquisitorial tribunal two years later. The Jaén tribunal remained active until 1495, when it was merged with that of Córdoba, and was primarily devoted to a hunt for Jewish belief and practice among *conversos*. The predecessor of the Toledan tribunal was set up in the La Manchan town of Ciudad Real in the autumn of 1483. On Sunday 14 September, the Feast of the Exaltation of the Holy Cross, the 'edict of grace' (see below) was read in St Mary's Church, and a further pursuit of heresy among the *converso* population was begun. At about the same time, inquisitors also established themselves at Guadalupe in Extremadura, apparently with the primary purpose of investigating supposed Judaism among the town's important community of Jeronymite friars. During the 1480s, further inquisitorial tribunals were set up, without arousing significant controversy, in Avila, Valladolid, Medina del Campo, Segovia and Sigüenza. The same could not be said of the crown of Aragon, to which the king and queen had every intention of extending their new creation.[10]

The first practical problem which Ferdinand encountered was the continued existence in Aragon, Catalonia and Valencia of tribunals which had been set up in the thirteenth century. As early as May

1481, the king took steps to gain greater control over the papal Inquisition within his hereditary domain and, characteristically, he set in place a double strategem. His ambassador to the Roman Curia, Comendador Gonzalo de Beteta, received two sets of instructions, one to be publicized and the other to be kept secret. Beteta's open commission was to approach the Dominican general, Salvo Cassetta, and the papal vice-chancellor, Cardinal Rodrigo Borja, with a request that, without any change to the existing Papal Inquisition, the Dominican inquisitor in Aragon, Maestre Vidal, who was also the order's provincial in that kingdom, should be replaced by Ferdinand's candidate, Fray Juan Orts. On the other hand, the ambassador's secret instructions were that, if these approaches, as well as an overture to the cardinal of Naples, proved unsuccessful, he was to obtain the requisite document directly from the pope. The king told Beteta that he also wanted Fray Juan Cristóbal de Gualbes to be appointed as inquisitor in the crown of Aragon, both friars possessing the same powers as their Castilian equivalents. The controversy over supposed inquisitorial excesses in Andalusia, and especially in Seville, and Sixtus IV's personal involvement in it, threatened to block Ferdinand's moves. Having never apparently been enthusiastic to grant the Castilian bull to Isabella in 1478, the pope was evidently not keen to spread the new institution to Aragon. In response, the king changed tack, and approached the Dominican general with a request that Fray Gaspar Juglar should be appointed as inquisitor in the order's Aragonese province, under existing rules. An important innovation was that Juglar would then appoint Ferdinand's nominees as his subordinate officials. This plan was accepted, and both Orts and Gualbes were duly appointed, though the relevant royal document, dated 28 December 1481, also contained, apparently without papal authority, a copy of the 1478 bull for Castile. Once apprised of this legal attack on papal prerogative, Sixtus dug in his heels and refused to abolish the old papal Inquisition in Aragon. More locally, Ferdinand identified the Dominican provincial in Aragon, Fray Francisco Vidal, as the main obstacle to his plans. In 1479, Vidal had, to the apparent annoyance of the king, been involved in a successful scheme to remove, with the help of forged documents, an inquisitor in Barcelona, Juan Comes. It was not until 25 May 1483 that Sixtus finally agreed that Gualbes should become inquisitor in Valencia, bypassing the Dominican provincial in an unprecedented way. On 17 October of that year, a papal formulary had permitted the Castilian inquisitor-general, Tomás de Torquemada, to act in that capacity and to appoint inquisitors in Aragon, Catalonia and Valencia. The lack of a papal document explicitly winding up the old Inquisition in the crown of Aragon, and ordering the establishment of a new tribunal on the Castilian model, thus became irrelevant to events on the ground.

In the meantime, and no doubt having observed the goings-on in Castile, *conversos* in the crown of Aragon began to protest to the papacy as soon as Ferdinand's appointees started work in Zaragoza, Barcelona and Valencia. Torquemada's appointment in Aragonese and Catalan lands, overriding as it did the complete legal and constitutional separation between the crowns of Castile and Aragon, was to create a storm which engulfed many others in addition to those New Christians who were accused of 'Judaizing'. The initial moves to revive the medieval Inquisition in Aragon and the Catalan territories, and even the strengthening of royal authority over its tribunals, had threatened only the *conversos*, but the appointment of Castilian inquisitors to posts in the neighbouring kingdom was quite another matter. In 1484–5, violent opposition was to break out against Ferdinand's Inquisition in many parts of his realm. The *conversos*, many of whom played a prominent part in both royal and local government, fought to be recognized as sincere Christians, and hence to retain the hard-won status of their families in society at large. Enough *autos de fe* had already taken place in Castile and Andalusia, and enough complaints had already been made to the Crown and the Papacy about acts of arbitrary cruelty committed by the inquisitors of that kingdom, for Aragonese and Catalan New Christians to have little doubt concerning the fate which awaited them if Torquemada's agents were allowed to act in Ferdinand's lands. It is also clear, though, that much resistance in these years to the new inquisitors came from those who claimed no Jewish origin, but objected to Castilian influence and defended their traditional charters (*fueros* or *fors*). On 14 April 1484, during a meeting of the Aragonese cortes at Tarazona, Torquemada began the process of spreading the Castilian Inquisition into the neighbouring kingdom by summoning a special meeting of representatives of the main towns of the crown of Aragon. At this junta he announced the appointment of new inquisitors to Zaragoza, Huesca, Teruel, Lleida (Lérida), Barcelona and Valencia. In early May, Gaspar Juglar and Pedro Arbués de Epila went to Zaragoza as inquisitors and immediately met stout opposition from *conversos* and constitutionalists alike. When their Basque Dominican colleague Juan de Solivera arrived in the fiercely independent Aragonese town of Teruel, on 23 May, he was refused entry, partly on the grounds that he was too young for the post in terms of canon law, and had to take refuge in the nearby town of Cella, where his fellow-inquisitor Martín Navarro was vicar. The councillors of Teruel had begun to explore with their legal advisers the possibilities of legal and constitutional resistance to the Inquisition as soon as their representatives returned from the Cortes, and the meeting with Torquemada, at Tarazona. Teruel was populated at this time by a mixture of Old Christians, New Christians, Jews and Muslims, and the ample surviving records suggest that the primary reason for the town's resistance to the Inquisition was the tribunal's perceived infringement of its ancient constitutional liberties, rather than the defence of the *conversos* as such. The brave resistance of the citizens proved unsuccessful, as Ferdinand refused all overtures from the town's representatives and instead ordered into action his own chief official in Teruel and its surrounding territory, or *comunidad*, the *capitán* Juan Garcés de Marcilla, whose post was similar to that of a *corregidor* in Castile. After a show of military force by the Crown, the two inquisitors were finally able to make their official entry into Teruel on 25 March 1485, though the area was not entirely pacified for another two or three years.[11]

Resistance to what was clearly perceived as Ferdinand's, rather than the Church's, Inquisition was no more effective in other Aragonese and Catalan towns. In Barcelona, the papal inquisitor Juan Comes had been at least nominally in post since 1461 and, as a result, the city sent no representative to Tarazona in 1484, to discuss the establishment of a new tribunal. Torquemada, however, appointed two new inquisitors for Barcelona nevertheless, and revoked Comes's appointment. The city councillors refused to accept the change and it was not until February 1486, in the reign of Pope Innocent VIII, that a legal device was put into practice to remove Comes and appoint his replacements. The pope formally removed from their posts all the inquisitors in the crown of Aragon, whether they occupied their posts under the new or the old foundation. Having thus cleared the field, he allowed Torquemada to appoint as inquisitor of Barcelona a Dominican friar, Alonso de Espina, namesake of the Franciscan author of the *Fortress of the Faith*. The flight of large numbers of New Christians from the city and the surrounding principate of Catalonia reduced the number of Espina's prisoners. In Valencia, the papal tribunal had in fact been active in the 1460s, for example trying fifteen *conversos*, between 1460 and 1467, for supposed 'Judaizing'. Orts and Gualbes, who had occupied their posts in this tribunal, amid controversy, only since 1481, were removed by Torquemada in favour of Martín Iñigo, who was a Valencian, and Juan de Epila, who was Aragonese. The latter appointment led once again to constitutional protests, on the grounds that the naming of a non-Valencian was illegal, but the resistance soon crumbled. As in other cases, Ferdinand was happy to argue that, if there were really no heresy in the kingdom of Valencia, as the local authorities claimed, then its inhabitants surely needed to have no fear of the new inquisitors. As elsewhere, the opposition was unsuccessful, and a vigorous new tribunal was set up in Valencia, later having oversight also of Teruel. The most dramatic resistance to the new foundation of the Inquisition took place in Zaragoza, the capital of the kingdom of Aragon. There the violence which had been talked about in Seville became a reality. It seems that the inquisitor, Pedro Arbués de Epila, soon realised that his life was genuinely in danger from a combination of *converso* opponents and Aragonese constitutionalists. On the night of 15–16 September 1485, Arbués prayed in Zaragoza cathedral, wearing under his clerical cap and robes a steel helmet and a coat of mail, but these precautions did not save him. Contemporary sources state that eight men, who had been hired by his enemies among the New Christians of the city, stole up and, having checked his identity, proceeded to stab him a number of times. The inquisitor lingered for another day, before becoming a martyr, in the eyes of the Inquisition and its supporters. The propaganda value of the death of Arbués to Ferdinand and his ecclesiastical allies was considerable. The new Inquisition had imitated the thirteenth-century original by acquiring its own 'protomartyr', and not only had resistance to the tribunals been utterly discredited in the eyes of many law-abiding citizens, but the inquisitors' claims concerning the threat posed by 'Judaizing' *conversos* to Spanish society appeared to be vindicated by this violent deed.

The Inquisition, by its very nature, continues in the present day to arouse strong passions among its opponents and defenders alike. It should be stressed that, although Ferdinand and Isabella's tribunal responded to the particular circumstances of their time, its procedures were directly descended from those of its medieval predecessor, which had been more or less established by the end of the thirteenth century. In addition to new papal and royal legislation which affected their work, Spanish inquisitors after 1478 had at their disposal two manuals of procedure which had come to be generally recognized. The first, which is normally known as the *Manual of the Inquisitor* (*Practice of the office of the Inquisition of heretical depravity*) was composed in 1323 or 1324 by a French Dominican, Bernard Gui, who acted against heretics in southern France. Much more influential, during Isabella and Ferdinand's reign and after, was the *Inquisitor's directory* by the Catalan Dominican, and inquisitor, Nicolau Eymerich, which was completed in about 1379. Both works consisted of a mixture of legal texts and commentary, and were primarily directed against Cathars, Waldensians, and the radical groups within or on the fringe of the Franciscan order, who were known as 'spirituals'. Also, in line with the prevailing thought among church leaders in the fourteenth century, both authors identified Jews and Judaism as particular dangers to Christian society, and regarded converts from Christianity to Judaism as the most dangerous of all. Thanks to its diverse origins in Scripture and in the early history of the Church, the Inquisition had become, by the late fifteenth century, an awkward mixture of a law court and a confessional. Officially, the aim of inquisitors had always been to restore Christian unity by bringing wandering souls back into the Church. In that respect, the Inquisition thus had a part in the administration of the sacrament of reconciliation, or penance, whereby a sinner confessed his or her sins to a priest, and was given penance for what was past and advice for the amendment of conduct in the future, before receiving absolution. In the confessional, the normal rules of evidence in a court of law did not apply, and thus a dangerous area of liberty was created for inquisitors, in Spain as elsewhere. The almost complete loss or destruction of the records of the Seville and Córdoba tribunals make it effectively impossible to substantiate accounts, in contemporary and later secondary sources, of the number of arrests and deaths which took place in the early days, though surviving documentation of other tribunals, such as Ciudad Real-Toledo, Teruel and Valencia, provide a clearer picture. Observers at the time estimated that, between 1481 and 1488, the inquisitors in Seville arrested and tried approximately seven hundred 'Judaizers', many of them in their absence. As with all the work of the new Spanish Inquisition, accusations of indiscriminate violence, combined with economic abuse and exploitation, quickly arose. In particular, the royal chronicler Fernando del Pulgar, himself a *converso*, protested to Cardinal Pedro González de Mendoza that while a minority of his fellow New Christians may have held Jewish beliefs and practised them in secret, most of those who found their way to Triana castle, and later to other castles and prisons, were guilty of no such offence. Contrary to the view held by some modern scholars, and in particular Benzion Netanyahu and Norman Roth, Pulgar did not conclude from the paucity of genuine Judaizers that all the rest of the *conversos* were whole and sincere Christians. Instead, he highlighted a social reality of the Andalusia of his own day, which was the considerable degree of domestic confinement to which women and girls were subject, protesting that many in such circumstances had no effective possibility of learning about the Christian faith, and should not be persecuted for their innocent ignorance. The new inquisitors' investigation of heresy began with the publication of an 'edict of grace', which was normally done in a large church, or in the sole parish church of a smaller place, to which the Christian people had been summoned by their own clergy. The ceremony frequently included a sermon, in which a representative of the Inquisition elaborated on the mortal danger which threatened all those who were guilty of the errors of religious belief and practice which had been outlined in the edict itself. The local population was given a period of either thirty or forty days during which individuals should come forward and confess whatever was on their conscience. In principle, at least, those who came forward during this interval and made a complete confession were to be fully 'reconciled', or reintegrated into the Church, suffering no further personal or economic penalty.

A crucial feature of the Inquisition's operation was that, in addition to being required to confess their own failings, individuals were told that their immortal souls would be in peril if they did not reveal what they knew of the heresy of others, including relatives and neighbours. Despite their supposed regulation by canon law, the medieval tribunals had developed a fairly relaxed attitude towards the status and value of evidence. The inquisitors of Isabella and Ferdinand's reign, like their predecessors in Spain and elsewhere, sought to uncover heretical networks, rather than simply to correct the errors of individuals. In practice, whatever the subsequent outcome, the financial consequences of arrest on suspicion, or admission, of 'heretical depravity' were immediate and drastic. The movable and immovable goods of the person concerned were confiscated immediately, and even those eventually declared innocent never received them back in full. The consequences for the relatives of those who were arresred and/or convicted were inevitably severe, in both economic and social terms. Although they were agencies both of the Church and of the Crown, the tribunals were effectively self-financing, which immediately and inevitably led to accusations that they were motivated by greed rather than their self-proclaimed zeal for the faith. Arrests of those who were only slightly (*de levi*) or extremely (*de vehementi*) suspected of heresy normally followed the sifting of denunciations and confessions by the inquisitors and their team. This consisted of two or three inquisitors, with academic qualifications in theology or law, a prosecutor (*promotor* or *procurador fiscal*), a notary to record interrogations, a constable (*alguacil*) and a receiver of confiscated goods (*receptor de bienes confiscados*). If the prosecutor could convince the inquisitors that there was sufficient evidence to make a case against a person, the constable would be ordered to arrest him or her. The Castilian and Aragonese tribunals followed their predecessors elsewhere in Europe in employing imprisonment as a routine punishment. This, as well as the need for the visible support and protection of the royal authorities, led them to resort to castles to accommodate them and their prisoners, though the latter often spent more time in the cells before they were convicted and sentenced than afterwards. There were frequently long intervals, which sometimes amounted to years, between interrogations, while further evidence was found, attempts were made to reconcile the testimony of witnesses, or the accused were broken down and induced to confess their guilt.

The 'inquisitorial' procedure itself, which was far from unique to religious tribunals, had as its object the discovery of the 'truth'. In accordance with the principles of civil and canon law, which were both derived from the codes and practices of the late Roman Empire, the inquisitor, having achieved this discovery, had to apply to the case the provisions of the written law. The examination of prisoners which took place in the Inquisition's dungeons was meant to proceed in accordance with rigid rules, under the direction of one or more inquisitors and in the presence of a notary to record the proceedings, sometimes including even the expression and manner of the participants. The prosecutor assembled out of the evidence before him a questionnaire to be put to all witnesses against the accused. Here was no dramatic cross-examination in open court, as in modern British and American justice, but the meticulous, and repetitive, application, in secret, of set lists of questions. One potentially important innovation of the post-1478 Inquisition in Spain was the introduction of professional lawyers to represent defendants. A defence counsel would begin to act for his client after the *promotor* had brought his case, established his list of prosecution witnesses and drawn up his questionnaire to be put to them. There were, however, significant weaknesses in the provision for the defence of the accused. Defendants had no say in choosing their counsel, but were forced to accept whomever was named by the inquisitors. In such conditions, it was unlikely that any lawyer who had hopes of a successful career would risk too robust a defence of a client who was accused of an evil and anti-social offence, though records show that a few did so. Worse, although the defence lawyer was provided with details of the prosecution case, this was done only after the accused had been interrogated, often over a long period, without knowing whether or not he had incriminated himself. In addition, on the pretext of preventing the intimidation of prosecution witnesses and their families, all names and other circumstantial detail which might identify them to the defendant was excluded. Under these restrictions, defence witnesses were gathered and a questionnaire was composed to be put to them. Defendants were entitled to name their 'mortal enemies', whose testimony was by canon law to be disregarded by the inquisitors, but this rarely saved a prisoner from punishment. Notoriously, inquisitors held in reserve the use of torture, in order to 'persuade' a reluctant defendant, male or female, to reveal the 'truth'. This possibility was inherited from the beginnings of the tribunal, but it is striking that those who publicly opposed the new Spanish Inquisition in its earlier years, before 1500, do not generally include the use of torture among their complaints, referring rather to false accusations and financial abuses. When all testimony for and against the defendant had been gathered, the inquisitors would then decide on his or her guilt or innocence (usually the former) and declare the appropriate sentence. This would be referred to a committee of assessors (*calificadores*), normally parish or monastic clerics and/or academics from the locality of the tribunal concerned, who would ratify or alter it, again generally the former. Assessors sometimes took part in the examination of cases before trials began, and were also entitled to attend interrogation sessions before a verdict had been reached. At this stage, the secretive proceedings of the Inquisition suddenly became public.[12]

Once the sentence against a prisoner had been agreed by inquisitors and *calificadores*, he or she was ready to process through the streets, usually from the Inquisition prison to a major public square, in order to take part in an *auto de fe*. As the institution of the 'Holy Office' of the Inquisition matured, in the middle to late sixteenth century, such *autos* became elaborately staged rituals, which might last for a whole day, and attracted both Spanish royalty and foreign visitors, whether approving or otherwise. In the early days of the inquisitors' assault on the *conversos*, on the other hand, *autos* seem to have been less like pieces of Renaissance and Baroque theatre, intended literally to 'act out' the unity of Catholic society, and more like the brutal penitential rites of the Church in earlier centuries. In contrast to the period after about 1550, the Inquisition in Ferdinand and Isabella's reign resulted in almost no artwork, and the early *autos* seem to have been austere and efficient 'processes' (in both senses of the word) of those convicted of 'Judaizing'. Contemporary accounts indicate that in Toledo, for instance, hundreds of *conversos*, including many of the wealthiest citizens and their wives, processed from the Dominican convent of St Peter Martyr to the main square, the Plaza de Zocodover. As involuntary penitents, their identities were visible to all, they were barefoot, and they carried large candles. When, over the years, such ceremonies became more established as a part of urban life and ritual, such prisoners wore mitres, which seemed to parody those of bishops, and robes, known as *sambenitos*, modelled on the priestly chasuble, indicating in graphic form the nature of their offence. After arriving in the square, they were forced to listen to a lengthy sermon, denouncing heresy in general and Jewish belief and practice in particular, and then their sentences were read out. Those who were held to have repented of their sins were 'reconciled' to the Church, at the price of financial ruin. Those deemed guilty of minor offences were subjected to further public ritual humiliation, in addition to participation in the *auto de fe* itself. Clad in *sambenitos*, they might be forced to attend the high mass for a period of time, or else despatched on pilgrimages to shrines. In more serious cases, they might suffer a lengthy period of imprisonment, or house arrest if prison accommodation was in short supply, as was often the case. In addition, their *sambenitos* were hung in their parish churches, to the eternal shame of their families, and often renewed or replaced when the fabric wore out. Those who were convicted of heresy for a second time were treated as 'relapsed', and it was they, generally constituting a small minority of those who paraded in the *auto de fe* procession, who were handed over ('relaxed', in the jargon of the inquisitors) to the secular authorities, or 'secular arm'. After a purely formal appeal for mercy by the ecclesiastical judges, who were forbidden to 'shed blood' themselves, though this did not prevent them from using torture during interrogations, the relapsed were taken generally to a place away from the site of the *auto* itself, where they were burned. As a further refinement, those who expressed repentance of their sins at this point, to the satisfaction of the attendant clerics, were killed by garrotting, while tied to the stake, before the fire was lit. The unrepentant were burned alive. Any attempt by historians to minimize the brutality of the Spanish Inquisition must nevertheless confront this reality, which was to be repeated hundreds of times, both in Spain and later in its imperial possessions, for centuries to come. What, though, was the religious identity of the *conversos*, who constituted by far the greatest proportion of those who were arrested and punished by Isabella and Ferdinand's Inquisition?

In recent years, a great deal of effort has been expended by scholars in attempting to discover whether the inquisitors of the late fifteenth and early sixteenth centuries were correct in their belief that large numbers of New Christians in Spain were in fact secret practitioners of the Jewish faith. The debate has frequently, and often with considerable and unedifying *odium academicum*, taken the form of a discussion of the value of the evidence accumulated by the inquisitorial tribunals. The two main flaws in most of the material which has been published on the subject are a tendency to deal in absolutes rather than nuances and an almost total unawareness of the work which has been done on the activities in the same period of the Inquisition in other countries, such as England, Italy and Bohemia, where 'Judaizing' was not an issue of any significance. The failure to question absolutes has shown itself in a tendency to treat all the testimony which was given to inquisitors by Spaniards in Ferdinand and Isabella's reign as either entirely 'true' or entirely 'false'. The consequence of the first case would be that there was indeed a massive Judaizing movement, both among those who had personally converted from Judaism to Christianity and among their descendants. If, on the other hand, the evidence collected by the inquisitors was entirely false, then they were guilty of the peculiar cruelty of unjustly persecuting sincere and genuine Christians. In this case, other motives than the honest defence of Christian orthodoxy would have to be ascribed to them, and the explanations most frequently offered are economic exploitation and an anti-Judaism akin to more recent racial anti-Semitism. A large proportion of the twentieth-century scholars who have tackled the question of the nature of *converso* religion would certainly or probably not subscribe to a Jewish or a Christian belief system which is comparable with those which presented themselves to fifteenth-century Spaniards. Yet, strangely, it is hard to find a scholar of the subject who does not implicitly accept at their face value rabbinical or priestly definitions of what it meant to be a Jew or a Christian. Torquemada's inquisitors inherited well-established theoretical notions of what constituted Jewish belief and practice. Based on the New Testament, they saw Judaism as a 'dead' and 'legalistic' religion, which was even diabolical in inspiration. Thus, in their gathering of evidence and in their interrogation of suspects, they concentrated on outward signs of Jewish observance, rather than the inner spiritual life which, as was admitted in manuals such as that of Eymerich, was in any case largely closed to the inquisitor. Thus the *demandas*, or lists of up to forty or fifty charges, which were drawn up by prosecutors against supposed 'Judaizers', consisted almost entirely of what were described as 'ceremonies of the Jewish Law (Torah)'. They concerned themselves little with theological matters, such as the nature of Christ and of the Virgin Mary, and the relationship between faith and works, which vexed bishops and inquisitors elsewhere in Europe, such as those who were concerned with Lollards in England and Hussites in Bohemia. The matters discussed in most Inquisition trials included the observance of the Jewish Sabbath and festivals such as Passover and Tabernacles, of Jewish dietary laws in the home, and even worship in synagogues by supposed Catholic Christians. Yet the rare survival of 'raw' witness statements from the tribunal of Soria and Burgo de Osma, between 1482 and 1506, reveals a rich variety of often quite sceptical and sophisticated religious views, even among people of humble rank. While much of this material did indeed concern adherence to Judaism and rejection of Christianity, it also contained materialistic and universalistic views of religion which have a remarkably modern air to them, and which were duplicated at the time in areas of Europe where the issue of conversion to Christianity from Judaism was not a major preoccupation.

In any case, the staff of the new tribunals of the Inquisition quickly came to the conclusion that, by their own lights, 'Judaizing' among *conversos*, by now the children and grandchildren of those who had personally changed faith, was rife in large areas of Castile and Aragon. In addition, the inquisitors decided that the main cause of this 'lapse' into the old faith was the continuing presence in the midst of Christian society of Jews, many of whom were personally related to the converts. Two years after the Inquisition began its operations in Seville, the Andalusian tribunals took action on this question. On 1 January 1483, the inquisitors of Seville and Córdoba ordered the expulsion from those dioceses, and also from the dioceses of Cádiz and Jaén, which fell under their jurisdiction, of their entire Jewish population, which was to be given just a month to leave for other parts of Spain. This initiative possibly originated with the king and queen rather than the Inquisition itself, as the tribunals had no jurisdiction over unbaptised Jews. In any case, the measure was clearly intended to assist the inquisitors with their work among Andalusian *conversos*, and was probably not unconnected with the Granada war, in which it seems to have been feared that, like their ancestors supposedly did in 711, they would side with the Muslims against the Christians. It is not known how many Jews in fact left Andalusia as a result of the 1483 expulsion order. Pulgar estimated that 4000 households departed, or approximately 20,000 people, while Isaac ibn Faraj made the much lower estimate of 5000 souls. In any case, despite some local opposition, notably in Jerez de la Frontera, a Jewish migration into Extremadura and Castile certainly seems to have taken place. As early as 8 January of that year, the town clerk (*escribano del concejo*) of Jerez records a 'movement of Jews' (*movimiento de judíos*), but the town council protested at the difficulty of liquidating the Jews' assets within the brief interval of a month. On 1 January 1484, Jacob Cachopo, who appears to have been the representative of the Jewish community in Jerez, obtained permission from the Crown for the exiles to return to the town in order to dispose of their property at reasonable prices. In the meantime, many Andalusian Jews seem to have moved to Segura de la Sierra (Jaén), and Llerena and Badajoz in Extremadura. This expulsion appears to have continued throughout 1484, but by the following year Jews had returned not only to Jerez but also to Moguer and Córdoba. In the latter case, the restored community contributed in that year to the cost of campaigns against Nasrid Granada. A further trial expulsion took place in Aragon in May 1486, when Ferdinand, by his direct royal authority rather than that of the Inquisition, ordered the expulsion of Jews from the dioceses of Zaragoza and Albarracin. This measure, which presupposed a direct and criminal link between Jews and *conversos*, was apparently taken in retaliation for the murder the inquisitor Arbués in Zaragoza, and the stout resistance put up to his colleague Solivera in Teruel. This edict, like that in Andalusia three years earlier, was only temporarily effective, as Jews were still in Aragon when the 'final' expulsion orders were issued in both Castile and Aragon on 31 March 1492 (see chapter 6).[13]

4

The War for Granada

According to the Castilian chronicler Alfonso de Palencia, Isabella and Ferdinand had a fixed purpose, during all their troubles both before and after Henry IV's death in 1474, to conquer and subdue the Nasrid emirate of Granada. In the traditional view, this sense of unity and purpose on the Christian side met indecisiveness and division from the Muslims. It now appears, though, that the role of dynastic intrigues in the fall of Granada has been exaggerated. The main causes of the Muslim kingdom's collapse were economic and demographic weakness, and in particular an effective Castilian campaign to destroy Granadan agriculture. With hindsight, Isabella's succession to the Castilian throne seems to have provided the necessary condition for the final denouement, but things certainly did not thus appear at the time. In her anxiety to secure the throne by eliminating her rival, Joanna, the queen signed two truces with the Nasrid emir, one in 1475, for a year, and one in 1476, for no less than five years. However, as in earlier periods of frontier history, the existence of a general truce did not prevent local incidence of violence, or even quite major expeditions, such as that of the marquis of Cádiz, Rodrigo Ponce de León, who captured Garciago late in 1477, killing 350 Muslims and seizing a considerable amount of booty. The Granadans retaliated in the following year by taking Cieza (Murcia), an *encomienda* of the order of Santiago, and leading 2000 of its inhabitants away as captives. Also in 1478, a new, three-year truce was signed between the emir Abu'l-Hasan (Muley Albuhacén in the Castilian sources) and the Catholic Monarchs, who were so anxious about the Portuguese threat that they were prepared to waive the normal annual tribute. When this truce ended, the marquis of Cádiz captured Montecorto, north-west of the town of Ronda, but it was re-captured by troops from Ronda on Christmas Eve, 1479. During 1480, when it appeared that their regime had been stabilized, with the final defeat of the Portuguese pretender and the setting out of their own programme for the government of Castile at the cortes of Toledo, Ferdinand and Isabella entrusted to the *asistente* of Seville, Diego de Merlo, the

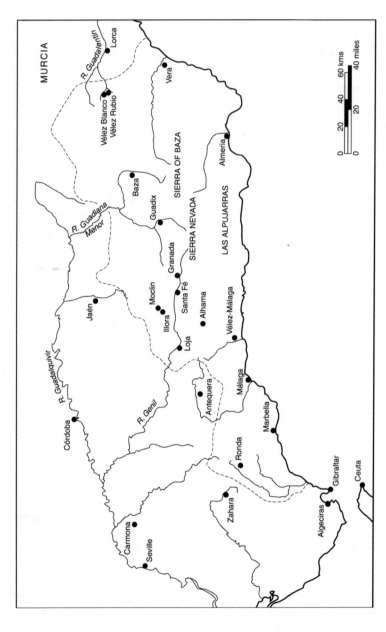

Map 2 The Conquest of Granada, Showing the Borders of the Emirate as They Were in 1482, based on J. N. Hillgarth, *The Spanish Kingdoms, 1250–1516,* ii. 1410 – 1516. *Castilian hegemony* (Oxford, 1978), p. 366.

supervision of the project to attack, and preferably subdue, the Nasrid kingdom of Granada. Merlo had already shown himself to be their faithful and efficacious servant, in the subduing of Córdoba and Seville, between 1476 and 1478, and his first task now was to attack and capture a Muslim-held stronghold, as a prelude to formally declaring war. Before he had established more definitive plans, Merlo mounted an attack on the village of Villalonga, in the territory of Ronda, using troops from Seville and those of the marquis of Cádiz, who was still anxious to ingratiate himself with the king and queen, in view of his ambiguous political conduct in previous years. The expedition, which continued to Ronda itself, suffered losses and made no significant gains, but although Merlo continued to assert that war had not been declared on Granada, a pattern had been set for the future. On the dark and stormy night of 27 December 1481, the Muslims, in a surprise attack, took without a fight the fortress of Zahara, in the same region, according to both Pulgar and Palencia because of the 'lack of diligence', or 'negligence', of the governor, Gonzalo de Saavedra, whose family had previously been in conflict with Ferdinand, but now lost control of the town for ever. The expedition, which was under the command of emir Abu'l-Hasan himself, indicates the Granadans' military strength and self-confidence. According to Pulgar, the emir had 'at that time more mounted troops and more artillery and all other things necessary for war than any of the other kings of Granada in times gone by. Trusting in his own strength, he made raids into Christian territory', mounting unsuccessful attacks on Castellar and Olvera. The main Arabic source for the period, the *Nubahut al-'asr*, and others, describe a kind of military tatoo, which Abu'l-Hasan arranged in April 1478, and which ended abruptly, at noon on 16 April, with a severe storm, causing severe flooding and mudslides, which washed away buildings and bridges. The emir appears to have suffered some kind of nervous breakdown as a result, and to have taken up a life of pleasure, instead of his previous military endeavour. The *Nubahuat*, which turns against Abu'l-Hasan at this point, accuses him of reducing his troops' pay and increasing taxes on civilians. The balance of power was about to shift decisively in the Castilians' favour. While earlier episodes of conflict, on or beyond the Granadan frontier, had failed to distract the king and queen from internal problems, the impact of the fall of Zahara was, in Azcona's expression, 'like dynamite'. According to Palencia, Ferdinand was particularly grieved at the loss because the town had been conquered, at great cost, by his grandfather Ferdinand of Aragon, who became known as Ferdinand of Antequera after capturing that crucial stronghold. The rulers quickly left Valencia, passed through and pacified Teruel, after troubles which had festered on there after the introduction of the new

Inquisition, and reached Medina del Campo on 1 February 1482. There, the penitential season of Lent passed in fasting, and in processions, which were intended to placate an apparently unfavourable God, but a military reply soon came from the Andalusian magnates and their men. In the meantime, in one of the quick reversals of fortune which were typical of traditional border fighting, Abu'l-Hasan recaptured Cardela and first lost and then regained Montecorto, from the marquis of Cádiz. The result was Alhama.[1]

The vast importance of the Christian capture of Alhama, a border town placed strategically in the the the centre of the Muslim kingdom, between Granada and Málaga, was not exaggerated by contemporary sources, either historical and literary. Although there were other routes between the two main cities, if the Castilians held Alhama, the town would serve as a base for further inroads into Abu'l-Hasan's territory. Being well aware of all this, the Andalusian nobility acted without waiting for the king and queen. Rodrigo Ponce de León, who by now had twenty years' experience of campaigning, kept his plans secret even from his own troops, as much to prevent his bitter rival, the duke of Medina Sidonia, from hearing about them, as to avoid signalling his intentions to his Muslim adversary. In the event, the marquis seems to have succeeded in assembling 2500 cavalry and 3000 infantry in Marchena, and taking them on two days' forced march, using mountain tracks, arriving within half a league of their target, before dawn on 28 February 1482. Using ladders, some scouts, led by a Leonese knight called Ortega de Prado, first climbed the town wall, and then entered the citadel, killing the solitary guard on duty, and also his companion who was asleep inside. At the time, the governor was away at a wedding in Vélez-Málaga, having left his wife in charge, and the defences were scarcely manned. The governor's wife and household were captured and the gates were opened to admit the marquis and the rest of his forces. Not unreasonably, given that Granada was not far away and reinforcements might be expected within hours, the Muslim population outside the citadel continued to bombard the Christians inside it with crossbows and *espingardas* (hand-guns or arquebuses), forcing them to break out literally through the castle wall to attack them. The Moorish resistance was fierce, and some unfortunates were burnt out of a mosque by Ponce de León's forces. Many died in the fighting, including the governor (*alcaide*) of Carmona, Sancho de Avila, and Christian captives were released from the town's dungeons. When Abu'l-Hasan arrived outside the walls on the following day, with several thousand cavalry and 50,000 or more infantry, according to the estimates of Palencia and Bernáldez, he found that numerous corpses had been tipped over the walls, and were being devoured by dogs. There seems to have been some confusion in the intentions of the Christians, as, while the strategic position of Alhama rendered it extremely unlikely that booty and captives could be brought unscathed to Christian territory, the *Nubdha* states that, when Abu'l-Hasan arrived, he found the expedition prepared to leave, as though retiring after a raid. Only when faced with a large Muslim army, and a barrage of arrows and arquebus fire, did Ponce de León's forces re-enter the town and prepare for a siege, though the need to emerge to secure water led to significant loss of life, and Pulgar asserts that members of the expedition had added to their own problems by previously destroying provisions, such as jars of oil and honey, and supplies of flour and grain, which had been stored there by the Granadan government. The emir and his massed forces ('the human wave') undertook a siege, but the Christian forces succeeded in sending messengers by night, telling their allies at home that their predicament would be hopeless if they were not rapidly relieved. The first response came from Córdoba, in the form of an army of about 1000 cavalry and 3000 infantry, led by Don Alonso de Aguilar and the city's *corregidor*, Garci Fernández Manrique. The Cordobans were beaten off by Muslim forces in the mountains, but, as a sign of the changed political conditions which pertained under Isabella's rule, the second, larger and successful, relief column, which the resisters had somehow managed to summon, was commanded by the marquis of Cádiz's arch-rival, the duke of Medina Sidonia, with the support of the count of Cabra, and others. This force succeeded in chasing Abu'l-Hasan away and temporarily relieving the siege, but once the main expedition had departed, leaving a garrison in place, the Muslim ruler returned with at least one artillery piece, a bombard, and renewed the siege, which was not finally relieved until early July. The marquis of Cádiz's success had been accompanied, somewhat belatedly, by action on the part of Ferdinand and Isabella. On 13 March, the representative at court of the Barcelona *conseller*s, Joan Bernat Marimón, was able to report that 2000 lancers had already left Medina del Campo in the Crown's pay, and that the largest levy of troops ever demanded in Castile was being assembled. Ferdinand himself duly left Medina the following day, and arrived in Córdoba, via La Rambla, on 31 March. The king then went to Alhama, and left supplies for the Christian garrison, but saw that, if the Castilian advantage was to be maintained, a further strategic point would have to be attacked. Although the general opinion of the Andalusian magnates was that the target should be Málaga, the king apparently took the advice of Diego de Merlo, and settled on Loja, the assault being planned for June.

One of the reasons why Abu'l-Hasan abandoned Alhama to the Christians was that, in the meantime, he had received intelligence that a Castilian force was indeed heading towards Loja. Ferdinand's army had been assembled from all over Castile, but it was badly prepared, consisting to a large extent of reluctant municipal levies, and the troops had left under the apparent ill omen of Isabella's giving birth, on 30 June 1482, to a stillborn twin sister to Princess Mary. More to the point, in military terms, was the fact that the Muslims were known to be forewarned of the expedition, which left Córdoba for Ecija on 1 July, and many advised that it should be used as a feint for an attack on Alora, near Málaga, which, if captured, could supply a springboard for an assault on the port itself. Thanks to disputes with the cities over payment, the Castilian expedition was much smaller than anticipated (5000 men-at-arms and 8000 infantry according to Palencia), and it suffered a humiliating reverse, because not only did the town's governor, 'Ali al-'Attar, put up stout resistance, but the emir's relieving force, which consisted of several thousand light cavalry (*jinetes*) and up to 80,000 infantry, succeeded in chasing the royal army away, and capturing a considerable quantity of artillery and siege equipment. In the process, the young Rodrigo Téllez Girón, master of the military order of Calatrava, was killed. Exploiting the disorderly retreat of the Castilian forces from their exposed position facing Loja, and also his own much shorter lines of communication, Abu'l-Hasan took the opportunity to raid a virtually undefended Tarifa, and drive off more than 3000 head of cattle. He achieved all this despite the fact that he had at the same time to contend with a rebellion by his son Boabdil (Muhammad XII), which was said in the *Nubaha* to have begun on the very day of the victory at Loja. From 1482 until the end of its independence, the Nasrid emirate was the scene of perpetual internecine conflict. Abu'l-Hasan established his capital, with his brother Muhammad al-Zagal, and his vizier, Abu'l-Qasim Venegas, in Málaga, while Boabdil, with his vizier Yusuf ben Kumasha (Aben Comixa) and the help of the clan of the Abencerrajes, expelled his father bloodily, and set himself up in Granada. After his defeat at Loja, and with the element of surprise, which had benefited the marquis of Cádiz at Alhama, no longer feasible, Ferdinand reverted to the traditional tactic of the *tala*, the burning of property and crops, including olives and fruit as well as grain, in the Vega of Granada. In Abu'l-Hasan's enclave, in the west of the territory, both sides attempted border raids and the capture of towns, with mixed success. Abu'l-Hasan captured Cañete with ease, but suffered defeat and heavy losses at Teba and Ardales, while Ponce de León failed at Setenil but gained a fortress in the Sierra de las Salinas. Ferdinand did, however, succeed in supplying Alhama once again, despite attacks en route by Moorish light cavalry (*jinetes*).

In 1483, the Castilian strategy, which had been planned in Córdoba during the previous autumn, seems to have been to capitalize on the success at Alhama by attempting to split the Nasrid kingdom into two halves, by attacking the Ajarquía, to the north and east of Málaga. Although the territory was already divided by the conflict between Abu'l-Hasan and his son, the former succeeded in demonstrating his power by attacking and looting the poorly-defended town of Cañete. Nevertheless, it is doubtful whether much could have been achieved by risking Christian forces in this difficult terrain, and the result was indeed disastrous for the attackers. First of all, Cañete was recaptured and refortified by its lord, the *adelantado* of Andalusia, with forces from other parts of the region, but Abu'l-Hasan attacked the castle of Turón, before making Guadix his base, as part of his conflict with his son. The plan agreed by the Andalusian magnates was to approach Málaga first through narrow rocky defiles and then by an easier passage along the coast. The first setback, however, occurred when troops from Seville failed to recapture Zahara, then joining the main army as it headed for the Ajarquía. At this point, disagreements broke out among the commanders as to the object of the expedition. While the marquis of Cádiz urged a direct attack on Málaga itself, many troops chose to attack the nearby Muslim strongholds, in search of booty. The local inhabitants took advantage of the Castilians' distraction to move into positions overlooking the invading army, while disagreement continued among the Christian commanders. In the event, the gloomy predictions of one of the factions in the preliminary council of war in Antequera were fully vindicated, when the apparently impressive Castilian army was ambushed in rocky terrain and its retreat blocked by rocks and missiles descending from a great height. Seeing that defeat was certain and a massacre probable, the highly experienced marquis of Cádiz accepted the advice of those who urged that he was indispensable to the Castilian war effort, and escaped by obscure paths, with the help of native guides and under cover of darkness. According to Palencia, when his departure was discovered by the rest of the army on the following day, 21 March, alarm and despondency did indeed break out. The retreat, through narrow defiles, was bloody, and a great deal of Christian booty was seized by the Muslim attackers. Many Christians were killed and more than a thousand captured according to Pulgar, two thousand according to the *Nubahat*. The leaders, including the master of Santiago, Alonso de Cárdenas, the *adelantado* of Andalusia, Pedro Enríquez de Ribera, and Don Alonso de Aguilar, retired to Antequera to join the marquis of Cádiz and to lick their wounds. The count of Cifuentes was taken captive, and handed over the Abu'l-Hasan in Málaga. The king and queen, who heard news of the disaster in far-off Galicia, decided to mount a new expedition at once and, as some compensation, Ferdinand did succeed in supplying Alhama, as well as carrying out another *tala* in Muslim territory.[2]

Apparently in order to take advantage of the Christian defeat in the Ajarquía, Boabdil, who was at this time in control of Granada, Guadix, Baza and other places, launched an attack on Lucena a month later. Thanks to the quality of his scouts, the *alcaide de los donceles*, Diego Fernández de Córdoba, who was lord of Lucena, was well prepared for the arrival of the Muslim army, on 20 April. Diego sent letters to the neighbouring lords and governors asking for help, and particularly from his namesake, the count of Cabra, who was in nearby Baena, and arrived the next day with 200 lancers and about 300 infantry. Having had time to prepare his defences and protect the more vulnerable among Lucena's population, the *alcaide de los donceles*, with the support and advice of the count of Cabra, was able to put up effective resistance. Not only did the Cordoban magnates save the town but they pursued the Granadans, who attempted to return home with booty across the Sierra de Rute towards Loja. While doing so, the Christians were themselves attacked at a stream which is named Garci González by Palencia, and Martín González by Bernáldez. Both Castilian and Granadan sources refer to the death or capture of large numbers, in conditions of confusion which mirrored the experience of the Christian forces in the Ajarquía de Málaga, and the Muslim prisoners included Boabdil himself, who was in disguise and not at first recognized. The self-proclaimed emir was first taken back to Lucena and then imprisoned in Porcuna, while the royal council decided what to do with him. According to Pulgar's account, the debate concerned whether to keep Boabdil in prison, and carry on with the conquest of the Granadan state, or whether to accept the captive emir's suggestion, and release him with military assistance to continue his war against his father. The advantage of the latter course was that divisions within the kingdom would continue, while tribute and the release of Christian captives might be achieved. After Ferdinand had referred the matter to his wife, the release of Boabdil was decided on. In the meantime, Abu'l-Hasan and his supporters had made some progress in re-establishing themselves in Granada, but his success was shortlived, as he fell ill with what the *Nubahat* described as a malady similar to epilepsy, and was deposed in favour of his brother, Muhammad XIII al-Zagal. While Boabdil was still in prison, Ferdinand launched a large expedition into Granadan territory, consisting of an estimated 10,000 light cavalry, 20,000 infantry, and no fewer than 30,000 extra men whose sole task was to destroy crops. There was also a support column for Alhama with 80,000 pack animals. Ferdinand's first attack was on Illora, where the local population was threshing grain as close to the walls as possible, for fear of the Castilian *tala*. When his troops were attacked from the battlements, the Castilian king drew up light cannon (*ribadoquines*) and cleared them with three-pound projectiles. He was not, however, in a position of sufficient strength to attempt the capture of the town. After a further major skirmish at Tájara, which was a source of supplies for Loja, and where the Muslims had a cannon of their own available, the reinforcement of Alhama was attempted. The journey there was difficult, and many horses died of thirst, but thousands of animals succeeded in bringing in supplies, and the garrison was increased by 1000, and placed under the command of Iñigo López de Mendoza, count of Tendilla. The king then continued to Alhendí, only 10 kilometres from Granada itself, and, in negotiations with Abu'l-Hassan's faction and with Boabdil's mother, Soraya, the latter offered a tribute of 12,000 *doblas zaenas* (about 14,000 ducats), the release of sixty prisoners a year for five years, and ten noble youths, including Boabdil's son Ahmad, as hostages. There was apparently an outcry in Granada, when the terms became known, and a surviving *fatwa*, signed by most of the Islamic religious leaders, declared that Boabdil was in rebellion against God and the Prophet. In the face of this hostility in the capital, the rebel son seems to have taken refuge in Guadix, by now almost certainly as a vassal of the Castilian crown. The Christian captives who were exchanged for Boabdil reached Córdoba on 31 August, and three days later, the self-proclaimed emir was formally sent on his way by Ferdinand. The legal ruler, Boabdil's father, Abu'l-Hasan, was not finished, however, and flexed his muscles by carrying out a *tala* of the lands around Teba and Antequera, with a large force of light cavalry and infantry, causing considerable damage to property. On 16 October, Abu'l-Hasan mounted another expedition in the direction of Utrera. The local magnates, including the marquis of Cádiz, and Luis Portocarrero, *corregidor* of Ecija, chased the Muslims away. The marquis meanwhile had it in mind to recapture Zahara, as the town was beginning to suffer grain shortages, and succeeded in his aim without the need for support from his noble Andalusian neighbours, who seem to have resented their exclusion.[3]

In the absence of Ferdinand in Aragon, primarily on Inquisition business in the Crown of Aragon, the first activity of the new season in Granada took place under the supervision of Isabella, who reached Córdoba at the beginning of May. The campaigning of 1484 may be divided into three episodes. First, the marquis of Cádiz and the master of Santiago, Alonso de Cárdenas, commanded an expedition of mostly Andalusian troops, with the aim of cutting the Granadan state in half. When their army reached La Churriana, to the west of Málaga, the plan was that it should receive supplies by sea, from Cádiz and Seville, but no attempt was made to capture any fortified places, as the primary purpose was to damage crops and property and put pressure on the inhabitants. When Ferdinand returned from Tarazona at the end of May, a council of war was held in Córdoba, to decide whether this policy of *tala* should be continued that summer, or whether a town should be besieged. The king somewhat implausibly maintained that the strategies could be combined, but, in any case, it was decided to follow the advice of the marquis of Cádiz, that Alora should be attacked, as the second phase of campaigning, in the last two weeks of June. To begin with, it was not obvious to the Granadans that the expedition had any other aim than to provide relief and provisions to Alhama, as a force of infantry cleared a way through the mountains to Antequera for the artillery. Thereafter, while the main target was in fact Alora, a *tala* was organized to divert the attention of Abu'l-Hasan. This dual strategy of destruction of crops and property, and siege warfare, was continued for the rest of the year, with the nobles and their retinues primarily responsible for the destruction of property, while the royal armies, consisting largely of infantry and artillery, undertook the sieges. Alora duly surrendered to Ferdinand, much to the fury of the Muslim defenders of Málaga, who refused to allow many of the refugees into their city. Towns near Alora, and particularly Coín and Casarabonela, sued for peace, but in reality gained Granadan reinforcements, under cover of the negotiations. During this time, on 21 June 1484, the young count of Belalcázar, Gutierre III de Sotomayor, was killed by a poisoned arrow in a skirmish near Casarabonela. After the count's death, and the evidence of Muslim double-dealing, Ferdinand pursued the *tala* near Granada with renewed vigour, and, having provisioned Alhama and left a garrison there, he attempted to provoke Abu'l-Hasan to battle by pitching camp outside the city, with a large force. The old emir did not respond, however, mainly because he feared attack from the supporters of his son Boabdil, and when the king realized this, he cut his losses and withdrew his forces to Córdoba, fifty days after he had originally left for Alora.

In the final campaign of the year, at the beginning of September, Ferdinand set out, once again on the advice of the marquis of Cádiz, with a considerable army, as well as artillery and siege machines, with the aim of besieging Setenil. The inhabitants unwisely trusted in the strength of their walls, and neglected to resist the placing of the Castilian guns, which eventually brought about the town's surrender. In addition to the royal forces, troops from Seville, Jerez and Carmona were assembled, under the command of the marquis of Cádiz and of the *adelantado* Pedro Enríquez, with the aim of preventing Muslim reinforcements arriving from the surrounding area. After some dissension in the camp, the king yet again accepted the advice of the marquis of Cádiz, and pursued the siege with determination. Setenil was a strategically important outpost for Ronda, and acted as a store of provisions for the inhabitants of the surrounding mountain areas, so that its surrender dealt a severe blow to the larger town. The king and queen spent the winter of 1484–5 in Seville, attempting to secure the succession to its archbishopric, and planning the following year's campaigns against the Nasrids. Meanwhile, Granadan politics were not developing to the Castilians' liking. Although Abu'l-Hasan, who lived on until 1495, had effectively been removed from the scene, his brother Muhammad al-Zagal, together with the Muslim religious leadership, succeeded in neutralising Boabdil, and in early 1485 drove him out of Almería. Up to this point, Castilians indeed had little to show for their massive expenditure of men and material, and the king was increasingly subject to criticism in some court circles. In the meantime, troops from Alhama, Setenil and Zahara inflicted losses in skirmishes with Muslim forces.

The new season, which was to prove crucial to the outcome of the war, started with an attack by the count of Cabra on the neighbourhood of Granada itself, which ended with defeat and significant losses. Also in January, Ferdinand issued a general summons to knights and their retinues to assemble in Córdoba. At this stage, the destination of the expedition, which left Seville on 20 January, was generally unknown, but when the combined municipal and seigneurial troops reached Antequera, they were ordered to attack Loja, though poor weather, and the difficulty of the enterprise, soon convinced Ferdinand of the need to withdraw. A further setback for the Castilian cause was the defection of the port of Almería from Boabdil to his father, but this was counterbalanced by the demoralization in Ronda which had resulted from the Christian capture of Setenil. In the second half of April, Ferdinand launched a further attack on towns and villages in the Málaga area, which resulted in the capture, after a siege, of Coín and Cártama, though with the loss of some of his best troops. Even so, although he was not yet ready to attack either Málaga or Granada directly, Ferdinand had now finally succeeded in splitting the emirate in half, and was able to turn his attention to Ronda. On 8 May, the marquis of Cádiz began a siege of the city, and its apparently formidable North African garrison, and, after artillery bombardments and the cutting of the water supply, its surrender took place in a mere fortnight. The effect was demoralizing, and after the fall of Ronda, numerous strong points in the surrounding region, the Serranía, sued for terms as well. Most of the population of Ronda was forced to leave, with what it could carry, but the Muslim *alguacil mayor*, Harvey thinks Ibrahim al-Hakim, was allowed to leave, and offered accommodation in either Seville or Alcalá de Guadaira. Other Muslim leaders were allowed to depart for North Africa, under a royal policy which appeared to be aimed at removing the traditional elite and subjecting the rest of the population to Castilian rule as Mudejar serfs (*siervos mudéjares*). The *alfaquís* and elders swore an oath on 'the unity of God, who knows what is public and what is secret, the living Creator, who gave the law to Muhammad his prophet', that they would be loyal vassals of the king and queen, doing military service and paying the same taxes and tributes as they had paid to their Muslim rulers. In return, Ferdinand agreed to allow disputes between Muslims to be settled by their own judges, according to Islamic law, the *sharia* and the *sunna*. The capture of Ronda was the first truly major Castilian victory of the war, and after the town had been secured, the royal army headed south-east to Marbella, and then along the coast towards the greater prize of Málaga. This display of military might, which was undertaken despite the difficulty of negotiating poor roads with heavy equipment, led to the rapid surrender of Marbella, on terms similar to those of Ronda, without any need for the deployment of the royal artillery. Despite this success, the Castilians had suffered serious losses on the way to the coast, particularly in the area of Mijas, so that Ferdinand decided he was not, at this stage, in a position to launch an attack on Málaga itself, and returned to Córdoba to plan a future campaign. In the meantime, in September 1485, an inconclusive night skirmish took place at Moclín, 25 kilometres north-west of Granada, ending with the count of Cabra running for his life, and Al-Zagal in hot pursuit. Nevertheless, the border fortresses at Cambil, Montejicar and Iznalloz were captured by Ferdinand, who spent the autumn in political rather than military manoeuvres. Boabdil was released again, and sent via Murcia to Huéscar, 40 kilometres north-east of Baza. According to the *Nubdat al-asr*, he offered immunity from Christian attack in return for support and, by the new year, he was back in Granada, on the Albaicín, where he started a military rebellion, in which his supporters were pounded by heavy weapons in the rest of the city.[4]

Ferdinand's main target in 1486 was Loja, which surrendered on 29 May, after an artillery bombardment. Among those captured was Boabdil, who had made peace with Al-Zagal, and was apparently patriotically defending his kingdom, though some supposed that he was still plotting with the Castilians. Once Loja had been taken, the Castilians were able to advance further towards Granada itself, from the west, by 20 June capturing Montfrío, Illora, Colomera and Moclín. On 11 June, Isabella paid her first visit to the front line, at Illora. Ferdinand spent some time in Galicia, during the summer, while the final assault on Málaga was planned in the rear base at Córdoba. In the meantime, a

naval blockade of the coast was undertaken, and some coastal inhabitants were driven inland. Raids also took place on the North African
coast. Internal conflict continued on the Muslim side, as Boabdil and
Al-Zagal reverted to their earlier disagreement.

In the new year, it was decided that the attack on Málaga should be
mounted from the east, in the Ajarquía, beginning with an assault on
Vélez-Málaga. A column set out from Córdoba on 8 April 1487,
arrived eight days later at Vélez, and at once began siege preparations.
Al-Zagal assembled as many troops as he could, and reached the town
on mountain tracks before the Castilian artillery had got through.
Having lit bonfires to summon the sparse inhabitants of the surrounding area to his support, he attempted to destroy Ferdinand's guns before
they could be brought into action. There was a night skirmish, apparently lit by the bonfires, but by the time that it ended inconclusively, Al-
Zagal had withdrawn, probably because he had heard of Boabdil's
victory at his expense in Granada, which almost certainly was indeed
plotted with the Castilian monarchs. In any case, Vélez surrendered on
27 April. Probably because they were anxious to move on to their main
target, Málaga, the victors unusually agreed to allow the defeated
inhabitants of Vélez to take their weapons with them, as well as their
goods and chattels. The rest of the Ajarquía surrendered at the same
time, and effectively acquired Mudéjar status. Once Vélez fell, a large
number of towns and villages in the surrounding area also surrendered.
After Al-Zagal had suddenly abandoned Vélez, and effectively withdrawn from the field, the Castilians had some hope that Málaga
would surrender without a fight, but the city's governor, Hemete Zeli,
who had been reinforced by Berbers, and also, according to Palencia, by
Muslim criminals from the Serranía de Ronda, as well as *conversos* who
had fled from the Andalusian Inquisition, refused to negotiate.[5] In these
circumstances, with both sides fully aware of the crucial importance of
the city, there were two possible strategies, either to mount a long-term
land and sea blockade, or to undertake a close siege and direct assault
on the city. The objection to a blockade was that it would be virtually
impossible to prevent small craft bringing in supplies from North
Africa, especially at night, and, in view of this, Ferdinand decided on
a direct assault. This was not only the most important operation of the
war so far, in terms of strategy, but also the most difficult. The city was
dominated by the linked castles of the Alcazaba, on the lower level, and
Gibralfaro on the higher. Gibralfaro was protected on the landward side
by steep slopes and, as the city was built on a narrow strip of land
between the mountains and the Mediterranean, these fortifications were
able to block east–west communication. There was a day of hand-to-
hand conflict on the slopes below Gibralfaro, in which many on both

sides lost their lives, the Muslims having demolished all buildings on the lower level to obtain clear sightlines. The Christians eventually drove the defenders back into the castle, and set about constructing, with remarkable speed, earthworks and a timber fortress to face the ramparts. It had room not only for artillery but for 2500 cavalry and 14,000 infantry, under the command of the marquis of Cádiz. This extraordinary building was surrounded by palisades and smaller constructions known as *estanças* (from the Italian *stanza*), which blockaded the city on all sides and were themselves protected by trenches. A static artillery battle then began, for which both sides had considerable resources, but the Christians soon acquired extra guns, both from the ships of the blockading fleet and from as far afield as Flanders. Stone cannon balls were brought from Algeciras. Nonetheless, the siege soon hit problems, with plague breaking out nearby, and some troops deserting to the Muslim side with lurid tales of the royal armies' discomfiture. Even the queen herself urged a withdrawal, and in order to convince her, as well as his Muslim opponents, who had every reason to hope for success, that his policy was correct, Ferdinand persuaded her to leave Córdoba, in June 1487, and join the troops in the field. A propaganda coup was urgently needed, as the harbour was still in Muslim hands, the defenders were bravely resisting the Castilian artillery barrage, and vast quantities of ammunition were being used up. In these somewhat worrying circumstances, some urged a rapid final assault on the city, before winter came, but instead a programme of tunnelling and sapping was undertaken under the walls. This was successfully countered by the defenders, however, and it was thus a great relief to Ferdinand when he heard that Boabdil had defeated a 'suicide' relief column, led by Al-Zagal, which had been heading in the direction of Málaga.

At this point, a man from Jerba in Tunisia, called Ibrahim al-Jarbi ('Abraen' to Pulgar), who had been living in a village near Guadix, assembled about four hundred Berbers and native Granadans, and set out across country with the aim of killing Ferdinand and Isabella. The contingent launched a dawn attack on one of the *estanças*, on the coast to the east of Málaga, and although half of them were killed, the other half were not, and succeeded in getting inside the perimeter works. While all this was going on, Ibrahim himself kept out of the fray, with the aim, not only of staying alive, but of getting himself taken prisoner. His prayerful attitude seems to have prevented his being killed by the soldiers who first spotted him, in a hollow near the lines, and he was taken to the marquis of Cádiz. Ponce de León seems not have been impressed at first with the apparently charismatic Muslim's claim that he had received a special revelation which he could only disclose to the king and queen, but nonetheless felt obliged to refer the matter to his sovereigns. They summoned Ibrahim, who was duly escorted into their presence, still dressed as he was when captured, in a burnous with a dagger in his belt. A large crowd assembled when he entered the royal tent, but Ferdinand was apparently sleeping off a large meal, and the queen did not wish him to be woken. Ibrahim was sent to another tent to wait, in the company of the marchioness of Moya and Felipa, duchess of Bragança. The Muslim apparently spoke no Castilian, and did not understand what was going on. Thinking that Felipa and her husband, Alvaro de Portugal, were the monarchs, presumably because of their ornate dress, he stabbed the duke in the head, nearly killing him, and lunged at the duchess. At this point, a royal treasury official, Ruy López de Toledo, rushed in and wrestled Ibrahim to the ground. Others then came into the tent, and the Muslim was quickly despatched. The pieces of his body were catapulted over the city wall, where the Malagans reverenced him as a martyr by sewing the corpse together with silken thread, washing and perfuming it, and gave it an emotional funeral. They then selected a Christian prisoner, whom they regarded as being of equivalent status, killed him, mounted his body on an ass, and sent him out of the city in the direction of the Castilian lines.[6]

As the siege went on, conditions inside Málaga steadily worsened, and a 'peace party' emerged, but the North African garrison in the Alcazaba remained determined to fight on. Eventually, two of the leading citizens, 'Ali Durdush and Amar Benamar, came out to the Christian headquarters and asked to become Mudéjar subjects of Ferdinand and Isabella, but they were told that the time to sue for terms had passed, and that their only choices were death or captivity. The response of the people of Málaga was to threaten to hang all their Christian prisoners from the battlements and burn the city, but they were informed by the Castilian rulers that, if they harmed a single prisoner, every citizen without exception would be killed. Eventually, the king and queen softened to the extent that safe-conducts were offered to those, like 'Ali Durdush, who were known genuinely to have sued for peace. After this, the Castilian forces entered the town, though the stench of the dead deterred the monarchs themselves from following until 18 August. The Muslim population, with the exception of 'Ali Durdush, were literally driven from their houses and corraled, until they could be allocated to their new captors. One-third were kept to be exchanged for Christian captives in North Africa, another third were given to those who had fought in the siege, and the rest went to the Crown to help defray the costs of the expedition. Male and female captives were also sent as gifts to various dignitaries, such as the pope, and the queens of Naples and Portugal. At the same time, complicated negotiations took place to ransom the Jewish community which had been trapped in Málaga during the siege. Boabdil's role in these events was ambiguous to say the least, and it appears that, in return for his assistance, the king and queen were prepared to cede to him, at least temporarily, a crescent-shaped area in the north and east of the Nasrid kingdom, including Guadix, Vélez Rubio, Vélez Blanco and Baza, as well as a strip southwards to the coast at Mojácar. Boabdil seems to have been a secret ally of the Castilians into 1488, though he was more loyal to the Muslim cause in the last years of Granada's independence. This change of attitude may be due, at least in part, to the fact that, after the Christian victory at Málaga, towns and villages in the area which had supposedly been assigned to him were among those which surrendered to the Castilian rulers without a fight. They included Vera, Cuevas, Huércal, Cabrera, Sorbas, Belefique, Níjar, Júrcar, Vélez Rubio and Vélez Blanco, Cantoria, Alboj and Galera.

As 1488 began, the conflict between El Zagal and Boabdil continued unabated, with the latter holding Granada and Almuñécar, not without difficulty, while his elder brother continued to control Almería, the Alpujarras, Guadix and Baza. The attempts of the royal captain-general, Fadrique de Toledo, son of the duke of Alba, to gain the allegiance of Baza simply led to a further loss of men and provisions, and the reaffirmation of El Zagal's control over the town. At this time, Juan de Benavides led a raid on Almería, while Ferdinand mounted a royal expedition later in the year, though events elsewhere in the Peninsula, as well as abroad, prevented the achievement of any significant result. By the following year, 1489, the Muslims only retained control over Granada itself, Guadix, Baza and Almería, and all except the capital were firmly held by Al-Zagal's supporters. Given that Almería was distant and well-protected, and Granada was clearly being left until last, the choice of target for the 1489 campaigning season was between Guadix and Baza, and the latter may well have been chosen because of recent Christian successes in the area around Vera. Baza, which was at the time under the command of Sidi Yahya al-Najjar and others, refused to surrender, and Ferdinand's artillery had to be deployed. The royal army first attempted to pitch camp in the irrigated *huerta*, but the ground, not surprisingly, proved to be much too soft, and the siege was soon restarted from a new site. No real progress was made between June and November, and the town's inhabitants began to hope that the Castilians would withdraw when winter came. The besiegers responded by building about a thousand mud-brick houses, though some fell down, killing their occupants. Meanwhile, the long and difficult supply routes, on which the royal army totally depended, became increasingly impassable as rain combined with the depredations of the vast trains of pack-animals. Once again, the queen and her ladies were brought in to raise the troops' morale, arriving on 5 November, and the conspicuous courtly display had a quick effect on the Muslim defenders. Within days, negotiations had begun between Sidi Yahya and Gutierre de Cárdenas, the *comendador mayor* of León. Both Arabic and Castilian sources indicate that the result, which was reached by the end of the month, was entirely to the advantage of the Muslim leaders, and in particular opened the way for Yahya to metamorphose into Don Pedro de Granada Venegas, while the ordinary people, who had valiantly defended the town, were left to their fate, the final surrender taking place on 4 December. Having arranged a generous settlement for his family, Yahya, whose conversion was still secret, went to see Al-Zagal in Guadix. No doubt impressed by the generosity with which the former commander of Baza had been treated, the self-proclaimed ruler of Granada had surrendered Almería by 22 December, and eight days later had given up Guadix as well, in return for the grant of a semi-independent statelet, including Andarax, Orgivas, Lanjarón, and other places in the Alpujarras, from which Christians were supposedly to be excluded. Al-Zagal was allowed to keep his weapons, and also received a payment of 20,000 *castellanos*, but, having become Ferdinand's vassal, he never occupied his mini-principality, and probably never intended to, but instead left for North Africa, quite probably, as some contemporary sources maintained, in an attempt to embarrass and shame Boabdil. Whatever the true motives of the Nasrids, Ferdinand must have thought that, with Guadix and Almería already in his hands without a fight, Granada would soon fall in a similar manner, but faction fighting in the city perversely helped to prolong its resistance.

Early in 1490, Boabdil sent his vizier, Al-Mulih, to negotiate with Ferdinand, who sent back with him to Granada two of his own men, with the task of preparing the political situation in the city for its final conquest. One was Martin de Alarcón, who had supervised Boabdil's imprisonment in Porcuna, in 1483, while the other was Gonzalo Fernández de Córdoba, who had been inside Granada already, in 1486, to support Boabdil against Al-Zagal. On this occasion, however, the negotiators failed, and Boabdil bit the hand that had fed him by counter-attacking. He appears to have been engaged in the forlorn pursuit of a supply route from the Mediterranean coast to his capital, attacking Padul and Adra successfully, and Salobreña in vain, in September 1490. The Castilians meanwhile engaged in a *tala* in the Vega of Granada, now directed against Boabdil and his men. After the virtual stalemate of 1490, the new year brought a much publicised 'final' assault on the city of Granada. The *tala* continued, and after the tented camp burnt down, a much more permanent settlement was built, with the name Santa Fe, using materials taken from demolished villages.

Isabella and her ladies appeared once again, and there were many famous deeds of valour on the part of the Castilians, but by August the commanders knew that the surrender of the Muslim capital was inevitable. Only Alfacar, among the neighbouring Muslim settlements, put up long and fierce resistance, which is stressed in the Arabic sources, but not in the Christian ones, because as long as the village remained uncaptured it was possible to bring supplies from the coast into Granada over broken ground. According to the *Nubdha*, as food became increasingly short, during the winter of 1490–1, the elders of the city went to Boabdil, and pointed out to him that their Muslim brethren in the Maghreb had not done anything to help them, and that the relative strength of the Christians was increasing all the time. They urged immediate negotiation, while Ferdinand and Isabella's armies were largely dispersed for the winter, on the grounds that no better terms would be on offer in the future. It appears that the Nasrid leaders, on the other hand, were afraid that, if surrender was contemplated, many of the common people would try to overthrow them and continue the fight. The resulting 'capitulations' of 1491 contain an incongruous mixture of petty and unrealistic points and the offer of genuine surrender which was Ferdinand's only aim in the entire campaign. Harvey argues convincingly that the weakness of these capitulations derived from the fact that they concealed the real agreement for the surrender of Granada, which had been made secretly between Boabdil and Ferdinand. The failure, after the eventual fall of the city in 1492, to implement the treaty which had been made in public was thus made more or less inevitable by Boabdil's flight to North Africa. Yet it could not be made to appear, to onlookers in both Spain and the rest of Europe, that the city had fallen because of treason and treachery within, rather than the bravery of the Christian attackers.

In view of the eventual victory of the Christian wars against the Nasrid kingdom of Granada, and the subsequent myth of national unity, supposedly achieved under Ferdinand and Isabella, it might be imagined that a homogeneous military force achieved this victory. Nothing could be further from the truth. The armies which took part in this series of campaigns inevitably reflected the political and social reality of the diverse regions of the crown of Castile. In theory, the Granada war was a 'feudal' conflict, in which the rulers summoned their vassals to help them regain control of lost territory, and these vassals, most of whom constituted the upper nobility, in turn summoned their own retinues to aid the royal cause. While the bases on which troops were recruited to serve in Granada were in fact much more diverse than this schema would suggest, it is nonetheless true that the vast bulk of the armies which fought in the campaigns fell into one of two broad categories, that is, royal or seigneurial troops. Nevertheless, the forces raised by the *concejos* of the larger towns, although in theory directly subject to the Crown, in practice originated locally rather than centrally.

The varied contingents which made up the forces of the Crown at least had in common the fact that the king and queen could summon them directly, without the need to refer either to the Cortes or to their leading noble vassals. First, the Castilian monarchs maintained, from their ordinary revenues, a regular, salaried contingent of men-at-arms (*hombres de armas*) and light cavalry (*jinetes*), known as *guardas reales*. It was during the civil conflict of the reign of Henry IV and the early years of Isabella and Ferdinand that these forces were reorganized and became fully professional, receiving regular salaries from the royal treasury. The royal guards were not a large force, numbering fewer than 900 during the Granada war, though more were recruited thereafter. During the campaigns of the 1480s, they fought alongside other contingents, and were organized into *capitanías*, with each captain commanding a squad of lancers, which commonly numbered between 100 and 200, either mounted or on foot. The military resources of the Holy Brotherhood (*Santa Hermandad*), which had been refounded on a national scale in 1476, were quickly diverted into the war effort against Granada, so that *capitanías de la Hermandad* were formed. Far from being humble local militias, as in earlier years, these contingents, which came from throughout the crown of Castile, were frequently commanded by courtiers, even including dignitaries such as the count of Tendilla and the marquis of Villena. They were organized in the same way as the *guardas reales*, and acted as garrisons in conquered territory until the Hermandad was wound up in 1498. Surviving accounts indicate that approximately 1500 lances and fifty *espingarderos* (hand-gunners) were contributed to the Castilian forces in Granada by this organization.[7]

In addition, Isabella, like her predecessors as 'feudal' monarchs, possessed her own personally-attached 'royal vassals' (*vasallos de la reina*), who received benefices (*acostamientos*) of lands, or more commonly cash, in return for direct service to the Crown. The Castilian *vasallos del rey* were survivals of earlier institutions, and were apparently seen by monarchs as a reliable source of additional troops, to be supplied by those who had a personal tie to their sovereign. Ferdinand and Isabella did not reform the royal vassals' conditions of service, which had been laid down by their predecessors since the reign of Alfonso XI in the fourteenth century, and continued to pay a daily wage (30 *maravedíes* for *jinetes* and 35 *maravedies* for *hombres de armas*) to those who responded to their summons. Ladero estimates that the *vasallos del rey* contributed over 1000 troops to the Granada campaign, and a total of 1067 is recorded in 1489. Documents from the period of the war indicate that the procedure for becoming a *vasallo del rey* was to be recommended for one's military skills, and many of those appointed appear to have been formerly squires (*escuderos*) in the royal guard. Lists from 1489–90 also show that they included leading magnates, such as the count of Cifuentes, lesser nobles such as Egas Venegas, lord of Luque (Córdoba), and prelates, including the bishops of Plasencia and Cuenca. There were also payments (*libranzas*) in the *acostamiento* system, for light cavalry and infantry from towns throughout the domains of Isabella and Ferdinand, from Andalusia in the south to Galicia and the Basque country in the north.[8]

Contemporary chronicles and documentary sources both indicate the extensive role played in the war against the Nasrid kingdom by contingents of troops led by members of the nobility, as well as the military orders. This method of raising armies, together with the 'chivalric' desire for honour and fame which it represented, reflected the practice of earlier centuries, in Spain and elsewhere. These traditional values were perhaps best represented by Don Rodrigo Ponce de León, marquis, and later duke, of Cádiz. Throughout the war, there is evidence of rivalry, in conspicuous display as well as military valour, between the various seigneurial retinues and levies. Sometimes, as in the case of the public reconciliation between the marquis of Cádiz and the duke of Medina Sidonia, which took place before Alhama, such conflicts were temporarily suppressed, but the monarchs had to pay constant attention to disputes over precedence, and often over strategy, which threatened the unity of the war effort. Among the nobility, a group of courtiers may be identified, including Gutierre de Cárdenas, *comendador mayor* of León, Enrique Enríquez, the king's *mayordomo*, the count of Tendilla and the marquis of Villena. The Castilian upper nobility, as a whole, responded to particular royal demands for troops, but did not attach itself permanently to the war effort, unless one of its number was given a specific role, such as Fadrique de Toledo as captain-general. Much more active in the various campaigns were the leading members of the Andalusian nobility, whose personal interests were evidently directly involved, such as the duke of Medina Sidonia, the marquis of Cádiz, the *adelantado* of Andalusia, Don Alonso de Aguilar, the count of Cabra and the *alcaide de los donceles*. The balance between cavalry and infantry in the contingents led by nobles showed a greater preponderance in favour of mounted troops than did the royal or municipal forces. This no doubt corresponded to the 'chivalric' ethic of that particular social group. The men-at-arms (*hombres de armas*), and the light cavalry who rode in the Moorish style with short stirrups (*jinetes*), were generally personal vassals or members of the household of the lord in question, including those who garrisoned his castles and fortresses. The infantry (*peones*), on the other hand, were either paid for their specific period of service or else levied in a 'feudal' manner from the towns and villages of his lordship (*señorío*). The costs of the seigneurial it forces were shared, by individual agreement, between the lord in question and the Crown. In addition, from 1485 onwards, the lesser nobility, those designated as *hidalgos*, began to contribute directly to the campaigns, being summoned personally to serve with their full weaponry.

The militias of the Castilian towns, like those of the other Christian kingdoms in the Peninsula, had a long history of helping to secure territory which had been conquered from the Muslims. The obligation of military service traditionally fell on all full citizens (*vecinos*), who resided permanently and paid direct taxes (*pechos*) in the town in question. These municipal forces might be either cavalry or infantry. All *caballeros* were required to respond to the call of their council (*concejo*) with their horse and weapons, and periodical parades (*alardes*), supposedly to demonstrate their readiness, were organized for these knights, who were known variously as *caballeros de premia, de cuantía*, or *de alarde*. In general terms, the direct summons of municipal forces, under the auspices of the councils of the royal towns, took place with regularity in Andalusia, and to a lesser extent in Extremadura, Murcia and New Castile. The local authorities were responsible for administering the Crown's global demands, and the result was generally a predominance of infantry forces over cavalry. This was particularly so in the case of the militias of the northern towns, including those of Galicia, Asturias and Vizcaya.[9]

In addition to the noble-led *capitanías*, which have already been referred to, from 1476 onwards, the three-yearly juntas of the Castilian Hermandad (there was a separate organization in Galicia) supported other 'law and order' activities. Between 1482 and 1490, the juntas took place more frequently, and effectively replaced the Cortes in the function of voting money to the Crown to supply additional resources for the Granada war. In 1482, for instance, the Junta of Pinto voted sufficient funds for the levy of 16,000 pack-animals and 8000 pioneers (*taladores*) to assist with the provisioning of Alhama in the following spring, while the Juntas of Alcalá de Henares, in November 1483, and Orgaz, in November 1484, voted similar sums. The Junta of Torrelaguna, in December 1485, saw a change of policy, in which the Hermandad began to supply combat troops, rather than auxiliaries and cash for the maintenance of Alhama. The 1485 junta voted money for 5000 infantry, in the following year this was doubled, and 10,000 became the annual figure up to 1490.

Another component of the Christian forces which should not be neglected is that of *homicianos*, that is, convicted criminals who were pardoned in return for military service. As in so many other cases, Ferdinand and Isabella did not innovate, but instead made full use of an existing practice. In March 1484, at the petition of the count of Tendilla, they granted a pardon to all criminals who served in Alhama for at least eight months, though the response, particularly in the Guadalquivir valley, was so great that, until the law was clarified later in the year, individuals seem actually to have regarded the provision as official licence to commit crimes. Thereafter, *homicianos* were to be found in many incidents of the war, and even in the permanent royal camp at Santa Fé, from which the city of Granada was finally captured.[10]

Despite the fact that its king was the overall commander, the territories of the crown of Aragon did not intervene as such in the Granada campaigns. This did not, however, mean that individuals and forces from the neighbouring kingdoms were absent from the conflict. When in Castile, Ferdinand had with him a group of courtiers, such as his *maestresala* (master of the hall), Pedro de Vaca, who did more than help him continue to administer his Aragonese domains. In particular, Catalan naval forces played an active part (see below), and Aragonese mercenaries seem to have fought in the 1482 campaign, though Catalan, Valencian and Aragonese nobles only took part on a significant scale in 1487.

The fact that Ferdinand and Isabella's campaigns against the emirate of Granada were designated as 'crusades' brought troops from outside the Spanish kingdoms to fight in the royal armies. Papal interest in the Spanish frontier against Islam and the *Reconquista* had already been rekindled in the 1430s. Martin V and Eugenius IV made successive grants of crusading indulgences to those who fought, and gave the traditional two-ninths' share of the Spanish Church's tithes (*tercias reales*) to the respective rulers of Castile and Aragon.[11] The Castilian clergy were taxed for the 'crusade' in 1431, further indulgences were granted and clerical subsidies demanded, in 1433, and a crusade was preached four years later. Unusually, a standard rate of payment was established for these indulgences, being lowered from eight ducats under Martin V to five florins by Eugenius IV in 1433, and to three florins by Nicholas V in 1448. The growing income from the sale of crusading bulls incited both the Papacy and the Spanish monarchs to greater enthusiasm and effort. As always, successive popes also had their own personal reasons for supporting military action in Spain.

Eugenius IV seems to have hoped that his financial generosity would prevent Castile from supporting his enemies in the council of Basel, which threatened papal supremacy, while Nicholas V and Calixtus III clearly saw the desirability of opening up a second front against Islam in the West, given the increasing Turkish threat in the eastern Mediterranean. Not only was the Spanish cause a good one in itself, but there was a hope that campaigns against Muslim Granada might shame rulers and subjects elsewhere in Europe into greater crusading fervour. In reality, despite his much embellished reputation for military as well as sexual impotence, Henry IV did mount campaigns against Granada between 1455 and 1458, as well as capturing Archidona and Gibraltar in 1462. Norman Housley compares Isabella and Ferdinand's renewal of the war effort with the very first designated crusade to Jerusalem, in 1096, in that a long-standing Muslim presence seemed suddenly to become so offensive that it had to be eliminated at all costs, at least politically if not, at this stage at least, in religious terms. Pope Sixtus IV issued the first crusading bull for war against Granada in November 1479, only two months after the signing of the treaty of Alcaçovas between Castile and Portugal. When campaigning began in earnest, in 1482, Isabella and Ferdinand asked for more generous terms, and Sixtus responded with a lengthy bull, *Orthodoxae Fidei* ('Of the orthodox Faith'). This opened the opportunity of crusading ordinances to a much wider public by introducing a scale of charges, which would enable even the most humble to participate, on payment of 2 *reales*, 'or as much as the [crusade] treasurers consider appropriate'. Even this rate would be lowered at later stages of the war, and another innovation, which was greatly assisted by the advent of printing, was the issue after 1483 of receipts or *buletas*, which were intended to ensure that even the humblest crusader would receive his indulgence. As well as being a huge Spanish effort, the Granada war also had an international aspect. Sixtus IV's lengthy bull of 10 August 1482 was addressed to 'the universal Christian faithful..., fighters and warriors and other assistance (*pugnatores et bellatores aliaque auxilia*), both from Spain...and from other nations'. The author of the standard history of the crusade bull in Spain, Goñi Gaztambide, has pointed out that it is hard to document precisely the contribution of foreign troops to the Granada campaigns. Contemporary sources suggest an individual rather than a mass response to the Spanish crusading bull, but troops certainly arrived to fight from various countries, including Germany, Switzerland, France, England, Ireland and even the most recent enemy of Castile, Portugal. There was, however, a certain routine aspect to calls to crusade in the fifteenth century and, after 1453, the fall of Constantinople to the Turks created a new and urgent call on military resources.[12]

Nevertheless, both individuals and contingents of troops from outside the Peninsula did arrive to fight in Isabella and Ferdinand's war, the most notable being Swiss. As early as 1483, the chronicler Fernando del Pulgar reported on the arrival of 'a people who are called the Swiss' (*una gente que se llamava los soyços*), who fought on foot, and showed their determination not to give ground to the enemy by wearing armour and protection only on the front and not the back. To Pulgar, although they were mercenaries, they were nevertheless good Christians, who rejected the contemporary military practice of living off the country by pillage and robbery. Although it seems unlikely that their tactics governed those of their Spanish allies, either during this war or afterwards, it is certain that companies of Swiss, and some German, mercenaries continued to gain employment in the successive Granada campaigns. They were present in 1482, staying in Alhama until two years later, and are to be found in the documents once again in 1491, when some of them received letters of commendation from the king. The personnel seems to have changed over the years. In 1482, a Master Johann was present with thirty hand-gunners (*espingarderos*) and fifteen pikemen (*piqueros*), while a Captain Georg and forty hand-gunners marched out of Alhama in 1484, and in 1491, Gaspar de Frey took part in the fighting with twenty-eight Swiss companions. On the sea, Italians came into their own, with a small number of Genoese captains working directly for the Castilians, even though their republic adopted no such firm stance. In 1484, for example, two Genoese carracks, the *Santa María* and the *Santa Brígida*, owned by Micer Pascual Lomelin and Giuliano Grimaldo, respectively, spent some time as guard vessels in the Straits of Gibraltar. It might appear surprising that the response of foreign troops, and in particular knights and nobles, to the Granada war was in fact so limited, since it was a papal crusade. Two likely reasons for the lack of appeal of Ferdinand and Isabella's campaigns to foreigners are a general European reluctance to respond militarily to the Muslim 'threat', which had led to a series of papal exhortations since the Turkish conquest of Constantinople, and a not unfounded perception that the war had a specifically Castilian, rather than a general Christian, intent. Nevertheless, there was some response to the papal call from north of the Pyrenees. Apart from the Swiss and German mercenary companies, there were also visitors from France and England.[13]

A member of the Woodville clan arrived from England in Lisbon in 1486, with the intention of fighting in the Granada war as a crusader. He is variously referred to by the Spanish chroniclers as 'Earl Rivers' and 'Lord Scales'. There continues to be some confusion in Spanish writing as to which Woodville made the voyage to Spain. Ladero states, citing Pulgar and Palencia, that the knight in question was Anthony, 'barón de Scales', apparently following Paz y Meliá, who notes, despite the fact that Palencia's text refers to 'Edward', that the Englishman was probably his brother Anthony, 'baron Scales, son of Richard Woodville and Jacquetta of Luxemburg'. Although he curiously refers, in his list of documented foreign participants in the Granada campaigns, to 'Woodville; Anthony, "lord" Scales', Benito states in his text, and surely correctly, that it was in fact Anthony's younger brother Edward who arrived in Spain with a company of soldiers. He is however wrong to state that Sir Edward Woodville's sister Elizabeth was married to Henry VII, as she was in fact Edward IV's queen. Edward, who took part in the Loja campaign, came from a family which had inevitably benefited from his sister's marriage, though not as much as its members might have expected. His eldest brother Anthony, who inherited the family title of Earl Rivers, seems to have been seen by some as a more attractive character than others of his relatives, who were regarded by contemporaries as greedy and over-ambitious. Long before his brother Edward, Anthony Woodville had strong connections with the Iberian peninsula. On 21 July 1471, he was appointed by his brother-in-law Edward IV to command a Spanish ship called *La Galante*, to trade with Spain and Portugal. It was not uncommon in the period for English trade with the Peninsula to be carried out in Iberian ships, even if the merchants who sponsored the voyage, in this case Robert Alcock and William Martyn, were English. In the event, Anthony Woodville appears not to have gone on this expedition. On 12 October, he obtained a new licence, which permitted him to go and fight the Saracens with Afonso V of Portugal, but he failed to make use of it because of the requirements of the English royal service. Early in 1472, he and his brother Edward were sent by the Yorkist king to assist Duke Francis II of Brittany in his war against Louis XI of France, Anthony taking with him, at his own expense, 1000 archers, most of whom were killed during the expedition. The new Lord Scales was, like his father, Sir Richard Woodville, an enthusiast for chivalric exercises, gaining thereby a European reputation. Such was Anthony Woodville's reputation at this time that he apparently figures in the Catalan Joan Martorell's novel *Tirant lo blanc*, as the *senyor d'Escala Rompuda*. As well as becoming a character in a highly popular chivalric novel, Anthony was a literary man in his own right. In the prologue of his translation of Tignoville's *Dicts and sayings of the philosophers*, Scales states that, in 1473, he went as a pilgrim to the shrine of St James at Santiago de Compostela. In the second half of the fifteenth century, the practice of combining pilgrimage with trade was growing among English visitors to Spain, and it is likely that Anthony made his voyage in this way. Two years later, he was one of a group of English nobles who went as pilgrims to Rome, and the shrines of southern Italy, including Bari, being robbed of an estimated thousand marks' worth of jewels and plate at the beginning of the return journey from Rome.

His younger brother Edward also played an active political role in the turbulent English politics of the period. He was admiral of Edward IV's navy, but fell out of favour with his successor Richard III, joining Henry Tudor, earl of Richmond, in exile in Brittany and France. It was after the battle of Bosworth field, on 22 August 1485, in which he fought, and Henry's subsequent accession to the throne, that Edward Woodville, who was rewarded with the governorship of the Isle of Wight, decided to go and fight in the Granada war. He appears to have 'borrowed' his brother Anthony's title of Lord Scales in order to cut more of a dash in the Iberian peninsula. According to the chronicler Palencia, Edward Woodville and his men came to Spain with the intention of expiating the sin of internecine conflict in their own country, the so-called 'Wars of the Roses'. Whatever the truth of this, the Englishman's company, which was estimated at approximately 300 archers together with supporters, left an unknown port on the south coast of England at the end of February 1486. The foreign troops which fought on the Christian side in the Granada campaigns have been variously described by Spanish historians as a 'foreign legion' and 'international brigades'. The army which Edward Woodville assembled in the Isle of Wight included not only local men but also troops from Scotland, Ireland, Brittany and Burgundy, as well as other parts of England. The expedition's first destination was Lisbon, where the reception committee was led by Fernando Lourenço, the treasurer and factor of the Casa de la Mina and the Guinea trade, who was no doubt interested in the competitive trading element of the impostor Lord Scales's fleet. Perhaps fearing controversy, King John II himself did not attend the subsequent lavish festivities, and by the beginning of March, the English company had set sail once again for Castilian territory. The chronicler and former governor of Puerto de Santa Maria, Diego de Valera, reported its arrival in a letter to Ferdinand and Isabella, dated the first of that month. According to Valera, some of the English merchants who accompanied Woodville and his men were already known in the port, economics once again sharing the space with crusading fervour. The party then sailed north to the duke of Medina Sidonia's port of Sanlúcar de Barrameda, travelled first to Seville to acquire further military equipment, and thence up the Guadalquivir to Córdoba, where they were received in the manner of royalty by the queen. Isabella, as a relative through the Lancastrian connection with which his family had earlier been allied, made various grants to Woodville, designated him as leader of the foreign knights, and presented him with lavish gifts, including a luxurious camp bed, two tents, four horses and six pack-animals, together with 2000 gold *doblas* in cash. After they had received such a welcome from the queen, Ferdinand naturally continued in that vein in the camp before Loja, where the royal army arrived in May. Woodville's company, which was estimated by contemporaries at between one and three hundred men, was said to have acquitted itself well in the fighting, which ended in the capture of the town on 28–29 May 1486. The Andalusian chronicler Andrés Bernáldez says that when 'Lord Scales' saw how things were going, he announced that he wanted to fight as he would in England, and dismounted. He proceeded to charge directly towards the Muslim defenders, in white armour, wearing a sword and carrying a shield, and accompanied by the rest of the English contingent with similar armour and weaponry. Thus encouraged, the Castilians similarly fell upon their opponents, and succeeded in entering the suburbs of Loja, after which the artillery secured the town's surrender. A number of Edward Woodville's English troops were killed on this day, and his captain, or second-in-command, was wounded. When Edward tried to scale the town's wall, defended only with a shield, he was knocked unconscious by a stone, and lost two or three of his teeth. The English knight now felt that he had achieved his aim and wanted to return to England, though various of his soldiers had died in the campaign, others having been captured by the Muslims and deported to Fez, in North Africa. Edward Woodville himself chose not to accompany the king and queen to La Coruña, but instead travelled to Seville and then Lisbon, where he was fêted by John II. The English crusader arrived back in England at the end of 1486 or the beginning of 1487, where he may have played a role in arranging the marriage of Ferdinand and Isabella's daughter Catherine to Henry VII's son Arthur, prince of Wales. In 1488, he died, repudiated by Henry VII, while fighting for Duke Francis of Brittany against the French crown. There is no other case of foreign participants in the Granada war to compare with the story of the false Lord Scales, but other troops from the British Isles, who are known to have participated in the 1486 and 1487 campaigns are William Marston, who is recorded as a groom of Henry VII's chamber, and Hubert Stanton, who was said to be from Ireland. French nobles were generally absent from the Granada campaigns, in contrast to their ancestors' extensive interventions in Spanish affairs in earlier decades. One Philippe de Shaundé ('Nicandel' in the Spanish sources), who was in the service of King Henry, was said to have contemplated bringing a force from England in addition to the Woodville company, but there is no evidence that it ever arrived.[14]

Until very recently, the notion has prevailed among historians, both military and general, that some kind of 'military revolution' took place in Europe after 1500. According to this thesis, there was little or no innovation in warfare between the fall of the Roman Empire and the Renaissance, when state armies reappeared. Only in the sixteenth century did the new power of massed infantry sweep away the force of 'feudal' knights and artillery gunners assume their subsequent role as 'angels of Death'. The beginning of this development has been variously linked with Charles VIII of France's invasion of Italy in 1494 and with Ferdinand and Isabella's Granada war. Such views owe much to simplistic notions of the Middle Ages as 'dark' and 'feudal', and the study of weaponry and its use indicates that much modern analysis is misconceived. Thus the methods and materials used by the armies which fought for the Spanish Christian monarchs against the Nasrid kingdom of Granada continued a tradition, rather than representing significant innovation. In this respect, as in so many others, Isabella and Ferdinand were conservative.

One of the most common units in the Castilian forces during the war was the 'lance'. Apart from the sword, the lance itself was the main offensive weapon of the medieval cavalry in western Europe. Until the beginning of the fourteenth century, a lance was normally just a pole, often of ash and about 3–4 metres long. By the early fifteenth century, as a result of improvements in body armour, the lance was normally placed on a special rest attached to the breastplate (known in French as the *arrêt de cuirasse*). Earlier technological developments, including the stirrup and the high-backed saddle, were intended to establish the knight firmly in his seat, so that he could deliver his lance-blow with the combined momentum of horse and rider. The purpose of these developments and tactics was to break up enemy formations, and allow lighter cavalry and infantry to engage more closely. The forces assembled for the Granada campaigns used all these categories of troops. The heavy lance nevertheless had its limitations, since it often broke on impact and needed to be replaced, which was easier said than done in the midst of a chaotic battle. Shortened lances were frequently used defensively by dismounted knights. The standby of the infantry, though, was the spear. In western Europe this was generally shorter than the cavalry lance, measuring about 2.75 metres, but a forest of spears wielded by an infantry unit often proved highly effective against a charge by horsemen. During the fourteenth century, the halberd, which was effectively an axe on the end of a long pole, became common among the infantry, while after 1400 the Swiss developed the massive pike, which could be up to 5.5 metres long, and caused a sensation in the Granada campaigns. This weapon was particularly associated with urban militias, and by the end of the fifteenth century, in Spain and elsewhere, the squares of pikemen were increasingly combining, and to deadly effect, with hand-gunners (see below). Swords, daggers and other kinds of knives were also regular parts of the infantry's armoury. According to some sources, Sir Edward Woodville's company, at Loja in 1486, included the longbow archers who had been typical of English armies, both at home and abroad, for several centuries. The longbow had a maximum range of as much as 400 metres, but was generally more effective at closer range. Within 60–120 metres, its arrows were capable of piercing chain mail, leather, and even poorer-quality plate armour. Such weapons played little part, however, in the Granada campaigns. The same could not be said of the crossbow, which had been used in Western Europe at least since the time of the First Crusade (1096–9). Evidence of mechanically-assisted bows dates back to at least 400 BC, in China and in the West, though the technology had been abandoned by western Europeans by the century before the First Crusade. Apart from having a similar power of penetration to the longbow, the crossbow, which was a normal part of the Castilians' weaponry in the Granada war, required less skill in operation than its older cousin, and was therefore suitable for use by the conscripted levies of the towns. It had some disadvantages, however, in field warfare, as had been discovered earlier, in northern Europe. In open country, cavalry might approach an opposing army at 250 metres a minute when trotting, and twice that in a gallop, which gave crossbowmen only 15–24 seconds in which to shoot, before the armies closed for battle. Thus the crossbowman could only hope for a second shot if he was able to fire the first at a range of 125–180 metres. Large, protected groups of crossbowmen, behind some kind of screen which was often carried by a shield-bearer, could hope to halt a cavalry charge in the field, but, for these very reasons, the crossbow was much relied on for defence in siege warfare. Indeed, in the conditions of the war in Granada, where sieges formed a major part of the action, the disadvantages of the weapon were less evident.[15]

It is generally agreed, both by contemporary chroniclers and by modern historians, that artillery played a crucial role in the Castilian victory in the Granada war, though siege engines of older types were certainly not abandoned, and continued to play a part in the campaigns. The traditional assessment of the balance between the various weapons used during the war is that the fortifications of the Granadan towns, which had been designed for defence against conventional infantry and cavalry, supported by siege engines and mines, were unable to resist the new threat of artillery and small firearms. The customary Granadan tactics of skirmishing and raiding by light cavalry were, in this interpretation, quite inadequate in the face of the new weapons of the Christians. There is indeed no doubt that the use of artillery by Ferdinand's armies increased steadily during the 1480s, and that the resulting destruction of Granadan fortifications enabled otherwise insuperable obstacles to be overcome, permitting the successful Christian advance into the heart of the Nasrid kingdom. The artillery pieces used in the war were made either of forged iron, or, increasingly, of bronze. The latter material was in use in the crown of Aragon by 1400, and appeared in Castile in the early fifteenth century. In each case, the founding was done with charcoal of pine, cork-oak or heather, using moulds. Traditionally, such guns were made in two pieces, known in Castilian as *caña y servidor*, the 'server', or breach, containing the powder charge, while the 'cane' or 'tube' (*trompa*) held the cannon ball. The two parts were lashed together with ropes on a wooden base, which could be adjusted to raise or lower the line of fire. Only at the end of the century did one-piece bronze guns begin to appear. The most established category of artillery weapon, when the Granada war began, was the bombard, lombard or gombard, a very wide-barrelled piece which fired large stone balls. Short and stumpy bombards were known as mortars, and there was a considerable overlap of nomenclature between these new weapons and their predecessors, which did not employ gunpowder. One variety of lombard, the 'organ' (*órgano*), was known in Castile by 1469, and consisted of three tubes bound together, and fired iron balls or the tips of lances, in quick succession, to immobilize enemy personnel. The *pasavolante* was in this period a small bombard, with a barrel more than two metres in length, and a calibre of 20 centimetres, though the more developed versions used during the Granada campaigns, which were made in one piece, had much longer barrels, measuring up to six metres, and a calibre of only 10 centimetres. Other similar guns were known as 'serpentines'. Perhaps the best known among the smaller weapons, from the beginning of the fifteenth century onwards, was the *ribadoquín*, which is frequently mentioned in the chronicles of the Granada war. It fired iron balls weighing three pounds, and had a larger version, with a calibre of about 4.5 centimetres, which was known as the *cerbatana*. The *falconete*, which was known in Aragon by 1413, fired iron balls covered with lead, weighing up to five pounds. In this period, a wide range of other names and nicknames were used to denote types and origins of weapons. Despite their extensive use, guns certainly did not replace siege engines, in the lengthy, and often faltering, Christian advance through the kingdom of Granada. One category, the so-called 'area' engines (*sectorias*), were intended to bring parties of infantry close to the besieged walls with less danger of injury from the defenders. They included the *bastida*, consisting of a wooden tower, with a hatch which opened to allow the soldiers inside to attack at the level of the top of the walls. The *escala real*, or 'royal ladder', had a compartment at its base, in which the attacking infantry travelled up to the wall, and which was then raised up on pulleys to the level of the defenders, under the covering fire of crossbowmen and hand-gunners (*espingarderos*). On other occasions, leather-covered constructions, variously known as *mantas*, *manteletes*, or *bancos pinjados*, were used to protect attacking troops at ground level, as they made their way towards the walls. In addition to cannons and handguns, various kinds of catapult, known as *magañas*, *algarradas* and *trabucos*, were used to fire projectiles into besieged towns and fortifications. The artillery was protected from the missiles of defenders by walls of shields.

Historians of warfare in the medieval period tend to discount the use of naval power, and those who planned the Castilian assault on the kingdom of Granada appear to have anticipated their preconceptions. On 10 February 1482, just after the Muslim capture of Zahara which initiated the war for the conquest of Granada, Diego de Valera wrote to King Ferdinand from his Andalusian vantage point in Puerto de Santa María. Assuming that his royal master would attack the Muslim kingdom that summer, Valera put forward a plan for the achievement of complete victory. The military man, diplomat and historian first proposed that the export of all grain from the crown of Castile should be banned, and that the available food supplies from Extremadura and Andalusia should be gathered on the borders of the Muslim kingdom. Naval warfare was to be given the highest priority in the forthcoming campaign. A strong enough fleet should be assembled not only to secure the strait between Spain and Africa but to patrol the coast of the Muslim state. Siege engines should be brought, as indeed they were, from as far afield as Galicia, Vizcaya, Asturias and Brittany, and the Genoese and Venetians should be urged to join in an economic blockade of Granada. Diego fully acknowledged the need for ground forces to carry out the traditional tactics of raid and destruction of enemy property (*tala*). Nevertheless, to him it was crucial that the port city of Málaga should be captured, and he was sure that this could only be done by means of a combined operation of forces on land and sea. The siege should involve an artillery bombardment of the city from two land batteries, one at Gibralfaro and the other on the coast near the city, but also from ten or twelve guns placed on blockships which would destroy the coastal defences. After this, well-armed infantry were to be sent in. At the same time, an assault should be undertaken from Murcia on the eastern port of Almería, thus isolating the Muslim capital completely. Diego de Valera's advice was not accepted in any systematic fashion, and the war lasted very much longer than he and others intended or wished, but his plan indicates the flexibility of at least some military thinking in the period. Based in the small seigneurial port of Puerto de Santa María, Valera was undoubtedly in a good position to comment on naval matters, and he had been in correspondence with Ferdinand on the subject at least since August 1476, when the war for the Castilian crown was in progress. Although his overall strategy for conquering Granada was rejected, Diego and his son Charles (the French and English version of this name was used routinely in contemporary documents), who had succeeded him as *alcaide* (governor) of the port, were given a supervisory role over maritime activity off south-western Spain when war against Granada began in earnest in 1482. Modern historians have generally regarded Valera's as the best plan, and Ladero has expressed the view that, if had been adopted, the crucial port of Málaga would have fallen in months instead of five years later, as in fact occurred. In general, despite effective operations by the Andalusian fleet off Spain and North Africa either side of the Straits of Gibraltar, naval forces were little used during the subsequent campaigns. The overall failure to deploy these resources efficiently was largely due, as Diego was well aware, to a lack of strategic awareness among Ferdinand and Isabella's courtiers, and an unwillingness on their part to make use of local expertise. In fact, the war was not systematically planned, but developed more or less spontaneously, after the capture of Alhama, a relatively unimportant town which was hard for the Christian forces to hold, and effectively wasted three seasons of campaigning. Diego de Valera had proposed that ships should be used not only to blockade the coasts of the Nasrid emirate but also to bring infantry reinforcements and war supplies to the land front from northern Spain. Both royal and municipal documents indicate the immense costs which Isabella and Ferdinand imposed on their subjects by their failure to heed this advice. The only area in which naval forces were used to some effect during the war was the blockade of Granada. Aragonese merchantmen, engaged in trade with the Barbary coast, were banned from the straits and the seas off the Nasrid state, but other Catalan and Aragonese ships were diverted from facing the Turkish threat in the eastern Mediterranean to help enforce the blockade. Eventually, after many expensive and destructive delays, the 1487 siege of Málaga duly vindicated Valera's approach.[16]

However effectively naval forces had been used, the clue to control of territory in the Muslim emirate of Granada was still the occupation of fortified places. The series of sieges which dominated the war serves to demonstrate this point. The quickest way of capturing a fortified place was to storm its walls directly by means of siege ladders, but this was not easy in the conditions of Nasrid Granada. Here, as in numerous earlier conflicts in medieval Europe, the techniques of lengthy and laborious siege warfare had to be employed. Apart from blockade, one of these was the mining of walls, for which purpose specialists were brought from Asturias and the Basque country. The usual technique was to dig a tunnel to a wall or tower, and hollow out a chamber under it. This would be held up by wooden props, which would at a suitable moment be set on fire, thus causing the building above to collapse. By the time of the Granada campaigns, gunpowder was beginning to be used in this process but, as in the case of twentieth-century 'escape' films, there was always a danger not only of discovery but of counter-tunnelling by the defenders. Miners could also be employed, as they were on numerous occasions during the Granada war, to make breaches in walls above ground. The miners and sappers who undertook such operations generally worked with picks or metal-tipped wooden rams, under the protection of sheds, sometimes on wheels, which were often known as 'mice'. After breaches had been made, siege towers were used to bring troops up to the walls in relative safety. If such methods proved ineffective, a blockade to starve the enemy into submission was often the only possible course. The level of organization and staying power which Ferdinand and Isabella achieved in the latter stages of the Granada war was not in fact atypical of such efforts in the medieval period. A remarkable level of discipline, on a regular basis, might achieve conquests even when technology failed, and the last days of the Nasrid dynasty demonstrated all too effectively that unity of purpose and strength of political will were also essential components of successful resistance.

In the study of western Europe as a whole, there has been considerable debate about the role of castles and other forms of fortification in the central and later Middle Ages. Robert Bartlett has pointed out that the relationship between castles and their attacks formed a large part of the dynamic of conquest and expansion between the tenth century and the fourteenth. Not only did the medieval castle have a considerable effect on the development of medieval warfare, but it quite evidently became not just a defensive but also an offensive weapon, this point being emphasised by R. C. Smail for the Latin Crusader kingdoms in the Middle East, and R. Allen Brown for England. More recently, Manuel Rojas Gabriel has applied such thinking to the fortifications of the frontier between Christian and Muslim territories in late medieval Andalusia. The traditional view has been that the frontier of the emirate of Granada formed a dense and co-ordinated system of defence which, along with the shifting balance of military and economic power and political alliances, determined the relative balance between the two adversaries. Here as elsewhere, castles and fortresses were indeed symbols of power and authority, and attracted to themselves various functions of government, as well as economic activity. They were also magnets for settlement, and the repopulation of abandoned frontier zones. What Rojas rightly seeks to modify is the established Spanish notion of a certain uniqueness in the character of the fortifications on the Granadan frontier. In reality, their density was highly variable, and a careful comparison between different sectors of the 'frontier' renders increasingly implausible, in this case, the concept of a co-ordinated system of defences. While the southern part of the modern province of Jaén, for example, was quite heavily fortified, the strategically important western part of the frontier, behind the Straits of Gibraltar, was poorly provided for. It is self-evident that, in the mountainous and variable terrain of the region, a short distance between points on the map might not necessarily betoken an easy link between castles or watchtowers on the ground. At the time when Ferdinand and Isabella's campaigns began, fortifications on the Christian side, in most cases accompanied by long-established centres of population, had evolved from earlier Muslim settlements. Despite the essential role of castles in holding and governing territory, there were some cases during the fifteenth century in which the Castilians did not maintain fortifications which they had captured. One such, which immediately preceded the Granada war, was the capture by the marquis of Cádiz, in 1477, of Garciago. Here, the fortified site was sacked and burned, and not maintained. In truth, according to the latest analysis, the military actions on the Granada frontier were not significantly different in character from those in other zones of conflict in the period. Studies, and surviving examples, of late medieval weaponry and fortifications indicate that, as a general rule, the advantage in warfare lay with defenders rather than attackers, which makes the outcome of Isabella and Ferdinand's 'crusade' all the more remarkable. It is clear that it took a long time, after its introduction to Spain in the late fourteenth century, for artillery to be employed effectively in sieges. An unavoidable fact is that, throughout the century which preceded the fall of Granada in 1492, the balance of military power overwhelmingly favoured the Castilians. During this period, the emirate was effectively unable to mount offensive operations, apart from minor raids and rustling expeditions, so that, in this comparatively safe situation, the Castilians built no new fortifications but devoted themselves to repairing existing ones. Complacency seems to have been the order of the day, however, and complaints reached the Cortes about the neglect of frontier defences, despite the many privileges which the Andalusian nobility received in order to maintain them. This seigneurialization of the zone was indeed a major factor in preventing the development of a co-ordinated defensive, or offensive, system. Governorships (*alcaidías*) came to be seen as honorific rewards rather than military posts, and in these circumstances, which lasted effectively until about 1480, it was comparatively easy for large, organized raiding parties to enter and leave Christian territory without coming into contact with either castles or their garrisons. Although the alert might be given by specialized scouts (*adalides*) or those working in the field, a rapid and co-ordinated response had traditionally been unlikely. This was partly because garrisons were normally too small to mount a counter-attack, but nevertheless, the limitation on the value of mobile warfare was that, if territory was to be held with any permanence, castles and fortresses would have to be captured.[17]

Although the frontier between the crown of Castile and the emirate of Granada remained largely static between 1369 and 1482, neither side recognized this as a permanent situation. The Christian 'crusade', which was to be spectacularly revived by Ferdinand and Isabella, remained a permanent option, while the Nasrids and their allies were always capable of resorting to the spirit of Muslim 'jihad', a concept of primarily spiritual warfare within the individual believer, which had a habit of becoming material and communal throughout Islamic history. Nevertheless, day-to-day arrangements were inevitably made for coexistence, so that the organization of peace was as important in this period as the more publicized 'organization for war'. When it began its existence, after Ferdinand III's spectacular conquests in Western Andalusia between 1230 and 1250, the new Nasrid state was in vassalage to the Castilian crown. Not only was this arrangement entirely contrary to Islamic law, which forbade a Muslim ruler to be subordinate to a non-Muslim one, but its terms were onerous and humiliating. The emir of Granada was required not only to attend the Castilian court, but also to supply troops to fight against fellow Muslims as well as Christians. In addition, Granada had to pay financial tribute (*parias*) to Castile, and in order to meet these demands, its rulers had to tax their subjects at higher rates than were permitted by Islamic law (*sharia*). In the turmoil which preceded and followed the arrival of the Trastamaran dynasty on the Castilian throne in 1369, these onerous terms were in practice relaxed, but fifteenth-century rulers did not abandon their claims, and their Muslim opponents failed to obtain any legal change in their relationship with the Christian kingdom. Between 1406 and 1481, a series of truces was established between Granada and Castile. According to the surviving records of the negotiation of such a truce in 1439, between Muhammad IX and John II, the Muslim ruler found it much easier to pay *parias* than to return Christian prisoners. Granadans were unwilling to hand over their captives without the payment of ransom, because they claimed that they needed this money to finance the freeing of their own relatives from Christian hands. To this the Castilian negotiators replied that the Muslims would have more resources with which to ransom their prisoners in Castile if they paid more attention to cultivation and stockbreeding, and less to raiding and rustling in Christian territory. It is evident from this account that each side had detailed knowledge of the internal political situation of the other, and the documents reveal that the Castilians were sensitive to their Muslim neighbours' legal situation. To avoid complications with *sharia*, the sections of truce agreements concerning the payment of *parias* and the handing over of captives were designated as 'gifts', and were not included in the main treaty. Common features of the truce agreements, from the beginning of John II's reign to the early years of Isabella and Ferdinand's, were determinations concerning captives, trade and arbitration. In the first case, it was mutually accepted that prisoners might legitimately escape to their home territory if they could, but if they brought stolen goods with them these would have to be returned. Ransomers, and others engaged in such humanitarian work, were to be allowed to cross and recross the border freely. As far as trade was concerned, and contrary to the general Christian canon law on the subject, merchants were allowed to trade across the border, provided that customs duties were paid, and forbidden commodities were not imported or exported.

For purposes of arbitration in cross-frontier disputes, judges might be named with the recognition of both sides, and with powers both to prosecute and to sentence offenders. Despite these apparently positive provisions, it has to be said that in the basic matter of military activity, these fifteenth-century truces, as well as temporary ceasefires, never succeeded in bringing a total end to fighting on and near the frontier. Any 'peace' achieved by such means was no more than nominal. Yet even up to the eve of the war for the final conquest of Granada, the mixture of licit and illicit trade, covert military activity, and traffic in deliberately or accidentally missing persons continued unabated. In 1478, for instance, the Catholic Monarchs granted to Fernando López de Alcalá the post of farmer and chief collector (*arrendador y recaudador mayor*) of the 'tenth and half-tenth of Moorish goods' (*diezmo y medio diezmo de lo morisco*), with the power to confiscate for himself any silk which had crossed the frontier illegally into Christian territory, without passing through a customs post. As an example of the kind of illicit military activity which went on across the frontier on the eve of the Granada war, at the beginning of 1480, the king and queen handed to Diego Hurtado de Mendoza, who was both *corregidor* of Écija and the chief magistrate in charge of the frontier posts with the emirate (*alcalde mayor de los puertos de la frontera con Granada*), a Muslim from Málaga called Ali Merchante. Ali had tried unsuccessfully to smuggle some lances and javelins across the border into the emirate under his saddle. The judge of the case, Licenciado Ledesma, acquitted his three accomplices, but convicted Ali himself of trafficking in forbidden goods (*cosas vedadas*), in this case military supplies.[18]

The taking of prisoners was clearly a constant feature of life on, and behind, the pre-war Christian–Muslim frontier, though more is known about Christian than Muslim captives in this period. Both ransoming and exchange were possible means of liberation, but Christian claims that prisoners were routinely put under pressure to convert to Islam seem to have been exaggerated. It evidently made more economic sense, from the captors' point of view, to obtain ransom for continuing Christians rather than acquire the responsibility for converts to Islam, but the generally desperate conditions of the prisoners seem to have led in some cases to conversions. It appears that, in many cases, Christian prisoners in the Nasrid emirate were imprisoned at night in improvized gaols, such as disused cisterns and silos, and employed during the day either as building workers, often in the construction and repair of fortifications, or else effectively as beasts of burden, operating irrigation pumps and mills. Given the lack of a fixed and fenced frontier, spontaneous escape was always a possibility. In the fifteenth century, the Christian-held fortress of Alcalá la Real, for example, was only 300 metres from Muslim territory, and displayed a light during the hours of darkness to assist fugitives. On some occasions, as has been noted, captives might be released under the terms of a truce, but more commonly they gained their freedom with the help of specialized negotiators, whether secular or religious. Since at least the thirteenth century, both the Castilian crown itself and some town councils had been in the habit of appointing professional ransomers, who were known as *alfaqueques*. They were generally merchants, who added the redeeming of captives to their trading activities and took 10 per cent of the ransom price as their commission. While the wealthy might be able to afford large ransoms, the same was evidently not the case for others. Poorer people would attempt to scrape together alms and legacies to pay for the release of their relatives, but the result was frequently inadequate. Because Muslims were similarly concerned to retrieve their own prisoners from Christian hands, complex bartering often developed, which the Castilian crown vainly attempted to regulate by limiting the possibility of owners' demanding extravagant prices in auctions of captives. Henry IV's government decreed that Christian owners of Muslim prisoners (for they were effectively treated as slaves), who had held them for less than a year, were not to charge more than a 30 per cent premium if the individual concerned was to be part of an exchange. If such prisoners had been held by Christians for more than a year, they might be sold at no more than half the original purchase price. The Church, too, was institutionally involved in the ransoming of Christian captives from Muslim Granada. Two religious orders were founded in Spain specifically for this purpose, and both originally in the crown of Aragon. The first, the order of the Most Holy Trinity (the 'Trinitarians'), was established in 1201, while the second, the order of St Mary of Mercy ('La Merced', or the Mercedarians), was set up by a Catalan layman, Pere Nolasc, in Barcelona in 1218. Yet, although there were Trinitarian and Mercedarian houses in the major 'frontier' towns, such as Murcia, Córdoba, Seville and Jerez de la Frontera, their activities do not appear in local records. This seems to be because the negotation process was centralized, and carried out away from the border with Granada, in annual chapters which nominated members of the order concerned to enter Muslim territory in order to carry out that season's negotiations. Sensing a lack of involvement, local authorities often took the initiative themselves, and appointed local *alfaqueques* to act on their behalf. The activities of these officials were regulated by the terms of Alfonso X's law-code, the *Siete Partidas*, which decreed that an *alfaqueque* should be trustworthy, not greedy, an Arabic speaker, diplomatic, courageous, long-suffering, and wealthy enough to act as a guarantor for ransom payments. *Alfaqueques* would enter Muslim territory under a safe conduct (*aman*) which was issued for a limited period. They were supposed to show respect for Islam at all times, and some Mercedarian friars lost their lives for ignoring this provision by administering the Christian sacraments to prisoners. Although Christian *alfaqueques* were required by law to travel amidst public display, including even the accompaniment of trumpeters, this appears not to have prevented them from acting not only as traders but sometimes as ambassadors, or even double agents. With the aim of establishing greater concern over these somewhat wayward and idiosyncratic officials, the Crown established the supervisory office of *alfaqueque mayor de tierra de moros*, which was held, at least from 1439 onwards, by members of the Saavedra family. Muslims were, of course, equally concerned about the condition and fate of their own co-religionaries in Christian hands, and appointed their own *alfaqueques*, who generally paid ransoms in silk, as Castile did not normally accept the depreciating Nasrid currency.

The *aman*, or safe conduct, was essential for subjects of the kings of Castile and Granada to enter each other's territory, because any illegal movements were liable to increase tension. In times of truce, however, legal trade between the two sides seems to have been quite extensive. This was inevitable, given that the Nasrid state was permanently short of home-produced grain, olive oil and cattle. The shortfall had to be made up by means of imports, often through Genoese intermediaries, and a customs tariff used in Alcalá la Real in 1476 indicates the nature of the traffic. Castile exported cattle, olive oil, woollen cloth (friezes), garments and honey to Granada, receiving in return sardines, silk, linen, dried fruit, sugar and Muslim garments, such as burnouses and veils. The strictures of both canon and civil law against the granting of any kind of aid to Muslim states turned all military supplies into contraband, even in 'peacetime', and the *alcaldes mayores* who had charge of the Christian *alfaqueques* also supervised trade across the frontier, in their capacity as *alcaldes de las sacas*, or 'magistrates in charge of exports'.

The border zone between Castile and Granada, in the years preceding Ferdinand and Isabella's onslaught, was dotted with offensive, or on occasions aggressive, fortifications, but it was also the scene of numerous and frequent human contacts, whether licit or otherwise. In addition, the interface between Christian and Islamic culture inspired a whole genre of literature which, though couched in the forms of medieval Western Europe, nonetheless appeared to show considerable admiration for a gallant and chivalrous Muslim enemy. But was the long border between Castile and Granada, in the last days of the Nasrid emirate, a 'frontier society'?[19]

In 1987, a group of scholars assembled in Edinburgh to deliver and debate papers which were later printed under the title *Medieval frontier societies*. In the final essay of the published collection, Robert I. Burns explicitly, indeed 'umbilically', relates the notion of 'the frontier' in medieval society to the theories of Frederick Jackson Turner, which were formulated in the context of the nineteenth-century American West. Focusing on the medieval frontier(s) between Christendom and the house of Islam in medieval Spain, and particularly on his own especial area of expertise in the thirteenth-century kingdom of Valencia, Fr Burns reasserts the validity of the notion that a 'frontier society' does indeed have, in principle, unique and distinctive features, even though Turner's own ideas on the subject have since been twisted, adapted, and sometimes rejected altogether. For Burns, no 'Turnerian' or, as he would prefer, 'neo-Turnerian' thesis can be applied and justified unless each case is considered on its merits. At least in theory, the Castilian–Granadan frontier was removed from history in 1492, though it remains to be seen whether this really happened. The question remains, however, whether it had ever been a 'frontier society' in any sense related to the 'Turner thesis'. Since 1989, revisionism has made further advances in this area of study, and it has recently been suggested, in a comparative essay by Nora Berend which uses examples from outside as well as

Plate 4 Portrait of a Man Said to Be Christopher Columbus (*c.*1446–1506), by Sabastiano del Piombo (Luciani) (1485?–1547). *Courtesy of the Metropolitan Museum of Art, New York*

within Europe, that, *contra* Turner, societies create frontiers rather than vice versa, and that Christian and Muslim propaganda, including even the apparently positive fifteenth-century ballads and romances, should be treated with caution as indicators of reality.[20]

5

Economy and Society

Despite their notorious climatic and geographical problems, the Spanish kingdoms, even excluding neighbouring Portugal, evidently had considerable potential, at the end of the fifteenth century, to become a power in Europe, and eventually the world.[1] The combined area of Ferdinand and Isabella's domains, 385,000 square kilometres in the crown of Castile and 110,000 square kilometres in that of the crown of Aragon, was almost equivalent to that of the mighty French kingdom, and equal to a large part of the fragmented Holy Roman Empire. Also, in view of the geographical position of the Iberian peninsula, with both Atlantic and Mediterranean coasts, a direct link with the rest of continental Europe, and a close proximity with Africa across the Straits of Gibraltar, Spain and its Portuguese neighbour had the evident potential to form a bridge between Europe, Africa, and later the Americas. In reality, though, the terrain of the Peninsula has more often proved to be a dividing than a uniting factor. In this process its great rivers and mountain ranges have played a part, but the somewhat insular character of Spain and Portugal is no doubt also due to the fact that seven-eighths of the Peninsula is bounded by sea. In addition, the land frontier with France was and is the broad and high range of the Pyrenees, which except for its western and eastern coastal extremities, in the Basque country and Catalonia respectively, to this day forms a complex structure of scarps and deep, almost impenetrable valleys. The major rivers and mountain ranges to the south of the Pyrenees form further barriers to communication from the north because of their prevailing east–west orientation. The size and height of the Cantabrian range near the north coast, the large central plateau known as the Meseta, and the southern Baetic mountains, make Spain, on average, the second highest country in Europe after Switzerland. The Iberian mountains at the eastern edge of the Meseta separate Castile from the Aragonese and Catalan lands to the east. As a further barrier to communication within the Peninsula, none of its five main rivers, the Douro/Duero, Ebro, Tagus, Guadiana and Guadalquivir, which drain from the Meseta and, with the exception of the Ebro, flow into the Atlantic, have ever been fully navigable. Thus Iberian rivers have generally been seen as divisive rather than unifying, as frontiers rather than channels of communication. In addition to the physical divisions within it, the Iberian peninsula was, and is, also affected by sharp climatic contrasts. The wettest area is to be found in the north-west, where there is no summer drought, but elsewhere in Spain rainfall is generally low and somewhat unpredictable. Indeed, some parts of the modern provinces of Murcia and Almería are still effectively semi-desert. Most of Spain is noted for ample sunshine and a piercing light, and the proverbial description of the Castilian tableland, with its hot summers and cold winters, is 'nine months of winter, three months of hell'. Though conditions are less harsh in coastal areas, Catalonia suffers in winter from a cold northerly wind known locally as the *tramontana*, as well as numerous mountain storms. The most fertile land in Spain is to be found in some coastal regions and in the large delta of the Guadalquivir, the latter being a major factor in the expansion of the Andalusian economy from the late fifteenth century onwards.[2]

In addition to these geographical and climatic difficulties, late medieval and early modern Spain also suffered from an endemic shortage of population, in relation to its economic potential. Reliable population statistics did not become available in the crown of Castile until 1528. When Isabella and Ferdinand enquired how many Castilians were available to serve in their Granada campaigns, they were told by their officials that there were about 1.5 million hearths (*hogares* or households) in the kingdom. The use of a demographic multiplier in the range 4.5 to 5 persons per household, despite its imprecision, would suggest a population of 6 to 7.5 million. However, the more precise calculations of the period 1528–36, which now included the former Muslim kingdom of Granada but excluded the approximately 180,000 inhabitants of the Basque country, came to no more than 4.5 million, which suggests that the earlier estimate was wildly inaccurate. In the absence of better evidence, it seems safe to assume that, around 1500, there were 4 million inhabitants, or slightly more, in the crown of Castile. Somewhat better statistics for the crown of Aragon suggest that, at that time, there were fewer than a million people (perhaps just over 850,000) in the kingdom of Aragon itself, approximately 120,000 in Navarre, and about a million in Portugal. This total was puny compared with that of France at the time, and clearly had implications for the balance of power in Europe. Although many Spaniards lived in urban settlements, only Seville, Barcelona and Valencia rated as large cities in European terms, with tens of thousands of citizens each. Isabella and Ferdinand's ambitions clearly faced physical and demographic difficulties, in addition to their political and religious problems.[3]

Although medieval and early modern governments expected, and were in turn expected by their subjects, to fulfil only limited and rudimentary institutional functions, one of these was to assure the basic nourishment of their people. In this respect, the situation of the Iberian peninsula was somewhat precarious. In a large part of the crowns of Aragon and Castile, the basis of agriculture was the three typically Mediterranean staples of grain, wine and olive oil, these being supplemented by fruit and vegetables and, in the south and east, some rice. Bread remained the essential food of most of the population, and the supply of grain was a constant preoccupation of the rulers, who did not have the level of control over the natural elements, or the vagaries of international trade, to which they aspired in the case of their own human subjects. In an average year, and many years during this period, especially in the early sixteenth century, were far from the average, there were wide variations in the agricultural productivity of the various parts of their realm. As far as grain was concerned, the valleys of the Duero and the Tagus, the southern part of Extremadura, and western Andalusia, especially around Córdoba, Seville and Jerez de la Frontera, as well as the middle section of the river Ebro, habitually produced good harvests. In contrast, the Basque country, Asturias and Galicia were regular importers of grain. In the crown of Aragon, Catalonia became an importer partly as a result of urbanization, and partly because of the use of land to produce commercial crops. Barcelona obtained much of its grain from the kingdom of Aragon and from Sicily, while Valencia also obtained imports from Andalusia and New Castile. Majorca, too, was a regular importer of grain. Over much of the south, the main arable crop was *pan terciado*, consisting of two-thirds wheat and one-third barley, while other grains, such as rye and oats, were also cultivated but generally for animal consumption. In areas of high grain production, as in other European countries, much land was used alternately for arable crops and pasture, in a system of two-crop rotation known in Castile as *año y vez*, which allowed the land to rest before producing a new crop. In less fertile areas, corn would be planted in one year, the land would lie fallow in the next, and livestock would graze on it in the third. There were variations in how arable land was used. In some cases, the whole of a property might be sown in one year and then kept fallow as *barbechos* in the next, but the more usual custom was to rotate land use within the estate on a fifty-fifty basis. The latter practice was particularly common in smaller holdings. The normal terms of the ecclesiastical tithe, two-thirds wheat and one-third barley (*pan terciado*), indicates the normal balance in grain production.

As well as being a staple of the agriculture of Spain, as of other Mediterranean countries, the olive provided Isabella's kingdom, in particular, with a valuable export crop, which required careful exploitation. At this stage, olive oil was not yet in habitual use by the 'Old Christian' majority for cooking, this custom being largely the preserve of the Jewish and Muslim populations, and of interest to the Inquisition as a possible method of identifying false converts. Instead, the oil, for example from the important area of production, near Seville, known as the Aljarafe, was largely used at home in the production of soap, and in Flanders and England as a detergent in the textile industry. Olive groves were ploughed twice a year, the first ploughing, in January, being deep and the second, in April, more gentle, though in alternate years only one ploughing took place. The ploughing of the grove had to be done in such a way as to avoid damaging the roots of the trees, so that the area around the trees themselves was hoed rather than ploughed, to gain full value from the spring rains. In areas with heavy soil, or in the rougher *monte bajo* (heathland), it was sometimes not possible to treat olive trees with this amount of care, and hence produce crops of high quality. Like arable land, olive groves (*olivares*) required to be subjected to *rozas* (stubble-burning), in order to remove other trees and shrubs. This was normally done in full every two years, with lesser tidying in the intermediate years. A more complex operation than maintaining the soil in the groves was the pruning of the trees themselves, to remove both dead olive wood and other vegetation which became entangled with the olive branches. This was normally the responsibility of tenants, and played a vital part in ensuring the quality of the resulting oil. Young growth was at a premium, and pruning was a skilled and delicate task. The olives were normally harvested between All Saints' day (1 November) and the New Year. They would then be treated with salt, to remove the dirt which they brought with them from the olive trees. The subsequent milling had to be rapid and precise, if the quality of the oil was not to be reduced. This was particularly important in the Seville region, where production was being expanded in this period for the export market.

Grapes, the third basic crop of Spanish agriculture, provided wine for export as well as the subsistence of the native population. As in the case of olives, there was an expanding market, both at home and abroad, so that new vineyards were being created, generally at the instance of landlords in the Church and among the upper nobility. The growth in wine production was especially pronounced in New Castile, in Extremadura and above all in the region around Seville, including Jerez de la Frontera, though there was also expansion of the area under vines, to meet local consumption, in lower Galicia, the middle section of the river Duero and the Rioja region. Where land was being cultivated in this way for the first time, contemporary documents state that it should first be cleared completely of existing vegetation and the soil hoed, all by hand. New vines would then be planted and the procedures of cultivation would begin. First the soil immediately surrounding the vines would be turned over and cleared, to allow better access for air and moisture to the roots. This was done every two years, but there were also annual tasks. Each year, the vines had to be pruned, and this operation generally took place after the vintage, in December and January in the south, and earlier in more northerly regions. After better growth had thus been ensured, the ground surrounding the vines was prepared for the next crop. This involved turning the soil over with hoes or mattocks, a procedure which was carried out twice during the growing season. In the important commercial wine-producing regions of Andalusia, the second digging was normally begun before Easter, and was to be completed by the end of May. In the early sixteenth century, and possibly to help meet increased demand for Spanish wine both at home and abroad, the practice developed of 'hooding' or 'covering' the vines (*encapucharlas o cubrir las viñas*), in order to make them grow outwards rather than upwards. The purpose of this measure was better to air the branches and to reduce the damage which the Spanish sun might inflict upon them. Another operation related to the quality of the product was the removal, while the vines were fruiting, of other wood or plants which had grown up between them. Numerous varieties of grapes were grown in Spain in this period, producing wine of varying quality, for the domestic and overseas markets. Vines were normally planted in non-irrigated land, though there is evidence of some being planted in irrigated areas in the Seville region. From time to time, the vine stock was renewed, in order to achieve fresh growth and assure the quality of the main product. This was done, for preference, during the winter, when the vines' cycle of germination had not yet begun. Cuttings from existing vines were used for this purpose, and were protected from the elements by covers made of cane, while they were still young and tender.[4]

The crop-producing lands which have so far been mentioned were generally tenanted properties, held in lordship from the Crown by ecclesiastical or secular individuals, or by corporations. Yet there remained, in Ferdinand and Isabella's reign, a tradition of communal ownership, which in the case of Castile was normally administered by municipal councils on the Crown's behalf. The 'documentary illusion', that a phenomenon which is nor described in writing does not exist, has at times led to the neglect of the practical rural uses and customs of late medieval Spain, in favour of the legalities of the better-recorded lord-ships (*señoríos*). Like rulers elsewhere in medieval Europe, the various Christian kings of Spain claimed notional overlordship in every part of their domains, but the special circumstances of the Reconquest had led them to claim direct lordship over all lands captured from Muslims. In Isabella and Ferdinand's time, and particularly in Castile, all lands which had not been assigned in some form of *señorío* were designated 'royal lands' (*tierras realengas*). Poor-quality land in this category, whether vacant or worked by individuals without a specific grant from the Crown, was known in Castile as *baldío*, or 'idle' land, and was basically regarded as being in public ownership. Thus the term was also used to describe lands which were administered by municipal councils, even though, in most cases, no individual or corporation had a legal title to them. Until recently, there has been a tendency among historians to regard *baldíos* as economically insignificant, but more extensive research in many regions has shown that they played a con-siderable part in the rural economy. They included the rougher land known as *monte alto* and *monte bajo*, and even quite fertile holdings in areas of sparse population. The most typical use of *baldíos*, however, was as pasture, and in some places the planting of crops on such common land was forbidden, though in others these areas were used to supplement crops from land of better quality. In other cases, as on the banks of the Guadalquivir near Córdoba, so-called *baldíos* could be some of the best land in Spain. There was also a long-established right of what was effectively squatting on unoccupied royal land, which was known in Castile as *presura*, from the words for seizure or capture. In the earlier Middle Ages this might be done with either the tacit or the explicit permission of the king. In some areas, such as the vineyards of north-western Spain, lands held by *presura* had by the fifteenth century become effectively, if not legally, private. A more extensive and signific-ant public use of seigneurial land was the grazing of stubble by flocks, a practice known in Castile as *derrota de mieses*, but also extensive else-where in Spain and in other parts of Western Europe. The practice effectively combined pastoral and arable agriculture as well as public and private ownership. In this system, individual rights to land were restricted to the period between the planting and harvesting of crops. After harvest, every holder of a grain field or pasture was obliged to open it to the flocks of the general public. This practice, which owed more to pragmatism than to legal theory, resulted from the need to maintain an adequate supply of pasture for the majority of Spain's flocks which were not involved in transhumant grazing. During much of the year, the *baldíos* and municipal pastures sufficed to maintain the flocks, but the dry summers in most of Spain greatly reduced their nutritional value. It was at this time that the stubble (*rastrojos*) and fallow land (*barbechos*) of the grain fields came into their own. The stubble contained green weeds as well as the dried remains of the corn, and Castilian peasants commonly delayed ploughing their stubble until the March following the harvest, so as not to lose its food value. The main advantages of the *derrota de mieses* to stockbreeders were that it saved them the cost of stabling their animals during the winter, and provided resources to farmers whose lands were fragmented by the customs and laws of property and inheritance.

Municipal involvement with the possession and management of rural property has already been noted. Among the goods, in Castile the *bienes propios*, with which the local councils (*concejos*) were endowed were frequently large or small parcels of land, ranging from the extensive *montes* of Toledo to small areas of pasture situated on the edge of centres of habitation. While town councils, large and small, were in theory free to dispose of their *propios*, they rarely did so, and in the time of Isabella and Ferdinand were still battling to defend them from the depredations of members of the upper nobility and their local allies. In addition to the lands which were administered by councils, many towns and villages also had the use of common grazing, known in Castile as the *ejido*. The name derived from the Latin *exitus*, and correctly indicates that this multi-purpose land was normally to be found on the road out of the centre of population concerned. Use of the *ejido* was normally restricted to permanent inhabitants (*vecinos*) of the place concerned, although, as with citizenship itself, such rights might be acquired by incomers and 'strangers' (*forasteros*) in return for the fulfilment of certain conditions. While the *ejido* was open land, other areas were enclosed as *dehesas* (from the Latin *defensa*, which had the same meaning). Nearly all Castilian municipalities had at least one common *dehesa*, though others might be part of the public *propios* or in private possession. Traditionally, the most common use for such an enclosure was as a *dehesa boyal*, to graze the plough oxen belonging to the town or village concerned. Such lands might also be used by butchers for the grazing of animals, or for horses and mules. Other enclosures, known in Castile as *cotos*, were often used for crops, while higher-quality pastures, or *prados*, generally beside rivers or streams, were also enclosed. The various types of *monte* were also normally open for common use, sometimes including the growing of crops, while better-quality cultivated commons were subject to complicated rules, because the cycle of their occupation was lengthy. A single area of pastureland might be used by a large number of animals, while only one individual or group could sow and reap a crop. In thinly populated areas, customs might remain simple and unwritten, but increasing pressure on space, especially around the larger centres of population, in the early sixteenth century, raised tensions generically between pastoralists and cultivators, and specifically between individuals and groups. In this sense, there were 'frontiers' throughout Spain, and not only on the border of the former Nasrid kingdom of Granada.

Few historians of any country can have achieved such a dominance over their subject as did Julius Klein, with his study, published in 1920, of the great Castilian association of graziers known as the 'Mesta'. Standard textbooks in English continue to reflect his overall conclusions concerning the character of the organization and the Catholic Monarchs' attitude towards it. Hillgarth affirms that 'The serious deforestation of Castile largely began with Isabella's laws favouring the Mesta. Any local attempts to improve agriculture, as in Murcia and Granada, were hampered because they interfered with the same organisation.' For Kamen, support of the Mesta was indeed an essential part of Ferdinand and Isabella's economic strategy. 'Through the Mesta the Catholic Kings got monopoly control of wool but their main objective was fiscal', in other words to increase their income from the main Castilian tax on the movement of livestock, the *servicio y montazgo* (see below). Yet he rightly observes that the traditional view of the Mesta as a general destroyer of agriculture is 'incorrect and misleading'. The organization of the Mesta, as classically defined by Klein and discussed by Jaime Vicens Vives, who described it as 'the most important and most original feature of the Castilian economy in the Late Middle Ages', adopted its national character in the thirteenth century. In 1273, Alfonso X consolidated existing local associations of shepherds and graziers as 'The honourable council of the Mesta of the shepherds of Castile' (*El honrado concejo de la Mesta de los pastores de Castilla*). The king's motive was evidently selfish and financial, and the main function of the new association was to organize and supervise the sheep-runs, or *cañadas*, which traversed the kingdom from north to south, and which were the routes of the transhumant flocks which migrated between their summer grazing in the north and their winter grazing in the south. The main *cañadas reales* were between León and Extremadura, between Logroño and the Guadarrama mountains via Avila and Segovia with various branches, and from Cuenca through La Mancha either to Murcia or to Andalusia. Flocks left their winter grazing in April, and were sheared of their vital wool crop while on the journey north. This was done either while they were crossing the sierra or once they had arrived, by August, in the summer pastures, or *agostaderos*. In 1492, the Catholic Monarchs issued a new statute to govern the operation of the Mesta, which probably largely confirmed the existing law of 1379. To be a 'brother (*hermano*) of the Mesta', one had to possess a transhumant, or migratory, flock and pay tax on it, the *servicio de ganado*, to the Crown. The brothers met twice a year, once in the south, in January or February, usually at Villanueva de la Serena where the Mesta archive was kept, and again in the north in September or later in the autumn, at various places including Segovia and Medina del Campo. To be quorate, forty brothers had to be present, though usually about ten per cent of the total membership of 3000 attended. Voting was by groups or *cuadrillas*. Though they also had to deal with the impact of royal legislation and protests about the behaviour of the Mesta flocks and their shepherds, internal affairs generally dominated the agenda. During Ferdinand and Isabella's reign, the old Castilian system of open elections was replaced by the drawing of lots from an urn, in the Aragonese manner. As with other aspects of the office-holding system of the period, the patronage of the high and mighty was an increasingly important aspect of the procedure. To support the *entregador principal*, or president of the Mesta, there were four *alcaldes de cuadrilla*, also known simply as *alcaldes de la Mesta*, who each had charge of one of the *cabañas* (León, Segovia, Soria and Cuenca), and also various judges, representatives of the brothers, and collectors of revenues. In his seminal study of the organization, Klein presented the Mesta as a democratic institution, in which the Castilian upper nobility had only limited influence, but later scholars, from Vicens Vives to Gerbet, have pointed out that the evidence does not sustain this interpretation. In reality, the flocks of the nobles, which might each number 30,000 or more, dominated the livestock industry and wool trade in the late fifteenth and early sixteenth centuries. Although the numbers of transhumant sheep seem to have declined during the turbulent years of Henry IV's reign, in 1477 the nontheless massive total of 2,694,032 head was recorded by the collectors of the royal *servicio y montazgo*, a tax paid at the passes (*puertos*) which constituted the official taxpoints. By 1519, the total thus recorded had reached 3,177, 669 head.[5]

The 1492 compilation of the laws of the Mesta, known as the 'law of possession' (*ley de posesión*), aimed to avoid all competition between the brothers themselves to secure winter *dehesas* or summer pastures. Mesta officials were to allocate pastures and brothers were not to dispute what they received. Both the laws of the national body and the considerable documentation which survives concerning local disputes indicate, however, that such conflicts over the allocation of grazing land were not confined to the brothers of the Mesta itself. In 1497, for instance, the Extremaduran town of Cabeza de Buey found itself in a legal dispute with the Mesta which reached the royal council. The national organization was accused of threatening local graziers that, if they did not become its 'brothers', they would be deprived of all opportunity to pasture their flocks elsewhere. Livestock owners who rented pasture faced fines if they did not join the Mesta. Within the brotherhood itself, disputes and legislation both before and after 1500 show that members were constantly seeking to secure the tenancy or possession of pasture at the expense of others, often 'reselling' such land for profit. By 1502, the leadership of the Mesta was aware that individuals who had only the most tenuous connection with the livestock industry were engaging in this kind of transaction. Although Isabella and Ferdinand are traditionally viewed as having been favourable to stockbreeders in general, and the national Mesta in particular, more recent research has suggested that the Crown, while evidently interested in the taxation revenue which was supplied by the movement of sheep, in the form both of *alcabala* and of *servicio y montazgo*, was also concerned to achieve a balance between pastoralists and cultivators. It is evident that a transhumant system of grazing, such as that of Castile, and the more localized arrangements which linked southern France with Aragon and Catalonia, depended upon the existence of arrangements for grazing in each place. In the case of Castile, while the national Mesta was established in 1273 at the latest, the early fourteenth century saw the growth of local 'mestas' in Andalusia, whose flocks were described as *travesíos*, and which, by 1500, extended throughout the region. A limited number of such institutions developed to the north of the Sierra Morena, in New and Old Castile. The Andalusian municipal mestas resulted from agreements between local municipal councils and stockbreeders, whose interests were generally well represented in those assemblies (*concejos*). As with the national body, they had a democratic appearance, even though so much of the land and assets of the region were in the hands of a small number of individuals and families who dominated both towns and countryside. Their primary purpose was to supervise all grazing and livestock within their jurisdiction, and they acted as a sort of buffer between the local graziers and the national Mesta, but also on occasions as intermediaries between humbler people with livestock and the leading stockbreeders (*señores de ganados*). Between 1496 and 1504, a number of local associations of this kind received royal authorization, for example in the area around Córdoba. Examples of such local associations in the north of Castile are to be found in the region of Soria, where non-transhumant flocks (*ganado estante*) achieved considerable numbers, alongside those which took part in the national system of Mesta *cañadas*. In addition to the Mesta flocks, it is estimated that there were two million head of *ganado estante* in Castile in this period. It is evident that livestock was taken out of Isabella's kingdom in this period, generally illegally, as such animals were normally included among the 'forbidden things' (*cosas vedadas*) which might not be exported.

Conflict between pastoralists and cultivators is already recorded in the book of Genesis, and was extensive in the Spain of Ferdinand and Isabella, not least because of the expansion of population in Andalusia. While sheep, and goats, are prominent in the documents, and hence in the historiography, there was also much demand in this period for grazing for cattle, including the plough oxen which have already been noted. In Córdoba, cattle not only provided meat and dairy products, but also supplied hides for the use of the leather industry, which in this period was increasingly using cow-hide rather than the product of sheep and goats. To meet the growing demand, ranching methods were developed in southern and western Spain which were later readily transferred to the New World. Especially in Andalusia and Extremadura, the general anxiety to increase the space available to graze cattle and sheep, which was stimulated both by an increasing population and by industrial demand, led to growing pressure to enclose land and thus deny historic common rights. The problem is illustrated by the series of documents which Ferdinand and Isabella's administration issued with the aim of protecting public lands and restricting the activities of private enclosers. On 28 September 1490, for instance, the Crown issued an order forbidding the citizens of Córdoba and its *tierra* to enclose more than a quarter of their land, and requiring them to allow the *vecinos* of the city and its outlying possessions to exercise traditional common rights. In the context of Andalusia, these consisted of hunting birds and rabbits (rights to hunt larger game were severely restricted), fishing, picking asparagus and other wild plants, gleaning and gathering hay. In November of that year, a further royal document mentioned explicitly the connection between the anxiety to fence in more land and Castile's expanding wool trade (see below). It referred to complaints received by the royal council that, during the preceding thirty years, certain citizens of Córdoba, whose flocks had repeatedly damaged cultivated land, had purchased the broken-down vineyards and olive groves at a low price and turned them into enclosed pasture, which they had then further expanded by annexing adjoining common land. The offenders were said to have deliberately left gaps in the fencing of their enclosures, so that flocks belonging to other owners might be tempted in, and fines collected under the terms of the municipal ordinances. The response of the Crown was to order that all unlicensed enclosures made in the area during the previous thirty years should be returned to common use. This is a good example of the balance which Isabella and Ferdinand's government attempted to achieve between conflicting demands for land. In the case of a second offence, the stock-owner was to lose all right to the land concerned. This policy was consolidated in a royal pragmatic, issued at Valladolid on 15 July 1492, which restricted the proportion of land held within the municipal boundary which might be enclosed in *dehesas* to a half for *vecinos*, a quarter for non-citizens resident in the town concerned, and an eighth for absentees. Further measures to obstruct the renting of grazing by outsiders were put in place in Córdoba in 1495 and 1499. Quotas were set for the import of stock to graze the city's *dehesas*. Evidently, such pressure on the use of pasture resulted from a combination of local demand and the needs of the national Mesta, which led both to attempted restrictions on the movement of livestock and to disputes over the boundaries between properties. In an attempt to reduce such local conflicts, the Castilian crown appointed professional judges, known as *jueces de términos*. These lawyers not only heard cases in the royal towns to which they were sent, but would frequently visit the disputed sites, sometimes hearing evidence and giving judgement seated on a boundary stone. In the years either side of 1500, municipalities were often forced to defend common land and *dehesas* against individual graziers of various social classes, though magnates and their lesser noble and mercantile allies, who were often themselves members of the city councils concerned, were the most conspicuous offenders. Against such political and economic might, municipal officials generally fought a losing battle, despite the intermittent assistance of the Crown's justices.[6]

In older Spanish historiography, there was a tendency to distinguish the Iberian peninsula from the monarchies to the north of the Pyrenees, on the grounds that the 'feudal' institutions of military service and land-holding which had developed in the Carolingian system and its satellites did not exist in the Christian principalities of northern Spain. Yet in all parts of the Peninsula, the vocabulary of what became known from the seventeenth century onwards as 'feudalism' was in common use. Men became the vassals of lords, to whom they owed military service and 'counsel', or advice, when required, and in return received, benefices in the form of lands and vassals of their own. During Ferdinand and Isabella's reign, their kingdoms remained a jurisdictional labyrinth, in which the main elements were lands directly under the Crown's legal control (*realengo*), lands under the lordship of secular nobles or the military orders, and lands in the possession of ecclesiastical corporations, such as cathedrals, bishops' households and monasteries (*abadengo*). Territory reconquered from Muslim states in the twelfth and thirteenth centuries was initially allocated by Christian rulers in accordance both with the need to retain and defend the new conquests and with current perceptions of the proper ordering of society. At earlier stages of the 'Reconquest', the part-time cavalry soldier had been given pride of place, though many peasants in the north of the Peninsula toiled on monastic estates. In the thirteenth century, however, the organization of landholding and government after the Castilian conquest of western Andalusia and the Aragonese–Catalan capture of the kingdom of Valencia both reflected changing approaches to tenure and social organization. In Córdoba and Seville, for instance, in the allocation (*repartimiento*) of land, which was carried out by agents of the Crown in the 1240s, holdings varied in size from the massive estates which were allocated to leading courtiers and foreign dignitaries, the latter quickly disposing of their gains and leaving the country, to small plots which were given to peasant farmers (*labradores*). Almost immediately, though, a property market developed in the region, and well before the end of the thirteenth century large tracts of land had been consolidated into estates which arrived in the hands of members of the nobility. While the late medieval Valencian nobility had jurisdiction over numerous vassals, many of whom were Muslims, in numerous Castilian towns and large areas of the countryside seigneurial jurisdiction had effectively replaced that of the Crown. Thus in Ferdinand and Isabella's Spain, in a manner comparable with other European countries in earlier centuries, the political and financial needs of their Trastamaran predecessors had greatly reduced the Crown's potential to control and direct the resources of the realm.

Although the whole of the fifteenth-century Castilian nobility claimed a common origin in the aristocracy of the Visigothic state, there was in reality little in common between its various components. The first such general characteristic was believed to be noble, or 'blue' blood. In his *Mirror of true nobility* (*Espejo de la verdadera nobleza*), Diego de Valera explained that in heraldry the colour blue represented a variety of concepts including heaven, divinity, loyalty and justice. Breeding, or lineage (*linaje*), thus remained an inspiration of much political and social activity. Nobility might also be conferred by the monarch, supposedly in recognition that the individual concerned, even though he was of lower status, possessed those intangible qualities of strength and virtue which made a person 'noble'. The second main characteristic of 'nobility' (*hidalguía*) was not moral but financial. *Hidalgos*, regardless of their actual wealth and status, were exempt from *pechos*, or direct taxes, levied by the Crown. While this privilege was of limited and diminishing economic value in Ferdinand and Isabella's reign (see below), it nonetheless retained its social cachet and was much coveted and fought for. Indeed, during the continued existence of the Muslim emirate of Granada before 1492, warriors (*bellatores* in earlier political treatises) continued to be regarded as the natural leaders of society. In particular, the small group of noble families which had been richly rewarded for their services by the early Trastamaran kings not only retained but strengthened their social and economic position during this period. Some, such as the marquises of Villena, the dukes of Medina Sidonia and the dukes of Medinaceli, succeeded, with the active help of their royal masters, in accumulating huge and continuous tracts of land, together with inland towns, ports and other economic assets, such as mills, wine-and olive-presses and even banks and brothels. The nature of the Reconquest meant that these upper noble families, some of which were to receive the title of 'grandee' (*grande*) during the reign of Charles V, tended to be concentrated in the southern half of the kingdom. In the north, things were different. In some areas, such as Asturias and the district of Trasmiera near Burgos, more than three-quarters of the population were designated as *hidalgos*, which inevitably meant that many or most of them were humble workers, engaged in non-noble occupations. In New Castile, Extremadura and Andalusia, the propor-tion of *hidalgos* to the overall population could be as low as 2.5 per cent. By law, a *hidalgo*, however humble his economic state, had in theory a direct relationship with the sovereign and might only be arrested by his or her express order. As a token of respect for his warlike calling, a *hidalgo*'s horse and military equipment were exempt from seizure for debt or for any other reason, and his supposedly noble blood meant that he was not to be tortured during any legal process. If a noble was condemned to death, he was beheaded rather than being subjected to the degrading punishments of hanging or garrotting. The government of John II of Castile had attempted to define the jobs, or 'offices', which degraded a *hidalgo* or, by being the occupation of the father of a prospective spouse, rendered such a marriage tie inappropriate. The examples quoted in the relevant law were those of tailor, leather-dresser, carpenter, stonecutter, digger, cloth-shearer, barber, spicer, retailer of goods and shoemaker. Less prosperous or dubious *hidalgos* might lose their tax-exempt status if they failed to maintain their horse and weap-ons or a permanent place of residence (*casa solariega*) in the place where they claimed exemption. The determination of disputed titles and the granting of new ones were the responsibility of royal magistrates known as the *alcaldes de los hijosdalgo*, who sat in a separate court, alongside the *oidores* of the *audiencia* or *chancillería*, in Valladolid.

Although, by the time of Ferdinand's death in 1516, about half the area of the crown of Castile was under seigneurial jurisdiction, only a small proportion of the kingdom's nobles possessed such a privilege, the rest living either in royal possessions or as vassals or servants of the great lords. As the main towns remained under the jurisdiction of the Crown, the lords exercised control over a minority of Castilians, and their legal powers varied considerably. In the early sixteenth century, some lords continued to possess their lordships (*señoríos*) as *solariego*, which was as near to full private ownership as late medieval and early modern states allowed, since it gave the lord direct possession of the land and habitations concerned, as well as jurisdiction over them and their population. In most cases, however, lords received from the Crown 'territorial' or 'jurisdictional' lordship (*señorío territorial o jurisdiccional*). This meant that the inhabitants of the towns and villages concerned did not necessarily become vassals of their new lord, in any personal sense, but simply went thereafter to the lord's court rather than the king's. A similar position existed in lands under the jurisdiction of the military orders. Some individuals did indeed become vassals of lords in the sense beloved of modern historians and in Castile, by the fifteenth century, they were generally rewarded for their services with payments in cash, known as *acostamientos*, in addition to the lord's protection. Also, some individuals entered into a personal arrangement of this kind with the monarch, becoming *vasallos del rey*. In their turn, leading magnates paid such *acostamientos* to their own crucial retainers, who had formed the backbone of the *bandos* which plagued much of Castile before the late 1470s. Most of the section of the population which was subject to seigneurial jurisdiction had no such personal ties to their lords. In the southern half of the crown of Castile in the late fifteenth century, this concept of 'territorial lordship' meant that the conditions under which the inhabitants held or worked their land were not altered when they were removed from *realengo*. Rather, the lord simply replaced the magistrates and courts of the municipal authorities which acted on behalf of the Crown. When a *señor* received the grant of a lordship, a specified number of *vasallos* might come with it, but they would form only a minority of the population concerned. This meant that most of those who worked the land within *señoríos* did not owe directly 'feudal' services to the lord, but instead had contracts under which they provided him with a share of the crop in return for long-term tenure, in the case of arable land, and shorter periods in the case of vineyards, olive groves and orchards or market gardens (*huertas*). Apart from overall control of their economic activities, lords received a share of royal sovereignty and jurisdiction, consisting of what was known to Castilian lawyers of the period as *mero y mixto imperio*, that is, criminal and civil jurisdiction. Such a delegation by the Crown of legal and administrative powers to nobles and military orders was in theory revocable but in Ferdinand and Isabella's reign it was almost unknown for such a 'feudal' right of a monarch to be exercised in practice. Notable exceptions were the removal from the Ponce de León family of the small but growing port of Cádiz, after the death of the hero of the Granada war, Marquis Rodrigo, in 1492, and the confiscation of Gibraltar from the dukes of Medina Sidonia in 1500. Under the rule of the Trastamaran dynasty, although the legal powers of the leading members of the seigneurial aristocracy were increased, the primary purpose of the development of the Roman, or civil, law in Castile was to strengthen the royal prerogative. Yet Roman law, as it had been developed by the administrative servants of the Crown, was in practice a two-edged weapon. Although it gave considerable sovereign powers to the ruler, it also permitted him (or her) effectively to dissipate that sovereignty, together with considerable social and economic resources, in grants of seigneurial jurisdiction. The recipients of such concessions of *señorío* also thereby gained authority over the collection of royal revenues within the territory concerned, and hence the possibility of siphoning off funds for their private use. In addition, Isabella and Ferdinand inherited a situation in which their predecessors had used their prerogative to assign additional royal revenues to individual nobles as *juros*. In this case, royal officials, or tax-farmers (see below) collected the money, at the Crown's expense, but paid it to the private beneficiary rather than into the royal treasury.[7]

Galicia, in the north-western corner of the crown of Castile, had a history, in the fifteenth century, of seigneurial violence, connected with the so-called *Irmandiños*, directed not only against the agents of the Crown but also at their own rural labour force. Although politically less significant than the upheavals in Andalusia, the disturbances in Galicia also required the attention of Isabella and Ferdinand at the beginning of their regime in Castile. Between 1467 and 1470, the activities of the *Irmandiños*, which were like an unruly parody of the Hermandades elsewhere in Castile, dedicated to undermining law and order rather than keeping the peace, were extensive. The *Irmandiños* were led by members of the lesser nobility of the region, who attracted support from the lower orders in both countryside and town, with the cry 'Long live the king and death to the *caballeros* (knights)'. During that period, the rebels destroyed over a hundred noble fortifications, forcing some of their neighbours to flee the region. Although the lords had largely regained control by the end of 1469, the potential for further violence in Galicia remained. Some of the lesser nobility in the region supported the cause of Joanna and Alfonso of Portugal in 1475, but once Ferdinand and Isabella had gained control, they were able to condemn the individuals concerned as rebels and traitors, using the opportunity to extend the power of the Crown. Most notably, they confiscated the possessions of the Crown's main representative in Galicia, Fernando de Pareja. Trouble continued, however, and in 1480, for example, the monarchs ended the long-standing insubordination of Hernando de Acuña, count of Camiña, whom they had previously named as governor (*gobernador*) of Galicia. Some individuals among the lesser nobility were executed as traitors, and forty-six seigneurial strongholds, or towers, were demolished on royal orders. The introduction of the new 'Santa Hermandad' to the region continued the task of restoring order and the Crown's authority, but this did not prevent Ferdinand from feeling the need, in March 1483, to visit Galicia in person, in an attempt to persuade the dissidents to recognize the authority of his governor, Hernando de Acuña. His efforts were only partially successful, however, and in 1485, rebellion broke out again among the Galician nobles, under the leadership of the count of Lemos; it was only a joint visit by the king and queen in the following year which brought the conflict to an end.[8]

The conflict which Ferdinand inherited in the countryside of Catalonia was of greater complexity than Isabella's problem in Galicia, in that it had some of the characteristics of a peasants' rather than a nobles' revolt. Although they never lived in legal servitude, for many centuries Catalan workers on the land, the *payeses*, had been subject to economic and social restrictions which paralleled those of France and Germany to a much greater extent than the equivalent conditions in Castile. The resulting laws and customs had become known to their enemies as *malos usos* (evil customs), and the most notorious of them was the *remença*, an often impossibly large payment which had to be made by a peasant or serf to his lord in order to be redeemed from his feudal obligations and gain freedom to leave the lord's land. Despite the devastating intervention in Catalonia of the Black Death, which severely affected the county-principality from the mid-fourteenth century, the condition of the rural labour force, which in other parts of Europe gained at the expense of their lords because of the resulting shortage of workers, did not improve. As far as the Crown was concerned, all exorbitant demands made of peasants were simply part of the lord's legal superiority over his tenant, which was known by lawyers, with disarming frankness, as the 'right of ill-treatment' (*ius mala-tractandi*). While, in the Middle Ages, the most downtrodden in society were not usually the first to rebel, the rural labour force of Catalonia, under the generic name of 'the Remenses', had already shown a willingness to resort to violence in the 1380s, a decade which also saw the Peasants' Revolt in England in 1381. As the fifteenth century proceeded, Catalan peasants continued to form illegal assemblies and organizations, with the dual purpose of finding ways of assembling sufficient funds to buy their freedom by means of *remença* payments, and of exerting pressure in other ways on their lords. As well as this serious social problem, Ferdinand II of Aragon also inherited a legal tradition which urged and supported the remedy of the Catalan peasants' grievances. While many lawyers backed the lords, others recognized the reality and the desirability of the right to freedom which was enshrined in the charters (fors). For example, the early fifteenth-century jurist Tomás Mieres, who helped to administer the royal estates, stated that the Remenses had the right not to accept laws which were contrary to the divine will, and that the king had a duty to intervene on behalf of any peasants who were oppressed by their lords, and if necessary free them from legal servitude. While such a stance might well have been based on moral criteria, it also offered economic benefits for the Crown, as did any measure which weakened alternative centres of power, such as the nobility, the urban bourgeoisie and the Church. Throughout the fifteenth century, up to the accession of Ferdinand with his wife Isabella, the peasants tended to distrust the Corts but put their faith in the Crown, as at least a potential protector.

In the mid-fifteenth century, the Remenses continued to be a well-organized group, and insofar as their anti-noble interests coincided with those of the Crown, they were able to gain some support for the redress of their grievances. By the 1450s, there were wide economic and social disparities among those who described themselves as 'Remenses'. While those from the Pyrenean region might be genuinely poor and under-privileged, others with lands in the fertile plains were very much more prosperous. As elsewhere in Europe, in that and the preceding centuries, it was the conflict between economic and social advancement on the one hand, and outmoded social divisions on the other, rather than straightforward poverty and oppression, which provided the main spur to rebellion. Ferdinand's uncle, Alfonso V, had generally sym-pathized with the grievances of the Remenses, since they did not, in any case, live on crown lands, though financial difficulties induced him to change tack from time to time, and give more support to the seigneurial nobility. Nevertheless, Alfonso never wholly abandoned his fundamental hostility to the Catalan ruling class, whether in town or country, and, at some point in the early 1450s, he received a delegation of Catalan peasants in Naples, apparently rebuking Italian courtiers for mocking their rustic manners. In 1448, Alfonso had put into effect a measure which had been proposed in the previous year, whereby pea-sants in Catalonia were allowed to form syndicates, which were to work towards the ending of abuses, and had the power to raise up to 100,000 Aragonese florins in compensation. Royal support for the efforts of Remenses to resist the institutions of servitude and buy out the lords' claims continued during the 1450s to be intermittent, and to correspond to immediate political and economic interests. Up to 1455, these were almost totally determined by Alfonso's need for money from the crown of Aragon to support his activities and ambitions in Italy. In that year, the king ordered the abolition of the *malos usos*, thus accepting the Remenses' petition of 1450, but this order was reversed in 1456, and once more reinstated two years later. During the Catalan civil war between 1462 and 1472, peasants in Old Catalonia had a chance to end, once and for all, the worst aspects of seigneurial power in the countryside. King John II undoubtedly needed the support of the Remenses in order to defeat the political elite in the Catalan *diputació*, but his allies received little reward for their efforts. Thus, while it should have been evident to observers that a solution of the problem of peasant conditions would form an integral part of any reconciliation between the Catalan nobility and the Trastamaran dynasty, no workable conclusion had been arrived at when the civil war came to an end. In fact, at a conference held either in 1474 or in 1475, John II made concessions to the nobles, allowing them to abuse their 'own men' (*homines proprii*) in whatever way they wished. He thus rejected one of the fundamental demands of the Remenses, and it was only after a further uprising, in 1484-5, that his son Ferdinand made a 'final' arbitration at Guadalupe, in Castilian Extremadura, on 20 April 1486.

Although the *sentencia arbitral* of Guadalupe appeared to be unique in medieval Europe, in that it abolished serfdom, at least in the case of Catalonia, the document neither ended seigneurial rights in general nor put a stop to the economic exploitation of the peasantry. In these respects, despite many decades of conflict, the parallels between Catalonia and the rest of Ferdinand and Isabella's domains remained close. It has been cogently argued that only the wealthiest Catalan peasants benefited from the Guadalupe *sentencia*, and that, as anti-seigneurial rebellions, the wars of the Remenses achieved only limited success. Although personal serfdom was abolished, the crushing apparatus of seigneurial rents and taxes, as well as other economic exactions, remained in place. Indeed, the Remenses were required by the sentence to pay compensation of 6000 Catalan pounds (*libras*) to the lords, for damage done to their property during the violence of 1484-5. In addition, the authority of the Crown was forcefully reasserted, with the imposition of a fine of no less than 50,000 pounds. On the other hand, the number of peasant rebels who were condemned to death was reduced from seventy-two to twelve, and the 50,000-pound fine payable to the Crown was balanced by the cancellation of the notional sum of 60,000 pounds which had supposedly been owed by the Remenses' organizations since the reign of Alfonso V. In addition, the time allowed for the collection of the money was delayed. In reality, though, Ferdinand's arbitration did represent a real setback for rural landlords in Catalonia. After decades of legal and physical battle, some arbitrary and abusive customs, such as the 'right of ill-treatment', as well as the notorious redemption payments, or *remenças*, themselves, had indeed been abolished. Like the laws which were issued in England after the Peasants' Revolt of 1381, restrictions which concerned social status, or the lack of it, were removed by the sentence of Guadalupe, while financial exactions, such as tithes, the lord's right to collect a share of the harvest, and payments for the use of seigneurial monopolies such as mills, as well as forests, pastures and other common land, remained in force. In rural Catalonia, as in so many cases during Ferdinand and Isabella's reign, if a revolution took place at all, it was a highly con-servative one.[9]

Despite the fundamental importance of the rural economy in Isabella and Ferdinand's kingdoms, their overall characteristics were those of a predominantly urbanized society. Although only two cities, Seville and Valencia, might be compared in size with the largest elsewhere in Europe, even the great bulk of the rural labour force lived in small towns and villages, rather than the scattered farmsteads and manors which were more typical of much of Northern Europe. A striking feature of urban society in fifteenth- and sixteenth-century Spain was the predominance of the military aristocracy in the towns as well as in the countryside. In Castile, the titled or upper nobility was very largely a creation of the Trastamaran dynasty. At Isabella's accession, in December 1474, there were forty-nine titled families, to which she added a further ten. The primary source of the wealth and power of these lineages was the Crown itself, and this royal largesse frequently included the opportunity to dominate, with complete legality, the gov-ernment of the royal towns. Although the possession of lordships (*señoríos*) by royal grant was evidently the basis of the upper nobility's activities, the grant to these magnates of offices which were in the Crown's gift, as magistrates (*alcaldes mayores*), or chief constables (*alguaciles mayores*), gave them a legal right to interfere in, and often to dominate, the affairs of the larger towns. While they possessed numerous castles and other fortifications in the lands under their seigneurial jurisdiction, the leading noble families commonly possessed houses, sometimes fortified, in nearby royal towns, which formed a convenient base for political as well as economic activities. They also benefited both from legal tax exemptions and from the ability to use surplus production from their estates to evade, and often control, the vagaries of the urban market. The stranglehold of the great families was thus almost complete, ranging from offices in the royal court, through the supervision of the government of the larger towns which remained under the direct jurisdiction of the Crown, to the control of human and material resources in the towns and countryside of thier lordships. In addition, their personal possessions, though not their royal offices, which nonetheless might be secured by means of the 'resignation' system (see chapter 2), were commonly transmitted to their heirs by means of the legal device known as the *mayorazgo*, or entail, which ensured that estates were transmitted intact to a designated heir. Combined with the readiness of both the Crown and the Papacy to legitimize their offspring when required, it was thus unlikely that a noble lineage would die out, and Isabella and Ferdinand did little more than confirm the power of the existing leading families. The financial fortunes involved, especially in the southern half of the crown of Castile, could be vast, though the limitations of the surviving records normally make it impossible to value the *mayorazgos* themselves in monetary terms. In Extremadura and Andalusia, for example, individual estates *excluding* the entailed property might in some cases be valued at over ten million *maravedíes*, as in the case of the dukes of Medina Sidonia. The goods included in the *mayorazgo* might be worth very much more, but the entail, being intended to keep the main family estates together, strongly favoured the eldest child over his, or occasionally her, siblings. The heads of these leading noble families, the future *grandes*, might have up to fifty specialized noble or non-noble servants (*criados* or *continos*), in addition to those attached to the households of their wives, whose responsibilities included the governorship of castles and fortresses, the magistracy of towns and the conduct of legal and administrative business in the *señoríos* concerned.

In the crown of Castile as a whole, although approximately ten per cent of the population in this period considered itself to be 'noble', the political and economic backbone was formed by the lesser seigneurial nobility. Like their richer and more powerful brothers, they employed the two devices of *mayorazgos* and the legitimization of bastard children to establish their dynasties and ensure their survival. In this process, too, the Crown co-operated actively, but in many respects the main beneficiaries were the leaders of the upper nobility. Not only did these 'middling' nobles, whether or not they possessed seigneurial jurisdictions of their own, form an essential element of the *bandos*, which dominated the politics of the earlier part of the reign and which were to reappear with a vengeance in the early years of the sixteenth century, but they also became the agents of the magnates on the ruling councils of the royal towns. Thus even when the Crown suspended upper nobles from their offices as magistrates and constables, as happened, for example, in Seville and Córdoba in the late 1470s, the magnates' friends, relations and allies remained as *regidores* or *veinticuatros* on the town councils concerned. Thus when the leading nobles began, around the year 1500, to intervene overtly once more in the politics of the larger Castilian towns (see chapter 9), they already had in place a solid network of patronage and power. Members of this group often possessed considerable fortunes in their own right. In Extremadura, although few of them had jurisdictional lordships of their own, an inventory of goods excluding the family house, composed on his decease in 1510, indicates that Hernán Gómez de Solís had possessions valued at over thirteen million *maravedíes*, a figure entirely comparable with those achieved by his social superiors. This fortune consisted of the lordship and castle of Salvatierra, worth 6,150,000 *maravedíes*, 2,400,000 *maravedíes* in *juros*, 1,750,000 in *dehesas* (see above), 2,600,000 *maravedíes* in the form of dowries for his daughters and 353,322 *maravedíes'* worth of movable goods. As in the case of the upper nobility, the value and income of lordship, the *señorío* itself, was by far the most important item. Among the non-seigneurial nobility, both in Extremadura and in other regions of the crown of Castile such as Andalusia, rents assigned on the royal revenues in the form of *juros* assumed greater importance, and while older notions of a 'service' nobility, in the sense of non-nobles who gained that rank as a direct result of royal service, may not be wholly applicable in the Castilian case, the dependence of all categories of the nobility on the Crown was undeniable. Even rulers with authoritarian instincts, such as Isabella and her husband, had neither the ability nor, probably, the will to prevent nobles from exercising political power throughout the kingdom. In the Andalusian city of Córdoba, for example, virtually all the leading noble families of the region were represented on the city council. The leaders of the two branches of the Fernández de Córdoba family, Don Alonso de Aguilar and the count of Cabra, whose *bandos* had plagued the city and its surroundings until the late 1470s, held special votes (*votos mayores*) in council meetings, in addition to their offices as *alcalde mayor* and *alguacil mayor*, respectively, from which they had been suspended by the king and queen. The latter measure scarcely limited their political influence, however, as this could effectively and easily be exercised through their faithful vassals and allies among the city's *veinticuatros*, against whom the Crown's *corregidores* found it hard or impossible to prevail. Thus it was not by means of possessing honorific titles that the Cordoban upper nobility exercised its regional power, but by 'retaining' lesser nobles (and all holders of public office in most royal towns in the southern half of the crown of Castile had to be nobles) with payments (*acostamientos*), as their *comensales* or *paniaguados*, who paid for their seat at the lord's table by voting the right way in the council chamber. The practice, whereby councillors and other office-holders in royal towns attached to themselves vassals or other retainers in return for payment, had been condemned as illegal by both John II of Castile and Isabella and Ferdinand, but the latter quite evidently connived at it in practice. While entry to the ruling oligarchies of the larger towns in New Castile and Andalusia was to become even more restricted in the late fifteenth and early sixteenth centuries, in the Castilian city of Valladolid, for instance, this period saw the increasing acceptance of those with genuinely mercantile interests among the 'lineages' which traditionally ruled the town. Already, in the 1430s, merchants, silversmiths and lawyers were to be found among the ruling elite, but the reign of Ferdinand and Isabella saw the 'new men' follow the precedent of the nobles and *caballeros*, in developing their own clienteles, though some of them, for example the merchant Luis de la Serna, came to the notice of the Inquisition in the late 1480s as possible 'Judaizers'.

In the crown of Aragon, the structure and activity of the cities and towns was as varied as the constitutional character of its distinct parts. In the inland kingdom of Aragon itself, although the population jealously guarded its political independence, the social and economic structure bore a strong resemblance to that of neighbouring Castile. Yet, apart from the highly controversial introduction of the Castilian Inquisition in 1484–5 (see chapter 3), this small and quite thinly populated kingdom had made little concession to the authoritarian inclination and policies of Ferdinand and his wife. The demands of the Granada campaigns had kept the king from Aragon, but the conquest of Málaga, in 1487, gave him the freedom to put this right, from his own point of view. On his arrival in that kingdom's capital, Zaragoza, in November of that year, he found much business to attend to. The kingdom was predominantly agrarian, and its seigneurial nobility, whose strength derived from the Crown, largely controlled the countryside and had significant influence in the few important towns, such as Teruel, Calatayud and Zaragoza itself. Yet the important difference between Aragon and its neighbour Castile was the much greater vitality of the kingdom's constitutional tradition, in which, as in some northern Italian cities and notably in Florence, nobles were not legally entitled to citizenship, even though they commonly had residences within them. As in northern Castilian towns such as Valladolid, mercantile, professional and, to some extent, industrial interests had long been directly involved in municipal government. The strength of the Aragonese constitutional tradition, which was to continue as a thorn in the flesh of Spanish monarchs into the early modern period, had shown itself in the controversy over the arrival in the kingdom of Ferdinand and Isabella's inquisitors. When the king reached Zaragoza in 1487, the resulting conflict still festered on, but he was quickly presented with an opportunity to reassert his authority. Two years earlier, on 5 January 1485, one of the constables (*alguaciles*) of his governor, who ruled in his absence, had come to blows with the senior councillor ('first *jurado*') of Zaragoza, Pedro Cerdán. The incident brought to a head all the existing tensions between the Aragonese constitutionalists and the Crown. While, at the time, the royal governor was forced to stand by while the *alguacil* concerned was tried and executed, on 14 January, for offences against the city, on 12 June of that year the main power behind the trial, the second *jurado*, Martín de Pertusa, was himself executed in retaliation. When Ferdinand arrived, in November 1487, his vice-chancellor in Aragon, Alfonso de la Cavallería, had acquired by means of the system of drawing lots, which was customary in municipal and other elections in the crown of Aragon, the office of first *jurado* in Zaragoza. The king took the opportunity, on 10 November, to force the city council to allow him to reform its ordinances, thus removing the influence of *caballeros infanzones*, the equivalent of Castilian *hidalgos*, from municipal office. With Ferdinand's presence during the late 1480s, the kingdom of Aragon, small in population but jealous of its constitutional rights and independence in a manner which perpetuated barriers to trade with neighbouring kingdoms, was partly brought into line with royal policies elsewhere. A Hermandad on the Castilian model was introduced, and the main institution of state apart from the Cortes, the standing committeè known as the *diputación*, was reformed. Little or nothing was done, however, to end the small kingdom's comparative economic isolation, and the merchants, lawyers, bankers and moneylenders, and other leading citizens of the main towns, continued to emulate, as far as possible, the values and way of life of their aristocratic neighbours, the *infanzones*, equivalent to the Castilian *hidalgos*.[10]

Inevitably, it was the much greater vitality of Catalonia which attracted most of Ferdinand's attention within his inherited domain. It has sometimes been suggested that Isabella's husband, influenced by his and his mother's experiences at the beginning of the civil war in 1462, conceived a great hostility towards the Catalans, but there is no solid evidence for this. Despite his lengthy absences during the Castilian succession wars and the Granada campaigns, he continued to take a close interest in Catalan affairs, and to raise hopes in the principality that he would regain the frontier territories of Cerdagne and Roussillon from the French, and restore the economy of Barcelona. When he succeeded his father as king in 1479, the great port was in severe economic crisis, while in the countryside the possession of large areas of land was in dispute as a result of the civil war between 1462 and 1472. While the grievances of the Remenses were still unresolved (see above), a bitter conflict had developed between the city government of Barcelona, led by the hundred or so *ciutadans honrats*, and the *diputació*. As soon as he became king, Ferdinand set about restoring alienated lands to those who had rebelled against the Crown during the civil war, and the *constitució de l'observança*, adopted by the Corts of 1480–1, largely favoured the former rebels. He also introduced, in the main Catalan towns, including Barcelona, Perpignan and Girona, an annual review of the membership of the body of leading citizens As far as rural matters were concerned, although a full settlement of the *remença* question was not to be reached for a further five years (see above), the economic difficulties of Catalonia had to be tackled at once. The export of saffron, traditional since the thirteenth century, had not taken place between 1477 and 1480, and German merchants had turned to Italy for supplies. Catalan coral fishers were suffering competition off Sardinia, and Barcelona was thus losing one of its staple trades. During the 1480s, declining trade and prosperity forced the city to abandon its merchant consulates around the Mediterranean, and traditional links with Muslim North Africa had largely been lost. In the central Mediterranean, Aragonese and Catalans were experiencing severe competition, from the Venetians in Sicily and the Genoese in Sardinia. During the Corts of 1480–1 the authorities in Barcelona told Ferdinand that artisans and their families were leaving the city permanently on every ship, and the king responded with a series of protectionist measures which the *consellers* had proposed. In 1482–3, the city council introduced its own programme of financial reforms and, despite continuing problems with the Remenses up to 1486, and the crisis over the introduction of the new Castilian Inquisition in 1484–7, the new measures were beginning to produce definite results by the early 1490s. Another delaying factor, however, was the rapid turnover of council officials and committee members, which resulted from the traditional system of annual elections. It may be argued that the recovery of the Catalan economy, known as the *redreç*, was already under way before Ferdinand intervened directly in Barcelona's city government. In 1485, cloth exports to Rhodes and Alexandria were resumed, and most of the consulates had been re-established by 1490. Ferdinand still felt it necessary to issue protectionist measures during the succeeding decade but, by means of a combination of his own efforts and those of the Catalans themselves, the Catalan economy after 1500 seems to have been in a very much stronger position.[11]

The relative success of the port of Valencia in the second half of the fifteenth century has generally been seen as at least in part the result of the problems experienced in Barcelona to the north. Historians have pointed to its comparatively stable currency and wages, and the massive loans which the city council was able to provide to the Crown in Ferdinand's reign. Yet the provision of these loans caused crises in the municipal finances, and had to be paid for by means of the assignment of a large proportion of the council's revenues to private corporations and individals. Thus, in Valencia as in Castile, public poverty came to coexist with private wealth. Money for public investment was scarce, and a highly necessary new port was not built. In addition, the kingdom of Valencia had long since ceased to be self-sufficient in grain, and shortages led to riots, for example in 1484 and 1503. The surviving registers of duty paid on maritime trade in and out of the port of Valencia, for 1459, 1488, 1491 and 1494, have the important limitation that clerks recorded only the last port of lading for each vessel, which was not necessarily the place of origin of the cargo concerned. With all their limitations, these statistics appear to show that, in the last quarter of the fifteenth century, Barcelona's share of maritime trade with Valencia declined from about a third to quarter, while the importance of Castilian trade increased at the expense of the Aragonese. Perhaps, however, it was the general buoyancy of Valencian economic activity which eased the king's difficulties in keeping the city under control, but in any case, the port was a bright light in the Spanish economy as a whole. It has rightly been stated on many occasions that Spain was a 'society organized for war', in which military and religious values prevailed over those of the market and the material. Yet even the activities of the eleventh-century 'Said' or 'Cid', Rodrigo Díaz de Vivar, and his cheating of the apparently Jewish merchants Rachel and Vidas, indicate inextricable links between the most idealistic crusading and what Marxists have called the 'material base'. The participation of mercantile interests in the government both of some northern Castilian towns and of the great ports of the crown of Aragon, Barcelona and Valencia, has already been noted. While the Catalan territories, including for this purpose the Balearic Islands, Sardinia and Sicily, remained locked into the Mediterranean trading system, with all its fluctuations, the economy of Castile in the fifteenth and early sixteenth centuries has been described as 'colonial' in character. The limited natural resources and the climatic conditions of that kingdom, together with its restricted industrial structure, opened up Castilian raw materials to exploitation by foreign manufacturers and consumers. By far the most important export commodity was wool, but Basque iron and Seville soap were also significant. Thus, although the growth of the Castilian economy as a whole had been fairly steady since before 1450, what was generally lacking was the exportation of finished products rather than raw materials. Even the massive production of merino wool in Castile, together with the fact that cloth manufacture was the most important industry in Isabella's realm, did not prevent massive imports of finished cloth from England, France, Flanders and, to a lesser extent, Italy. It has been suggested that Castile lacked a mercantile 'class', other than Jewish or *converso* financiers and traders, but the cases of Valladolid and Burgos suggest otherwise.[12]

By the mid-fifteenth century, there was a well-established mercantile group in Valladolid, which was regularly strengthened by new arrivals from other parts of Castile and sometimes from abroad, in particular from Flanders, France and Italy. The newcomers were attracted by the economic possibilities of a well- established urban centre, with the presence nearby of several noble households, regular visits by the Royal Court, the permanent presence of the high court of justice, the *chancillería*, and the holding of regular trade fairs. Nearly 150 names of such traders are recorded in this period, and they included cloth merchants, furriers, jewellers, silversmiths, spicers, moneychangers and two leading armourers. In about 1450, these major traders came to be known as merchants (*mercaderes*) rather than stallholders (*tenderos*). Whatever the economic activity in which they were engaged, as a group, these individuals and their families showed a strong sense of cohesion which, as in the case of knights and nobles, manifested itself in the dynastic accumulation and transmission of goods. In this process, they began in this period to purchase vineyards within the territory of Valladolid city council, though they do not appear to have invested in arable land or orchards and market gardens (*huertas*). In Burgos, too, members of the city elite had long been engaged in national and international trade, not least in the Spanish merino wool and in imported cloth from the Netherlands and England, which were traded at the great fairs in nearby Medina del Campo (see below). The mercantile interest was well represented among the *regidores*, and, as in other Iberian cities, there was a strong tendency for those who were successful as traders, bankers and lawyers to imitate the lifestyle of the nobles and *caballeros*, seeking landed estates and, where possible, marriage into the older aristocracy. By the late fifteenth century, merchants from Burgos had formed themselves into companies (*compañías*), on the model of the Italian *aziende*, and sought to control the towns on the Cantabrian coast, including the Castilian port of Santander and its Basque neighbours, Bilbao and San Sebastián, which possessed the fleets which landlocked Burgos required to transport its goods. This process involved political difficulties, especially in the case of the Basque ports, which jealously regarded their autonomous rights against Isabella and her Castilian subjects, but in the long run, the merchants of Burgos experienced no more difficulty in exploiting their inland site in international trade than had their Florentine colleagues since at least the thirteenth century, with Pisa as the equivalent of Santander and the Basque harbours. As well as seeking maritime outlets to the north, the municipal elite of Burgos sought to gain greater control over the production of the essential raw material of their trade, merino wool, whether from transhumant Mesta flocks or from *ganados estantes* or *travesíos*. As a result, Burgos merchants became particularly active in Andalusia. Their main settlement was in Seville, where they had become, by the end of the fifteenth century, the third most important mercantile community after the Genoese and the Andalusians themselves. No fewer than ninety-two Burgos merchants are recorded in Seville between 1489 and 1515, and they were involved with every commodity which was traded internationally from that city, including agricultural and textile products as well as raw wool. Further up the River Guadalquivir, Córdoba had, by Isabella and Ferdinand's reign, become an important centre for the collection and sale of the wool of all categories of merino flocks, from as far afield as Baza in the kingdom of Granada. The first recorded appearance of Burgos merchants in a contract for the purchase of wool in Córdoba was in 1486, but by 1515 traders from that city had apparently achieved a virtual stranglehold. The outsiders from Old Castile seem to have offered no significant price advantage to producers over local Andalusian cloth-merchants, but by the time of Ferdinand's death they felt strong enough to make contracts in advance to purchase the entire wool-crops of individual graziers for two or three years at a time. A number of the Burgos merchants, although they did not normally renounce their citizenship (*vecindad*) or, in some cases, their muncipal offices, in the northern town, nonetheless established regular contacts with Córdoba and district, either personally or through agents. Their importance to the local economy was evidently recognized by the city council, which of course contained a large number of wool-producers. Alonso de Castro, for example, was given permission to built a washing-house (*lavadero*), beside the Guadalquivir at Córdoba, to process the wool-crops which were purchased by him and his colleagues from Burgos. After the establishment of the merchant consulate (*consulado*) in Burgos, in 1494, several of its priors and consuls were recorded as trading in wool at Córdoba.[13]

Throughout southern Spain in the late Middle Ages, the most significant foreign merchant group were the Genoese. Their connection with the city dated from the later thirteenth century, by which time Seville was already the only regular stop for Genoese ships and traders on their way to England. In the fourteenth century, Egidio Boccanegra helped to establish the Castilian royal galley fleet there, becoming its admiral. By the time of Isabella's accession, Genoese merchant companies had established themselves not only in Seville, but also in Cádiz, and in Muslim Málaga and Almería. Genoese merchant companies (*aziende*), which were headed by a senior partner, or *maggiore*, gave their outlying branches a considerable degree of autonomy. Members of firms who were stationed in western and north-western Europe, from Almería to London and Bruges, were responsible not only for trading but also for gathering political and economic intelligence, so as to avoid crashes such as those suffered by the Florentine firms of Bardi and Peruzzi in the 1340s. Several factors attracted the Genoese to Spain, encouraging them to develop permanent colonies. These included the greater economic sophistication of the Mediterranean economy in this period, when compared with the Atlantic and Channel coasts, and limitations on Genoese expertise. While the citizens of the Ligurian republic benefited from the economic experience which they had accumulated over several centuries, they nevertheless required Portuguese and Basque ships to carry their goods. Also, Genoese ships were generally too small to sail up the Guadalquivir to Seville itself, calling instead at Cádiz or Sanlúcar de Barrameda, to load cargoes of grain, wine, olive oil, tunny fish, fruit, cochineal, wax, leather and silk. Both before and after the Christian conquest of 1492, Genoese ships also picked up silk, sugar and fruit from the kingdom of Granada.

The Genoese were mainly concerned, however, with precious and semi-precious metals. Among Spain's own natural resources were lead and silver mines near Cartagena, on the east coast, and important mercury mines near Almadén, on the northern edge of Andalusia. Earlier in the fifteenth century, the Genoese obtained from the Crown a monopoly of the Almadén mercury production, exporting much of it to southern Germany. The main attractions, though, were gold and silver, the hope being that African gold would balance their Venetian rivals' dominance of central European silver production. It was primarily for this reason that the Genoese established significant economic relations with the Muslim emirate of Granada, their main base there being the port of Málaga. The Christian merchants exported dark blue woollen cloth, Granadan silk, copper vessels and porcelain from there to Africa, the goods travelling along well-established trade routes to the Sudan. The main partners of the Genoese in this trade were the Muslim Maghreb kingdoms of Tunis and Tlemcen, and most of the African gold was landed in Málaga, Cádiz and Valencia. Already, by the late fourteenth century, Spain was the source of nearly all the gold and silver which were imported into Genoa and, in the 1490s, Ferdinand and Isabella's kingdoms, and Seville in particular, remained one of the main centres in Europe for the distribution of precious metals. Genoese merchants imported gold from Africa to Seville and exchanged it for silver, which was then exported to Genoa itself, to assist the republic in its trade with the eastern Mediterranean. This silver was often exported in the form of coin (*blancas*), which enabled the Genoese to profit from Castile's monetary problems in the mid-fifteenth century.[14]

The Genoese presence in the Andalusian ports of Seville, Cádiz and Málaga followed the same basic pattern. Seville was by far the most important Genoese settlement on the trade route between Genoa itself and northern Europe. Between 1489 and 1515, no fewer than 437 merchants from that city are recorded in the notarial records (*protocolos*) of Seville, though most were visitors (*estante*) rather than citizens (*vecinos*). A street, the Calle de los Genoveses, was named after them, they had their own church, and their statue of the Virgin remains in the city's cathedral. It is reasonable to assume that all, or virtually all, the males concerned were engaged in some kind of mercantile pursuit, and their colleagues and relatives also worked in the smaller ports of lower Andalusia, including Cádiz and Puerto de Santa María, as well as Jerez de la Frontera, which had a jetty, El Portal, on the river Guadalete. The Genoese community in Seville, with a permanent membership of about a hundred, was much the largest in the region, and even those of its number who did acquire citizenship there retained close ties with their home city, and, despite some intermarriage with the local lesser nobility, remained on the fringe of the oligarchy which ruled Seville, though a few became councillors in Cádiz and Jerez. Like their Spanish colleagues and relatives, the Genoese who settled in Christian Andalusia, before 1492, aspired to the lifestyle of the nobility, increasingly becoming rentiers of urban and rural properties. It seems that those who settled in the Nasrid kingdom of Granada pursued a similar course. In the last days of Muslim rule, there was a colony of about forty Genoese merchants in Málaga, under the authority of a consul and four councillors, which retained close links with Genoa itself. A few Genoese became involved in the economy of the inland city of Córdoba, including one of the ubiquitous Spinola family, Batista, who is recorded as a citizen (*vecino*) there in 1485–6. The importance of Genoese in the local economy in this period was out of all proportion to their numbers. As well as supplying imported grain to the area, and collecting the crusade bull in Córdoba diocese on behalf of the Church and Crown, they provided loans both to the city council and to members of the local nobility, as well as trading in cloth and silk, and supplying dyestuffs to the struggling Cordoban cloth industry. The services of one Genoese, 'Miçer Christoval', were so valued by the city's *veinticuatros* that he was made a full citizen (*vecino*) in June 1498, while in 1500, he and his compatriots were exempted en bloc from direct royal taxation (*repartimientos*), as though they were Spanish *hidalgos*. Florentines were also trading in Spain in this period, but their presence was insignificant compared with that of the Genoese, as were the other foreign mercantile contingents, including the French, Bretons, English and Irish.

While merchants, both native and foreign, were achieving dominance over essential trades and industry, such as wool and textiles, the Castilian crown retained considerable control, at least in theory, over crucial sectors of the economy. In the crown of Aragon, and particularly in the great cities of Barcelona and Valencia, mercantile elites had effectively seized this authority, though a strong guild structure remained as a thorn in their flesh which might be exploited, from time to time by the Crown. The nature of the Reconquest in earlier centuries had left rulers, and their national and local agents, with an interventionist attitude towards the rural, and especially the urban, economy. In the great cities of central and southern Spain, for example Toledo, Córdoba and Seville, Christian rulers in some cases inherited from their Muslim predecessors direct control over economic assets, such as markets for luxury goods (alcaicerías), central grain markets (alhóndigas) and workshops (realejos). However, just as the original distribution (repartimientos) of agricultural land after the conquest of western Andalusia was quickly altered in favour of the aristocracy, so in the towns themselves the royal economic properties soon found their way into the hands of nobles. In Ferdinand and Isabella's time, urban economies on both sides of the Castilian–Aragonese border displayed a sometimes uneasy mixture of public and private control. Both in Castile and in the kingdom of Aragon, a municipal official, known in Castilian as the almotacén, was responsible for the supervision of markets and trading standards. As its name implies, the office originated in the Islamic world, apparently in Syria, and its powers were extensive. In Córdoba, for example, although it had been in private hands earlier in the century, during Isabella and Ferdinand's reign the office was administered by officials (fieles) on behalf of the city council. Municipalities throughout Castile exercised the royal responsibility to assure, as far as natural conditions allowed, the sustenance of the whole population, but the political and economic power of the local nobility severely restricted the effectiveness of public regulation. Price controls on basic commodities, such as grain, wine and meat, frequently disintegrated, especially during the crises of the early sixteenth century.[15]

Similar tensions between government control and local and individual enterprise affected the labour market. Smaller centres of population throughout the Peninsula combined rural and urban occupations, while larger towns acted as marketing as well as political centres for their surrounding districts. Though the rural labour force was largely regulated by the seigneurial system, the traditional medieval organization of industrial and craft workers, in Spain as elsewhere, was the guild or confraternity. Although guilds in Castilian towns did not generally achieve the economic power and political influence which they had obtained in Catalonia and Valencia, they were a common feature of urban life. The late medieval guild commonly combined the functions of a workers' association, with the aims of securing fair conditions of trade and levels of remuneration. As a religious association, a guild had the additional purpose of providing for its members during life and praying for their souls after death. In Castilian, such bodies were known indiscriminately as *gremios* (guilds) and *cofradías* (confraternities). It has sometimes been suggested that Ferdinand and Isabella saw guilds as an obstruction to royal power and sought to weaken them, but evidence in the textile industry does not support such a vew. In Castilian towns such as Valladolid in the north, and Córdoba in the south, cloth-workers were organized into guilds by trade, for example weavers, dyers, fullers and shearers. Responsibility for regulating the industry was shared between the guilds and the municipal authorities. In Córdoba, the 1435 ordinances were confirmed by Ferdinand in 1483, but all the cloth-manufacturing cities were subject in 1500 to a royal examination of the regulation of the industry. The result of this investigation was greater municipal control, the guilds being required to co-operate more closely with the councils and their inspectors (*veedores*). Both royal and local authorities intervened in this period in an attempt to control and improve the quality of the cloth produced, and to regulate the dyestuffs which might greatly increase its monetary value. New royal ordinances for the regulation of the Castilian cloth industry were produced in 1511.[16]

In the Castile of the Catholic Monarchs, that part of the urban population which did not belong to the nobility or knighthood, the latter being obtainable by means of wealth in the form of *caballería de cuantía*, formed what was known as the *común* or *communidad* ('commune' or 'community'). Excluded from the political power which was exercised by the knights (*caballeros*), leading citizens (such as the *ciudatans honrats* of Barcelona) and merchants were the 'middling' people (*medianos*), who constituted about fifteen or twenty per cent of the population of the larger towns. This commonly recognized social category consisted of master craftsmen, small traders, and members of the professions, such as doctors, lawyers and teachers. The fairly comfortable economic state of the *medianos* was not matched by political power, and, especially in the first two decades of the sixteenth century, this situation increasingly caused discontent and instability. The rest of the so-called 'community' consisted of labourers in town and country and more marginal elements, often associated not only with poverty and illness, for which monasteries and privately-endowed hospitals made extensive if haphazard provision, but also with crime and prostitution. 'Travellers' (*vagamundos*), who often took to the road as result of the wars, and the social and economic dislocation, which were features of Isabella and Ferdinand's reign, were feared and legislated against by royal and local authorities. Prostitutes and their pimps (*rufianes*) haunted city centres, often, as in Seville and Córdoba, in the vicinity of cathedrals, and attracted at least the public expression of ire by churchmen and local councils. The Santa Hermandad did not lack custom among the bandits of the highways and countryside, for example in the Sierra Morena on the northern edge of Andalusia, and the arrival of Ferdinand and Isabella's firmer regime did not entirely end the attachment of straightforward criminals to the political factions of town and country. Efforts were made to regulate prostitutes (*mujeres públicas*) by concentrating them in public brothels, while periodic efforts were made by the constables to round up *rufianes*. Another element in urban society, particularly in the cities of the south and on the east coast, was slavery. In addition to Muslim captives, taken during the Granada campaigns, who were frequently ransomed in exchange for Christians, black Africans were brought to Spain and Portugal as slaves, mainly for work in households. In Isabella and Ferdinand's time, there were probably up to a thousand domestic slaves in Seville, including Muslims, black Africans and occasionally natives of the Canary Islands, and a similar number in Valencia, all apparently kept as much for social prestige as for their value as labourers. Few worked on the land, though the duke of Medina Sidonia owned 200 Muslims for this purpose.[17]

Acutely aware, both of Spain's importance in the distribution of gold and silver and of the need for a stable currency to foster international trade, the Catholic Monarchs took an active interest in the value of the coinage of their realms, as was their 'regalian' right as sovereigns. In this respect also, the crowns of Castile and Aragon remained entirely separate, since, while the currencies of Aragon and the Catalan territories formed part of the Carolingian sterling area, the Castilian currency was derived from the historic monetary system of western Islam. In Ferdinand's hereditary domains, all circulating coins were valued in terms of pounds, shillings and pence (*libras*, *sueldos* and *dineros*) as a money of account. Thus the Aragonese gold florin, which was a reliable trading currency based on the Florentine original, was valued at 16 *sueldos*, while the silver groat (*croat*) was reckoned at 1.5 *sueldos*. In Castile, on the other hand, the money of account in Isabella and Ferdinand's reign was the *maravedí*. Although it had long since ceased to circulate as coinage, the Castilian *maravedí* originated in the reign of Alfonso VIII, who, at the end of the twelfth century, issued a gold coinage of equivalent weight and value to the dinar which had been

minted in Spain by the Almoravid dynasty. During the thirteenth century, a coin equivalent to a half-dinar was minted in Castile, but also
called a *maravedí*. At this time, the Muslim dinar began to be referred
to as a *dobla*, a term still used in Ferdinand and Isabella's day to
describe a different coin. Not only did the Castilians imitate the earlier
Muslim currency, but they also continued to use the Islamic 'mark', or
mitcal de la ley, to weigh the metal content of coins. The Castilian mark
was thus smaller than that used in the rest of western Europe. Very early
in their reign, Isabella and Ferdinand issued a pragmatic, at Segovia on
20 February 1475, in which they made their first attempt to stabilize the
Castilian currency after the monetary turmoil of John II's and Henry
IV's reigns. They fixed the values of the gold *dobla*, or *excelente*, and
the silver *real* in terms of the *maravedí*, which had degenerated by the
fifteenth century into a base-metal currency as well being as a money of
account, at 870 and 30 *maravedís* respectively. Also in circulation in
Castile were gold coins of lesser value, the *enrique* and *castellano* (435
maravedíes) and the *dobla de la banda* (333 *maravedíes*). The most
important measure taken by Ferdinand and Isabella in monetary matters was, however, the pragmatic which they issued at Medina del
Campo on 13 June 1497. Its main provision was the replacement of
the *dobla excelente* by the ducat (*ducado*), based on the Venetian
original, as the main Castilian gold coin and measure of value for
internal and external trade. This internationally respected coin had
been imitated in Valencia in 1477 and in Catalonia, as the *principat*,
in 1493. The minting of double ducats and half-ducats was ordered, the
former becoming the most common. A revaluation in terms of the
money of account also took place, the new gold ducat, or *excelente
de la granada*, being rated at 375 *maravedíes* and the silver *real* at 34
maravedíes. Although the currency and valuations which were fixed in
1497 lasted until 1566, the Medina del Campo pragmatic was less
successful in stabilizing the base-metal currency, or *vellón*, which was
of much greater concern to the bulk of the population than the bimet-
allic ratio of gold and silver which preoccupied the wealthy in general,
and international traders in particular. At the cortes of Toledo in 1480,
the *procuradores* complained at a shortage of *vellón* in circulation,
which was making life hard for the poor. The specific problem was a
lack of small change, which was necessary for the transactions which
concerned most ordinary people, the practical solution being to import
low-value coins from other countries, such as France, Béarn, Brittany
and Flanders. Neither the 1480 ordinances of Toledo nor the 1497
pragmatic of Medina del Campo solved this problem, however, and
foreign small change continued to circulate in Castile for many decades.
Nevertheless, Ferdinand and Isabella did make a major contribution to

the well-being of their humbler subjects by ending the debasement of low-value coinage which had been an oppressive and destabilising feature of previous reigns.[18]

Although mercantile groups, both native and foreign, achieved some success and influence in certain towns, such as Burgos and Seville in Castile and Barcelona and Valencia in the crown of Aragon, the Spanish financial market in Isabella and Ferdinand's reign was not fully integrated for the purposes of international trade. Most financiers in town and country, especially in Castile, were either Jews, up to 1492, or *conversos*, who, if they traded at all on their own account, did so in local markets. Ample private capital was available to finance the farming of royal taxation (see below), but trading transactions between regions within the Peninsula or with foreign countries could usually only be settled at the periodic fairs, which were held throughout Spain. The most famous and important of these were the fairs at Medina del Campo, in Old Castile. Thus although banking operations, whether by Spaniards or Italians, were extensive, they did not constitute a coordinated system. It would be wrong to suppose, though, that sophisticated banking techniques were not used in Spain in this period. A case in point is Seville which, in the fifteenth century, was with Cádiz the country's 'gold capital', possessing the most important Castilian mint. The imports of African gold were primarily required to finance the activities of merchants, and many of them were valued at millions of *maravedís*. The Genoese needed the bullion to finance their trade deficit, since Spanish exports routinely failed to match the value of imports. The Seville banking system in the late fifteenth and early sixteenth centuries was somewhat primitive in comparison with those of Barcelona and Valencia. Throughout the fifteenth century, most of the lenders and changers of money in Seville were *conversos*. From 1445, they were under the authority of Juan Manuel de Lando, the governor of the city's royal castles and dockyards (*alcaide de los alcázares y atarazanas*), who was succeeded in 1482 by his son-in-law Gonzalo Ruiz de León, one of the king and queen's guards (a *guarda real*) and as well as being a councillor. The governor was responsible for licensing money-changers (*cambiadores*), for which purpose candidates had to provide financial guarantees. The approval of the city council was also required, and no one without a licence might set up 'a table, balance and chest to change [money]'. Seville banking in this period was almost entirely a local affair, just two Genoese becoming *cambiadores*, in 1500 and 1501, respectively. Those money-changers who did not work in the open air rented accommodation for their tables, balances and ledgers in private houses and shops. Little record survives of banking transactions in Seville in this period. The next category of banker above the *cambiador* was the merchant banker (*mercader-banquero*), who engaged in international trade. Successful transactions across political boundaries required links with other trading sites, in which the official prohibition of lending at interest by or to Christians was circumvented by skilful use of the currency markets. Thanks to the efforts of the Genoese, Seville had regular trading links not only with Barcelona, Valencia and Majorca, in the crown of Aragon, but also with major trading centres elsewhere in Western Europe – Florence, Venice, Pisa, Rome, Avignon, Bruges and London. In this way, Andalusia was fully integrated into the European economic system, though the flowering of the Seville banking system took place only after trade with the Americas was opened up by the Crown in 1504.[19]

Given the disproportionate survival of royal archives, compared with other documentary sources, there is a natural tendency among historians to see taxation not as a restraint on trade but as necessary for the peaceful and orderly functioning of society. Late medieval governments naturally encouraged this view of their activities, but, since the aims which they set themselves were almost entirely limited to the necessities of defence and law and order, it is questionable whether the revenues which they raised did much more than foster their own selfish interests. Nevertheless, the civil wars which preceded the accession to their respective thrones of both Isabella and Ferdinand provided a highly plausible reason for paying close attention to the royal finances, which were in a neglected and decayed state in both kingdoms. The possibilities and prospects in Castile and Aragon were, however, very different.

Not only were the Aragonese and Catalan lands smaller in area than Castile, but they traditionally resisted, through their constitutional representatives, the handing over of taxation revenue to their rulers. When Ferdinand came to the various thrones of this group of territories in 1479, Catalonia and the Balearic Islands were slowly recovering from the rebellion and civil conflict of recent years. As was traditional in medieval monarchies, financial aid to the king might be provided either by parliamentary vote or by means of loans. Subsidies voted by the Cortes or Corts of the different parts of the Crown of Aragon were notoriously hard to collect, and even the large loans made to the king by the city of Valencia paled into insignificance beside the revenues which might be extracted from Castile. The Castilian crown had established a strong system of revenue collection even before the accession of the first Trastamaran king, Henry II, in 1369, and no further innovation of any importance was to made in the structure of taxation until after the death of Ferdinand in 1516. In contrast to some other Western European monarchies, Castilian rulers, although they claimed 'natural lordship' over their entire kingdom, did not possess a personal domain of family estates, from which they might directly extract revenue under seigneurial jurisdiction. Although *realengo* was extensive, and contained the main towns of the kingdom, it did not normally provide 'feudal' dues in the manner which was customary in neighbouring kingdoms. The basis for the collection of most of the royal revenues in late medieval Castile was the Roman law principle that rulers might collect taxes by 'eminent right' (*ius eminens*), which was a political concept, not linked directly to the possession of land. What seigneurial rights continued to be enjoyed by fifteenth-century Castilian rulers were relics of an earlier period and of little current monetary value. They had, in practice, been replaced by the subsidies (*servicios*) which were voted by the Cortes. Up to the beginning of the Granada war, Castilian monarchs were also in receipt of the traditional *parias*, which had been offered by the Nasrid emirs to stave off Christian attack. Like other medieval rulers, the kings of Castile retained a set of 'regalian' rights of a financial nature, which were reserved to the Crown and provided further income and political influence. These included salt and the revenue from its workings and sale, the minting of coins, and special taxes and rights concerned with Muslims and Jews who lived as subjects of the Castilian crown. The poll tax (*pecho*) on Jews and Muslims was regarded as part of the royal treasury, in parallel with the Muslim tradition of treating Christians and Jews, the other 'Peoples of the Book [i.e. the Bible]' as subordinate and in error, but nonetheless entitled to religious freedom and restricted human rights. Thus the *pecho* on Muslims and Jews, which helped to finance the Granada war, was an equivalent of the Muslims poll tax, or *jizya*. In addition, and also on an earlier Muslim model, Castilian rulers claimed a fifth share, the *quinto real*, of all booty captured in war. This regalian right was to be of immense significance when Spanish 'discoveries' in America began to yield riches. The main basis of the royal taxation system in late medieval Castile, from the thirteenth century, was indirect, that is, taxes and dues on transactions involving goods and services, rather than direct taxation in the form of the extraction of revenue from subjects in cash form. Although most local tolls had been alienated to the councils of royal towns or to lords, the Crown retained the *servicio* and *montazgo* on the movement of livestock, as well as various internal and external customs dues, such as the *almojarifazgo* in southern Spain. In addition, the recognition by the Papacy of the Spanish Reconquest as a crusade had allowed the kings of Castile and Aragon to extract further revenue from the Christian clergy, in the form not only of the crusade tax (*cruzada*), but also of two-ninths of the tithe (the *tercias reales*), a device which was not available to their contemporaries in neighbouring countries.

Between the accession of John II in 1406 and that of Isabella in 1474, there was a decline of up to two-thirds in the taxation revenues of the Castilian crown. This catastrophic loss was mainly caused by the collapse of the yield from the main indirect tax, the *alcabala*, This was a notional tax of 10 per cent on sales and purchases, similar to the modern value added tax in the European Union, which had been established since the 1340s as the most important source of income for the Crown. Nevertheless, during Henry IV's reign, the *alcabala* still provided about four-fifths of the royal income, with various customs duties accounting for a further eighth, even though some such taxes, for example the duty collected on sea traffic in the Cantabrian ports, the *diezmos de la mar de Castilla*, had been granted to private individuals. During Ferdinand and Isabella's reign, the income from salt-pans and salt amounted to no more than 3–3.5 per cent of the total and that from the taxes on the movement of livestock to 2.5 per cent. Even before the approval by the Cortes of the ordinances of Toledo in 1480, the government of Isabella and Ferdinand had begun to restore the royal revenues to their former levels. Nevertheless, it was not until 1504, the year of the queen's death, that the yield once again attained its level of a century previously. Even then, the great bulk of the Crown's income came from 'extraordinary' levies, such as the income generated by the Santa Hermandad and the *pedidos y monedas*, or *servicios*, which were voted by the Cortes. Without these revenues, wars such as the expensive Granada campaigns could not have been fought. Even then, a heavy price had to be paid for the loyalty and military support of the seigneurial aristocracy, which continued to receive a large slice of the taxation revenue which was supposedly directed to the Crown. Such monies were paid out either as salaries for military posts, such as the governorship of royal castles and fortresses, or in the form of *juros*. Although the Catholic Monarchs made an assault on the practice of granting *juros*, under the terms of the ordinances of Toledo, financial necessity soon forced them to revert to the practice of Isabella's predecessors and make further grants of this kind, which were in effect sales rather than gifts.

The collection of royal revenues was always problematic, given the inadequacy of the royal bureaucracy. The farming-out of the collection of taxation proved to be the most efficient method of raising money, whether nationally or locally. In Ferdinand and Isabella's time, the collection of individual rents in Castile was auctioned nationally, once a year, in Valladolid. The successful bidders, who were generally a group of wealthy financiers, then subcontracted parts of the tax concerned to the localities. Thus the vital *alcabala*, which was supposedly a

single rent, was in fact subdivided by commodity, the rent for a particular commodity covering all trades associated with that particular
material. Thus shoemakers and tanners, for example, would pay the
alcabala on leather. It was evidently not possible for the bureaucracy of
a late medieval or early modern state to administer a tax on every
individual transaction, and in practice, local contractors for the collection of the *alcabala* would come to agreements with individual traders,
for payment by instalments, based on estimated annual turnover. The
collection of direct taxation, mainly *pedidos y monedas*, was delegated
to municipal councils, which were responsible for drawing up tax-lists
(*padrones*) of those who were liable to pay. The scope for abuse of this
system by the leading families is obvious and was not conducive either
to royal financial efficiency or to urban peace. In addition, the fiscal
burden in the crown of Castile varied widely between regions, largely
according to the government's view of their relative importance in
political and economic terms. Thus Galicia, as well as parts of Asturias
and the Basque provinces, were allowed to escape the payment of direct
taxation in the form of *servicios*, or their component *monedas*. Given its
overwhelming financial importance to the Crown, it was, however, the
alcabala which provided the best guide to the overall distribution of
the tax burden in Castile. The economic and demographic heart of the
kingdom was a band of territory running from Burgos in the north, via
Valladolid and Segovia, to Toledo, Córdoba and Seville. While Galicia's
contribution to indirect, as well as direct, royal taxation was relatively
small (4–5 per cent), the north-eastern dioceses of Burgo de Osma and
Calahorra, and the eastern dioceses of Sigüenza, Cuenca and Cartagena,
together provided about fifteen per cent of the total yield from indirect
taxation.

Even more fundamental than this conspicuous lack of equity between
regions was the gross unfairness of the distribution of the tax burden
within local communities. In addition to their responsibility for the
collection of money voted by the Cortes in the form of *servicios*, the
councils of Castilian royal towns had the power to raise, without
reference to higher authority, additional taxes or assizes (*sisas*) on
essential commodities, including foodstuffs, in order to supplement
their permanently inadequate public revenues. The need to levy *sisas*,
or *imposiciones*, arose from the inability either of the Castilian crown
or of its local authorities effectively to tap the resources of their wealthiest subjects and citizens. As early as 1438, a committee of the town
council of Jerez de la Frontera debated frankly a proposal in a petition
from two of its citizens that no council officer should use his authority
to gain exemption from taxation. These Andalusian petitioners thus
identified what was perhaps the main flaw of the Castilian taxation

system in the late Middle Ages. This was that, instead of making a larger contribution than their fellow-citizens to the public purse, the wealthiest Castilians used their power and influence, either legally or illegally, to pay less. The Jerez magistrates and councillors of 1438 admitted that they possessed no means of relating tax demands to ability to pay, and this situation had certainly not improved by Isabella and Ferdinand's reign. The issue was discussed again by councils, for example in Jerez and Córdoba in 1496 and 1508, but nothing was done to remedy this inequality. At the beginning of Spain's imperial period, exemption from taxation continued to be regarded as the natural accompaniment to financial and social success, and attempts to place information on private wealth in the hands of local, let alone royal, authorities were steadfastly resisted. In such circumstances public finance inevitably remained the poor relation of private wealth, and all measures to remedy this situation were thwarted by the largely unquestioned assumptions which prevailed concerning the nature of society. Rich men, whether Andalusian nobles or Catalan merchants, were indeed prepared to contribute, on occasions, to the public good, but they insisted that this should be done voluntarily, by means of loans and gifts, and not in the form of regular and compulsory taxation.[20]

In many respects, the conquest of the Canary Islands illustrated the problems which were later to appear in the Americas. The first agreement for the capture and occupation of Gran Canaria, in 1477, entrusted the enterprise to the bishop of Lanzarote, Juan de Frías, and Juan Rejón as military commander. In June of the following year, Rejón established the first Spanish town on La Palma, named Real [Camp] de La Palma. He had, however, to accept a royal governor, Pedro de Algaba, and disputes between the two men postponed the conquest for a further year. In 1479, Rejón raised further forces, with the help of Bishop Frías and a Genoese from Cádiz, Pedro Fernández Cabrón, but in the following year a new royal governor, Pedro de Vera, was despatched to the islands. He came with an impressive array of titles *gobernador real*, *corregidor* and *alcaide* – and a new expedition which was jointly financed by Fernández Cabrón and the Crown, funds from the latter source being administered by the chief royal accountant (*contador mayor*), Alonso de Quintanilla. Having unseated Rejón, who had previously had Algaba, Vera's predecessor as royal governor, executed, the new occupant of the post launched a war of conquest against the native Gran Canarians. By April 1483, success had been achieved, partly thanks the division of Vera's opponents into two parties, supporting as ruler Telde and Galdar, respectively. It took longer to subdue the native inhabitants of La Palma and Tenerife. Not until June 1492 did one of the victors of Gran Canaria, Alfonso Fernández de

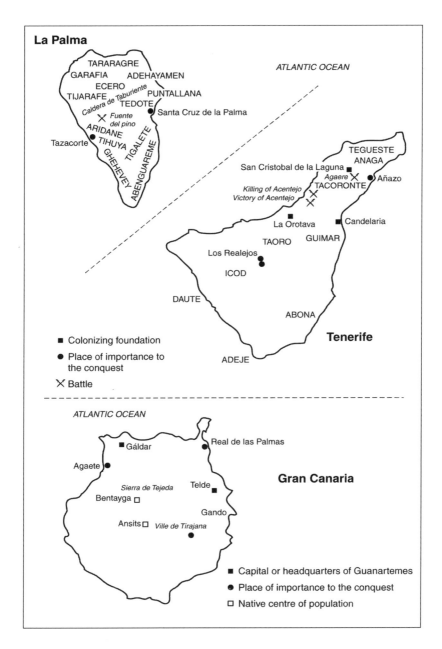

Map 3 The Conquest and Colonization of the Canary Islands, based on Miguel Angel Ladero Quesada, *La Espana de los Reyes Católicos* (Madrid, 199), p. 478.

Lugo, come to an agreement with the Crown for the launch of an expedition to conquer La Palma. This was undertaken by Lugo himself, with finance from a syndicate of Genoese merchants, began in September of that year and was completed in May 1493. Success was achieved with the help of Christianized inhabitants of the island, who fought with the Spaniards against their 'pagan' neighbours. Lugo then embarked on a similar enterprise in Tenerife, with new Genoese financial partners. In December 1493, he gathered a substantial army of 150 light cavalry (*jinetes*) and 1500 infantry, on board thirty ships. Once again, the help was sought of 'friendly' groups among the native population, especially those who were supposedly in the process of being converted to Christianity. The strongest opponents of Spanish colonization, who dominated the north of the island, inflicted a major defeat on the invaders in May 1494, at Acentejo, and the survivors were forced to retreat to Gran Canaria. In the autumn of 1495, Lugo returned better prepared, and this time succeeded in defeating the native Canarians at Agüere. Near the site of this battle, the town of San Cristóbal de la Laguna was founded, and soon afterwards, Lugo had the satisfaction of avenging his 1494 defeat at the very same spot, Acentejo. In May 1496, all the remaining leaders of the 'Guanches' surrendered to the Spaniards.

It is natural that the relationship between the Spanish colonists and the native Canarians in the late fifteenth and early sixteenth centuries has been compared with the situation which was soon to develop in the Americas. In both cases, Iberians met unfamiliar population groups, who could not be categorized either as 'Moors', the Muslim enemies of the Reconquest, or as *negros* (black Africans), with whom they increasingly traded in gold and human beings. There were, however, important differences between the respective situations of the Canaries and the Caribbean, where the Spanish first met those who were to become known as 'native Americans'. The Canaries, while being situated close to the African coast, were on average less than a week's voyage from southern Spain. They were also, of course, a very much smaller and more compact territory even than those parts of the Americas of which the Spaniards were then aware. The ethnic origin of the native Canarians is disputed, the main suggestions being either that they descended from prehistoric Cro-Magnon man (a suggestion also made concerning the Basques in Spain and France), or else that they were related to the Berbers of North Africa, who had colonized large parts of Spain during the period of Muslim rule. Whether or not for this reason, intermarriage between Canarians and Spaniards seems to have begun at once, though assimilation was not completed until long after Ferdinand's death. Given that the Canaries became, and indeed remain, a wholly Spanish, or Castilian, province, it now requires some imagination to realize that pre-conquest society in the islands was diverse and complex. It has already been noted that divisions between indigenous leaders, over politics and the adoption of Christianity, made the task of the Spanish *conquistadores* much easier. Perhaps surprisingly, despite their geographical situation, the native Canarians appear not to have been great sailors, and the communities on the different islands had generally developed in ethnic and cultural isolation from one another, for example the Mahos in Lanzarote and Fuerteventura, and Guanches in Tenerife. Not only that, but each island, apart perhaps from El Hierro, was riven by *bandos*, on a pattern not dissimilar to that which had been the scourge of Castile itself until the early years of Isabella and Ferdinand's reign. It now appears that earlier estimates of the pre-1477 population of the Canaries as between 80,000 and 100,000 are greatly exaggerated. In reality, it is unlikely that even the most densely populated islands, Gran Canaria and Tenerife, contained more than about 10,000 people each, and these figures were to fall quickly as the result of the introduction of European diseases, which at once reached epidemic proportions. By 1500, the population of the islands seems to have shrunk to a mere 7000, including some migrants within the archipelago, such as the people from Gran Canaria and Gomera who assisted the Spaniards in the conquest of Tenerife. The clash of economic and cultural systems which took place in the Canaries clearly announced the problems which were subsequently to face Spaniards and native Americans on a very much larger scale. In general, the islands before the conquest had lived in 'prehistoric' conditions, according to European criteria. Only in Gran Canaria and Tenerife had Majorcan missionaries in the fourteenth century achieved a degree of economic development on the European model. On those islands, barley was grown, hand-milling took place, figs were cultivated, there was coastal fishing, and European livestock, including sheep, goats and pigs (*ganado menor*) was reared. Nowhere in the archipelago, however, were the islands' immense forest resources exploited. As was soon to occur in the Americas, there was no will or desire, in contacts between conquerors and native inhabitants, for comprehension, let alone tolerance, of conflicting beliefs and customs.

The motives of the Spanish conquerors and colonizers consisted of the same mixture of 'material' and 'spiritual' motives which was to baffle modern students in the case of America. At one level, straightforward greed, as well as a desire to conquer, subjugate, exploit and enslave, dominated the minds of the settlers and the backers at home. Yet evangelization, the conversion of the Canarians to Christianity, which had been a priority in the fourteenth-century expeditions to the islands, still loomed large in Ferdinand and Isabella's reign. As was to happen soon afterwards in America, Spaniards, whether clergy or laymen, did not regard the religious beliefs of the native Canarians as serious or worthy of respect. In contrast with Judaism and Islam, the monotheistic faiths which had been their bitter rivals in the Peninsula itself, Isabella and Ferdinand's Christian subjects saw the pagan inhabitants of the archipelago as empty of 'religion' and ripe for the reception of the Gospel. Whatever Spanish prejudice towards them, the Canary Islanders did not possess any kind of religious organization to match the militant representatives of the hierarchical Roman Catholic Church. Instead, Christian missionaries were given free rein to work in the Canaries, and did so on the basis of a Castilian legal device which was to be much employed in the Americas, the *requerimiento*. This procedure, which was extensively used at home, consisted of the publication of a legal demand, often by reading aloud, by one party against another. In municipal government, for example, town councils might issue *requerimientos* against magnates or neighbouring councils, over disputed lands and boundaries. Within the Castilian legal system, the recipient of such a document was required to make a response in law. It is evident, though, that those who had such documents issued against them in the Canary Islands, and later in America, were in no position to make such a response effectively. In the case of the Canaries, the royal governor, Juan Rejón, issued a *requerimiento* which demanded that the indigenous inhabitants, being godless pagans, should accept both the Christian Gospel and the sovereignty of the Castilian crown. As in America in subsequent years, church leaders did, however, adopt, as part of their evangelistic role, a responsibility for protecting the native Canarians from abuse by secular colonizers. Without this ecclesiastical intervention, it is likely that those of the native population who survived the onslaught of disease would have been systematically enslaved, despite the prohibitions of the Papacy, issued in 1434 and 1462, and those of the Catholic Monarchs themselves in 1470, 1490 and 1499. Although many atrocities were committed against the native Canarians by their new Spanish masters, there was one feature of the post-conquest settlement in the archipelago which differed from the situation which arose later in America. In the case of the Canaries, the limited number of the native population who survived the tribulations of the period of conquest were successfully integrated into the settler community.

Nevertheless, by the time of Ferdinand's death, in 1516, the identity of the former peoples of the Canaries disappeared, either because of demographic collapse or through assimilation. As in the contemporary 'repopulation' (*repoblación*) of the former Muslim kingdom of Granada, subjects of Ferdinand and Isabella who came to settle in the Canary Islands did so on legal bases which had been laid down in earlier phases of the Reconquest in the Peninsula itself. Prospective colonists had to agree to accept parcels of land from the Crown on condition that they remained in them for at least five years, and took their families with them. It appears that similar rules applied in those islands which remained under seigneurial jurisdiction. Both Crown and settlers benefited in certain respects from the distinctive situation of the islands in which, unlike that which prevailed in the Peninsula itself, it was possible to built an almost entirely new society. The monarchs were thus able to evade traditional rights and practices which might have restricted their plans if such a thing had been attempted in Europe, while the settlers, of mixed origins themselves and in some cases inter-married with the survivors among the native population, were able to demand a light regime of rent and taxation. Nevertheless, the society which developed in the Canaries under Castilian rule bore an uncanny resemblance to its peninsular antecedent. Perhaps inevitably, a 'nobil-ity', not all of it with a legal claim to *hidalguía*, quickly arose among the settlers, including those Andalusians and Norman French who estab-lished themselves in Lanzarote and Fuerteventura, as well as the holders of the largest properties (*datas*) in Gran Canaria, Tenerife and La Palma, who also occupied administrative posts in the islands. The vital role of Italian and Flemish merchants, and their capital, merely served to emphasize that the Canaries were fully a part of the Spanish, and especially the Andalusian, economic zone. At the same time, many other settlers, both in the 1490s and later, received only small pieces of land and, as in the Peninsula itself in earlier centuries, some were reduced to working as labourers on the lands of others. Most of these humbler settlers seem to have come from Andalusia and Extremadura, but a number of Portuguese also settled in Tenerife and La Palma, generally to develop the cultivation of grain or sugar, the latter becom-ing an important industry in the islands. One result of the conditions of relative flexibility and freedom which reigned in the new colonies seems to have been that, at least in the early years, Jewish Christians (*con-versos*) were able to establish themselves. The Inquisition was not to arrive in the Canaries (Las Palmas) until 1507. Genoese merchants became highly influential in the society and economy of the archipe-lago, being largely instrumental in developing the sugar industry, which soon attracted mercantile investors from other parts of Europe as well.[21]

By the time of Ferdinand's death, the first phase of the Spanish *repoblación* of the Canary Islands had effectively been completed. The population of the islands was now approximately 25,000, a quarter of whom were native Canarians. These limited demographic resources restricted economic development and even the largest towns, La Laguna and Las Palmas, numbered no more than 3000 inhabitants. Tenerife was able to export grain well into the sixteenth century, because of its small population, and another consequence, which was a precursor of later developments in the Americas, was the importation of black African and Muslim slaves to supplement the islands' labour force. The shortage of workers also meant that the contracts obtained by Spanish and Portuguese settlers, as tenants and sometimes sharecroppers (*aparceros*), tended to be more generous than those available in the Peninsula. As the sixteenth century began, apart from sugar, the main exports from the Canaries were forest products, especially wood and resin, fish, and the valuable *orchilla* lichen, which was used in Spain to make dye for red and purple cloth. The islands were self-sufficient in basic foodstuffs, but it was mainly the sale of sugar, produced on much of the best land, which paid for the importation of manufactured goods, and led to the development of an infrastructure of harbours and roads. It was because of sugar that the Canaries became an integral part of a mercantile capitalist system which extended not only to Spain and Portugal but as far as Italy and Flanders. The islands also became staging posts on the increasingly important trading routes between Europe and the west coast of Africa. During the lifetime of Isabella, and even that of Ferdinand, although the Canaries experience provided some pointers to the future colonization of America, the island chain was mainly seen as an extension of the European economic system and a link with Africa. To emphasize the latter point, between 1499 and 1502, governor Lugo attempted to construct towers and establish enclaves on the West African coast between Cape Nun, at the southern boundary of the Muslim kingdom of Fez, and Cape Bojador, to the south.

The government of the Canary Islands, after the final surrender in 1496, continued to be fully integrated with that of Castile itself. The royal council of Castile retained jurisdiction over, and appointed governors for, the entire archipelago, also naming governor Lugo *adelantado real* of Tenerife and La Palma. The charter known as the *fuero de Canaria* was issued in the same form to the new Christian towns of the kingdom of Granada after the 1492 conquest, and the town ordinances of La Laguna and Las Palmas appear to have been strongly influenced by those of Seville. *Señoríos* in the Canaries were granted in exactly the same terms as in Castile itself. In addition, as in the case of the newly-conquered kingdom of Granada, the Catholic Monarchs obtained from Alexander VI the *patronato*, or right to appoint to all ecclesiastical posts in the islands (see chapter 6). Here, indeed, was a clear and direct link between European and American experience.

Despite efforts to claim him for Catalonia, or even as a crypto-Jew, there seems to be little doubt that Christopher Columbus was born a Christian in Genoa, probably in 1451, the year of the birth of Isabella, the queen who eventually sponsored his project to seek a westward route to Japan (Cipango) and China (Cathay). This scheme, which was based on a gross underestimate of the distance between Europe and East Asia (2400 nautical miles instead of 10,000), as well as complete ignorance of the intervening land-mass which was soon to become known as America, does not appear to have ripened until the late 1470s. Other notions which appear to have gripped Columbus, such as the possibility of meeting the mythical black Christian emperor, Prester John, who was believed to live in Africa, and the renewal of the Crusade in order to defeat Islam and restore the 'Holy House' in Jerusalem (apparently the former Jewish Temple), also seem to have matured as the explorer's career developed. In any case, it is evident that Columbus never realized that he had discovered a continent, and indeed, in the whole of Isabella and later Ferdinand's reign, the theme, let alone the reality, of America remained almost entirely marginal to Spanish life. Detailed study of Columbus's reading and thought has revealed that he absorbed a wide range of religious ideas and literary motifs from earlier centuries. He was influenced by earlier legends of the discovery of lost lands in the Atlantic, such as the story of the Irish St Brendan and the tale of the 'Fortunate Islands', a name which had earlier been applied to the Canaries. With the help of religious advisers in Seville and the Franciscan convent at La Rábida, near Huelva, Columbus also combed the Bible for messianic and eschatological prophecies, which he increasingly interpreted as referring not only to his royal master and mistress but also to himself. By the early sixteenth century, the Genoese adventurer appears to have believed not only that the last days of history were approaching and the second coming of Christ was imminent (beliefs which were common at the time; see chapter 6), but that he himself had a vital role to play in precipitating these events.

In more mundane terms, Christopher Columbus's first connections in the Iberian peninsula were with Portugal rather than Spain. In 1476 he settled in Lisbon, where he married Felipa Perestrelo y Moniz, the couple then moving for a while to the Portuguese Atlantic island of Madeira. When Columbus sought Portuguese sponsorship for his proposed voyage to Cipango and Cathay, the kingdom was engaged not only in a battle with its Castilian neighbour for maritime supremacy in the Atlantic, but also in a struggle for total control over its larger rival. By this time, Alfonso V had abdicated, and Portugal was ruled by his son John II, who had opposed the invasion of Castile, and was hardly

Plate 5   Arms of Ferdinand and Isabella, with (*lower left*) those of Prince John and Margaret of Austria, and (*lower right*) Philip of Habsburg and Joanna, later King and Queen of Spain from Queen Isabella's breviary. *Courtesy of the British Library*

likely to support a highly ambitious expedition which would very probably lead to further conflict with the increasingly successful regime of Isabella and Ferdinand. The treaties of Alcaçovas, in 1479, put an end to any such hopes, but this was not the only reason for the Portuguese rejection of the scheme. In addition, some of John II's counsellors believed, rightly, that Columbus's calculation of the distance between Portugal and Japan was wrong, and the conclusive factor was that news was expected imminently of the Portuguese' own expedition to India, which had taken the easterly route round the Horn of Africa. As the doors in Lisbon were clearly closed to him, and his wife was dead, Columbus crossed the border into Castile. He first sought support from magnates with interests in Andalusia and its maritime trade, the dukes of Medinaceli and Medina Sidonia, but was received by the king and queen at Alcalá de Henares, in January 1486. A new committee of experts was set up, but it came to the same conclusion as its Portuguese equivalent, and in 1488 Columbus abandoned Castile and returned to Portugal, though he also made unsuccessful overtures to the French and English courts. Finally, however, it was the Catholic Monarchs who gave the Genoese his chance. In the autumn of 1491, they came to an understanding with Columbus, which was implemented after the conquest of Granada, in an agreement (*capitulaciones*) made at Santa Fé, the former royal camp outside the city, on 17 April 1492. The Crown was to provide nearly three-quarters of the costs of the expedition, which were estimated at two million (*maravedíes*), and two caravels, the *Pinto* and *Niña*, based in Palos, while Columbus himself provided the *Santa María*. The generous treatment which the Santa Fé agreement gave to the explorer was no doubt due to the fact that neither he nor the monarchs and their advisers had any notion of the nature and significance of what he was about to discover. Columbus was granted the exalted title of 'Admiral of the Ocean Sea' (*Almirante del Mar Océano*), with the same powers in his particular sphere of operation as were possessed in Spain by the hereditary admirals of Castile, the aristocratic Enríquez, who were related to the king and queen themselves. In addition, he was given both the Aragonese title of viceroy (*virrey*) and the Castilian office of governor (*gobernador*) in all the lands which he might discover, with authority to appoint subordinate officials and jurisdiction in all trading disputes. The Admiral was to receive a tenth of all goods obtained as a result of his voyage or under his jurisdiction, and he was permitted to invest up to eight per cent of the capital of any company or enterprise which was set up to trade with the lands which he discovered.

Columbus finally set sail from Palos on 3 August 1492, his three ships containing a total crew of fewer than ninety men. The expedition headed initially for the Canary Islands, setting out westwards from there on 6 September. Just over a month later, on 12 October, they landed on the island of Guanahani, and named it San Salvador, today Watling Island, in the Bahamas. The ships then travelled past other islands in the chain and along the coast of Cuba, which they named Juana, before landing once more, on 6 December, in the island which they named La Española (Hispaniola), now Santo Domingo. There he left part of his crew, before returning across the Atlantic, first to Lisbon, and then, in April 1493, to Barcelona, where he and members of his expedition, together with some representatives of the native Caribbean population, were formally received by the king and queen, in the royal palace. Even though they did not realize the significance of Columbus's achievement, to the extent that the term 'Indies' was thereafter to be attached to the Caribbean, and later to the American mainland, Ferdinand and Isabella seem to have seen their own strategic interest at once. They sought diplomatic titles to the new discoveries from Pope Alexander VI, and attempted to renegotiate the demarcation of their interests in the Atlantic with their Portuguese rivals. Between May and September 1493, Alexander obliged with bulls which guaranteed Spanish rights of conquest over all the newly- discovered territories and gave them the authority to convert the inhabitants to Christianity. The terms of these grants were similar to those which had previously been made to Portugal in the case of Guinea. Alexander established the right of the Castilians (not the Aragonese or Catalans) to sail and conquer to the west of a meridian 100 leagues (550 km) to the west of the islands of the Azores, which were a Portuguese possession. John II did not accept these terms, however, holding to those of the 1479 treaty of Alcaçovas, and he succeeded in having the dividing line between the Spanish and Portuguese spheres of influence moved westwards to 370 leagues west of the Cape Verde islands, which were also Portuguese. It is possible that, apart from wishing to defend existing Portuguese interests to the south of the Canary Islands and along the Guinea coast, John was also aware that some of his mariners had already advanced as far as the coast of Brazil, although the beginning of that colony is officially dated in 1500. In any case, the famous treaty of Tordesillas (1494) established the partition of lands, seas and political economic interests between the rival Iberian kingdoms which has influenced world history until this day.

Columbus had in the meantime set sail, in September 1493, on a second and much larger expedition, with 17 ships and about 1500 men. Although his main aim was to colonize his existing discoveries, he also found more Caribbean islands and what was to become Puerto Rico. On his third voyage, which began in May 1498, he headed further south, discovering Trinidad, and navigating the estuary of the Orinoco, which he took to be one of the rivers of Paradise, and also part of the coast of modern Venezuela. By this time, however, Columbus's political fortunes had already begun to decline, and, apart from the efforts of explorers working for other countries, such as John Cabot and Vasco da Gama, by 1499 the newly-designated 'Catholic Monarchs' were themselves authorizing others to make expeditions to what was soon to become known as the 'New World'. Thus, as the sixteenth century began, Alonso de Ojeda, Juan de la Cosa, Pero Alonso Niño, and Vicente Yáñez Pinzón succeeded in exploring the entire coast of America between Trinidad and the Amazon. Meanwhile, in 1501 and 1503, under Portuguese patronage, the Italian explorer who was to give his name to the continent, Amerigo Vespucci, sailed along the coast of Brazil. Thanks to the efforts of these explorers, and in particular of Vespucci and Juan de la Cosa, the realization dawned that the new discoveries which were being made by the Iberian kingdoms and their agents were not in Asia but in a previously unknown contient. Indeed, it was Cosa who, as early as 1500, produced the first map of the 'New World'. Still, though, in his fourth and last voyage, in 1502, Columbus explored the coast of modern Honduras in the vain search for a passage westwards to his Asian dream. Events had, by this time passed the brave 'Admiral' by. Between Isabella's death in 1504 and that of her husband, twelve years later, a succession of explorers visited and mapped out the entire Caribbean, still looking for a way through to the Spice Islands and Asia. In 1513, Vasco Núñez de Balboa had his first view of the Pacific Ocean, which he called the 'Mar del Sur' (Southern Sea), while Juan Ponce de León began to explore the coast of modern Florida, and, in 1516, Juan Díaz de Solís reached the River Plate (Río de la Plata), between modern Argentina and Uruguay.

Apart from his enthusiastic self-education, his mystical and visionary religious views, and his impressive ability as a sailor and leader of men, Christopher Columbus did his best to exploit his position as viceroy and governor. He set up his headquarters in Hispaniola, with the help of his brothers [Bartolomé], whom he made *adelantado*, and Diego. In his obsessive quest for wealth in general, and gold in particular, which were needed to satisfy his masters and public at home as well as his own greed, Columbus and his regime were guilty of committing, or at least of condoning, grave abuses against the native inhabitants of the Caribbean. The exploitative working practices, even on occasions including slavery, although this was officially banned by Ferdinand and Isabella, soon led to violent confrontations between Spaniards and Caribs, as well as disease and often death. Christopher's powers were confirmed by the Crown in 1497, but complaints against his administration mounted, and conflicts soon broke out among the colonists themselves. A new royal governor, Francisco de Bobadilla, was sent out, and in 1500 he went so far as to send Columbus back to Spain in chains, to be tried and punished for his misdemeanours. In the event, the great discoverer lost all his governmental powers and rights, but was allowed to keep his title of admiral. In 1501, Bobadilla was succeeded as governor in Hispaniola by Nicolás de Ovando, but in 1508 the office of viceroy was restored and given to Christopher's son Diego, who held it until 1515, but with much reduced powers. As a further check on the activities of the colonists and their local officials, a new High Court (Audiencia Real) was set up in Santo Domingo, in 1511. Although some discoverers were allowed to become governors, on behalf of the Crown, of the lands which they had found, the growth of royal control over the New World was inexorable. As early as 1503, overall control of all trade between the colonies and Spain was vested in the Casa de Contratación in Seville, which in 1510 issued a set of ordinances to regulate it. The future bishop Juan Rodríguez de Fonseca, and the royal secretary Lope de Conchillos, worked to ensure that the royal exchequer duly received its fifth share, the *quinto real*, of the proceeds from the New World, especially precious metals.

By the time of Ferdinand's death, the outline of the problems which were to afflict the American colonies of Spain was already in place. Those of the Catholic Monarchs' subjects who went west to settle in the Caribbean islands (and demand for such colonizers grew in proportion to the decline of the indigenous population through exploitation and disease) inevitably took with them the values of their home society. Given the prominence of Andalusia in the political, military and economic activity of Ferdinand and Isabella's Spain, it was perhaps inevitable that most of the trade with the Indies should be carried from Seville and its outports, including Huelva, Palos, Sanlúcar de Barrameda and Cádiz, and that large numbers of settlers should come from that region. Also prominent as a source of colonists was Extremadura, while others emigrated from Castile itself and León. Aragonese and Catalans were conspicuously absent in the early years of the enterprise. A conflict quickly arose, not simply between the colonists and the Crown, which attempted, often vainly, to control them, but also over the ethical standards which were to be applied in the new settlements, especially towards the indigenous population. The junta of Burgos, in 1512, established laws which were intended to regulate such matters and, although European diseases, such as smallpox and the plague, before long eliminated the native Caribbean population, with the help of the cruelty of the colonists, such legal and humanitarian standards were to remain on the Crown's political agenda during the succeeding centuries.

Behind the concerns of the Catholic Monarchs and their successors for the good of native Americans was the religious priority, which was to spread the light of the Christian Gospel among them. While the long-term economic consequences of the new Spanish Empire were yet to be realised or understood, its religious imperatives were already firmly in place when Ferdinand died.[22]

6

Christians, Jews and Muslims

No country in late medieval Europe had a more self-consciously Christian identity than Spain. To the cost of adherents of the other two mono-theistic faiths of the family of Abraham, Jews and Muslims, the Christian majority among the population of the Spanish kingdoms defined its own identity in terms of opposition to the 'enemies of Christ', among whom their non-Christian neighbours were included. The warfare for which medieval Spanish society was organized was thus what had been known since the eleventh century as the Crusade against the infidel. Isabella and Ferdinand inherited a part of the Catholic Chruch within their boundaries which was wealthy, powerful, and deeply rooted within the institutions and values of their kingdoms. As in the rest of the Western Church, the Christian population of Spain was organized into territorial units, modelled on the provinces of the late Roman Empire. As in Roman times, these units, or dioceses, were grouped into 'provinces'. Each of these dioceses was headed by a bishop, or 'overseer', whose office and role were modelled on the practice of the Early Church, as it had been described in the New Testament of the Bible and developed over the subsequent centuries. The holder of the one bishopric in each province which had superiority over the rest was known as an archbishop. In the late Middle Ages, bishops retained a crucial role as chief pastors of their diocese, with ultimate responsi-bility for the Christian life of all those within their area. The importance of such appointments had inevitably attracted outside influence, how-ever, and Spanish bishops in the fifteenth century were commonly 'provided' to their posts (as was the current jargon) by an uneasy combination of influences which emanated from the popes in Rome and the rulers of the peninsular kingdoms. Such appointments were to be a matter of continuing controversy in Isabella and Ferdinand's reign. In geographical terms, until two new ones were created in 1492, there were four ecclesiastical provinces in the crown of Castile. That of Toledo was headed by the diocese of Toledo itself, which was led by an archbishop who was also 'primate', or chief bishop, of Spain. It contained the Castilian dioceses of Palencia, Segovia, (Burgo de) Osma, Sigüenza and Cuenca, and the Andalusian dioceses of Córdoba and Jaén. In the north and west of the crown of Castile, the province of Santiago de Compostela (St James of Compostella, containing the shrine of the apostle James the Great) consisted of the archdiocese of that name, and the dioceses of Badajoz, Plasencia, Ciudad Rodrigo and Coria, in Extremadura, Avila in Old Castile, Salamanca and Zamora in the ancient kingdom of León, and Tuy, Lugo and Mondoñedo in Galicia. The province of Seville, in western Andalusia, contained only the neighbouring diocese of Cádiz, which was administered together with it, and the diocese of the Canaries. After the conquest of Granada in 1492, a new province was created in the former Muslim emirate, containing the archdiocese of Granada itself and the dioceses of Guadix, Málaga and Almería. In addition, some Castilian dioceses were attached to provinces in neighbouring kingdoms, Calahorra to Zaragoza in Aragon, Cartagena to Valencia, and Astorga and Orense to Braga in Portugal. Outside the provincial system altogether were the dioceses of Burgos, León and Oviedo, which were directly subject to the pope's jurisdiction.

In the kingdom of Aragon, as well as the Castilian see of Calahorra, the province of Zaragoza contained the archdiocese of that name, and the dioceses of Segorbe-Albarracin and Tarazona. The ancient Catalan province of Tarragona consisted of that archdiocese, and the dioceses of Barcelona, Girona, Lleida, Urgel and Vich, as well as Elne in Roussillon, which was disputed with the archdiocese of Narbonne. In 1470, apparently in recognition of its growing economic and political importance, Pope Paul II removed the see of Valencia from the province of Zaragoza, placing it directly under papal jurisdiction. In August 1492, Valencia was elevated to the rank of a metropolitan see, at the head of a new province which consisted of the dioceses of Cartagena and Majorca. Pamplona, which was the only bishopric in the small kingdom of Navarre, on either side of the Pyrenees, came under the ecclesiastical authority of the French see of Bayonne. During Ferdinand and Isabella's reign, pressure grew for Spanish dioceses not to be subjected to foreign archbishops, but significant developments in this direction were postponed to a later period. In the Americas also, episcopal structures were established later, but the Canary Islands already had a considerable ecclesiastical history before the final surrender of the native rulers in 1496. The attempt to evangelize the Canaries had begun in the 1340s, most of the missionaries coming from Majorca, and in 1351, Clement VI appointed as first bishop of the Canaries the Carmelite friar Bernardo Gil, who established his see at Telde in Gran Canaria. During the succeeding decades, the fortunes of this diocese, as well as the missionary dioceses of San Marcial and Rubicón, had been variable, but in

1485, Innocent VIII authorized the transfer of the main bishopric to Las Palmas in Gran Canaria, which incorporated the see of Rubicón.[1]

Within the territorial scheme of church government, dioceses were subdivided into smaller units known as archdeaconries, which were in turn divided into deaneries. By the fifteenth century, the basic unit in each of these larger areas of government was the parish which, in towns, might be small but densely populated, while in the countryside the parish church often served as the centre of worship for widely dispersed settlements. Christian tradition taught, however, that the Church consisted primarily of people rather than land or buildings, and alongside its governmental organization there was a complex structure of personnel. Within the whole body of Christians, which was indeed the 'Body of Christ', a fundamental distinction existed between the clerks or clergy, all male, and the laity. 'Lay' men and women were those members of the Church, without regard for their social rank, who had not dedicated their lives fully to Christ by means of vows and the reception of 'major orders', that is, as deacons, priests or bishops, or 'minor' ones, for example as sacristan or acolyte (server). The only groups which transcended this barrier between the laity and an all-male clergy were the male and female religious communities, who also dedicated their lives wholly to God, under the vows of poverty, chastity and obedience. In Spain, as elsewhere in western Europe in the late Middle Ages, the social distinctions among the clergy, who underwent the tonsure (*corona*), or removal of hair from the centre of the scalp as a sign of separation from the world, were as great as those among lay Christians. Contemporaries recognized as the 'higher clergy' (*alto clero*) those who staffed the cathedrals, the collegiate churches, and certain important parishes in the larger towns, while the 'lower clergy' (*clero inferior*) consisted of the bulk of those who had the care ('cure') of the souls of the faithful in the parishes, as well as large numbers of chaplains who were paid by individuals or confraternities to say masses for the souls of the departed. The reward for a man who held a senior post in this clerical hierarchy was a feudal *beneficium*, or benefice, in land and/or cash, but the bulk of the pastoral work was usually done by vicars, or deputies, known as *plebanos* (those who looked after the people) in urban parishes and *abades* (not monastic abbots but secular priests, as in the French *abbé*) in the countryside. Like the bishops, the higher clergy, on the other hand, were fully integrated into the seigneurial system. Bishops had revenues assigned to them personally, for the running of their households (the *mesas obispales*), but also, in some cases, administered massive revenues which were assigned to their dioceses. The rest of the higher clergy, assembled in corporate bodies such as cathedral chapters and colleges, similarly possessed towns, fortresses, vassals and rents, and exercised secular legal jurisdiction over lay people, under the regime of *abadengo*. As an indication of the immense wealth which was vested in cathedral chapters in the late fifteenth century, ten Castilian cathedrals, including the primatial see of Toledo, between them had jurisdiction over thirty-one towns and villages and over 2300 vassals. Although, as has been noted, even rulers such as Ferdinand and Isabella were, in terms of ecclesiastical law, lay people and, in that sense, as inferior to the humblest tonsured student as any peasant or artisan, such a theoretical view accorded ill with political and social reality. Trastamaran notions of the 'natural lordship' and 'absolute power' vested in kings had as much difficulty in accommodating the exercise of clerical privileges and jurisdictional powers by bishops and ecclesiastical corporations as they did the pretensions of the secular nobility, or the leading citizens of the towns.

As in other western European kingdoms in the period, conflict between Crown and Church over the exercise of legal and financial powers festered constantly in Isabella and Ferdinand's realms. The king and queen did not attack the property of the Church, but they deeply resented the institution's intervention in the keeping of law and order, which they regarded as the Crown's prerogative. When bishops or cathedral chapters acquired immovable goods in *señorío abadengo* they thereby received, in addition to the towns, villages and lands concerned, the total yield, in cash or kind, of the properties which came directly into their hands, as well as the one-third shares of the tithe on all other production to which bishops and cathedrals were respectively entitled. Such grants of lordship also included rights of vassalage, such as customs dues (*portazgos*) and some urban taxes (*minucias de la ciudad*). The jurisdictional rights of the Church, which caused perennial conflict both with the Crown and with the jurisdictions of royal towns and secular lords, included legal fines, the granting and sale of the offices of notary or public scribe (*escribano público*), and the appointment, in practice frequently for money, of other officials, including magistrates and constables (*alguaciles*). As in the case of grants to secular lords, bishops and higher clergy (*prelados* or prelates) received from the Crown full jurisdiction or, in the customary phrase, 'civil and criminal jurisdiction, high and low, and *mero y mixto imperio*', the latter being another legal expression for civil and criminal jurisdiction. This situation inevitably meant that bishops and other senior clergy, as well as having a spiritual and pastoral role as Church leaders, effectively became part of the seigneurial class, gaining secular, material benefits and demanding rents and services from their vassals and tenants. The secular possessions of the archbishops of Toledo matched those at least of the lesser seigneurial aristocracy, while the archbishops of Santiago had lordships *ex officio*, not only within their own diocese but also in those of Zamora, Salamanca and Palencia. Among the rest of the dioceses in the crown of Castile and Galicia, the exempt papal sees of Burgos, León and Oviedo were next in wealth from secular possessions, but a long way behind the leaders. Ten Castilian cathedrals, in León, Astorga, Palencia, Zamora, Salamanca, Segovia, Sigüenza, Toledo, Cartagena and Seville, between them held lordship (*señorío*) over more than thirty towns and villages, containing a total of about 2300 vassals in *abadengo,* in addition to inhabitants with whom they did not have direct feudal ties. The bishops of the kingdom of Aragon, on the other hand, were not always effective in exploiting their seigneurial rights, unlike their equivalents in Catalonia, while nothing is known of the situation in Majorca and Valencia. The bishops of Pamplona, in the much poorer Navarrese Church, could boast just one lordship, consisting of the Aragonese castle of Navardún.[2]

The nature and degree of episcopal supervision of dioceses varied according to particular circumstances, both personal and material. Although full possession of the rights of each see was vested in the diocesan bishop, who might or might not be resident in his diocese, another bishop might be named as coadjutor, to help him, or an auxiliary bishop might be appointed. It was also possible for another person, who did not have the orders, or the 'cure of souls', which normally went with the oversight of a diocese, to be granted the administration of its property, and secular jurisdiction, where appropriate, these rights and powers being known as 'temporalities'. In such circumstances, the 'spiritualities', or strictly ecclesiastical and pastoral duties attached to the relevant office, were intended to be delegated to suitably qualified persons. The possibility of abuse in these arrangements was evident, and had already led to demands for reform, in Spain as elsewhere, long before Martin Luther appeared on the European scene. A further hazard to the dignity of the episcopal office was the existence of men in bishop's orders who were neither diocesan bishops nor administrators of dioceses. Some such did have notional dioceses *in partibus infidelium,* that is, historic sees which were out of the control of the Western Church, in areas of Africa and Asia which had been conquered in earlier centuries by Islam, or else were under the control of Orthodox Churches. Many of these bishops proved to be useful deputies, for example administering the sacrament of confirmation of behalf of diocesans who found themselves caught up in secular political and governmental roles, as was frequently the case in Spain, as elsewhere, in Ferdinand and Isabella's time. There were also, however, roving bishops *de anillo* (a phrase which referred to the episcopal ring, which served as a sign of their office), who obtained their episcopal orders directly from Rome, often, it appeared, in dubious or suspect circumstances.

It was the appointment of bishops to dioceses which most preoccupied late medieval rulers, and Ferdinand and Isabella were no exceptions in this respect. As a result of the developments which had taken place during the preceding centuries, three parties had a legitimate interest in the choice, or election, of diocesan bishops, the first being the Papacy, the second, the Crown and the third, the relevant cathedral chapter. The one missing element in the process was the voice of the Christian people. Particularly since its period of exile from Rome in Avignon, between 1305 and 1378, the Papacy had fought to centralize appointments to senior posts in the Church, especially those of bishops, channeling them through the college of cardinals, or consistory. Medieval secular rulers, in Spain as elsewhere, had refused to concede the principle of papal provision to bishoprics, both on theoretical grounds, in that a king should have absolute jurisdiction within his own kingdom on God's behalf, and, more practically, because bishops possessed a great deal of political and economic power which should not, and could not, be beholden to an external source. In this sense, there was nothing new in the disputes and polemics of the subsequent Reformation era. Cathedral chapters, on the other hand, had clearly lost ground, during the fourteenth and fifteenth centuries, in their struggle to control episcopal appointments. In earlier centuries, they had had the freedom to elect (in French, *congé d'élire*) their bishop, but, in Spain as elsewhere, this privilege had been questioned, and largely lost, in the longstanding struggle between the opposing forces of popes and kings. Nevertheless, cathedral canons in Isabella and Ferdinand's reign still retained considerable nuisance value, in the matter of the appointment of bishops.[3]

The strong interest taken by the Catholic Monarchs in the better governance of the Church, or *reformación* (in Latin *reformatio*) as it was known at the time, was first and quickly revealed in Castile by the calling of the national council of clergy in Seville in 1478. Ever since the Conciliar movement of the early fifteenth century, in which general councils of the Church attempted to heal the papal schism, had threatened the powers, and at times even the existence, of the Papacy as an institution, a standard item on the reforming agenda had been the purification of the office of bishop as pastor of the Christian flock. Bishops were to be pastors and not landowners or politicians. They were to reside and work in their dioceses, and not to spend their time in royal courts, on the battlefield, or in the hunting forest. They were to be appointed by the clergy themselves, and not by lay rulers, to be leaders of the whole Christian Church, on what was believed to be the model set out in the New Testament, above all in the early apostolic letters. Yet such aims were much easier to state than to achieve. In her tortuous journey to the throne, Isabella herself owed a great deal to political prelates, in particular Archbishop Carrillo of Toledo and Cardinal Mendoza of Seville, and it was not long before ideals met pragmatic reality in the provision of new bishops to Spanish sees. During the latter part of Henry IV's reign in Castile and of John II's in Aragon, the two main protagonists for control of such appointments had been the popes and the cathedral chapters concerned. Pius II (1458–64) and Paul II (1464–71) had rejected the results of chapter elections in Barcelona in 1463, Sigüenza in 1465, Oviedo and Tuy in 1468, and Cuenca in 1469. Spanish chapters fought back, however, in turn resisting papal appointments in Zamora (1468), Santiago de Compostela (1469), Coria and Burgo de Osma (1475), Palencia (1476) and Calahorra (1477). The canons failed, however, to exploit the political and social turmoil of these two decades in order to regain their lost right of 'free' election, being defeated by a combination of papal sanctions and, in some cases, the physical efforts of the 'secular arm', or royal and local authorities. In Córdoba, for instance, the chief magistrate (*alcalde mayor*), Don Alonso de Aguilar, drove Bishop Pedro Solier y Córdoba, who was also his relative, out of the city altogether in the latter part of Henry IV's reign. If papal power within their domains was to be controlled and possibly reduced, it was certainly not the intention of the new king and queen that the resulting gain of secular over papal power should go to anyone other than themselves. As early as 15 January 1475, in the concordat of Segovia (see chapter 1), they agreed that the queen would take the initiative in the provision of bishops and other senior clerics in Castile, the dual purpose being to strengthen royal power over the Church and to improve the quality of those appointed to sees. With this aim in mind, the Segovia agreement stated that bishops should in future be university graduates (*letrados*). Thus it was clear, right at the beginning of Isabella's reign, that the Crown was determined to reduce, if not eliminate, the powers of both the Papacy and the cathedral chapters.[4]

In the event, the first conflict between the royal couple and the pope over the appointment of a bishop took place in Aragon rather than Castile. The Franciscan Della Rovere pope, Sixtus IV (1471–84), refused to accept the nomination as archbishop of Zaragoza of Ferdinand's illegitimate child Alfonso, who had been born of his mistress Aldonza Roig de Iborra. Instead, the pope named to the see Auxias Despuig, who though a Catalan was bishop of an Italian see, Morreale, and also Cardinal of St Sabina. Both Sixtus and Ferdinand's father, John II, dug in their heels, and the dispute was not settled for three years.

Eventually, Despuig, whose family assets had meanwhile been threatened by the Aragonese crown, withdrew his candidacy, and on 14 August 1478, Sixtus issued a bull appointing the nine-year-old bastard to the see of Zaragoza. The child was dispensed from the legal impediment of his birth, and the pope stated that he would be entitled to legal possession of the spiritualities and temporalities of his bishopric when he reached the age of twenty-five. In the meantime, he was to maintain himself and his household from other ecclesiastical benefices which he had already been granted. Ferdinand and Isabella seem to have decided, as soon as the trouble over Zaragoza occurred, that they would do everything they could to avoid such difficulties in future. On 5 June 1475, they issued new instructions to their ambassador in Rome, García Martínez de Lerma, which mainly concerned provisions to ecclesiastical benefices. This issue was raised again by Isabella in her instructions to a further envoy, Pedro Colón, whom she sent to negotiate with Sixtus over her difficulties with her former ally Alonso Carrillo, archbishop of Toledo. The Crown aimed to control completely the provision of bishops and other senior clerics, and the matter was placed on the agenda of the Seville council in July 1478. Thus, while the pope may have obliged Isabella and Ferdinand in the matter of the Inquisition, this acquiescence certainly did not bring other conflicts between them to an end.

Indeed, trouble over episcopal appointments broke out only two days after the Seville council closed. On 3 August, the death occurred of the bishop of Cuenca, Cardinal Antonio Giacomo Venier (de Veneris), who had acted as papal legate in Spain since 1460. Only ten days later, Sixtus named as the new bishop another Italian, his own cousin Raffaello Sansoni Riario, but the king and queen decided to stand their ground. It would hardly demonstrate their moral and political constancy, at a time when their regime was still under some threat from dissident magnates and the Portuguese, if they immediately conceded the papal preorgative, used nepotistically on behalf of a foreigner. They put negotiations in the hands of a new embassy to Rome, which consisted of Diego de Muros, bishop of Oviedo, Juan Arias, canon of Seville, and Rodrigo de La Calzada, abbot of Sahagún. The dispute between Sixtus and the Monarchs became ever more acrimonious. Diplomats on each side were arrested, and the keeping of law and order in the diocese of Cuenca was placed in the hands of the Santa Hermandad, to ensure that the episcopal rents were duly collected and to prevent violence. Nevertheless, the deadlock continued into 1481, when the matter of Cuenca was entrusted to Alfonso de San Cebrián, a Dominican who was on the way to Rome for the general chapter of his order. After further lengthy negotiations, an agreement was eventually reached in Córdoba on 3 July 1482, whereby the Curia accepted Isabella's provisions of Alfonso de Burgos to Cuenca, the grant of the see of Osma as an additional office and benefit for Cardinal Pedro González de Mendoza (so much for the need for resident bishops), and the appointment to Córdoba of Tello de Buendía, and of the pope's nephew, Cardinal Riario, to Salamanca. In return for these concessions, the Castilian crown granted Sixtus a tax on clerical pensions and also the chance, at least, of a third share of the kingdom's tithes and the revenues from the crusade bull (*cruzada*). Significantly, however, the Papacy conceded nothing of its right to appoint bishops in Castile, and relevant bulls for the four sees make no reference whatsoever to a royal role in the provisions. A new crisis soon developed, however, with the death of the archbishop of Toledo, Alfonso Carrillo. Isabella and her husband immediately moved to replace their ally and scourge as primate of Spain with Cardinal Mendoza, and Sixtus had no difficulty in accepting this. The problem arose with the consequent vacancy of Seville. Feeling that, despite its international reputation as a university city, Salamanca was an insufficient reward for his nephew Riario, the pope proposed that at least he should receive the see of Osma, if not the rich archdiocese of Seville itself. On this occasion, success was shared, the king and queen obtaining their choices for most of the vacant sees, while the pope's nephew was given much-disputed possession of the bishopric of Salamanca, which Isabella had first requested for her confessor, the Jeronymite friar Hernando de Talavera, later to be archbishop of Granada. In the summer of 1484, Sixtus's successor Innocent VIII immediately faced a new conflict with the Castilian monarchs when the see of Seville fell vacant once again, as a result of the death of Bishop Iñigo Manrique de Lara. At Rome, this wealthy bishopric was coveted by the papal vice-chancellor, the Valencian Rodrigo de Borja [Borgia], but his suit was implacably opposed by Ferdinand and Isabella. As a pre-emptive measure, they ordered the arrest of his son, Pedro Luis de Borja, and the confiscation of the Spanish possessions of the entire family. Pope Innocent took these measures as a personal affront, but the Castilian rulers were immovable, and Rodrigo had no choice but to renounce his claim to the see of Seville, which was instead conferred, in August 1485, on Diego Hurtado de Mendoza. Although he conceded defeat in the matter of personnel, Pope Innocent refused, in the relevant bull of provision, to allow any legal role to the Crown in the appointment of bishops. In practical terms, however, the royal administration profited handsomely from the revenues of the archdiocese of Seville during the preceding interregnum. Such conflict with Spain did not, in any case, prevent Innocent from granting to Isabella and her husband the *patronato*, or right to provide to all the bishoprics and clerical benefices in the newly-conquered kingdom of Granada.

It might be supposed that, given the treatment which he received from them over the bishopric of Seville, Rodrigo de Borja would have been little concerned to oblige Isabella and Ferdinand, when he became pope, as Alexander VI, in 1492. Indeed, problems over provisions to Spanish dioceses quickly arose. No doubt as part of his election 'campaign' in the consistory, the new Borgia pope had promised the see of Cartagena to Cardinal Orsini, that of Majorca to Cardinal Savelli, and the archdiocese of Valencia to his own son Cesare. Although the king and queen were prepared to accept this notorious figure of the Italian Renaissance in Valencia, they successfully demanded Cartagena for Bernardino López de Carvajal, of whom more will be heard, and Majorca for Guillermo Ramón de Moncada. Thereafter, no doubt in his anxiety to obtain Spanish support in his Italian conflicts (see chapter 7), Alexander gave the king and queen what they wanted, not only in the Peninsula but also in the New World. His successor, Julius II (1503–13), nephew of Sixtus IV, began by behaving in an equally accommodating manner towards the Spanish monarchs. On 4 November 1504, shortly before Isabella's death, Julius's consistory not only appointed the king and queen's candidates to the bishoprics of Seville, Córdoba, Palencia and Cartagena, but also granted the Crown a special tithe to finance war against the 'infidel', renewed the royal *patronato* over all the churches in the kingdom of Granada, and granted the Crown power to fill various minor benefices. Less pleasing to the king and queen, however, was Julius's continuation of the practice of appointing foreigners to Spanish bishoprics which fell vacant owing to the death of their holders while in Rome. At the time of her death, Isabella was still pursuing, by diplomatic means, the goal of reserving such appointments to the Crown. A month later, however, on 26 December 1504, Julius named Cardinal Luis de Aragón as bishop of León, one of the dioceses traditionally reserved to direct papal jurisdiction, the previous bishop having died in Rome. Ferdinand had a different candidate, Diego Ramírez de Guzmán, bishop of Catania, and pursued diplomatic and financial measures against Luis de Aragón and his successor as papally-approved claimant, Cardinal Vera. The pope remained obstinate, however, and on 10 May 1507 provided to León another foreigner, Cardinal Alidosi, bishop of Pavia. This lengthy and often acrimonious dispute eventually ended on 16 June 1511, when the Italian was succeeded by Luis de Aragón. During the period of turmoil in Spain which followed Isabella's death (see chapter 9), there was conflict with Rome over every episcopal vacancy which had to be filled. In addition, cathedral chapters took the opportunity to assert once again their historic power of election, the most notorious case being that of Zamora. When the bishop of that diocese died, Antonio de Acuña was in Rome on diplomatic business. He seized his opportunity, gained the provision under the traditional papal prerogative, and proved to be a violent thorn in the flesh of the Castilian government for many years (see chapter 9). Relations between Crown and Curia deteriorated further when the see of Sigüenza fell vacant, near the end of Julius's reign, in 1513. The matter was complicated by the fact that the town was under the bishop's secular as well as ecclesiastical jurisdiction, and its authorities had tried to enlist the Crown's support for transferring itself to royal jurisdiction, that is, from *abadengo* to *realengo*. So violent and acrimonious was the exchange of written missives between Spain and the Curia that Ferdinand even threatened to break with Rome, withdrawing from the pope both the obedience of Castile, where he was governor, and that of Aragon, where he ruled as sovereign. The political situation in Italy forced Julius to adopt a more conciliatory attitude. Nevertheless, when the pope died, in 1513, two further disputes over episcopal provisions were in progress in Spain, one concerning the see of Burgos in Old Castile, and the other that of Tuy, in Galicia.

The bishop of Burgos, Pascual de Ampudia, had died in Rome, and Julius used his traditional prerogative to replace him with Cardinal Jaime Serra. The succession in Tuy had been in dispute since 1506, when Juan de Sepúlveda had been appointed by the pope but rejected by the Castilian crown. The new Medici pope, Leo X (1513–21), tackled these two problems in the conclave which elected him, but his relations with Ferdinand remained stormy, in this and other matters, until the Aragonese king's death in 1516. In addition to Burgos and Tuy, the bishopric of Sigüenza became a bone of contention when the Cardinal of Santa Croce, Bernardino López de Carvajal, was deprived of this see, as well as numerous other ecclesiastical offices and benefits, after taking a leading part in the illegal church council of Pisa in 1511–12. After the cardinal had made an act of contrition to the pope, Leo wanted to restore Carvajal's position, yet not only had his offices been granted to others but Ferdinand was reluctant to let the budding reformer (see below) off so lightly. In any case, he had granted the bishopric of Sigüenza to Fadrique de Portugal, and the resulting dispute continued under his successor as 'regent' of Castile, Cardinal Cisneros and into the reign of Charles I and V. During this series of conflicts between the Spanish crown and the popes, the threat of withdrawal of the Spanish Church from obedience to Rome was made more than once, though never carried out.[5]

All Spanish rulers jealously guarded their *patronato*, or general patronage of the Church within their frontiers, but they were equally anxious to express it in the appointment of senior clergy. Church law forbade the exercise of such powers by a layman over a cathedral or collegiate church, in other words, one which was operated by a chapter of canons. Kings might claim customary rights in such matters, but these were hard and laborious to defend, and although popes had the power to grant such privileges, it was not until Leo X's reign that Spanish rulers began to receive the power of appointment, or 'presentation', other than in the kingdom of Granada and in the Canaries. Ferdinand and Isabella's efforts to turn patronage into presentation received the support of enthusiastic canon lawyers and other bureaucratic servants of the Crown. In 1487, Juan de Castilla stated, from his professorial chair at Salamanca university, that any provisions to churches in Castile and León which were made by the pope without the consent of the king and queen should be regarded as null and void. This mode of royal thought appears to have been acceptable to the leaders of the Spanish Church who, at the council of Seville in 1478, supported the exercise of royal patronage in this way. There were, however, moves, in sermons and other documents, to urge Ferdinand and Isabella to use their powers in order to appoint better candidates. As the system functioned during their reign, the relevant royal chancery would draw up a document which named a person to the vacant see. This would then be sent to Rome by means of an ambassador, who would refer the presentation in question to the Curia. Approval of the appointment required a vote by the cardinals in consistory. The ideal specification for a Spanish bishop was set out early in Isabella and Ferdinand's reign, clearly with their personal involvement and concern, in addition to the advice of spiritual counsellors, such as Hernando de Talavera, who was to become archbishop of Granada after the conquest in 1492. A fundamental criterion was that diocesan bishops should be natives and subjects of the Spanish rulers. It was argued that, since their dioceses possessed fortifications and vassals, it was essential that they should be held on behalf of the Crown by reliable individuals, this being particularly important in frontier regions. There was also a perception that foreign bishops would inevitably export revenues from Spain, beyond those to which the papacy was in any case entitled. The 1478 assembly at Seville asked that all bishops appointed to Spanish sees should be resident in the country, but political realities meant that Ferdinand and Isabella had to make exceptions for Italian cardinals, who might be useful allies at Rome.

During the fifteenth century, and more particularly in the period of what was to become known as the Reformation, there was much concentration, in both ecclesiastical and secular thought and writing, on the personal failings of bishops, which were held to affect the whole life of the Church and its members. Isabella appears to have shown a genuine concern for the moral rectitude of those whom she recommended as bishops, though Ferdinand, as the case of his illegitimate son Alfonso has shown, was less solicitous in this regard. It is true that, at the time of her accession in Castile, it was common knowledge that the holders of some of the most important bishoprics of that kingdom, too, for example the archbishops of Toledo, Seville and Santiago de Compostela, not only made no pretence of living a celibate life but even used ecclesiastical revenues to support their children. It might be argued that these particular prelates were in some sense relics of a previous age, yet the queen, like so many of her contemporaries as European rulers, was soon to discover that she too had to confront the domestic failings of some of those whom she herself had chosen to be spiritual leaders. Ferdinand, having begun with the promotion of his bastard son to the archdiocese of Zaragoza, continued to display less concern than his wife over the moral qualities of bishops, including those whom he was involved in appointing in Castile after his wife's death. It is clear, though, that given the personal and institutional foibles of the Roman pontiff and his cardinals at the time, it was easy for the king and queen's attempts to place 'honest' and 'virtuous' candidates in Spanish bishoprics to become in practice a weapon for asserting and exercising royal supremacy over the Church. In a memorandum which he sent to the Castilian royal council in 1512, as part of the preparation of the Spanish position for Leo X's Fifth Lateran Council, the bishop of Burgos, Fray Pascual de Ampudia, denounced those of his fellow-diocesans who continued to parade their mistresses (*mancebas*) at Court, and to obtain lucrative posts for their offspring. In practice, though, the fact that a bishop failed to live up to the personal standards which were theoretically expected of his office did not necessarily preclude his active support for reform. In Ferdinand and Isabella's Spain, traditional Christian teaching concerning the availability of God's grace to the repentant sinner was generally held to apply even to the most hardened of prelates.

A feature of the fifty years or so before 1475, in both Castile and Aragon, was the direct involvement of bishops in political violence, and it has already been seen that prelates took part in the war of the Castilian succession which dominated the first years of Isabella's reign. Despite their clerical status, bishops were often natural allies of rebellious nobles, because they were of the same social rank and frequently came from the same families, which were often also related to the Iberian royal dynasties. One reaction of rulers to this situation was to appoint diocesans from a lower social category, who would perhaps have fewer pretensions, and avoid political entanglements, at least with opposition groups. This notion appears to be behind Juan de Castilla's urging, in Ferdinand and Isabella's time, that the appointment of bishops should be entirely under the control of the Crown. Another requirement which became increasingly important in the late fifteenth century was that bishops should be *letrados*, or university-educated, the supposition being that candidates from such a background would be less aristocratic and less militaristic. By the end of Ferdinand's reign, it was becoming increasingly necessary for episcopal candidates to have previously attended either the university of Salamanca or, latterly, that of Alcalá in Spain, or else those of Paris or Bologna abroad. As the Lutheran Reformation approached, the required activities of Spanish diocesan bishops had changed from those of their often warlike predecessors, and had also become more extensive. In addition to preaching, and controlling and sanctifying the faithful, they were now expected to publish books and papers, to edit liturgical and classical texts, to improve churches and episcopal buildings, and to patronize the fine arts (see chapter 8). Isabella's personal preference seems to have been for graduates of the college of St Bartholomew (San Bartolomé) in Salamanca, although, after her death, the college of St Ildefonso in Alcalá perhaps represented her ideals even more completely. Ferdinand, too, recruited graduates from Castilian universities to fill vacancies in Aragonese and Catalan sees, though he also appointed, as bishops and abbots, products of the Catalan university of Lleida, as well as some who had obtained their degrees abroad.

The change in the social rank of those appointed as diocesan bishops in Isabella and Ferdinand's reigns should not be exaggerated. Members of upper noble families, whose titles sometimes went back to the beginnings of the Trastamaran dynasty in the fourteenth century, continued to be appointed to sees in Castile. Cases in point were the Enríquez, Manrique, Zúñiga and Alvarez de Toledo. The situation was similar in the crown of Aragon, where bishops were appointed from the Fernández de Heredia, Cardona, Despuig and Borja families. Out of a total of 132 men provided to Castilian and Aragonese bishoprics in the period 1474–1516, thirty-two came from the upper nobility of the respective kingdoms. Over half the appointments, seventy-four, were made from the lesser nobility and the 'professional' classes, mostly lawyers, who together formed the backbone of both the royal and the municipal administration. Just eight bishops were of a still lower social rank, while twenty were either Italians or else Spaniards who had previously held Italian bishoprics in order to work at the Curia. As to their educational, rather than their social level, apart from a few of the nobles, all were *letrados*, who had undergone higher education. The largest contingent consisted of graduates in 'both laws', canon and civil, of Salamanca or else of foreign universities. In the time of the Catholic Monarchs, theologians formed a minority on the bench of bishops, though it should not be assumed that those who had been trained in law were necessarily any less devoted as Christians. As regards their previous employment, the great majority of Ferdinand and Isabella's bishops came from the service of the Royal Court, whether lay, as the sons of officials or themselves officials of the chancery, or else clerical, as chaplains, diplomats or inquisitors. A significant number of bishops came from professorial chairs in the universities or from teaching posts in graduate colleges (*colegios mayores*). There was a contingent of members of religious orders, who generally had served in noble households, or else as royal confessors. Although many successful candidates had previously held ecclesiastical benefices, almost none of them had any direct pastoral experience in the care of the faithful. None of those who were raised to the episcopate during the reigns of Isabella and Ferdinand have since been recognized as saints by the Roman Church. This is not to say, however, that there were not able and dedicated prelates, who served Church and State effectively. Lack of subsequent interest in Rome might appear to suggest that these Spanish bishops gave high priority to their sovereign's wills.

Important as bishops were in the government and character of the Church, they could achieve no effectiveness without the aid of the rest of the clerical estate. Most prominent among them were the cathedral chapters which, like their diocesans, had a large stake in the jurisdictional structure of Ferdinand and Isabella's kingdoms. This, rather than the wealth of the Church in itself, was the main cause of friction between secular and ecclesiastical officials and judges. The 'high' Trastamaran doctrine of monarchy, to which both rulers were firmly wedded, brooked no interference with the royal prerogative, and the conflicting jurisdictional claims of the Church and secular authorities were painfully worked out, day by day, in Spanish villages, towns and cities, in disputes of varying degrees of pettiness or importance. Each side defended its corner with the best weapons at its disposal. The Crown could summon churchmen to appear in its courts, and punish the recalcitrant with the confiscation of goods or with imprisonment. The Church was able to retaliate with its 'spiritual' weapons, the excommunication, or withholding of the sacraments, from groups or individuals, however mighty, and, in extreme cases, an 'interdict', which meant the withdrawal of the services of the clergy from an entire community, or even a whole kingdom. As in the case of other Western European countries, what the Spanish rulers objected to was the fact that, in some places, the Church exercised civil jurisdiction over its nonclerical vassals, as well as the populations of ecclesiastical lordships (*abadengos*). The theorists and practitioners of monarchy, and especially those in Castile, although similar tensions arose in the crown of Aragon, were scandalized by the fact that bishops and ecclesiastical corporations might thus exercise control over every aspect of lay people's lives, both during their time on earth and in the life which followed. On a day-to-day basis, non-clerics brought secular cases to church courts, while ecclesiastical judges regularly and systematically interfered in civil matters, such as debt, thus straying into the normal sphere of royal and secular seigneurial courts. As in other Western European countries, the use and abuse of the right of sanctuary, or immunity from secular justice by means of remaining in designated ecclesiastical sites, was another continuing cause of friction between Church and State. In addition, the accumulation of possessions in the hands of ecclesiastical institutions, as a result of donations from lay people in return for the spiritual aid of the Church, had created a forest of jurisdictional immunities which offered numerous opportunities for abuse. Ferdinand and Isabella were keenly aware that, important as it undoubtedly was to restrain the ambitions of nobles and prelates, the daily battle on the ground against ecclesiastical lords and courts, as well as their secular seigneurial equivalents, was equally essential to the consolidation of their regime. Inevitably, many cases involved 'mixed jurisdiction', that is, both secular and ecclesiastical, and the Crown was determined to keep these pleas within its own grasp. In a pragmatic, issued in Seville on 23 June 1500, the king and queen ordered ecclesiastical lords in Galicia, including bishops, abbots, cathedral chapters and collegiate churches, to appoint laymen to deal with such cases on their behalf. If they continued to insist on appointing clerics as judges, these officials were no longer to be allowed to exact spiritual penalties, including excommunication, and the accused were to be entitled, in every case, to appeal to the secular courts. In 1502, these rules were extended to the rest of Castile and to Aragon. As a symbol of their predominance, only lay judges were allowed to have the wand, or staff (*vara*) of justice carried before them.

The use and abuse of the clerical tonsure, the *corona*, was another regular cause of strife in Spain, as elsewhere in western Europe. The administration of the tonsure had to be carried out by a bishop, but he did not have to be a diocesan, and roving prelates were prepared to carry out the ceremony in return for a monetary consideration. The scope for abuse was obvious, and seems particularly to have irked Ferdinand and Isabella, who raised the issue both in their church assembly in Seville in 1478 and two years later, at the cortes of Toledo. In succeeding years, their ambassadors in the Roman Curia continued to pursue the matter. In the early sixteenth century the king and queen remained convinced that, in large parts of their kingdoms, the clerical *corona* continued to be made available without any kind of test of suitability. They were equally preoccupied with clerical dress, which had traditionally been intended to set the clergy apart from the rest of Christian society, and hence to ensure proper decorum The 1478 assembly in Seville ordered that bishops should investigate the situation in their dioceses. Within thirty days, clerics were to produce certificates to demonstrate their entitlement to the tonsure, which was to be of a specified minimum size (that of an 'old *blanca*', a small coin representing a fraction of a *maravedí*), and to wear robes which should hang at least four fingers' length (*cuatro dedos*) below the knee, and should be in dark rather than gaudy colours. The bishops were slow to implement these regulations, however, and Isabella and Ferdinand eventually obtained, on 27 July 1493, a bull from Pope Alexander VI which reinforced them. Nevertheless, many clerics continued to defy all requests that they should be tonsured, that their remaining hair should not be too long, and that they should wear dark academic gowns, reaching close to their feet. Evidence from Córdoba, for example, suggests that these injunctions were honoured more in the breach than the observance.

Efforts to obtain a clergy which was more *honesto* also proceeded at provincial level, for example in the councils of Aranda in 1473 and Seville in 1482, and in the dioceses themselves. After 1474, it was clear, though, that much of the reforming initiative came from the Crown, which exercised immense influence through its patronage and its ability to affect the decisions of the popes. Isabella and Ferdinand's purpose was to spread to the whole of the clergy the standards which they were attempting to impose on the bishops. One of the methods which they used was to work for the reduction of papal influence in appointments to senior posts, such as canonries in cathedral and collegiate churches. After the queen's death, Ferdinand pursued this issue until the end of his days. In particular, he fought to prevent the appointment of non-Spaniards to benefices in Castile and Aragon, although, on 17 July 1514, Leo X defied him by issuing a brief which deplored lay influence in clerical appointments, and accurately pointed out that many Spaniards benefited from holding posts in other countries, not least in Rome itself. Another aspect of the king and queen's campaign for a more 'honest' clergy was the question of celibacy, and purity of life. If bishops were parading their mistresses at court, it was hardly surprising that many of their diocesan clergy were also in such relationships. Accusations of sexual and other impropriety were also frequently made against members of the religious orders, including those which supposedly lived in enclosure, as well as the mendicant friars. Evidence of such clerical misconduct comes from all parts of Ferdinand and Isabella's domains, and the very fact that the secular and ecclesiastical legislation on the subject was so often repeated bears testimony to its limited effectiveness. At the 1478 church council of Seville, the monarchs attempted to make a hardly generous deal with the clergy over their mistresses. In return for repealing various laws which were irksome to the clergy, in particular one which required a tax of a mark of silver from their *mancebas*, Isabella and Ferdinand required them to live in future as celibates. Under the pretext of this new church law, royal constables (*alguaciles*) raided, and sometimes ransacked, the houses of the clergy, humiliating them in public. The legislation was incorporated into secular law at the cortes of Toledo in 1480, but had to be repeated in instructions which were issued by the Crown in 1500 to its *gobernadores* and other officials. The penalties for the mistresses of secular clergy, friars, or even married men were strengthened. For the first offence there was to be a fine of a mark and a half of silver and one year's banishment from the locality, for the second a fine of one silver mark and two years' banishment, and for the third a silver mark, a public flogging of a hundred strokes and banishment for a year. It should not, however, be assumed that the obstinacy of the Spanish clergy in this matter was simply a matter of mindless self-indulgence. Despite centuries of papal requirements on the subject, the view that celibacy should be voluntary among the parochial clergy, which had been advanced by distinguished canon lawyers, was still espoused by some. Among the population in general, as the Inquisition discovered, the view was all too common that sexual activity among the unmarried was, in any case, not a sin.

The Catholic Monarchs were concerned that the diocesan clergy, like the bishops and canons, should be well educated, though their success in this regard was limited. They were also anxious that clergy who were recruited to important posts in cathedral, collegiate and parish churches should be well educated, and in some cases of noble rank, but, despite their sterling battles with the papacy, their influence over such appointments was limited. In Burgos, Palencia and Calahorra, for example, the right of provision to many benefices belonged to the relevant bishop, who was required to appoint natives of the diocese concerned. It was not necessarily the case, however, that initiative in reform was left entirely to the Crown. Provincial councils and diocesan synods were held from time to time, most frequently in the province of Tarragona. In the huge archdiocese of Toledo, although Archbishop Carrillo's provincial council at Aranda de Duero, in 1473, seems to have been submerged by the political turmoil of the time (see chapter 1), the national council in Seville in 1478 took up the main issues which had been raised. It was only under the tutelage of Francisco Jiménez de Cisneros as archbishop that synods were called together more regularly in the archdiocese of Toledo, two closely related gatherings being held at Alcalá de Henares in 1497 and at Talavera in the following year. The resulting legislation paid a degree of attention which was unusual for the period to catachesis, or the teaching of the Christian faith to both children and adults, as well as urgent demands for the reform of the clergy. Although the impact of Cardinal Cisneros's measures was reduced virtually to nothing by his long and acrimonious dispute with Toledo cathedral chapter, the Franciscan archbishop, and inquisitor, was not alone among diocesan bishops of the period in pursuing such reforms. Efforts in this direction were also made by two Dominican prelates, Diego de Deza of Seville, who succeeded Tomás de Torquemada as inquisitor-general, and Pascual de Ampudia, who called four synods in his diocese of Burgos, in 1498, 1500, 1503 and 1511.[6]

It would be wrong to suppose, however, that initiatives for church reform in this period came only from the Crown or zealous bishops. The subject of spontaneous reform among the Spanish clergy in general has so far received limited attention, but it does appear that there continued to be meetings, of clerical juntas, confraternities and 'congregations', which were not concerned solely with the defence of rights and privileges against the representatives of other jurisdictions. It is true that economic and jurisdictional matters predominated in the assemblies of the fifteenth century, as well as that held in 1505, but the 1478 Seville council legislated on many other matters as well, while the main purpose of the 'Catholic congregation' which gathered in Burgos in 1508 was to investigate the conduct of Diego Rodríguez Lucero, inquisitor of Córdoba (see below).

The 1478 meeting at Seville made pronouncements on political matters, for example that clerics should not intervene in the current disturbances in the kingdom, which resulted from Joanna's claim to the throne. The clergy were told that they might have no temporal lord apart from their monarchs and the pope. Bishops were to reside in their dioceses and carry out visitations in a conscientious manner, while all clergy were to be tonsured and wear suitable clothes. They were not to adopt secular lifestyles. The 1482 assembly in Córdoba, on the other hand, concentrated mainly on economic matters. It decided how payment of the clerical subsidy to the Crown should be distributed among the dioceses, and also raised a series of issues in defence of the liberties of the clergy, both financial and legal. These included the taxation of church property by secular authorities and clashes between lay and ecclesiastical judges. At the meeting of clergy held in Medina del

Campo, in 1491, further issues were raised, in particular, the relationship between the secular clergy and two other organisms in the Spanish Church, the religious communities and the military orders. The Medina meeting interestingly asserted that the reform of the Church was being set back by the running disputes between bishops and cathedral chapters which have already been mentioned. The 1505 assembly, while bombarding the respective governments of Castile and Aragon with demands for juridical and economic freedom, was still apparently pursuing a parallel agenda of reform. A series of complaints were made to the Roman Curia about the poor quality of some of some of those appointed by the popes to benefices in Spain, and the resulting failures in pastoral care. The secular clergy were not alone, however, in seeking a purification of the Church, in the years surrounding 1500.

By the time of Isabella's accession to the throne of Castile in 1474, a division had become established in most of the orders of monks, friars and nuns who lived and worked both within that kingdom and in the crown of Aragon. The distinction concerned was between the so-called *claustrales*, or *conventuales*, and the *observantes*, or *reformados*. The former were dedicated to maintaining the way of life, or 'rule', which had been handed down to them, while the latter, on the pretext of returning to the original instructions and intentions of the founders of their orders, had in fact acquired new rules of life within their respective traditions. Both positions were sanctioned by the Papacy, which had overall control of all religious orders, but, by the late fifteenth century, the Observants, with the active support of the Crown, were steadily gaining ground at the expense of the Conventuals. Traditional monasticism, derived from St Benedict (*c*.480–*c*.530), also maintained a significant presence in the Spain of Ferdinand and Isabella. Benedictine and Cistercian monasteries, as well as those of the austere Carthusian order, remained as complex, and often economically powerful, communities. These hierarchical structures, headed by an abbot and the 'choir monks' who had taken the full monastic vows of poverty, chastity and obedience, also contained lay brothers, including *donados*, who possessed benefices from the monastery, and lay servants, together with their families. By the late fifteenth century, whatever the earlier 'community' sense of Spanish monasteries, based on the Benedictine tradition, may have been, the primary concern of the traditional monasteries often appeared to be economic self-interest. Individual monastic houses were effectively running as economic corporations, with less and less emphasis on the spiritual life which was meant to be at their core.

Alongside the enclosed male communities were churches which had been staffed, some of them since the twelfth century, by colleges of 'regular' canons, so called because, although they were secular priests and not monks, they lived under a rule which was traditionally, but inaccurately, ascribed to St Augustine. Such collegiate churches were less hierarchically organized than the monasteries, and more open to the world, in that they more often undertook parochial work. Only the Premonstratensian canons, named after their mother house at Prémontré in northern France, had the autonomy of a rule of their own. This was also the case with the *conventos*, or friaries of the Mendicant orders. Not only had the Dominican, Franciscan and 'eremitical', or hermit Augustinian orders of friars been established in Spain since the thirteenth century, but native orders of friars had also developed in the Peninsula. These included the 'ransoming' orders of Mercy (La Merced) and the Trinity (La Trinidad), the function of which was to redeem Christians from Muslim captivity, and the semi-eremitical order of St Jerome, the Jeronymites (Jerónimos), which received considerable royal favour in the fourteenth and fifteenth centuries. Unlike the various Benedictine orders, the friars retained a strong community tradition, with considerable influence remaining in their provincial and general chapters, the latter involving their brothers in other countries. Alongside the male monasteries and friaries was a structure of houses for female religious. In the context of late medieval and early modern society, there was no female equivalent of the communities of canons or friars who lived in the secular world. Instead, in every religious order, women lived, at least notionally, an enclosed life, in a tightly-knit community, with male secular priests or religious to provide the sacramental services, especially confession and mass, which could not, under church law, be provided by women.

Both in the reforming literature of the period, and in much modern scholarly work, the 'conventual' religious life, both in Spain and elsewhere, has generally not been highly regarded. In fact, though a global picture is not yet possible, and may never be, there were wide variations in the quality of monastic life at this time, between and within the religious orders themselves and between the various peninsular kingdoms. In 1400, perhaps the most obvious evidence of the presence of traditional monasticism in Spanish society was still its exercise of lordship and jurisdiction over some towns, villages and lands. Yet the economic power of the larger monasteries was under threat, in this period, from the spread of the *encomienda*. Under this arrangement, a monastery's estates might be entrusted, either to abbots or priors of other orders, or to secular nobles, who thereby gained an opportunity not only to exploit the wealth of the community concerned but also to interfere in its internal affairs. Even without papal or royal initiatives, attempts were made in the fifteenth century to reform the Benedictine and Cistercian communities, which were mostly situated in the northern half of the Peninsula. The aims of this internal reform seem to have been more concerned with the basic devotional functions of the monks, which were concentrated on the performance of the elaborate Benedictine liturgy in the monastic church, than with other aspects of traditional communal life, such as private study and manual work, which had fallen into decline in the preceding century. In the larger and wealthier Benedictine monasteries, such as Santo Domingo de Silos in Castile and Montserrat in Catalonia, meticulous observance of the liturgy was accompanied by excellent cuisine, including banquets on festivals, regular supplies of outer and inner clothing, shaving, nightlights, and heated rooms, in particular the dining hall. The Cistercian order, which had begun in the Benedictine reform of the eleventh and twelfth centuries, presented a rather more spiritually inspiring example in the fifteenth century. In the kingdom of Valencia in this period, for example, the Cistercian houses appear to have been well-ordered and prosperous, even if they lacked the charisma of the austere Carthusians and the fashionable Jeronymites. Nonetheless, despite papal and royal attempts to end the practice, the Cistercians, like other orders, continued to suffer the effects of *encomiendas*, under which secular outsiders administered their properties. By Ferdinand's reign, the lack of community sense in the order's Spanish houses prevented external visitors from identifying and correcting their abuses: admonitions and advice were simply rejected out of hand. Nevertheless, the Cistercians took a full part in the reforming effort which was so powerfully sponsored by Isabella and her husband. The Spanish abbots of the order held an assembly at Valladolid, in 1493, under the presidency of the abbot of the mother house of Cîteaux. This meeting both formulated a response to the monarchs' reforming programme and ensured that the Spanish houses would not secede from the main order, which had been a danger. Nevertheless, the weaknesses of 'conventual' life remained plain for all to see. The liturgy was often poorly performed, and the communal austerity of traditional Cistercian monasticism had become a matter of single rooms instead of dormitories for the monks, the rule of silence in the house was systematically flouted, and frequent disputes within communities often verged on rebellion against abbots. Conventual Cistercian nunneries seem to have been equally lax, in many cases. The peculiar features of traditional female religious communities, in this and other enclosed orders, were their use as residences for female members of the upper classes who frequently had no discernible vocation to the religious life, and imported the social customs of their rank in the outside world, often including luxurious private accommodation, and the effective employment of lower-class and poorer sisters as servants. In the time of Ferdinand and Isabella, however, such behaviour was becoming increasingly unfashionable, especially in male houses, and the days of 'conventual' Cistercianism in Spain were effectively numbered. With active use of royal patronage, the great houses of Poblet, in Catalonia, and Las Huelgas, in Old Castile, for example, became pillars of the Observance. The lax customs of these monasteries, and of their daughter houses, increasingly fell foul of newly austere abbots and prelates.

The conflict, as it often became, between conventuals and observants passed some religious orders by, for example, the military orders and the ransoming orders of Mercy and the Trinity, but it reached its greatest heights in the mendicant orders of friars. The notion that true 'observance' of the founder's rule was the only proper goal of a friar's life had been prevalent ever since Dominic and Francis established their respective orders, with papal approval. By 1300, the Dominicans and Franciscans, and to a lesser extent the eremitical Augustinians, had achieved considerable influence not only in the religious life of the Spanish kingdoms but also in the academic and political spheres. It was in the latter part of the fourteenth century, however, that a new movement for observance began, especially in the Franciscan order. It first arose in Italy, but soon spread to other provinces of the order, including the three in Spain. In the Franciscan 'religion', as each particular Christian devotion was known in the period, the greatest stress was placed, among the traditional monastic vows to poverty, chastity and obedience, on the first. Francis of Assisi had advised his 'little brothers' (*Fraticelli*) to regard money as of no more value than stones, and saw no great need for the lay brothers of his order to learn to read, if they were able to praise God without, but his rapidly expanding movement soon faced a demand for compromise. Franciscans felt an urge to study God's word, which brought them into the environment of the partly secular universities, and led them to want to acquire property, in the form of books. More fundamentally, however, the massive support which they began to receive from other Christians, many of them wealthy, increasingly expressed itself, as it had done for the earlier, monastic orders, in the form of gifts of money and property. Conventual Franciscans continued, in Ferdinand and Isabella's time, to accept these apparent necessities, so that their practice departed from the austerity which their order's founder had demanded from others, as well as himself. By the late fourteenth century, however, the desire among some Spanish Franciscans to return to earlier standards, as they saw them, was beginning to show itself in a rejection of the revised rule to which their houses were then subject. By Isabella and Ferdinand's reign, the conventual tradition in Spain's religious orders seems to have lost faith in its own survival. Only a few, marginalized conventual houses were left in Castile, while the observants advanced dramatically, with the strongest royal support. In this 'offensive' against the conventuals, the existing Franciscan provincials, for example, took an active role, despite Pope Sixtus IV's legislative attempts to protect conventual institutions and property. In Ferdinand's crown of Aragon, the conventual communities put up more of a fight, and were not to be incorporated into the Observance until the late sixteenth century. These houses, and in particular the nunneries among them, were enabled to mount such resistance largely because they continued to receive the support of the wealthier mercantile families. Nevertheless, a number of houses of male Franciscans and female Clarisas, in Aragon, Catalonia and Navarre, were permanently destroyed as a result of the military conflicts of the second half of the fifteenth century. In the long run, despite Sixtus IV's efforts to protect conventualism in the Franciscan and Dominican orders, and to a lesser extent among the Augustinians and Carmelites, the victory was to go definitively to the Observance. Permanent integration of the two groups took place in the Dominican order in 1504, and seven years later among the Augustinians. A major effort was made, at this time, to achieve a similar result among the Franciscans, but this failed during Ferdinand's lifetime, largely as a result of resistance in the Italian provinces of the order.

It is, notoriously, very much easier to register institutional changes in religious organizations than transformations in their spiritual life. Throughout the Church's history, those who were dissatisfied with its quality have attacked their opponents in vigorous and lurid terms, thus obtaining much greater attention from scholars than their more conventional brethren. The possibility of such documentary distortion should be borne in mind in any consideration of the 'reform' of the Spanish Church in fifteenth- and sixteenth-century Spain. It is undeniable, though, that a revival of spiritual life did take place in this period, especially in the religious orders, so that the disputes which arose were not solely concerned with institutional and economic matters. One important development was the growth, from the late fourteenth century onwards, of a desire to return to the eremitical traditions of the earliest Christian monasticism. During the late fourteenth and fifteenth centuries, this tendency developed strongly, not least in the Jeronymite order, which became highly influential in the Iberian peninsula. Its original character was a combination into cells of individuals who had previously lived as hermits, and who took as an inspiration their notional founder, Jerome, the author of the Latin, 'Vulgate' translation of the Bible. The new Jeronymite houses quickly attracted the patronage of the rich and famous, as in the case of the Madrid convent, which was founded by Henry IV of Castile in 1461.

It is evident that the Catholic Monarchs inherited a powerful movement for both spiritual and institutional reform, which had strengthened the observance of founders' rules, as well as the contemplative aspects of the religious life. The 1478 council of Seville, as well as providing the impetus for the introduction of the Inquisition to Castile, included the religious orders in its comprehensive campaign to improve the quality and discipline of the clergy. Particularly active at the council was Fray Hernando de Talavera, a Jeronymite friar who was by then Isabella's confessor and main spiritual adviser, and later became the first archbishop of Granada, after the conquest in 1492. Other leading reformers in the Spanish hierarchy were the Dominican Pascual de Ampudia, who has been compared to his contemporary of the same order in Florence, Girolamo Savonarola, and carried out reforms in his diocese of Burgos between 1496 and 1512, and, of course, the great Franciscan Cardinal Francisco Jiménez de Toledo, who was archbishop of Toledo between 1495 and his death in 1517. In 1479, after the Seville council was over, Ferdinand and Isabella petitioned the pope to license bishops in Castile and Aragon to reform religious houses in their dioceses, on the lines already described, and forbid the entry of lay people to female convents, which had been leading to notorious abuses. Although both Sixtus IV and his successor, Innocent VIII, jealous for papal prerogatives, refused such blanket permission, the rulers were not deterred. One line of attack was, as has already been seen, to influence, and if possible control, episcopal appointments, while a consequence of their official support of the observant movement in the religious orders was to restore the right of free election of the superiors, or heads, of monasteries and convents. This policy was clearly intended to lead to the appointment of reforming abbots, abbesses and priors, but such measures were strongly resisted by the Papacy, which feared the loss of income as well as power. Religious reform was often linked with the monarchs' efforts to restore and maintain order in their kingdoms. Thus the attempt to quell noble rebellion in Galicia (see chapter 1) was accompanied by the despatch of monks from the reformed Benedictine house of San Benito in Valladolid to visit their order's houses in the region. One result was that all the Benedictine nuns in Galicia were congregated in a single convent, where 'observant' discipline was to be assured. In Catalonia, Ferdinand personally supervised the reform of nunneries, sending out twenty-four edicts on the subject in November and December 1493. In both regions, however, the rulers met the problems which had vexed earlier reformers. Nuns who had lived for many years in a lax environment, which made their convents seem almost like hotels, were often reluctant, in the extreme, to submit to strict enclosure. They could, and did, claim that they were 'observant' too, but of the laxer, 'mitigated' rule in which they had professed. Many reacted by escaping from their convents and leaving the religious life altogether. Events in the 1490s, as in earlier decades, revealed the problems and limitations of the official programme for 'reformation' of the Church. As with the introduction of the new Inquisition from 1484, a major cause of resistance in the crown of Aragon, especially in Catalonia, was that reformed nuns, who were intended to act as examples to the backsliders, were commonly Castilian, and therefore 'foreign'. Isabella and Ferdinand seem to have learnt their lesson from the initial contretemps, and attempted to employ local reforming groups thereafter, but progress in Aragon and the Catalan lands remained slow. In Castile, though, by the time of Ferdinand's death, it was possible to point to some achievements. Although efforts to reform the great Cistercian convent of Las Huelgas had reached stalemate, the order's Spanish houses had finally achieved effective independence, in the reforming cause, from the mother house at Cîteaux. Attempts to found new Cistercian colleges, at Salamanca and Alcalá, appear to indicate a revival of enthusiasm in the order at the beginning of the sixteenth century.

Perhaps a sign of renewed enthusiasm for the Cistercian life, in this case for women, was the choice by Beatriz de Silva, who had formerly been a lady-in-waiting to Isabella's mother, of the rule of that order for her convent of the Conception (Concepción) in Toledo, which received papal authorization in 1489. The house in question, which later became mother to the new order of the Conception, retained some Cistercian hallmarks, even though it had been influenced from the start by Franciscan spirituality and in 1511 was made administratively subject to the observant Franciscan order.[7] As far as the established orders of friars were concerned, in 1496, at the same time that he granted the title of 'Catholic Monarchs' to Ferdinand and Isabella, Alexander VI appointed Cisneros to supervise the reform of the Spanish Franciscans, and Fray Diego de Deza, to perform a similar role among the Dominicans. Deza was shortly to succeed Tomás de Torquemada as inquisitor-general, however, and most of the task of reform devolved upon Bishop Pascual de Ampudia. Despite some last-ditch resistance from the Franciscan conventuals, which was, paradoxically, supported by the pope, Cisneros achieved practical, if not legal, victory, with massive royal support. The queen took a personal interest in the success of the Observance, to the extent of herself becoming a 'tertiary', or member of the lay Third Order, and eventually being buried in a Franciscan habit. In the Franciscan province of Castile, the conventual houses were all effectively taken over by the observants, though less success was achieved in the provinces of Santiago and Aragon. The Catholic Monarchs' reform programme was most effective among the religious orders. In the case of the Franciscans, they gave support to reforming groups, such as the 'congregation', after 1517 elevated to the status of a province, of St Gabriel, in Extremadura, which became a nursery of missionaries to the New World, such as Fray Toribio de Benavente 'Motolinía'. Isabella and Ferdinand had also supported the Franciscan congregation, known as the 'Amadeites', which had been founded during Henry IV's reign by Fray Amadeo de Silva, brother of the foundress of the Concepción convent in Toledo. Amadeo's radical Franciscan group, which continued to be active in the early decades of the sixteenth century, was based in the convent and church of San Pietro in Montorio, on the Janiculum in Rome, and had a strong apocalyptic strand in its devotion.[8]

Although efforts to reform the secular clergy, who manned the parish churches and cathedrals, had continued intermittently for centuries, the report which was composed for Isabella at the beginning of her reign, by her confessor Hernando de Talavera, suggested that little, if anything, had improved. Clergy, and especially the higher clergy such as bishops, continued to be absent from their posts on a large scale, such jobs continued to be bought and sold, and greed and scandal were not hard to find. To Talavera's Jeronymite eyes, the lower ranks of the clergy presented an even more dismal picture, which was the target of measures passed at Aranda in 1473 and five years later, in Seville. Clergy were not looking after their altars and sacred vessels properly, were collecting money from the laity during the celebration of Sunday mass, and allowed lay people not only to transact secular business during services, but even to dance to the music of church organs. It should be borne in mind, when reading such accounts, that reformers, such as Talavera proved to be when he took on the archdiocese of Granada after 1492, are not necessarily the best guides to the religious life of the great bulk of the population. Nevertheless, the violent resistance which was put up to reforming bishops, for example in Salamanca, Astorga and Vizcaya, suggests that the pessimism of the Jeronymite's observations was not without justification. Even the energetic Cisneros, preoccupied with political business and the reform of the religious orders, did not visit his archdiocese of Toledo for two years, and could do no more than try to enforce the programme for clerical and lay discipline which had been set out by the Roman Church at least since the thirteenth century. At the end of Isabella and Ferdinand's reigns, the separation of the clergy, in their way of life as well as their office, from the rest of the population was still a largely unachieved aim. The monarchs seem to have had a somewhat rigid notion of what the religion and morals of Spanish society should be. This view was perhaps better adapted to the more centralized and disciplined religious orders, with which they achieved a significant degree of success, than to the secular clergy and the lay majority. After some disagreements with Sixtus IV and Innocent VIII, Ferdinand and Isabella found the Valencian Borja Alexander VI very much more co-operative, in matters of Church reform, as in the operation of the Inquisition and in the evangelization and control of the New World. The king and queen were also very much influenced by their chosen ecclesiastical advisers, and a distinct change of emphasis has been observed after 1492, when Talavera was replaced by Cisneros as the main confessor and counsellor in such matters. It has been suggested that the Franciscan cardinal brought a more 'nationalist' emphasis to Spanish church policy, though, like other late medieval rulers, Ferdinand, in particular had long since shown inclinations in this direction. There is also some evidence that husband and wife differed somewhat in their approaches to the question of church reform. In the first years of the sixteenth century, Ferdinand seems to have been willing to allow conventual Franciscans to live unmolested in his kingdom of Valencia and, after his wife's death, he attempted to moderate the zeal of the ecclesiastical reformers, though such action had already been urged by Isabella herself, in a codicil to her will. In any case, in the latter years of his reign, after the failure of the attempt to merge the conventual Franciscans with the observants, Ferdinand pursued the former with as much vigour as his wife had done.

It should not be supposed that, even in its most nationalistic mood, the effort to reform the Spanish Church during Ferdinand and Isabella's reign took place in either an intellectual or a geographical vacuum. Spaniards had been active in moves to end the schism of the Catholic Church, and in attempts to reform it, since at least the early fifteenth century. When the first of these aims was achieved, at the council of Constance (1414–18), with the establishment of Martin V (who reigned 1417–31), there were hopes that such councils of the leading clergy, with lay advisers, would become a regular part of the government of the Church. Under the terms of the decree *Frequens*, which was issued at Constance on 9 October 1417 as a 'perpetual edict', the next council was to meet five years after the end of the current one, the second was to be held seven years after that and, thereafter, similar assemblies were to be convened at least every ten years. Although *Frequens* was never fully implemented, councils were indeed held, at Pavia and Siena in 1423–4, at Basle intermittently between 1431 and 1447, and in Ferrara and Florence in 1438, with a remnant continuing until 1447. Martin V and his successors soon demonstrated, however, that they had no intention of relinquishing their hard-won papal prerogatives, or of sharing them with a general council. Thus although it was not until January

1460 that Pius II, in his bull *Execrabilis*, formally condemned conciliar theory, the disputes, and increasing militancy, which had developed during the years of the Basle council had effectively discredited 'conciliar' theory in eyes other than those of the popes.[9] Nevertheless, the yearning for reform refused to die away in the Church, and many, including some secular rulers, continued to believe that abuses 'in head and members' would not be confronted effectively unless a new 'ecumenical council' was assembled to guide the hand of the successor of Peter. This was to be one of the constant aims of Isabella and Ferdinand. The period between 1414 and 1460 did, however, see an important crystallization of certain aspects of Roman Catholicism which were to exert influence long after the death of the king of Aragon in 1516. In 1438, for example, the council of Florence, which was sponsored by Pope Eugenius IV (who reigned 1431–47), formally established the list of seven Christian sacraments – baptism, the eucharist or mass, confirmation, ordination, penance or confession, extreme unction and matrimony – the latter five of which were to cause such dissension during the Protestant Reformation and thereafter. The years preceding Isabella's accession to the Castilian throne also saw considerable development of the Church's views about the role and significance of Mary, the mother of Jesus. In particular, the mid-fifteenth century saw a growth in support for the belief that, in order to be a suitable vessel for the birth of Jesus, who was 'true God and true Man', Mary must not only have been a virgin throughout the process of conception, pregnancy and birth, as the New Testament, and in particular Matthew and Luke's gospels (Chapters 1ff. in each case) state, but also herself born free of the taint of 'original sin', inherited from Adam and Eve, which affects every other human being. This doctrine of the 'Immaculate Conception' had, in the past, been opposed even by such devotees of the Virgin Mary as St Bernard of Clairvaux (1090–1153), and was not to be declared dogma until 1854, during the reign of Pius IX. Nevertheless, this teaching received solid support from the council of Basle, which declared that Mary's 'immaculate conception is a pious opinion, consistent with the worship of the Church, to Catholic faith, to right reason, and to Holy Scripture', and decreed that the liturgical feast of the (Immaculate) Conception should henceforth be celebrated each year on 8 December. Despite the conflicts which engulfed the Basle fathers, and the eventual repudiation of that council by the Papacy, this commemoration became a permanent part of the liturgy of the Roman Catholic Church, when it was approved by Sixtus IV in 1476. The Franciscans, among whom this pope was included, had long been strong supporters of Marian devotion in general and the Immaculate Conception in particular. It is clear that such views were shared by

Isabella herself, as she supported her mother's former lady-in-waiting, Beatriz de Silva, in her project to found a religious order of the Conception, and also, with her husband, paid for a new façade for the 'Amadean' Franciscan Church of San Pietro in Montorio. Perhaps paradoxically in modern eyes, the increasingly ornate presentation of papal Rome, during Isabella and Ferdinand's reigns, was accompanied with a high regard, on the part both of these rulers and of some popes, for poverty and austerity in the Christian life. Another common thread in both Italian and Spanish church life was a concern to read, and if possible to understand, the 'signs of the times'.[10]

It has been suggested that the Spain of the Catholic Monarchs was suffused with prophecy. The accession of the two sovereigns to their respective thrones had been accompanied by an upsurge in political prophecy and messianism, which was matched by Alfonso V of Portugal, when he invaded Castile on behalf of his new wife Joanna. As early as 1472, when Ferdinand of Sicily was little known outside his own sphere, an Aragonese poet had hailed him as a future ruler of the world, while propagandists for the Portuguese king announced, in 1475, that he, in turn, was the 'hidden', or 'hooded' king (el rey encubierto), who was prophesied by many writers as the coming deliverer of the kingdom from tyranny and evil. In 1486, during the Granada war, one of the leading commanders, the Andalusian magnate Rodrigo Ponce de León, claimed to have been personally assured, by 'a very knowledgeable man and Catholic Christian', that Ferdinand of Aragon (his queen was not, apparently, mentioned in this prediction) would not only drive the Muslims out of Spain, but would go on to conquer the whole of Africa, destroy Islam completely, reconquer Jerusalem and the holy places, and become 'emperor of Rome, and of the Turks, and of the Spains'. It might be argued that the words of the anonymous seer were fulfilled, at least in part, by Charles V, rather than his grandfather, but there is convincing evidence that Ferdinand himself believed until his dying day that he would not die until he had personally conquered Jerusalem. Thus he would not only avenge the defeat of the crusaders in the thirteenth century by restoring the third Muslim holy place to Christendom, but also demonstrate the folly and impotence of Judaism. The high status which was granted to political prophets in the Spain of Isabella and Ferdinand is indicated by the exceptional favour which was received by Sor María de Santo Domingo, known as the 'Beata de Piedrahita'. Although a laywoman in the Dominican 'Third Order', Sor María not only made public predictions which seemed to correspond closely to the Aragonese king's overall ecclesiastical and secular aims, but also became, with the support of the Franciscan Cardinal Cisneros, reforming visitor to the male Dominican houses of Castile. When the 'beata's' ministrations were subjected to ecclesiastical investigation, in 1509–10, her supporters included the duke of Alba, Cisneros, and Ferdinand himself. 'Prophecy' was more likely to be listened to in high places if it supported existing policy, and, in Sor María's case, this included statements on behalf of Cisneros's 'crusade' to capture the Muslim city of Oran in 1509.[11]

If the written words of Christopher Columbus are to be accepted at face value, and there is no serious reason for not doing so, the 'discoverer' of the New World of the Americas took seriously the notion of Spain's role, and in particular his own, in the world's preparations for the future coming to earth of the Antichrist, and the subsequent Last Judgement of all humankind. Even if the explorer was not totally convinced of his personal role in the process at the time of his first westward voyage in 1492, six years later, in his written acknowledgement of royal permission to establish an entailed estate (*mayorazgo*), he referred to his own long-standing campaign for the recapture from Muslim control of the 'Holy House' in Jerusalem. In 1500, a year of extensive prophetic activity in the Peninsula, Columbus drew up for the king and queen a memorandum entitled 'The reason I have for believing in the restoration of the Holy House to the Holy Church militant'. In this document, he claimed that he relied 'entirely on holy, sacred Scripture and certain prophetic texts by certain saintly persons who by divine revelation have had something to say on this matter'. While it may be excessive to argue that such religious beliefs were the mainspring of the Genoese adventurer's enterprises, they undoubtedly influenced him increasingly. As an external sign of his Christian adherence, and in accord with the spiritual climate of the years around the turn of the sixteenth century, Columbus was commonly seen at Court in a Franciscan habit. In particular, the Franciscans of the Andalusian house of La Rábida, near the port of Palos de la Frontera, from which he departed on his first voyage, had provided vital intellectual and spiritual support to his search for a royal sponsor. Nevertheless, between 1500 and 1502, when the discoverer was actively propagating his own, and Spain's, role in the forthcoming Apocalypse, the main religious influence on him seems to have come not from Franciscans but from an Italian Carthusian, Gaspar Gorricio, who was based in the order's house of Santa María de las Cuevas, Seville. Gorricio seems to have been largely responsible for the compilation of extracts from Scripture and the writings of the Church Fathers which seems to have been completed by 1503.[12] The Franciscan millenarian spirituality, which greatly affected Columbus, as well as his Spanish royal masters, had been influenced since the thirteenth century by the ideas of the Calabrian Benedictine abbot, Joachim of Fiore (*c*.1132–1202). Thus, by taking up

Joachim's ideas, Columbus fitted readily into the religious atmosphere of Isabella and Ferdinand's court, which envisaged the general reform of the Church under the ageis of the 'last [Holy Roman] Emperor', as a preparation for the coming of the world's final days. In reality, much that was ascribed to Joachim in late fifteenth- and early sixteenth-century Europe was written by others, and the specific links between Spain and prophecies for the end of time, which were so much favoured by Isabella and her husband, should be ascribed to the Catalan physician and mystic Arnold of Vilanova (c.1240–1311). Columbus seems to have gained his belief in the messianic and eschatological role of Spain, and hence of himself, from Arnold's *Vaticinia de summis pontificibus* ('Prophecies concerning the supreme Pontiffs [popes]'). In his *Lettera rarissima* ('Very rare letters'), written to Ferdinand and Isabella during his fourth, and last voyage, the admiral of the 'Ocean Sea' stated that 'Jerusalem and Mount Zion are to be rebuilt by Christian hands, and God through the mouth of the prophet in the fourteenth psalm said so. The abbot Joachim said that this man was to come from Spain.' Columbus further states, in the *Book of Prophecies*, that 'We read that Joachim, abbot of Calabria, predicted that someone from Spain would recover the wealth from Zion.' In reality, this prophecy seems to come from Arnold of Vilanova's *Vae mundo in centum annis* ('Oh world, in a hundred years!'), which had spread from radical Franciscan to Aragonese political circles by the end of the fourteenth century. The climate of prophecy in Spain during the latter part of Isabella and Ferdinand's reigns affected not only Old Christians, but also Jews and *conversos.*[13]

During the 1480s, although the work of Torquemada's expanding Inquisition was, in law, directed at converts to Christianity and not at those who remained faithful to Judaism, the conditions for Jewish life in Castile and Aragon began to deteriorate. Earlier Castilian ordinances, such as those enacted by the government of John II at Valladolid in 1412, and the 'sentence of arbitration' announced in 1465 by the commissioners who had been appointed by a reluctant Henry IV, had been of only limited effect. Equivalent laws in the territories of the crown of Aragon seem to have been equally ineffective. Yet even before their epoch-making visits to Andalusia in 1477–8, Isabella and Ferdinand had included in their programme for the wartime cortes of Madrigal, in 1476, measures to enforce long-standing provisions, in both ecclesiastical and secular law, dating back to the Fourth Lateran Council in 1215. These were intended to restrict social contact between Jewish and Muslim minorities on the one hand, and the Christian majority on the other. The cortes of Toledo, in 1480, confirmed the policy of *apartamiento*, which disrupted the lives of many urban communities by laying upon *corregidores*, and other royal and municipal officials, the duty of forcibly confining the Jewish and Muslim minorities, or *aljamas*, within their towns to existing, or newly delineated, walled enclosures, the ancestors of the Venetian ghetto of the sixteenth century. What followed, in many places, was a lengthy and painful process of 'urban renewal', in which streets were blocked, windows walled up, and families and communities split. It was already clear that the price for Christian social and religious unity was to be paid by the remaining members of the minority communities, in their *juderías* and *morerías*. As the decade of the 1480s progressed, the conditions for the life of these groups, together with social cohesion in both Castile and Aragon, were to deteriorate further. The raising of tension against Muslims, which had begun before 1480, was inevitably increased by the ten-year war to end the existence of the Muslim kingdom of Granada. During the period of these exhausting and expensive campaigns, the inquisitors pursued their investigation into the lives and religions of innumerable descendants of those who had converted from Judaism to Christianity. The tribunals of the Holy Office claimed to have discovered evidence which corroborated the assertions which had been made by advocates of a new Inquisition in Castile, and a revived one in the crown of Aragon. They came to two conclusions, as the testimony of thousands of defendants and witnesses, collected from virtually all corners of Ferdinand and Isabella's domains, demonstrated. The first of these was that many, if not all, *conversos* continued to believe in and practise Judaism, under a cloak of Catholic conformity. The second, which was to be of the greatest significance in the near future, was that these 'New Christians' were being drawn back into their ancestral faith by the continued existence in Spain of legal and practising Jewish communities, often consisting of their own family relations.

In June 1490, at a tavern in Astorga, some inebriated travellers claimed to have discovered, in the luggage of a *converso* wool-comber called Benito García, a stolen eucharistic host, the consecrated bread of the Catholic mass. One of the local bishop's officials, the vicar-general Dr Villalba, was informed, and García was arrested and immediately tortured. The prisoner appears to have been a Christian, very probably a *converso*, and to have been travelling back to the Toledo area from the shrine of St James at Compostela, with a mixture of *converso* and Jewish companions. This combination of religious affiliations was to be of the essence of the story of the case, which was later to be publicized, to deadly effect, in both Castile and Aragon. What is known today of the case which came to be known at the time and later, as that of the 'Holy Child of La Guardia' (*Santo Niño de La Guardia*), is mainly to be found in the records of the subsequent trial by the Inquisition of one of

Benito García's companions, the Jew Yuçe Franco. By the time that the diocesan authorities handed the case over to the Valladolid tribunal of the Holy Office, a further charge against the Jewish and *converso* group had been added. In addition to the accusation, which had become a standard one against Jews in large areas of western and central Europe in the late Middle Ages, that they had misused a eucharistic host and hence blasphemed against the Christ whom it embodied, they now fell foul of the other charge which had become, since the twelfth century, a regular part of the so-called 'blood libel' against Jews. This was that the group had kidnapped a young Christian boy, an inhabitant of the small town of La Guardia, south-east of Toledo, and had then proceeded to torture and finally crucify him, in imitation of the sufferings which had been inflicted on Jesus. The case, which seemed to demonstrate that New Christians did indeed appear to have retained the devilish nature of their Jewish ancestors and living friends and relations, quickly attracted interest at a higher level. Contrary to normal practice, the papers and defendants were transferred to the neighbouring tribunal in Avila, the base of the inquisitor-general, Tomás de Torquemada. During the next year and a half, the inquisitors struggled to gain confirmation from both defendants and witnesses of their double charge of 'ritual murder' and host desecration. In their effort to secure a coherent story which could lead to conviction and sentence, they not only resorted to torture, but went against Torquemada's own procedural instructions to the Inquisition by deliberately bringing defendants together, in an effort to reconcile their obstinately conflicting statements. As a result of this confrontation, which took place in Avila on 12 October 1491, three of the accused, Benito García, Yuçe Franco and Juan de Ocaña, professed to agree that they had taken part in the crucifixion of the boy, early in 1490, in a cave outside La Guardia. Not only that but six months later they had met again, somewhere between that town and Tembleque, and given Benito the stolen host, which he was to take to a rabbi in Zamora, for use in spells to 'drive the Christians mad' (*'para que raviasen los christianos'*). However, agreement concerning what had happened was still not complete, and the inquisitors of Avila referred the case to a committee of assessors (*calificadores*), who were academics from Salamanca University. The scholars declared that, on the basis of the evidence before them, the Jew Yuçe Franco was indeed guilty of aiding and abetting the *conversos* in their atrocious behaviour. Events now moved rapidly towards their violent denouement. On 2 November, a final attempt was made to torture the defendants into conformity with the Inquisition's story of child murder and blasphemy. By this time, though, inconsistencies in the evidence were no longer regarded as obstacles to a guilty verdict and, on 11 November, the Avila tribunal placed the papers in the hands of their regular *calificadores*, who were local clergy law-yers. This panel convicted the accused, both New Christian and Jewish, of the double offence of ritual murder and host desecration. On 16 November 1491, an *auto de fe* was held in Avila, after which Benito, Juan and Yuçe, together with a number of others who are not specified in the incomplete surviving records, were burned to death.

The trial of the supposed torturers and murderers of the so-called Holy Child of La Guardia had various remarkable features, by the standards of the jurisprudence of the Inquisition during Ferdinand and Isabella's reign. The irregular confrontation of witnesses, which at a stroke undermined the isolation of prisoners and secrecy of interroga-tion which were much-prized features of the Holy Office until its last days in the early nineteenth century, has already been noted. Perhaps even more striking, however, was the continued absence, both during the trial and afterwards, of any evidence either of a missing boy, alive or dead, or of any parental report of a lost child. The reason why such details were regarded as irrelevant, in the context of the last phase of the Granada war, was soon to be revealed. The publicity of the case began at once. On 17 November 1491, the day after the *auto* in Avila, one of the town's notaries, Antón González, wrote to the municipal council of La Guardia enclosing a copy of the Inquisition's sentence against Benito García, as well as an eyewitness account of the ceremo-nies of the previous day. In this the notary stated that Benito died as a Catholic Christian, and that Juan de Ocaña and Juan Franco had also expressed repentance for their acts, though the other defendants had been put to death on a slow fire. The future development of the legend of the 'Holy Child' was indicated, at this early stage, in the Avila notary's suggestion to the authorities in La Guardia that the local delegate of the Inquisition in the child's home town, Alonso Domín-guez, would tell them exactly where the lad had been crucified, though only divine revelation would indicate where his remains might be found. Evidently, the Holy Office had plans for the deceased 'child', and Torquemada soon ordered that the Avila proceedings should be translated into Catalan, evidently for distribution and publicity in Fer-dinand's hereditary domains. At the same time, a small painting was prepared, which survives in the Archivo Histórico Nacional in Madrid, showing the child on the cross, surrounded by the supposed conspira-tors, who are named in the picture. The message which Spaniards and their rulers were to receive was clear. It was that Jews and *conversos* were working together to destroy Isabella and Ferdinand's kingdoms. Royal action was soon to follow, on 31 March 1492.[14]

On that date, the king and queen issued two parallel edicts, through their Castilian and Aragonese chanceries. Under the terms of both documents, which differed somewhat in emphasis as well as terminology, the Jewish subjects of the two monarchs were to be forced to make an epoch-making decision, both for their personal lives and for their communities. If they had not been baptised as Christians by 31 July, they were to leave Isabella and Ferdinand's domains and not return. Any Christian who assisted a Jew to break the terms of the relevant edict was to lose his own property, as well as other royal favours. Jews who refused to convert were also permitted by royal licence to take their movable goods out of Spain. They were not allowed to take with them commodities which might not normally be exported (*cosas vedadas*), such as horses and mules, bullion, and Spanish coins. Local authorities were ordered to give their fullest support to the implementation of the royal order. Although there was some delay in the issue of the relevant instructions throughout Castile and Aragon, this merely served to reduce the time available for the disposal of property by those who preferred to leave Spain as Jews rather than convert. Given the nature of the edicts of 31 March 1492, the resulting disintegration of what had been, for many centuries, the largest Jewish community in Europe has naturally been ascribed to the initiative of the king and queen, and their government. Yet the efforts of the Inquisition, particularly in the two preceding years, should not be forgotten, and, in the triumphalist circumstances of the approaching end of the centuries-old Reconquest, the royal measures were an all too natural sequel to the 'evidence' which had been garnered in the trial of the supposed crucifiers of the Holy Child of La Guardia.

The more than suspected involvement of the Inquisition in the monarchs' decision, which had its precedents in the local expulsion of Jews from parts of Andalusia and Aragon in the preceding decade (see chapter 3), also raises a question about the traditional description of the 31 March measures as 'expulsion edicts'. On the face of it, this is precisely what these documents were. Jews were told that they had to convert or leave, and many undoubtedly did so. Although estimates of the total number who departed have tended to decline, in recent years, from the figures of between 100,000 and 300,000 which were suggested by Christian and Jewish contemporaries, to something between 50,000 and 70,000, it remains evident that a very large forcible movement of people, in difficult and sometimes tragic circumstances, took place in Spain in the summer of 1492. Observers, of both religions, described the painful departure of Jews, both rich and poor, to the neighbouring kingdoms of Portugal and Navarre, to Italy, and to the Muslim lands of North Africa and Ottoman Turkey. The Andalusian priest chronicler, Andrés Bernáldez, gleefully recounted the killing and robbing of the refugees in the kingdoms of the Maghreb, while other Jews were parted from their remaining possessions by the ship's captains who transported them across the Straits of Gibraltar or the Mediterranean. Less dramatic, but also a cause of great distress, was the treatment meted out to those who departed by land. Problems began at once, when it became generally known that Isabella and Ferdinand's Jewish subjects would have to convert or leave. The fact that those who made the latter decision were forced to dispose of their houses and lands inevitably sent property prices crashing, and neither royal orders nor local authorities could prevent Christians from squatting in houses which had been abandoned. Yet when Jews finally left their home towns and headed, for example, for the Portuguese border, their difficulties continued. Subsequent investigations by ducal officials in the lands of the duke of Béjar, who had jurisdiction over various towns in the areas of Salamanca and Cáceres, reveal that, during the passage of the refugees between April and July 1492, abuses had been rife. The officials' questions suggest that Jews' Christian neighbours had not only illegally seized houses and lands, but had also stolen synagogue ornaments. On other occasions, Christians seem to have given active assistance to Jews, legally carrying, or else smuggling, their goods into Portugal. Officials, too, were not above exploiting the situation. As soon as customs officers in the border town of Ciudad Rodrigo heard of the Castilian expulsion edict, they raised the tax on passengers into Portugal from one *real* to four-and-a-half. In October 1492, royal investigators reported that abusive duties had been collected from Jews who departed through this customs post. Subsequent evidence from Inquisition sources indicates that some of those who removed their goods to Portugal had travelled from as far away as Soria and Burgo de Osma, in north-eastern Castile. Yet not all Ferdinand and Isabella's Jewish subjects took the option of departure. As soon as the royal edicts reached the towns and villages of Castile and Aragon, reports began to emerge of campaigns of preaching, aimed at persuading Jews to convert to Christianity and stay. The unsympathetic Christian commentator, Andrés Bernáldez, states that these efforts were sponsored by the Crown, and there is some evidence that they achieved immediate success. According to Elijah Capsali, a contemporary Jewish commentator, 'thousands, and even tens of thousands' of Jews responded to the evangelistic call, which, if true, would mean that the events of 1390–1420, when such numbers had undoubtedly been baptised, were repeated in 1492. More specifically, in the Aragonese town of Teruel, which had earlier been the scene of stout resistance to the introduction of the Castilian Inquisition (see chapter 3), local sources indicate that the whole Jewish community, numbering up to a hundred souls, which had returned to the town after the temporary expulsion of 1486, was converted and baptized in a single morning.[15]

Such events should have surprised no one, given the terms of the two orders of 31 March. While the Aragonese version, issued by Ferdinand for his hereditary domains, rehearsed traditional Christian hatred of Jews, largely on religious grounds, the Castilian document explicitly stated that the spiritual and social state of the *conversos*, and hence of the kingdom as a whole, was threatened by the continuing links between New Christians and Jews. Whatever the degree of accuracy of contemporary accounts of the events of mid-1492, the clearest supporting evidence that Isabella and Ferdinand intended their March edicts to bring about the conversion rather than the expulsion of their Jewish subjects may be found in a further royal order, which was issued on 10 November of that year. This measure offered a royal safe conduct to all Jews who returned to Castile and Aragon as baptised Christians. In order to enable them to restart their lives, these New Christians were to receive back all the property which they had been forced to sell earlier in the year, though they were required to compensate the owners of the property in the meantime for any improvement (*mejoramiento*) which they had made. According to the terms of the November edict, the baptisms in question might take place either in Portugal (Navarre is not mentioned) or in Castilian border towns, such as Ciudad Rodrigo and Zamora. Christians who had bought property from Jews after 31 March of that year would be required, if and when the previous owner returned, to appear before the relevant local authorities in order to hand over the goods in question in due legal form. A series of royal documents, dated between December 1492 and April 1494, indicate that the royal 'law of return' was not intended to be a dead letter. Examples of its application during this period are to be found in Ledesma, Atienza, Cuéllar, Segovia, Zamora, Logroño, Santaolalla and Sepúlveda. It is clearly impossible to provide reliable statistics of those Jews who returned to Castile as converts at this time. Inquisition records, for example from the tribunal in Soria and Burgo de Osma, indicate that returns of this kind were a well-recognized phenomenon, which might even be used to date other events. Years later, in evidence to the Soria Inquisition, Juan de Salzedo referred to 'the time when the Jews returned from Portugal', and similar phrases were used three years later by other witnesses. While the Crown concerned itself primarily with economic matters, the inquisitors, whose policy of ensuring that all people of Jewish origin within Castile and Aragon were at least nominally Catholic Christians, and hence under their jurisdiction, inevitably questioned the orthodoxy of the new converts. Given the circumstances in which the returns took place, the accusation of insincerity, due to a desire for social and economic advancement, which had damaged Spanish *conversos* for many decades, inevitably arose once again. It should also be noted that, during the last years of the fifteenth century and the beginning of the sixteenth, while *judeoconversos* were being arrested and investigated by the Inquisition for supposed 'Judaizing', royal officials were selling documents of 'rehabilitation' (*habilitaciones*) to those who wished to have their dealings with the Holy Office expunged from the record, and were prepared to pay for the privilege, at rates set according to their degree of wealth. The government of Ferdinand and Isabella seems quickly to have become aware that the loss of productive citizens, many of them of considerable ability, whether Jews or *conversos*, was not conducive to the future health of kingdoms which were, at that very time, intended by their rulers to become significant powers in the world. In addition to internal Spanish factors, it may also be desirable, however, to look at the situation in the neighbouring peninsular kingdoms to which many Jews initially migrated in the summer of 1492 – Portugal and Navarre.[16]

Like its Spanish neighbours, Portugal in 1492 contained a significant and well-established Jewish community, numbering approximately 30,000 people, or 3 per cent of the total population. As elsewhere in late medieval Europe, Jews predominantly lived in towns, and up to a tenth of the population of the main towns, Lisbon and Oporto, may have been Jewish. In its treatment of Jews, as in all other aspects of policy, Portugal stoutly maintained its independence from its overbearing neighbour, Castile. Thus the newly-established royal house of Avis reacted to the sufferings of Castilian and Aragonese Jews in 1391 by affirming, in the following year, its protection of the religious and social status of its own Jewish subjects. Indeed, during the 1390s, some Spanish Jews took advantage of this policy to emigrate to the neighbouring kingdom. However, serious tensions began to develop within Portugal during the 1480s, when Torquemada's inquisitors began their work in the neighbouring Castilian territories, in particular Andalusia and Extremadura. This time, the immigrants were *conversos* rather than Jews, and violence soon began to occur between the Spaniards and the native population, especially in Lisbon. King John II responded to this situation by setting up a new panel of inquisitors, to police the 'New Christians', and by inviting the 'asylum seekers' to leave, on condition that they went to another Christian country. The new Portuguese inquisitors soon began trials of *conversos*, and some convicted 'Judaizers' were burnt in Lisbon and Santarém. Also, ominously, a small number of Portuguese Jews were arrested and imprisoned at this time, for supposedly proselytizing on behalf of their faith among the Spanish *conversos*. Before 1492, there was no particular pressure on native Portuguese Jews to convert to Christianity, but events in the subsequent decade were to change this situation drastically. As tensions increased, the Old

Christian majority in Portugal began to blame the established Jewish population of the kingdom, as well as the Spanish *converso* immigrants, for the country's current problems, even including outbreaks of the plague. Even before the Spanish edicts of 31 March 1492, preaching campaigns had begun to convert Portuguese Jews, but the situation became much more fraught during the summer months of that year, when it is estimated that between 20,000 and 30,000 Jews crossed the border from Castile. As a result, the Jewish population of Portugal was rapidly doubled, and another outbreak of the plague served to increase further native, including Jewish, hostility to the newcomers. With an eye to financial advantage, John II's government was happy to allow 600 families from among the richest Spanish émigrés to settle in the kingdom, at the price of 6,000 *cruzados* per household, and some less wealthy families were allowed to settle in return for lesser sums.

Wealthy Jews, contrary to what was believed in many Christian circles, seem to have constituted only a small minority among the refugees, but this did not make the acceptance of the Spaniards into Portuguese society any easier. The influx of artisans from Castile created tensions in the labour market, and those who had avoided extortion at border posts by entering Portugal illegally thus rendered themselves liable to exploitation. Their former sovereign's offer of return to their former lives and property may well have seemed attractive in these circumstances, even at the heavy price of Christian baptism. Inquisitorial duties, in Portugal at this time, largely remained in the hands of bishops, rather than specialized tribunals and, as they were still Jews, the newcomers were largely unaffected by the normal ecclesiastical courts. It may have appeared to some that the prospect of living a Jewish life in Portugal, as they had previously done in Spain, was good, but any who believed such a thing were soon to be disillusioned. Like his royal neighbours, John II seems to have been primarily interested in the conversion of the Jews in his kingdom, beginning with the recent influx from Spain. When Jewish immigrants failed to pay the minimum entrance fee of eight *cruzados* per head, or else were found to have entered the kingdom illegally, their younger children began to be forcibly removed from them, and despatched to the island of São Tomé, off the west coast of Africa, where they were to be indoctrinated in Christianity and set to work in the developing sugar industry. As a slightly more emollient inducement to convert, on 19 October 1492, the king ordered that Spanish-Jewish parents, and their remaining older children, would be guaranteed social and fiscal privileges if they accepted baptism. Faced with the choice between these dubious offers, which at least appeared to save them from an Inquisition such as awaited them if they returned to Spain, and continued legal servitude to the Portuguese crown, many were indeed baptized. As early as 1493, John II appears to have considered copying Ferdinand and Isabella's orders of the preceding year, and forcing the established Jewish population of Portugal either to convert or to leave. Although such a measure was, in the event, to be postponed until 1497, the king proceeded, in 1493 and 1494, to put pressure on individual Jews to convert or emigrate, though he continued to be grateful for financial help from the wealthy members of the community. John died on 25 October 1496, and was succeeded by his brother-in-law, Manuel, duke of Beja, who to begin with adopted a more conciliatory policy towards his Jewish subjects. He took measures to stop Christian violence against Jews, guaranteed their existing privileges, and freed those who had previously been in royal servitude. Jewish hopes of a new and more peaceful era were dashed, however, when Manual contracted to marry Isabella, the daughter of Ferdinand and Isabella, for which the expulsion or conversion of the Jews of Portugal was made a precondition. As in Spain, conversion was clearly the primary aim, as those in Portugal who accepted baptism were to be exempted from inquisitorial action for a period of twenty years from 1497, when the edict, which was dated 5 December 1496, came into effect.

The document gave Portugal's Jews most of a year in which to convert or leave, and was accompanied by a parallel order to the kingdom's remaining Muslims. Whereas the Muslims were allowed to leave Portuguese territory, in April 1497, without any attempt being made convert them, and they travelled, ironically, with a safe conduct from the recent victors of the Granada war, the treatment of the Jews was to be very different. Manuel seems originally to have planned a gross act of deception, which was to take place on Easter Sunday 1497, but leaks by his councillors led to its being brought forward by over a month, to the beginning of the Christian penitential season of Lent. The Jews of Portugal were told to assemble in the capital, Lisbon, and encouraged to believe that they would be allowed to leave the country, with their families and movable goods, following the recent Spanish example. In the event, what happened was horribly different. First, a process began of forcibly separating Jewish children from their parents, for indoctrination as Christians, on the model of the earlier deportations to São Tomé. According to Portuguese Christian writers of the time and later, some parents suffocated or drowned their own children, rather than allow them to be taken away and baptized, while some Jewish children were taken and hidden from the authorities by Old Christians; however, in view of the fate which was about to befall their parents, this act of kindness and humanity very probably did not save these children from the font. According to traditional accounts, the adult Jewish population was ordered to assemble in Lisbon for embarkation, but instead was forcibly baptized. Given the limited administrative efficiency of late medieval and early modern governments, it is not surprising that recent revision has suggested that the Lisbon 'coup' did not in fact include all the Jews of Portugal, either numerically or geographically. Nevertheless, two long-term consequences of Portuguese policy in the years either side of 1500 are undeniable. First, the closure of the Portuguese frontier, after 1496, to those Spaniards who wished to live an open and legal Jewish life, put further pressure on those who remained in the country to come to terms of some sort with Christianity, The second result of King Manuel's actions was to create, in his own kingdom and empire, a largely, if not wholly unwilling 'New Christian' population which was to be influential, both in the mind and in action, during several further centuries of Iberian life.[17]

Despite its legal independence, which lasted until 1512–13, the Pyrenean kingdom of Navarre, which was the second main destination of Jewish émigrés in 1492, had unwittingly become involved in the affairs of Ferdinand and Isabella's Inquisition, when the assassins of Pedro Arbués, inquisitor of Zaragoza, fled across the border to Tudela, in September 1485. This town, with its long-established Jewish community, violently resisted the efforts of Inquisition officials from the neighbouring kingdom of Aragon, with which Navarre was dynastically and politically connected, not only to retrieve those suspected of Arbués's murder, but also to arrest other Aragonese *conversos* who had sought sanctuary across the border. Despite the intervention of Pope Innocent VIII, in April 1487, ordering Navarrese officials to assist the Aragonese inquisitors in every way, on pain of excommunication, it was only in February of the following year that a compromise was reached between the representatives of Tudela and Ferdinand and Isabella, which effectively allowed the agents of the Aragonese Inquisition to pursue their business in the neighbouring kingdom. Given the manifest threat of interference from across the border, it seems surprising that, in 1492, the rulers of Navarre, Cathérine and Jean d'Albret, initially welcomed Jewish refugees from Castile and Aragon. The refuge proved to be short-lived, however, and in 1498 Navarre issued its own expulsion edict, which closed the last door to an open and legal Jewish life in the Iberian pennsula. The final extinction of the very independence of Spanish Navarre itself was not to be long delayed (see chapter 9).[18]

When Jews began to leave his native land of Andalusia and cross to North Africa, as a result of the Castilian edict of 31 March 1492, the chronicler Bernáldez, in the mocking manner which he customarily adopted where the people of Israel were concerned, commented on their prevailing mood and attitude. By his account, and others from both Christian and Jewish sources, many of those who left Spain in that year believed that they were destined to experience what Moses and the Children of Israel had experienced in their Exodus from Egypt. They would, in Bernáldez's words, 'go out with much honour and riches, without losing any of their goods, to possess the Holy Promised Land, which they confessed to having lost through their great and abominable sins, which their ancestors had committed against God'. Early sixteenth-century Jewish writers, such as Solomon ibn Verga, Elijah Capsali and Isaac Abravanel, were clearly convinced of the spiritual significance of the 1492 expulsion from Spain, but similar feelings and experiences seem also to have affected their *converso* brothers and sisters.[19] Between 1499 and Lent of 1502, what was described by the then inquisitors of Córdoba, the notorious Diego Rodríguez Lucero and Dr Ludovico, as a 'Judaizing' messianic movement developed in the small seignorial town of Chillón, to the north of that city. It was said that the Messiah, accompanied by the prophet Elijah, would come in March 1500, but violent inquisitorial repression led to two *autos de fe*, in 1502, causing the deaths of no fewer than 130 people. The investigations which led to this bloodthirsty outcome were largely carried out by Lucero, who was eventually removed from his post in 1508, after the direct intervention of Ferdinand as *gobernador* of Castile. While it is generally accepted that Lucero's notion of the scale of the 'Judaizing' *converso* movement in Córdoba itself, which he believed to include a synagogue in the house of one of the city's parish councillors (*jurados*), Juan de Córdoba, was false, the interest of at least some *conversos* in Jewish prophecy seems to have been genuine enough. Already, in 1464, the papal Inquisition in Valencia claimed to have discovered that a group of New Christians, apparently from Córdoba, who had been in contact with Jews and with local *conversos*, had been talking of a Messiah who would lead them – as Jews, not Christians, traditionally believed – to the Land of Israel, via Venice or Constantinople. The new foundation of the Inquisition in Castile soon discovered similar evidence, and in 1486 a Toledan *converso* told the tribunal in that city that many New Christians in Córdoba, at the time of the riots in 1473, believed that the Turks, who had conquered Constantinople twenty years before, were the precursors of the Jewish Messiah, who would be an earthly ruler in the Land of Israel.

The most significant movement which received the Inquisition's attention involved the followers of Inés, who became a prophetess in the town of Herrera del Duque, at the southern edge of the Spanish Meseta. The Toledo Inquisition tried more than thirty of Inés's followers, and the relevant documents provide some indication of the character of the visionary and her community. According to the testimony of Juan de Segovia, a shoemaker in Córdoba, Inés's prophecies were directed particularly to *conversos*. She told her listeners that, before the Messiah came, for the first time, and not the second, as Christians believed, angels would appear, and there would be other signs in heaven. The Messiah would take the Spanish *conversos* to the Promised Land, where they would eat from golden plates, 'and she said because she was a sinner she could not see them, and wept for it'. Inés claimed that her dead mother had come to fetch her, and had taken her up to heaven. She ascended, holding her mother's hand, with an angel for company, and also a boy whom she had known, and who had died some years earlier. Inés passed through Purgatory, in which souls were suffering, and then, reaching heaven, saw other people, 'on golden chairs, in glory'. The angel told her that they had been persecuted by the Inquisition. 'Friend of God, those who rest up there are those who were burned on earth.' The visionary and prophetess claimed to have received signs from heaven, an ear of corn, an olive and a letter, to authenticate her experiences in the eyes of her listeners. Witnesses later told the Inquisition that she soon claimed to be visiting heaven every week, and that she led a movement, first in the area to the north of Córdoba and then in the city itself, which had distinctly 'Judaizing' tendencies. Inés was said, by Luis Guantero of Herrera, to have claimed that 'no one could be saved without keeping the Law and believing the Law of Moses', which was precisely the offence with which *conversos* were frequently charged by the Inquisition. In the two years before the authorities in Córdoba began to repress the move-ment, Inés and her followers seem to have begun to behave in the manner of an apocalyptic cult. Luis claimed that people in the district, inspired by Inés, and including children as young as seven or eight, were engaging in fasts, and disposing of their property, 'in the hope that they would be taken to the Promised Land, and because God had made a most excellent city in heaven, which would be transferred to earth, where all the *conversos* would dwell and live in great abundance'. The group led by Inés, in the area of Herrera, Chillón and Almodóvar del Campo, seems to have been effectively suppressed by the Toledo Inquisition, though the supposed equivalent movement in Córdoba created a much greater storm, and resulted in several more years of violent inquisitorial repression. The religious content of the statements and claims made by Inés, at least as they were recounted to the Inquisition, give a vivid impression of some of the spiritual currents in the Spain of Ferdinand and Isabella. Not only do they have a strong apocalyptic flavour, but they also blend a Jewish view of the events of the last days with material which appears to be derived from the last book of the Christian New Testament, the Apocalypse, or Revelation of

St John. Jewish eschatology is present, not only in the demand for strong adherence to the Mosaic law and in the notion of an earthly Messianic kingdom in the land of Israel, where the *conversos* would live in peace and prosperity, but also in the statement that the prophet Elijah would return as the precursor of the Messiah. The evidently Christian elements in accounts of the Herrera movement include the mention of Purgatory, the heavenly banquet of the martyrs, and the notion of the celestial city coming down to earth, which is the final image of the book of Revelation.[20]

As Christians, both 'Old' and 'New', awaited the coming of the half-millennium, and Jews attempted to comprehend the meaning of their expulsion from Spain, the year 1492 was also a crisis for Muslims. Uniquely in the history of Islam, territory which had once been Muslim had been lost, with the fall of the Nasrid emirate. Thus Muslims, too, were forced to ponder the spiritual, as well as the political meaning of a traumatic disaster. Both the edicts for the conversion or expulsion of the Jews, and Christopher Columbus's first landfall in the Americas, in turn had a bearing on the fate of Ferdinand and Isabella's Muslim subjects, both those conquered in the kingdom of Granada and those living as *mudéjares* in other parts of Spain. The relevance of the Jewish case is obvious, in that the treatment of the *conversos*, both before 1492 and after, provided an actual precedent for the fate of converts from Islam, *moriscos*, throughout the sixteenth century. Muslims, and Muslim converts to Christianity, were also directly affected by the political and military consequences of Isabella and Ferdinand's victory in Granada. The fate of the Nasrid dynasty had in part been sealed by the weakness of the Muslim states of the Maghreb, and their consequent failure to intervene in defence of their religious brothers. After the fall of Granada, apart from the subjugation of the emirate itself, which had only been a totally independent Islamic state, free from tribute, for ten years, Muslims elsewhere in Castile and the crown of Aragon experienced the consequences of Spain's growing military might, first in Europe, and then worldwide. The events of 1492 thus combined to seal the fate of those Muslims who did not leave at the time of the conquest. Yet the conversion, subjection, and subsequent expulsion, early in the seventeenth century, of the *moriscos* should not obscure the fact that, in the early years after the conquest of Granada, such an outcome did not appear likely.

The 'capitulations' (*capitulos*), or treaty, whereby the Muslim authorities surrendered power in Granada to the crown of Castile, were initially respected by the conquerors. Although many of the former religious and secular leaders emigrated, for eight years the city itself remained predominantly Muslim, in social composition, belief and practice. A small Christian ruling class, effectively Castilian, was introduced, consisting of military men, lawyers and clergy, but a contemporary list survives of twenty-one Muslim leaders who continued to be active in the government of the city. Many, if not all, of them had held secular or, mainly, religious office under the previous regime. Other Muslim dignitaries, including Boabdil himself, were allowed to live in some state outside the city, though the former military aristocracy was encouraged to emigrate to North Africa. It is true that a desire to convert the leading Muslims who remained was evident from the beginning in royal and ecclesiastical circles, but the choice as first archbishop of Granada of the elderly Jeronymite, Hernando de Talavera, who had formerly been Isabella's confessor, appeared to indicate a conciliatory religious policy. All evidence suggests that he observed the *capitulaciones* to the letter, allowing religious freedom to Muslims in his new diocese, though working and praying for their conversion by a combination of teaching and example. Talavera made it his policy to meet regularly with Muslim religious leaders (*alfaquíes*). He founded a school of Arabic, although he himself seems not to have progressed beyond the first nouns, and he sought the uttainable goal of an Arabic-speaking clergy. He built a home for 'poor' Muslim children, whom he is said to have 'indoctrinated' personally, and, in parallel with measures in previous centuries to separate Jewish converts from their communities, he set up houses for Muslim women who became Christians. One was for those who became nuns, while the other provided food and shelter for the rest. The archbishop, no doubt affected by the Christian perception of Muslim polygamy, as well as the dislocation of Granadan society which no doubt followed the Christian conquest, sent out his servants to bring in children from the street, so that they might receive clothing and shelter, but above all Christian teaching. It is thus wrong to suppose that the conflict which arose between Talavera and Archbishop Cisneros, over the approach which should be adopted towards the Muslim population of Granada, concerned the need for mission and conversion. Both bishops totally agreed on this aim, though they fundamentally disagreed over tactics, and the question of recognizing the integrity of Islam, in its own right, did not arise in either case. Talavera and Cisneros were both reformers of the Church, who anticipated many developments which were to become the policy of the Roman Church, especially after the council of Trent. Nevertheless, political events in Granada overtook Talavera's gentler proselytizing methods. A rebellion by Muslims in the Alpujarras, in 1499, allowed Cisneros, as inquisitor-general, to intervene in Talavera's diocese. Just as the *capitulaciones* in western Andalusia in the thirteenth-century reconquest had been abrogated after the Muslim rebellions of 1264, the 1492 agreement was unilaterally declared null and void by Isabella and Ferdinand's government once violence broke out in the kingdom of Granada. A policy of forcible baptism was introduced, to replace the conversionist opportunism which characterized Talavera's independent management of his diocese. The travail of the *moriscos* had begun.[21]

7

Spain in Europe

The kingdoms which Ferdinand and Isabella inherited had been integrated, at least since Roman times, not only with their neighbours in the Iberian peninsula but also with many aspects of the life of the continent to the north of the Pyrenees. Even the fullest extent and strength of Muslim rule in Spain, or Al-Andalus, in the ninth and tenth centuries, could not and did not sever these European links, though they also brought the Peninsula into a cultural, economic and political world which stretched from the Atlantic to the Indian Ocean. The new sovereigns of Castile and Aragon, in 1474 and 1479, respectively, inherited intimate political, economic, social, religious and cultural ties both with their Iberian neighbours and with the other kingdoms of Western Europe, in particular France, England, the various states of Italy and the Holy Roman Empire, as well as the Papacy. Within the Peninsula, Portugal had intruded immediately upon the consciousness of the Castilian queen and her consort, while the Muslim kingdom of Granada awaited their attention until the treaties of Alcaçovas and Toledo had been signed, in 1479 and 1480, respectively. It was, in turn, only after the fall of Granada in 1492 that Ferdinand, in particular, was able to involve himself more fully in policy outside the Peninsula. Well before 1493, however, the historic political and diplomatic differences between Castile and Aragon, territories which had spent more than two centuries struggling for Iberian hegemony, resurfaced, and it is impossible to understand Spanish involvements in European events between then and 1516 without a recognition of that fact. France, with its overpowering demographic, economic and military resources, was to be crucial in all that followed. Ever since the Trastamaran victory in the Castilian civil war of the mid-fourteenth century, which formed the basis of both Isabella's and Ferdinand's power, Castile had been allied with France, while Aragon and Catalonia were historically opposed to their overbearing northern neighbour. At the same time, for geographical and economic reasons, Castilian interests gravitated towards the Atlantic, with a logical outcome when Columbus voyaged towards the Americas,

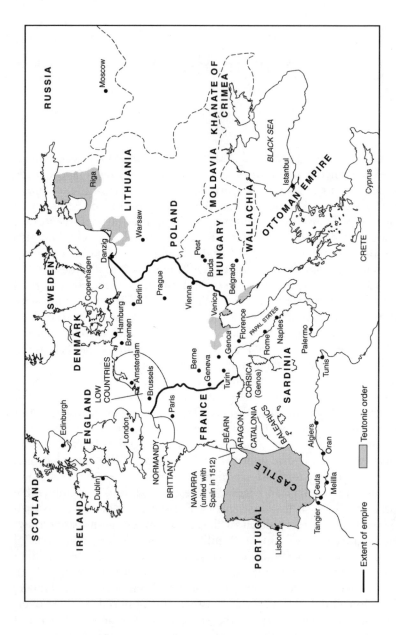

Map 4   Europe in 1500, based on Ernest Belenguer, *Fernando el Católico* (Barcelona, 1999), p 393.

while Aragonese and Catalans naturally looked towards the Mediterranean. From the 1490s onwards, although Castilian interests in North and West Africa and the Atlantic islands certainly did not disappear from the agenda, there was a strong tendency, under Ferdinand's guidance, for Aragonese opposition to France to direct foreign policy. The other main strategic aim, in which Isabella and her husband coincided, was to achieve dominance in the western Mediterranean, and block the further expansion of the Ottomans to the east. Manifestations of this overall strategy included attempts to control the seas from the Straits of Gibraltar to Tunis, thus reducing piracy and the traffic in Christian captives in the North African slave-markets, and increasing intervention in Italy, including the establishment of a kind of protectorate in the kingdom of Naples. Supposed divisions between 'Castilian' and 'Aragonese' foreign policies should not be exaggerated. The dynastic union of the two groups of territories forced a co-ordination of what had previously been disparate, and often opposing, aims. Contemporary foreign commentators, both inside and outside Spain, tended to see one 'Spanish' policy, and indeed, the use of the term 'Spain' to describe the dual monarchy was becoming general well before the Habsburg succession in 1516. Nevertheless, it is possible to detect a Catalan – Aragonese 'bias' in the two monarchies' external relations, except in the cases of the two remaining independent Iberian kingdoms, Portugal and Navarre, to which attention will now turn.[1]

Once the treaties of Alcaçovas had been signed, relations between Castile and Portugal returned, for the most part, to their traditional good-neighbourliness, which dated from the former's reluctant acceptance of the latter's independence, after the Portuguese victory at Aljubarrota/Batalha, in 1385. During the 1480s, peace between the two kingdoms was generally maintained, while Ferdinand and Isabella pursued their military campaigns in Granada. Nevertheless, the residence in Portugal of the Castilian queen's defeated rival, Joanna, continued to be a point of friction. As long as the unfortunate princess, who was known to the Portuguese as 'the excellent nun' (a excelente freira), remained alive in monastic confinement, and later, until 1530, in more luxurious accommodation as a excelente senhora, she posed a potential threat to Isabella, and the stability of her regime. Even if Joanna had not existed, other personal and public relations made it inevitable that Castile should become involved in Portuguese affairs. It had been decided in 1479 that royal ties would prevent further conflict between the two kingdoms. Ferdinand and Isabella's daughter, also called Isabella, was betrothed to the eventual heir to the Portuguese throne, Prince John's son Afonso, with whom she was indeed briefly married, between 1490 and his death in the following year. The first crisis in Castilian–

Portuguese relations was not long delayed after Alcaçovas. The accession to the Portuguese throne of John II, in 1481, ushered in a period of arbitrary royal violence which was somewhat reminiscent of that of Peter of Castile between 1350 and 1369. Although he was known to Portuguese chroniclers as 'the perfect prince', even before he succeeded his disillusioned and increasingly godfearing father, Afonso, John had begun to reveal distinctly absolutist tendencies. In 1478, Lopo Vaz de Castelo-Branco, governor (*alcaide*) of Moura castle, went over to the Castilian side. Afonso started negotiations with him and reached a compromise, but the then Prince John had him killed. Once king, John soon excited opposition, which centred around his cousin, and brother-in-law, Fernando, duke of Bragança, an illegitimate descendant of John I. The duke was accused by the king of *lèse-majesté* and of negotiating secretly with Castile and Aragon. He was arrested in May 1483, after which his family fled to Castile, and after a trial was beheaded at Evora, on 20 June 1484, with the accompaniment of an ostentatious display of grief on the part of the king. John's next victim was Diogo, duke of Viseu, his cousin and another brother-in-law, whom he suspected of plotting to avenge the duke of Bragança. This time, the king did not trouble himself with a judicial process, personally stabbing Diogo to death, in August of the same year. The execution and imprisonment of other nobles, accused of being part of the conspiracy, continued into 1485. The bishop of Evora, Dom Garcia de Meneses, was shut up in a cistern in the castle of Palmela, where he died, while other likely victims fled across the border to Castile. Thus Isabella and Ferdinand were able to claim, not unreasonably, that they had no choice but to continue their involvement in Portuguese politics. A further provocation to the Trastamarans was the departure of Joanna, during 1483, from her convent in Coimbra, apparently with at least the approval of John II. In response, the Castilian court sheltered numerous Portuguese exiles, many of whom were particularly congenial to their new hosts because of their known opposition to further maritime exploration and expansion on the part of Portugal. John II was strongly committed to this activity, especially after his son Afonso died, as a result of a riding accident, in July 1491. A condition of Alfonso's marriage to Isabel had been that Joanna would never again be allowed to leave her convent. The prince's untimely death left his father without an heir, male or female, and his closest surviving blood relation, after the carnage of the previous years, was yet another brother-in-law from the Bragança line, Dom Manuel, duke of Beja, whose own brother John had personally murdered. Perhaps not surprisingly, given his treatment of the other male members of the family, John did not trust Manuel, and tried to keep him from the throne. Instead, he promoted his own illegitimate son, Dom Jorge (George), whose mother was his mistress Dona Ana de Mendonça. In 1492, following Prince Afonso's death, John obtained from Pope Innocent VIII the grant to Jorge of the government and administration of the military orders of Avis and Santiago (the Portuguese order of that name). Despite these efforts on behalf of Jorge, Manuel duly succeeded John as king in 1495, though the conflict over the succession once again caused a serious split in the Portuguese aristocracy and among leading churchmen. In 1497, he married the widow of Prince Alfonso, Isabella, a move which precipitated the expulsion of the Jews from Portugal, or their forced conversion (see chapter 6). After the sudden death, in that same year, of Ferdinand and Isabella's son John, it looked for a time as though Manuel and the young Isabella's son Michael (Miguel) would eventually inherit Castile and Aragon, as well as Portugal. The cruel luck of the Trastamarans struck again, however, and Manuel was first left a widower, in 1498, and then lost his son, in 1500. In the latter year, he married Ferdinand and Isabella's fourth daughter, Mary, after which the possibility of the unity of the three Iberian kingdoms was put off, in the event until 1580. During this period, the Catholic Monarchs and Portugal avoided any major peninsular conflict, despite their competing interests in Africa and the Atlantic.

Not only did Spain (primarily Castile) and Portugal oppose one another in the seas to the east and south of the Iberian peninsula, but the question of further maritime adventure was also a cause of division within the Portuguese court. In the mid-1480s, while John II appeared to anticipate, in some respects, the plot of Shakespeare's *Macbeth*, and Diogo Cão and his men were advancing ever southwards along the coast of Africa, the matter of entering the Indian Ocean rose up the political agenda. The turning point in Portuguese seaborne expansion proved to be the voyage of Bartolomeu Dias, with the king's support, to the Cape of Good Hope, in 1487–8. Until then, the prevailing strategy, as proposed by Prince Henry 'the Navigator', had been to pursue a southerly course along the coast of Africa in order to discover the limits of Islam and, if possible, to find allies such as the legendary Christian emperor, 'Prester John', who might attack the 'Moors' from the opposite flank. Faced with a confusing and contradictory set of rumours, which had accumulated during the medieval centuries from the German historian Otto of Freising, in 1145, to the Genoese merchant and explorer Antoniotto Usodimare in the 1450s, John II was cautious in his support of the 1487 expedition. Dias seems to have been a professional mariner, rather than a noble, and was sent with three ships to explore the African coast beyond the point which had been reached by Diogo Cão. By January 1488, he had achieved this goal and rounded the tip of the continent, returning to Lisbon in December of that year, before the eyes of Christopher Columbus, among others. In May 1487, John II also sent an expedition over land, via Spain, Italy and Alexandria, to India, with the aim of observing the spice trade from its source. Despite these voyages of exploration, Portuguese policy towards Asia was divided and hesitant in the last years of John's reign. One reason for this was fear of the difficulty of sea rather than land routes to the east, but another was fear of a renewal of hostilities with Castile, after a relatively peaceful period since the trade-war over Guinea. Tensions between the two kingdoms began to revive in April 1493, when Martín Alonso Pinzón brought back news of Columbus's first discoveries. Throughout the reigns of Isabella and Ferdinand, the bulk of the Portuguese nobility, with its interests primarily based in landed estates, tended to sympathize with Castile and resist the martime adventure which was to lead to Vasco da Gama's voyage into the Indian Ocean in 1497–9. The recognized need for an accommodation with Castile resulted in the treaty of Tordesillas, in June 1494. This established a demarcation line between Spanish and Portuguese interests, situated 370 leagues west of the Cape Verde islands. The North African coast east of Morocco, including Melilla and Cazaza, was reserved for Spain, in effect Castile, while Portugal retained its interests in West Africa. Imperial conflicts were, however, to revive in the latter years of Ferdinand's 'governorship' of Castile.[2]

The strategic position of Navarre, on the western Pyrenean frontier between Spain and France, remained a potential or actual problem for Ferdinand and his wife. When Ferdinand acceded to the Aragonese throne in 1479, Navarre was ruled by Madeleine, sister of Louis XI of France and widow of Gaston V Fébus, count of Foix. Between then and his death in 1483, their son Francis Fébus was accepted as king both in Spanish 'upper' Navarre, and in French 'lower' Navarre. When the succession thus passed to Francis's sister Cathérine, difficulties arose which involved both the neighbouring powers. First, a collateral line, headed by Gaston V's brother Jean, contested Cathérine's claim to the county of Foix, on the basis of Salic law, which forbade female succession to territories within the historic French kingdom which claimed separate sovereignty, as was the case in Béarn, in lower Navarre. The decision in the case of the succession to Foix thus rested with the Parlement in Paris, which provided the French crown with a convenient weapon to keep Madeleine and her daughter in order in their Pyrenean kingdom. The dying Louis XI had no great wish, however, to uphold Jean de Foix's claim, because this would effectively recognize the sovereign status of Béarn, and procrastination was the policy pursued. If France gained a legal passage into French Navarre, so went the reasoning in Paris, Ferdinand of Aragon might feel justified in achieving a similar result. The Trastamaran connection to the kingdom was intimate and long-standing, including the rule, or claim to rule, of Ferdinand's own father, John II of Aragon, between 1441 and 1479. Thus as 'spider' King Louis came to the end of his life, in the summer of 1483, and his eldest daughter Anne de Beaujeu prepared to assume the regency on behalf of her brother Charles VIII, Ferdinand and Isabella tried to exploit the political vacuum. Like the French in the country of Foix, the Spanish king and queen aimed to turn the small but strategically important kingdom of Navarre into a kind of protectorate. Madeleine and Cathérine, resident in the castle of Pau, were in an unenviable situation, and the likelihood of their holding on to both parts of their inheritance, north and south of the Pyrenees, seemed to be decreasing by the day. If they left Pau, the Paris Parlement was likely to take the county of Pau away from them, yet if they failed to show themselves in Navarre, and its capital Pamplona, Ferdinand was waiting to pounce.

The ambitions of the Spanish monarchs were assisted by the internal political situation of Navarre, in which two noble factions, the Agramonts and the Beaumonts (Beamontes), were struggling for supremacy. In the mid-1480s, Isabella and Ferdinand encircled the kingdom with troops, based in the Basque provinces, Castile and Aragon, which might intervene directly at any time. In addition, they offered their son John as a husband for Cathérine, the plan being that the couple would be recognized as rulers of Navarre at a specially convoked cortes in Estella. Isabella, who appears to have taken the lead in these negotiations, attempted to exploit the constitution (*fueros*) of Navarre in order to manipulate the succession. The Castilian and Aragonese case was that the queen had to marry, under the terms of the *fueros*, and if she did not do so, her subjects were entitled to elect someone else as their ruler, in this case the prince of Asturias, who was in any case the grandson of their former king, John II. In the event, a combination of political turmoil within Navarre and a counter-offer from the French side saved Cathérine and her mother from the unpalatable Spanish option. By refusing to attend, the Agramonts prevented the Cortes from meeting in Estella, though the Beaumonts did assemble at Puente la Reina. Madeleine thus felt able to reject Ferdinand and Isabella's 'offer', the ostensible reason being age difference. Instead, by means of a contract signed at Orthez on 14 June 1484, Cathérine was married to the only candidate who was acceptable to both Spain and France, Jean d'Albret, a noble of a junior line, with substantial possessions in south-western France, but not suspected of gross political ambition. The new king consort of Navarre was the son of Alain d'Albret, who was active in local resistance to the complete incorporation of the duchy of Brittany into the French crown. The fact that Jean was thus not particularly amenable to French manipulation naturally made him more acceptable to the Spanish rulers. The intrusion of the Aragonese Inquisition from 1485 (see chapter 6) indicated all to clearly, though, that the threat of annexation of the kingdom by either Aragon or Castile was not removed by Cathérine's marriage. Apart from seeking the murderers of the inquisitor Pedro Arbués, and other refugee *conversos*, Ferdinand made a series of demands on the Navarrese monarchs which were ominous for the future. First, Jean and Cathérine had to agree that their Spanish territory, which was effectively governed by Jean's father Alain, would never be used as a base for operations against Isabella and Ferdinand's domains, and even that the governors (*alcaides*) of their fortresses should do homage (*pleito-home-naje*) to the Catholic Monarchs. In particular, after 1488, Viana and Tudela fell effectively under the control of their overbearing neighbours. Ferdinand and Isabella's second demand was that they should have a veto over the marriages of any children who might be born to Cathérine and Jean, and the third was that they should move their residence from the French side of the mountains to Pamplona. Thus, by means of treaties signed at Valencia in 1488, outside Granada in 1491, Pamplona in 1493 and Madrid in 1495, Navarre effectively became a Spanish protectorate. Nevertheless, the final extinction of its independence was not to begin until 1512 (see chapter 9).[3]

Navarre was far from being the only area of dispute between Ferdinand and Isabella's kingdoms and France. When Ferdinand became king of Aragon in 1479, the Catalan counties of Cerdagne and Roussillon had been in French hands since 1462, apart from a brief interval in 1472–3. As historic possessions of the counts of Barcelona, these territories, which were as strategically important in the eastern Pyrenees as Navarre was in the west, constituted a lingering source of conflict with Spain's powerful northern neighbour. John II of Aragon had been allied to the rebel Valois duchy of Burgundy, with its wealthy and powerful group of territories which straddled the frontier between France and the Holy Roman Empire. Ferdinand cautiously refused to renew his father's alliance with Duke Charles the Bold of Burgundy's daughter Marie, and her husband Maximilian of Austria without guarantees on their part. Thanks to the emptiness of the Aragonese and Catalan exchequer, together with Castile's new war against Muslim Granada, the possibility of fighting for the two lost counties appeared remote. In 1483, the dying Louis XI, as a part of his effort to regulate his accounts before meeting his Maker, ordered that the territories should be returned to Ferdinand, but his daughter Anne refused to comply. The Aragonese king was unable to force her to change her mind, because the Aragonese cortes of Tarazona, in 1484, refused to vote the necessary supplies, and his own wife was unwilling to divert Castilian resources from the Granada campaigns. Ferdinand was thus reduced to copying the policy of his father John II, attempting to 'encircle' France by means of alliances, both political and mercantile, with its traditional adversaries, England and Burgundy. One consequence of this policy was to be close Spanish involvement in the fate of the duchy of Brittany.

The southern Breton port of Nantes was a traditional stop on the trade route to England and the Low Countries, in which Castilians and Basques actively participated. In 1483, Ferdinand and Isabella's ambassador, Juan de Herrera, signed a treaty of friendship with Duke Francis of Brittany, thus cementing both economic and political links, in opposition to the Valois monarchy, which was determined to bring the duchy into line with its other feudal dependencies. The strategic importance of Brittany was equally obvious to France's enemies, and Ferdinand and Isabella, frustrated in their efforts to regain Cerdagne and Roussillon, sent Castilian troops to help Francis resist the regency of Charles VIII in the so-called 'mad war' (*guerre folle*), starting in 1484, which was to lead to final defeat for the Bretons and their allies, including dissident members of the French nobility such as Louis, duke of Orléans and the count of Dunois, in 1488. In September of that year, Duke Francis died, leaving his daughter Anne as his unmarried and vulnerable heiress. In an attempt to stave off French annexation of the duchy, in the latter part of 1489 Isabella and Ferdinand, together with their new allies Henry VII of England and Maximilian of Austria, king of the Romans, sent troops to 'defend' duchess Anne. Each ruler had his or her own selfish motive. The head of the new and insecure Tudor dynasty hoped to regain Guyenne and, above all Normandy, which had been lost by the English at the end of the Hundred Years War, while Maximilian sought those parts of his wife's Burgundian inheritance which had been seized by Louis XI, after the death of her father, Charles the Bold, in 1477. For Ferdinand and Isabella, the existing links between Brittany and Navarre, in the person of Alain d'Albret, opened up the possibility of an anti-French coalition of territories on the Atlantic coast, which they might hope to dominate. Nevertheless, the primary aim of Spanish intervention in Brittany was to regain Roussillon and Cerdagne. The 'triple alliance' was consolidated by the treaty of Okyng, in September 1490, but it was trumped in December of the following year, when Duchess Anne married Charles VIII, thus integrating Brittany fully with the French crown. The French king then proceeded to pick off his enemies, first Henry VII, by the treaty of Etaples in November 1492, then Isabella and Ferdinand, by the treaty of Tours –Barcelona in January 1493, and finally Maximilian in the following May. Charles had Italian adventures in mind, and needed peace on his other boundaries. The main consequence of the treaty of Barcelona for Ferdinand and his wife was that the two lost Catalan countries were returned peacefully to the crown of Aragon.

For largely commercial reasons, political links between Castile and England, which had been extensive throughout most of the fourteenth century, were already being strengthened when Isabella became queen in 1474. Treaties between the two kingdoms had been signed in 1467 and 1471, while more local arrangements were also made by groups of merchants. In 1483, for example, the traders of Guipúzcoa, in the Basque country, made their own agreement with the government of Richard III, aimed at setting up a system of arbitration between English and Spanish merchants. This was intended to avoid the traditional, and somewhat hit-and-miss, system of 'letters of mark and reprisal' (*cartas de marca y represalia*), under which, if a merchant committed an offence abroad, the authorities in the aggrieved country might seize any compatriot of the offender in retaliation, thus severely disrupting international trade. While the English and Spanish crowns were becoming jointly involved in the affairs of Brittany, Richard III was defeated and killed on Bosworth Field, in 1485, and Henry Tudor effectively ended the Wars of the Roses by setting up a new dynasty. There had already been some discussion, in the reigns of Edward IV and Richard III, of the possibility of matrimonial ties between the two royal families, and the joint alliance with Brittany, together with the developing economic links between Spain, England and Maximilian's prosperous territories in the Low Countries, made such a prospect ever more attractive. The two sides got down to business in July 1488, when a political and economic agreement was reached in London, between Ferdinand and Henry, to parallel the treaty which had been made in Valencia, in January of that year, between the Aragonese king and Alain d'Albret, on behalf of the Bretons. The existing close economic ties between England and the Iberian peninsula were thus supplemented by a common political interest in restraining, and if possible controlling, the immense power of a France which was successfully recovering from the devastation of the Hundred Years War. According to the instructions which he gave to his ambassador in London, Rodrigo González de Puebla, Ferdinand was anxious to point out to the English king the disastrous effect which French control of Brittany would have. He also warned of the dire consequences which would follow if the French managed to seize the remaining Burgundian territories, and in particular the Low Countries ports. The result of Puebla's labours was a treaty, signed at Medina del Campo in March 1489, whereby each party undertook to make war on France and not to make peace without the consent of the other. The war aims of each country, Guyenne and Normandy in the case of England and Cerdagne and Roussillon in the case of Spain, have already been noted, but there were also important reasons of economic policy. The new alliance was to be crowned, literally at some future date, by a marriage between Arthur, prince of Wales, and Catherine, daughter of Ferdinand and Isabella. These terms were confirmed, at Okyng, later in that year, but it was not to be until 1501, in very different political circumstances, that Catherine was despatched to England, to become first a widow and then a divorcee.

The third signatory of the Okyng treaty in 1489, Maximilian, duke of Austria and king of the Romans, was in some respects a problematic ally for Ferdinand and Isabella, even though the houses of Habsburg and Trastámara were soon to be interlocked on a permanent basis. Geography and politics, especially in central Europe, frequently diverted Maximilian from his alliance with Ferdinand and Henry, while poor personal relations created problems between the three rulers. At the same time as the Bretons were failing to make progress in the 'mad war', Maximilian was found to be negotiating with Anne de Beaujeu, behind the backs of his allies, following a teasing suggestion that France might be prepared at least to consider restoring to him the French inheritance of his wife Mary of Burgundy. The offer was, of course, spurious, but it succeeded in creating confusion among France's opponents. In his plan to prevent further French expansion, Ferdinand also had to contend with the opposition of his own wife. Isabella was totally committed to the final conquest of Granada, believing that the capture of Málaga in 1488, and Baza in the following year, clearly indicated divine support for the enterprise. In addition, the Castilian queen seems genuinely to have believed that Anne of France would hand over Cerdagne and Roussillon peacefully, in early 1490 persuading her husband to agree to the French regent's offer, accompanied by a personal letter from the young Charles VIII, of an interview at the Franco-Spanish border, in order to settle the matter. Negotiations were placed in the hands of two members of the religious order of Minims, which derived from the Franciscan tradition and was founded in 1435 by St Francis of Paula. Jean de Mauléon represented France while the Catalan Bernardo Boil spoke for Ferdinand and Isabella, and the talks continued even during the most difficult phases of Franco-Spanish relations. Whether or not Anne de Beaujeu genuinely wished to hand back Cerdagne and Roussillon, the opposing alliance was weakened by her namesake of Brittany's refusal to marry the recently widowed Maximilian, and by the impossibility of the duchess of Brittany's securing Spanish troops to aid her cause, as the Granada war reached its climax in 1491. In any case, France took charge of events, as Charles VIII brushed aside plans for Anne of Brittany to marry the king of the Romans and took her for himself. French troops entered Nantes in February 1491, and within a few months had secured the entire duchy. Though Ferdinand and his wife could not have known it, a new phase in European politics was about to begin, and to last long after the deaths of both monarchs.

The crucial factor seems to have been the coming of age, in that year, of Charles VIII. The young king had no sympathy with the painstaking diplomacy of his sister, which dealt in protracted negotiations and conciliation, with the occasional exchange, with neighbouring powers, of small pieces of territory and border fortresses. After cutting the Gordian knot by seizing Brittany, Charles began to eye the prospect of expansion in Italy, where Ferrante, king of Naples, a cousin of Ferdinand of Aragon, appeared not to have long to live. Charles and his advisers doubted whether Ferrante's heirs would be capable of defending the kingdom against serious attack. Nevertheless, the three years following the fall of Granada, at the beginning of 1492, might be seen in retrospect as the most tranquil period of Isabella and Ferdinand's joint reigns. The rulers were largely able to devote themselves to internal matters in their respective kingdoms, including the assimilation to Castile of the kingdom of Granada, as well as attempting to exploit the gain of territory from Islam by establishing a stronger presence in North Africa (see chapter 9). After the victory celebrations in Granada, Isabella accompanied her husband into his hereditary domains where, in August 1493, a twenty-five-year commercial treaty was signed with Barcelona's traditional trading partner, the republic of Genoa. Relations with Navarre also seemed to be improving as, in January 1494, an agreement was reached with Cathérine of Foix and her husband Jean d'Albret that no 'foreign', in other words French, troops would be allowed to pass through their kingdom into Spain. There were additional, though hypothetical plans for a marriage alliance, in which Cathérine and Jean's daughter Anne would marry an unspecified grandson of Ferdinand and Isabella. In the meantime, the main Aragonese and Castilian tactic was to support, as a counterbalance to the d'Albret, the Beaumont faction, led by the count of Lerín. All these activities in the Peninsula were about to be overshadowed, however, by the activities of Charles of France in Italy. Already, in January 1492, he had made an alliance with Milan, while the death of Lorenzo de' Medici, in April of that year, threatened to destabilize not only the Tuscan region but the whole of Italy. The Spanish monarchs had high hopes of the election, in August 1492, of Rodrigo de Borja as Pope Alexander VI, but various initial friendly gestures, such as the grant in 1493 of ecclesiastical privileges in Spain and the Indies, did not prevent both parties from being sucked into the morass of Italian politics. Ominously for the future, Ferdinand's ambassador to the Curia, Diego López de Haro, soon had to inform Alexander that his master regarded the succession in Naples as a Spanish affair. Ferdinand – and to the outside world he was the sole activator of policy beyond the Pyrenees – was also worried by a political realignment which was being prepared in Italy. Since the peace of Lodi, in 1454, the Peninsula had been led politically by an alliance of Milan, Florence and Naples, but now the Papacy was intervening more directly, with the formation of a new grouping connecting Rome, Milan and Venice.

In these changing circumstances, including the imminent decease of Ferrante, the kingdom of Naples increasingly appeared to be the most likely area of conflict, which would bring foreign powers directly into Italian affairs. No mention of the southern Italian kingdom, which had been in Trastamaran hands for fifty years, was made in the treaty of Tours – Barcelona in 1493. Nevertheless, in August of that year Ferdinand gave an undertaking to Charles VIII that he would not oppose any attempt which the French king might make to exercise rights which were legally his in Naples. He also agreed not to forge any further matrimonial links with the family of his cousin Ferrante, who had reigned there since his father Alfonso died in 1458. How Ferdinand would react in the face of a French military invasion remained to be seen, as he retained a claim of his own to Naples in his capacity as heir of Alfonso in the crown of Aragon. The test of all intentions came when Ferrante died, in January 1494. Pope Alexander, as suzerain of Naples, immediately declared Ferrante's son to be king, as Alfonso II, and announced that all other claims, in practice those of Charles and Ferdinand, would be subject to legal process. Tension was great, however, as a Spanish fleet patrolled Italian waters, to provide protection against the Turks, and Cardinal Giuliano della Rovere, the future Pope Julius II, felt the need to flee to his allies in France. The Turkish threat, which was genuine enough, provided the pretext for many of the events which followed. Charles VIII justified his efforts to implement his claim to the Neapolitan throne by stating that the kingdom would be a base for a crusade against the Ottomans and the restoration of Jerusalem to Christian rule. The arrival in France, in April 1494, of the defeated candidate in the papal election of 1492, Giuliano della Rovere, who was about to be arrested for disloyalty by Alexander VI, seems to have persuaded Charles to break the diplomatic equilibrium in western Europe, and launch a military invasion of Italy. While the French king hoped for a crusade and to become king of a Jerusalem newly restored

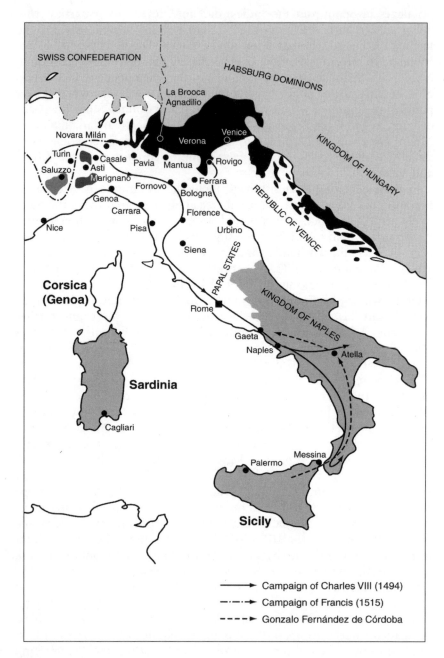

Map 5 The Italian Wars, based on Ernest Belenguer, *Fernando el Católico* (Barcelona, 1999), p. 394.

to Christendom, Giuliano wanted a new general council of the Church, which would preferably elect him as pope.

When Charles asked his commanders, in November 1493, what resources they would require for a major campaign in Italy, France had been directly involved in the affairs of the Peninsula for over two centuries. Since the time of the First Crusade (1096–9), the popes had claimed both Naples and Sicily as their own fiefs, with the right to choose the rulers of the two kingdoms. In 1265, Clement IV granted both to Charles of Anjou, a brother of the crusading king of France, (St) Louis IX. In the following year, Charles duly occupied his new possessions with French troops, and in 1277 another significant development took place when he bought the legal right to the former crusader kingdom of Jerusalem, which by that time had effectively disappeared from the map of the Middle East. Both these claims were to be resurrected by Charles of Anjou's Valois descendant, and namesake, in 1494. Aragonese claims to Naples and Sicily, of which Ferdinand claimed to be the heir, in the late fifteenth century, were equally venerable. In 1282, the Sicilians rose up against their French masters, in what has become known as the rebellion of the 'Sicilian Vespers'. Support for the rebels came from the Aragonese and Catalans, as Peter III of Aragon himself claimed the Sicilian crown, through the descent of his wife Constance, daughter of Manfred, the last Hohenstaufen king of Sicily. Two decades of warfare left the house of Anjou with Naples and the house of Barcelona in control of Sicily, and this state of affairs continued until the death of Queen Joanna II of Naples in 1435. Using resources from his other Iberian and Mediterranean territories, Alfonso V of Aragon then asserted his long-standing dynastic claim to the kingdom by invading southern Italy, from his base in Sicily, finally capturing Naples in 1442. In her will, however, Joanna had left her titles to her collateral relative, René I of Anjou, count of Provence, after which the French claim to Naples pursued a tortuous course, until it eventually reached the hands of Charles VIII. René disinherited his grandson, the duke of Lorraine, and bequeathed his Italian titles to his nephew Charles of Maine. When Charles died, in 1481, his claims to Naples and Jerusalem, as well as Provence, went to King Louis XI. Initially, Louis could only immediately implement his claim to Provence, but his acquisition thereby of the port of Marseilles provided practical encouragement to the French desire for military and political adventures in the Mediterranean. When, as a child, he succeeded his father in 1483, the young Charles VIII duly took the titles of king of Naples and Jerusalem. He appears to have become convinced that he was the true heir of Ferrante of Naples, despite the latter's investiture by Pius II, as overlord of Naples, and in January 1494, the moment to act seemed to have arrived. In this respect, the son put aside the caution of his ailing father, Louis, who had made it his priority, in over twenty years on the throne, to work for the restoration of the integrity of the historic kingdom of France, which dated from the death of Charlemagne in 814. Louis appears to have realised that he had nothing to gain from further conflict in Italy, even agreeing to lease Genoa to the neighbouring duchy of Milan and thereby ending a long-running and rancorous dispute which had been fuelled by endemic feuding among the leading Genoese families. The father evidently had little interest in pursuing the late René of Anjou's agenda in Italy, but his small and ill-proportioned son was determined to take upon himself the mantle of his illustrious namesake, the first Holy Roman Emperor.

Charles VIII, like many of his contemporaries, including Isabella of Castile (see chapter 8), was an avid reader of chivalric romances, but his practical adventures were not merely quixotic, as they reflected historic aims of the Capetian and Angevin dynasties. The growing Turkish threat, in the central and western Mediterranean, served to add credibility to what might otherwise have seemed a far-fetched scheme. With the ending of Breton independence, Louis's agenda of reunifying France appeared to be complete, and the time appeared to be ripe for his son to claim, if necessary by force, his 'Sicilian' inheritance, Naples being regarded, then as later, as one of the 'two Sicilies'. Southern Italy was to be the base for achieving the historic Catholic aim, much beloved of popes since the thirteenth century, of defeating Islam and regaining Jerusalem for Christ. In this respect, as in so many others, the 'Most Christian' king of France and the soon to be 'Catholic' king of Aragon had very much in common. In the event, however, the opening for French military action was provided not by external aggression but by an Italian, Ludovico Sforza, 'Il Moro', of Milan. It is doubtful whether Ludovico wished to see French domination of Italy. More probably he merely sought support from across the frontier in his own struggles to make good his claim to investiture as duke, in succession to Giangaleazzo, and to defend it against Italian rivals, and against his Catalan enemies, whose soverign was Ferdinand. The Milanese duke would have to do business with whomever was king of Naples, and had no special interest in seeing either a Valois or a Trastamaran ruler there. To other Italian powers, Ludovico later presented himself as victim of French aggression, who was forced by long-standing ties of alliance to support Charles's claim to Naples, and saw no other way in which to hold on to Genoa. Alexander VI, as overlord of the southern kingdom, tried to play off France and the Aragonese against each other, while secretly assuring the latter that he would help defend them against aggression and publicly permitting the coronation of Alfonso, duke of

Calabria, as Ferrante's successor. In any case, the 1494 invasion was to change the Italian political landscape beyond recognition. When news arrived of French plans, the major Italian states found themselves in varying dilemmas. Piero de' Medici, the still insecure son of Lorenzo, was torn between responding to Napolitan appeals for support and a desire to maintain historic political and economic ties with France. The 'most serene republic' (*Serenissima*) of Venice refused all appeals, on the grounds that Turkish attacks in the Balkans, which had reached the 'Terra Ferma', the Venetian lands in north-eastern Italy, prevented it from intervening in internal Italian affairs. The most obvious military method for preventing the invasion was for the French fleet to be defeated, and preferably sunk, off Genoa, before its artillery could be landed. Two attempts by Alfonso of Naples's brother Federigo to gain a foothold on the Ligurian coast were unsuccessful, however, and the entry of the French army was unimpeded.

By early September 1494, Charles's troops were in Asti, and nothing appeared to stand in the way of their southward march towards Naples. The French army was more impressive for the quality of its troops and equipment than for its sheer numbers. Its discipline and tactics were more than a match for the Italian mercenary companies which opposed it. Charles paid a courtesy call to the ailing Giangaleazzo in Pavia, where the duke's wife, the Neapolitan princess Isabella, in tears and at his feet, begged the French king to spare her Aragonese relatives in the south. Her appeal was in vain, and when the duke died, a few days later, Ludovico persuaded the Milanese council to name him as duke, instead of Giangaleazzo's infant son. Il Moro strictly had no further need of Charles, though he was glad to receive from him, a few weeks later, investiture as duke of Genoa. The supposed allies soon began to quarrel, for example over control over the small towns on the coast of southern Liguria and Tuscany, but Ludovico did not suffer the drastic fate of his Florentine neighbour Piero de' Medici, who was overthrown by a coup as a result of the French invasion. Charles's army continued its relentless advance, however, and Alfonso of Naples's son, Ferrante, duke of Calabria, commonly known as Ferrandino, fell back with his troops, while Pope Alexander stood impotently to one side, awaiting the outcome. When the French king entered Rome near the end of the year, Alexander was forced to promise him Naples and also, as a token of the Church's approval of his much vaunted crusade against the Turks, handed over to him the Ottoman Prince Jem, who had been in Christian captivity for some time. It was clear that the final assault on Naples would take place in the new year, and Alfonso appeared to be resigned to defeat. He became preoccupied with his own sins, and soon abdicated in favour of his son Ferrandino, who became King Ferrante II. The formerly great commander, a terror to his people, withdrew to a convent in Sicily, where he soon died. He appears not to have intended Charles to take his kingdom but rather to give his son a chance to win the support of his people and defend it successfully. In the event, however, Ferrandino was forced into a slow and steady retreat, as the French army worked its way southwards in February 1495, winning over defectors at every stage. The Neapolitan king fled to Ischia, with his uncle Federigo and the rest of the family, hoping only for a recall when his subjects tired of the arrogance of the French. Charles solemnly entered Naples on 24 February 1495, quickly gaining at least the apparent allegiance of most of the kingdom, though a few coastal towns remained loyal to the Aragonese cause. The permanent establishment of a French regime would not be so easy, as although Charles inherited a fairly efficient governmental system in Naples, disloyalty and faction fighting were traditionally rife. Ferrandino and his uncle refused either to remounce their claims to the throne or to hand over their large Neapolitan estates, in return for large holdings in France. Charles evidently did not intend to stay long in the kingdom, appointing Gilbert de Montpensier as his deputy, and proposing to win over the local aristocracy with grants and rewards. He was crowned in May 1495 and left Naples, never to return, on 20th of that month. His return journey to France was to be very much more difficult than his triumphal southward progress.

Not only had Pope Alexander omitted to confer the kingdom of Naples on Charles in feudal form, but an Italian league, consisting of various smaller states under the leadership of Venice and Milan, formed to prevent his passage through the Peninsula. On 6 July an inconclusive battle took place at Fornovo, in the Apennines, and although the French fought well and were able to continue on their way, this sign of native resistance prompted Ferrandino to return to what he still regarded as his kingdom. It was at this point that Ferdinand of Aragon entered the fray. Although his ultimate ambition was to obtain the Neapolitan kingdom, or at least the duchy of Calabria, for himself, Ferdinand at first appeared to support Ferrandino, in March 1495 sending a small fleet carrying about 300 light cavalry and 2000 infantry to aid him, under the command of the Cordoban magnate, Gonzalo Fernández de Córdoba, later to become known, on the basis of his Italian exploits, as the 'Great Captain'. As a sign of future intentions, according to his private instructions, any fortresses which Gonzalo captured were to be held not for Ferrante II but for Ferdinand himself, and during April five forts in Calabria were treated in this way. Apart from this Spanish help, Ferrandino also gained an alliance with Venice, by ceding to the *Serenissima* some Apulian towns to add to that republic's line of defence on the Adriatic against the Turks. The 'legitimist' forces advanced steadily northwards, from bases in Calabria and Apulia, and in the following year Ferrandino re-entered Naples in triumph, though he died soon afterwards, at an early age, on 7 October 1496. His successor was his uncle Federigo, who, much to Ferdinand's annoyance, was recognized as king by both the pope and Venice. The war over Naples not only reactivated the alliance of Spain, England, the Empire and other powers to encircle France, but also combined Mediterranean and Atlantic dimensions, in a manner which was to be characteristic of the following century.

A new turn occurred when Charles VIII died prematurely, on 7 April 1498, after hitting his oversized head on a door jamb in the royal château of Amboise. Like Ferrandino, Charles had no direct male heir, and was succeeded by his cousin, the duke of Orléans, who thus became Louis XII. It was as a result of the new king's invasion of Italy, in 1499, that Spain intervened directly in that peninsula's politics, quickly achieving a dominance in the south which would last well into the Habsburg period. Although he had felt constrained, as he was no doubt intended to be, during Charles VIII's irruption into Italy, by the recent return of the longed-for counties of Roussillon and Cerdagne, Ferdinand continued to care for his interests in the region. In 1497, for example, at Alcalá de Henares, he persuaded Charles VIII's negotiators to agree to a partition of southern Italy, in which he would receive Calabria, but by the treaty of Chambord – Granada, signed in October and November 1500 with Louis XII, he was promised Apulia as well. The partition of Naples caused much surprise at the time, both in Italy and abroad. Most regarded it as a blunder by Louis, who had no need, from a position of greatly superior strength, voluntarily to let the Spanish into southern Italy on a legal basis. The consequence, which soon followed, was that when Louis mounted his new invasion, capturing and attempting to remove Ludovico il Moro from Milan, to which his house of Orléans asserted a claim, before heading south to restore the French position in Naples, the Aragonese were there waiting for him. Early in 1500, the Great Captain was sent to Sicily with a large fleet, but a fairly small army of 300 men-at arms, the same number of light cavalry and 4000 infantry. He was first sent to Corfu, which, with Venetian help, he saved from the Turks, conquering Cephalonia in December of that year. Eventually, in the summer of 1501, Ferdinand's Cordoban general invaded Calabria, but by this time virtually all the kingdom was in French hands. Sensing superiority, Louis's army fought back and, between September 1502 and April 1503, blockaded Gonzalo in Barletta, where he apparently employed himself profitably in devising a new type of infantry on the German model. This consisted of a combination of pikes, short swords and hand-held firearms. Partly as a result of the use of the new techniques, the Spanish beat the French in the battle of Cerignola, on 28 April. As a result, Naples fell on 16 May, so that, by the end of 1503, the whole of southern Italy was in the hands of Ferdinand himself, and not of his proxy, Federigo of Naples, who had by this time been pensioned off. Louis unsuccessfully tried to use Ferdinand's inexperienced son-in-law, Archduke Philip, whose son Charles of Ghent, later to be king of Spain and Holy Roman Emperor, was now betrothed to Louis's daughter Claude, to obtain a better settlement than was justified by events on the ground, and then sent a further force to Italy. This influenced the election, in August 1503, of Giuliano della Rovere as Pope Julius II, to succeed Alexander VI, and then proceed to confront the Great Captain in Naples. At first, the Spaniards and their allies were bottled up once again, but they eventually broke out and, on 28 December of that year, won a decisive victory over the French at Garigliano, after which Louis made a three-year truce with Ferdinand. Louis's attempted diversions on the Catalan frontier, in particular his attacks on the castle of Salses, failed to alter the outcome. The pattern of sixteenth-century Italian politics was beginning to be set, though the immediate future of Ferdinand's Italian policy remained uncertain, when his beloved wife died in November 1504.[4]

8

Cultural Life: Spain and the Renaissance

Until quite recently, it was generally accepted that the 'Renaissance' was a purely Italian phenomenon, which came to Spain during the reign of Ferdinand and Isabella. According to this view, cultural developments were largely governed by politics, so that, as far as Castile was concerned, although Isabella's father, John II, and half-brother Henry IV, were known to have artistic interests, their 'misgovernment' of the kingdom largely prevented indigenous cultural developments. Only the restoration of order after 1474 enabled Spain to become more fully integrated with the rest of Europe. In brief, the cultural history of the reign of Ferdinand and Isabella, in this interpretation, largely began after the conquest of Granada in 1492. Thereafter, the Italian Renaissance was introduced into Spain on the initiative of Isabella and her husband. The queen established a school at court, in which Italian humanists, the Geraldini brothers, taught her own children and those of members of the upper nobility. An important role in the raising of the cultural level, especially of Castile, has traditionally been allotted to Cardinal Francisco Jiménez de Cisneros. The Franciscan prelate introduced educational as well as general ecclesiastical reforms (see chapter 6), and founded the university of Alcalá de Henares, where Italian-trained humanists prepared the edition of the Bible with Hebrew, Greek and Chaldean (Syriac) texts, as well as Latin, which was known as the 'Complutensian Polyglot', from Complutum, the Roman name for Alcalá. According to the traditional view, the initial influx of Renaissance ideas in Isabella and Ferdinand's reign came to full flower under Charles V. This assessment of the nature of Spanish culture between 1474 and 1516 evidently contains a judgement on the whole achievement of the reign, and thus makes political as well as cultural presuppositions. It is, however, based on contemporary claims, notably by the Italian humanists who were imported to the court of the Catholic Monarchs, such as Pietro Martire d'Anghiera (de Angleria) and Lucio Marineo Siculo, as well as the Florentine ambassador Francesco Guicciardini. Such an interpretation is also based on the long outdated assumption that the Italian Renaissance began in the late fifteenth century. If terms such as 'Renaissance' and 'humanism' are to be used in relation to education and the arts in Ferdinand and Isabella's Spain, they clearly need to be placed in their original Italian context.

It has become clear, over several decades, that the Italian Renaissance was primarily religious, as scholastic as any other part of medieval intellectual life, and innovative in many artistic and scientific fields which were to develop spectacularly after 1500. The main motivation for Petrarch (Francesco Petrarca, 1304–74), who may be regarded as the first 'Renaissance man', was to tackle the religious and social malaise which afflicted most of western Europe as a result of the Black Death. Petrarch thought that the only solution to society's problems was for people to come to an inner conviction of Christian truth and thus discover and follow the rules for leading a good Christian life. He tended towards feeling and the emotions, rather than reason alone, as the solution to the problems of human existence, which during his lifetime seemed particularly acute. He and his companions also took a sensual delight in the Latin Classics, which filled them with divine joy. The point was to be important for the cultural life of Isabella and Ferdinand's Spain. The first 'humanists', in fourteenth-century Italy and Provence, saw the 'reborn' Classics not in opposition to Christianity but as increasing faith in the Triune God. They hoped to transfer their own happy experience to others by returning to their 'purest' form the Classical texts which were known in the Middle Ages, by discovering more such texts, and by composing their own imitations. Although Petrarch wrote as a private citizen, his ideas and work were particularly taken up by servants of a state, the Florentine republic. Notable among them were Coluccio Salutati (1331–1406) and his intellectual heir Leonardo Bruni Aretino (c.1370–1444), who both adopted and adapted the ideas of Petrarch and his circle to help Florence resist the 'tyranny' of its powerful neighbour, the duchy of Milan. The 'study of humanity' (*studium humanitatis*) thus involved action in the world, the *vita activa*, as well as intellectual study, and was later to be used as a stick to beat the 'contemplative' religious orders, not least in Spain, up to the nineteenth century. From the late fourteenth century onwards, it also greatly influenced the writing of history. The 'humanists', as they were coming to be called, at first in Italy and soon elsewhere, including Spain, went back to the primary sources which they saw as truly valuable, these being the living faith of the early Christians, the ethical behaviour of the republican Romans before the corruption which came later with the Empire, and the eloquent and persuasive oratory of the senators and legal advocates of the late Roman republic, in particular Cicero. The result of their deep study of Classical texts, each in its entirety, was a view of human history which did not in any way devalue the role of God as arbiter, but nonetheless regarded every episode in the lives of individuals and societies as intrinsically interesting, and not simply an inert piece of a divine canvas.[1]

Early in the fifteenth century, Spain was commonly regarded by other Europeans as a land of mystery and not a little barbarism, full of 'Saracens' (Muslims), Jews and Christian frontiersmen. Not for the last time in Spanish history, the responsibility for such myths and clichés lay not only with prejudiced foreigners but also to some extent with the Spaniards themselves. By 1500, some of the old prejudices about Spain may have survived abroad, but the realms of Isabella and Ferdinand could no longer be regarded as marginal to the general concerns of Europe, whether political or intellectual. 'Humanists' in the Peninsula readily claimed responsibility for this transformation, but their social and intellectual character merits closer examination. To begin with, it is important to remember that 'Renaissance' Italian humanism was not the bearer of the Classics to Spain. Hispania had contained some of the most Romanized provinces of the republic and Empire, and much of this heritage had been preserved, first by the Visigoths and then by Muslim conquerors. In a manner which, to say the least, lacked scholarly rigour by the best standards of contemporary Italy, the former senatorial colony, and later caliphal capital of Córdoba proudly boasted, in the fifteenth century, that it was not only the home of a 'wonder of the world', the great Mosque-cathedral (*Mezquita-catedral*), but also the birthplace of numerous philosophers, including the Romans Lucan and Seneca, the Muslims Avicenna and Averroës, and even, according to the Cordoban poet Juan de Mena, the scholastics' hero, Aristotle himself. Mena (1411–56) was a chronicler as well as a poet, and also secretary for Latin letters to John II of Castile. He and his contemporary, Iñigo López de Mendoza, marquis of Santillana (1396–1458), as accomplished poets in a new Latinate Castilian style, were examples of Italian influence in Spain long before Isabella's accession. Santillana had a large collection of Florentine manuscripts, although, after his death, the Florentine bookseller Vespasiano da Bisticci said that the marquis could read Tuscan Italian well but not Latin. In this respect he was typical of his era. The main thrust of 'humanism' in early and mid-fifteenth century Spain was the translation into the vernacular, and the adaptation, of Classical Greek and Latin works, mainly for the entertainment and enlightenment of nobles and military men (*caballeros*) rather than the scholars who populated the universities, church circles, and the royal administration. Many of these texts were translated into Castilian not from the originals but from sometimes false adaptations in Latin or Italian by contemporary Renaissance humanists, in Florence and elsewhere. The efforts of the Castilians would not, however, have been regarded by their Italian contemporaries as the 'rebirth' of Classical letters in Spain. Rather they represented another form of Renaissance, a late medieval revival of an idealized Antiquity, which was able to thrive well into the sixteenth century, quite independently of the efforts of professional humanists who worked in Latin.

The latter began to appear on the Castilian scene with the great *converso* family of Burgos, the Santa María, formerly Ha-Levi. Alonso García de Santa María (1384–1456), bishop of Burgos, baptized as a child after the conversion in 1390/1 of his father, who was first a rabbi and then bishop of that city, made direct contact with Italian humanistic ideas in Italy during the 1420s, and seems genuinely to have absorbed them. He accepted Cicero's view of the positive value of rhetoric, which was essential to the Italian Renaissance of his period. Although his lack of interest in another vital facet of Italian humanism at that time, philology, brought him into polemical conflict with Leonardo Bruni, Alonso de Cartagena may nonetheless be regarded as a founder of a disitinctive Iberian humanism. His important contribution was to stress that philosophical meaning mattered as much as philology and rhetoric in the study of Classical texts. Also typical of humanistic learning in fifteenth-century Spain was Cartagena's readiness to produce vernacular works, for example his Castilian translation of Seneca's *On Providence*, in parallel with those which he produced in Latin. The careers of two other Castilian scholars, the Cordoban Nuño de Guzmán (*c*.1405 – after 1467) and Rodrigo Sánchez de Arévalo (1404–70), bishop of Palencia, demonstrate the growing vitality of Castilian humanism during the reigns of John II and Henry IV. Nuño was a traveller and book-collector, who commissioned from the Florentine humanist Giannozzo Manetti a biography of the Stoic philosopher Seneca, who was born in Córdoba. He was delighted to inform Manetti of the supposed site of Seneca's house, which was treasured by the people of his native city. Guzmán helped to start a trend in which Spaniards began to match their Italian humanist conemporaries by taking a growing interest in antiquarian sites, both in their own country and abroad. The Spanish envoys at Pius II's church council of Mantua (1459–61), called in a vain attempt to organize a crusade against the Turks, took full advantage of their time in Italy to undertake such pursuits. Rodrigo Sánchez de Arévalo worked in the Roman Curia in the time of Pius II (1458–64) and Paul II (1464–71). In 1470 he finally published the first printed *History* of Spain, which was dedicated to Henry IV of Castile. The work had two main purposes, the first being to announce to a Christian Europe which was reeling from the Turkish advance, and in particular the fall of Byzantium/Constantinople to Islam in 1453, that the true hope of a Christian recovery lay with the kings of Spain/Hispania, and their historic mission to 'reconquer' Muslim Granada. This much he inherited from Alonso de Cartagena, but Rodrigo, bated by Italian humanists' mockery of Spanish cultural achievements during the council of Mantua, went further by claiming that Hispanic civilization derived from the Trojans, and was thus more venerable even than that of Rome. The growth in Spanish self-confidence was evidently well under way by the time Isabella became queen of Castile.

Given their close historic links with Italy, it was inevitable that the lands of the crown of Aragon would also be affected by cultural developments in Italy, from the time of Petrarch onwards. As in Castile, the Royal Court of Aragon–Catalonia played a crucial role in the reception of ideas from the neighbouring peninsula. Petrarch and Boccaccio had Catalan followers in the chanceries of John I (1387–95) and Martin I (1395–1410), who wrote to each other in Latin and attempted to 'purify' their style. A Catalan Renaissance looked to be on the cards, but the arrival on the Aragonese throne of the Trastamarans from Castile, after Martin's death had extinguished the house of Barcelona, was a grave setback. The new dynasty continued to support indigenous arts, but in 1432, Alfonso V left for Italy, never to return. He gathered a crop of Italian humanists in Naples, but centres such as Barcelona, Valencia and Majorca went into decline, though in Navarre Prince Charles of Viana did become a patron. John II of Navarre's accession to the thrones of the crown of Aragon, after Alfonso's death in 1458, brought about a revival of the arts. Humanistic circles developed once again at the courts of Zaragoza and Barcelona, Italian books were printed, and a royalist and nationalistic school of historical writing had already developed in Aragon and Catalonia, when Ferdinand married Isabella in 1469. From then on, a united humanistic and historical tradition developed within the couple's territories. With Rodrigo Sánchez de Arévalo at the council of Mantua in 1459–61 was the Catalan cardinal bishop of Girona, Joan Margarit (c.1421–84), who had been educated at the Spanish College in Bologna and for many years worked at the Roman Curia on behalf of Alfonso V and John II of Aragon, continuing in the service of Ferdinand and his wife. Margarit worked for over twenty years on a history of what he called the 'pre-[Visi]-gothic' period in Spain. This he wrote to counter the growing Castilian mythology of the time, which suggested that all that was good in Spain, including its current aristocracy, derived from the country's Germanic heritage. Such a historical view was evidently as unattractive to Catalans and Aragonese as it was to *conversos* all over Spain, including the Santa María family. Nevertheless, Margarit, perhaps because of the time which he spent abroad, did not become embroiled in Catalan regionalism, and remained a loyal supporter of the Trastamaran dynasty until his death. Like some of his Castilian contemporaries, and with the advantage of access to the best sites in Italy, the bishop of Girona joined in the developing craze for sightseeing and archaeological discovery and investigation.[2]

Also among the Spaniards who attended Pius II's council at Mantua was Alfonso de Palencia (1424–92), who was almost certainly born in the Castilian city of that name, and in 1441 became a member of the household of Alonso de Cartagena, bishop of Burgos. Between about 1447 and 1453, he was in Italy, partly on cathedral business, meeting, in Rome and Florence, many of the leading lights of the Renaissance, including the Greeks, Cardinal Bessarion and George of Trebizond, as well as Leonardo Bruni, Poggio Bracciolini and Vespasiano da Bisticci. Returning to Spain in 1453, he joined the household of Alfonso de Velasco, who was a *veinticuatro* of Seville. In 1456, he moved to join the retinue of Alfonso de Fonseca the elder, archbishop of Seville. At this point, Palencia's career took off. He replaced Juan de Mena as Latin secretary to the king, now Henry IV, and apart from a diplomatic trip to Rome in 1464, spent the rest of his life in Seville. Palencia was probably the nearest to a full Italian humanist that Spain produced in the second half of the fifteenth century. He was the author of numerous works of history and geography, political theory, and what was beginning to be known as 'antiquarianism', though his works on this last subject are largely lost. He produced witty letters in Latin, and also Castilian translations of Classical texts such as Plutarch and the Jewish historian Flavius Josephus. He was also a lexicographer, and in some sense a precursor of the grammarian of Isabella's day, Antonio de Nebrija. His greatest work, however, was his Latin history of Spain up to his death in 1492, the *Gesta hispaniensia* ('Deeds of the Spaniards'), commonly known, from the title of its Roman model by Livy, as the 'Decades'. This learned and often polemical work not only provides a mordant survey of the Spanish history of his day, but also devotes considerable space to events in neighbouring countries, as well as a full appreciation of the significance of the arrival of the Ottoman Turks in the eastern Mediterranean. Isabella had sacked him from his post as chronicler, apparently for his excessive independence and perhaps for his misogyny, during the cortes of Toledo in 1480. Palencia died in 1492, just as his sovereigns, whose strength of purpose he had so much praised, were beginning to consolidate their conquest of Granada.[3]

The towering scholarly figure of Spanish humanism during the reign of Ferdinand and Isabella, not only in his own eyes, was Antonio of Lebrija (1444–1522), who wished to be known as Nebrija. He was educated at the Spanish College in Bologna and could fully match the efforts of any of his Italian contemporaries. 'Nebrija' was a master of self-publicity, who began his own reinvention by dropping his original surname, the humble Martínez, in favour of the splendid sobriquet *Aelius Antonius Nebrixensis*, after the imagined Roman origin of his native town in Andalusia. Although he made it his policy never to acknowledge predecessors or influences, Nebrija very probably knew Alfonso de Palencia, and owed a great deal to Alonso de Cartagena. The Andalusian scholar was interested in antiquities, and in 1498 prepared a short treatise on the subject for Isabella, supposedly as a sample of a much longer work, which never appeared. On his return form Bologna in 1470, Nebrija settled in the University of Salamanca, supposedly to combat scholarly obscurantism there. In 1481, he published an introduction to Latin grammar for students, which was intended to replace existing textbooks. The 'Introductions' achieved great success, and in about 1487, a bilingual edition was produced for Queen Isabella. Later editions were sold all over western Europe, including England, though the book was not nearly as 'original' as its author claimed, growing to over three hundred pages of traditional Gothic type, and using well-established medieval techniques, such as mnemonic rhymes for grammatical points and lengthy marginal notes, or glosses. The fact that Nebrija's Latin grammar was much criticized in the sixteenth century is perhaps a backhanded compliment to its very success, which turned it into a monument to be targeted. The power of language was deeply appreciated by Nebrija, who expressed much of his approach in his St Luke's Day lectures as a professor at Salamanca. He lambasted the scholarship of most of his colleagues, which he regarded as barbaric, and enunciated his own belief that a grammarian, a humanist *grammaticus*, should be a polymath, whose superior knowledge of the Latin language and literature enabled him to dominate all other academic disciplines, rather as theologians were traditionally supposed to do.

Yet the cultural heritage of Isabella and Ferdinand's Spain, in part thanks to the long coexistence of the three faiths of Abraham in the Peninsula, was much more diverse in subject matter than the discussion so far may suggest. The Muslim heritage, in which Jews had historically been extensively involved, bequeathed expertise in medicine, astronomy and agricultural science. The revival of Christian studies, particularly in the university of Salamanca, during the fifteenth century, which could not all be ascribed to the influence of the Italian Renaissance, did not totally efface these earlier cultural and intellectual influences. Some Spanish scholars, such as Enrique de Villena (1386–1434) and later Fernando de Córdoba (1423–86), sought to marginalize the traditionally respectable study of astrology and alchemy, in favour of a quest for a 'universal science', or system of knowledge, in the tradition of the earlier Catalan scholars, Ramón Llull and Arnold of Vilanova. Fernando de Córdoba, who lived mainly in Rome, joined the circle of Cardinal Bessarion and became a committed neoplatonist. Such individuals were not typical, however, of the bulk of educated people in the Iberian peninsula itself. Although its faculties of civil and canon law were increasingly becoming a nursery for bureaucrats in the Church and public administration, Salamanca university also offered in this period teaching in medicine, astronomy, natural philosophy, Hebrew and music. In the Renaissance period, in Spain as elsewhere in Europe, astrology remained a respectable academic discipline, and the holder of the first chair in the subject at Salamanca was a Pole. Members of the university, such as Diego Ortiz de Calzadilla, who were engaged in theoretical astronomy, co-operated with Portuguese colleagues in Lisbon, who profited from the direct experience of that kingdom's maritime voyagers. Abraham Zacuto (c.1452–c.1522) spent some time in Salamanca, before becoming court astronomer to Manuel of Portugal, while Nebrija himself became involved in the burgeoning production at this time of works of cosmography. Perhaps in part because of the Muslim heritage, medical studies in Spain were rather more empirical in bias than those in many other parts of Europe, and did not only take place in the universities. From about 1460, for instance, the Jeronymite monastery of Guadalupe had a well-known medical school in addition to its hospital. It appears that one of the reasons for the strong interest in this particular monastery of Isabella and her husband was its medical expertise. The queen employed the products of its medical school as her personal physicians, and the royal architect, Juan Guas, built a hospice there in the late 1480s. The Crown tried to control the medical profession in general by means of a licensing system, in March 1477 appointing four medical doctors as royal 'chief magistrates and examiners' (alcaldes mayores y examinadores). The system of control for the medical profession was to be similar to that which applied to other professional and trading guilds (gremios). In theory, these officials were to license every medical practitioner, from the court physician to the humblest purveyor of herbal remedies, but in practice the system did not extend far beyond the court and the universities. Agricultural practice was also regarded as a sphere of scientific, as well as social and economic, interest, and in 1513 Gabriel Alonso de Herrera published his 'Book of agriculture' (Libro de agricultura), which distilled the experience of Spanish farmers, from the Romans to the moriscos of Granada in his own day, and which remained a standard work of reference up to the nineteenth century.

It is probably fair to say that, at the time of Isabella's accession, innovation was not the hallmark of theological and philosophical studies in Spain. The syllabuses of the schools and universities were rooted in the scholastic theology of the thirteenth century and earlier, with little concession even to the 'nominalist' philosophy of the fourteenth. Some indication of the conditions in Castilian universities in the time of Ferdinand and Isabella may be found in royal documents. Government control of the 'old' universities of Salamanca and Valladolid was increasingly the norm in this period, in return for royal recognition and privileges. The cortes of Toledo in 1480 ordained that only the degrees of these two establishments were henceforth to be recognized in the kingdom, and this measure was subsequently clarified in a series of royal pragmatics, between 1481 and 1497. Among the more important provisions were those made in an attempt to assure the quality of graduates (*letrados*) who were entering the public service in increasing numbers. They were to have been for at least ten years at a university (*estudio general*), this implying postgraduate study, and to be at least twenty-seven years old before they could become involved in the administration of justice. While granting exclusivity within Castile to Salamanca and Valladolid, the Crown also intervened in the internal running of the universities. Measures were taken to assure the independence of electors to chairs, to reduce the lavishness of the feasts and celebrations which those elected subsequently had to offer to the electors, and to pay the examination fees of poorer students. This royal protection, whether effective or not in practice, was in principle necessary in what proved to be a period of university expansion. Salamanca university, which in Isabella and Ferdinand's time contained twenty-five professors and about 7000 students, was governed by statutes which had been granted to it by Pope Martin V in 1422. During that century, a massive building programme took place, including the major and minor schools, the university hospital of St Thomas Aquinas and an extension to the university library. A later sixteenth-century building still displays a medallion including a portrait of the Catholic Monarchs and, in Greek, the motto 'The kings to the University and the University to the kings'. Valladolid university had also been growing since the arrival on the throne in the mid-fourteenth century of the Trastamaran dynasty, and the establishment in the town of the *audiencia*, or high court. Valladolid thus specialized in law, though theology was taught there after 1418. The expansion of higher education in Castile during Ferdinand and Isabella's reign also involved the establishment of new foundations, such as the university of Sigüenza (1477). Dominican colleges were planted in Avila, Valladolid and Seville, where a new university was set up in 1502, and Cardinal Mendoza had earlier founded the college of St Cross (Santa Cruz). Diego de Muros, who was bishop first of Mondoñedo in Galicia, and then of the Asturian see of Oviedo, set up the university of Santiago de Compostela in 1504, though it did not begin to function until 1525, and later established the Colegio de San Salvador de Oviedo, in Salamanca. In the same period, beginnings were made in the foundation of universities in the crown of Aragon. Arts faculties (in effect undergraduate colleges) were set up in Zaragoza and Valencia in 1474, the latter becoming a university by papal licence in 1500, at the order of the Valencian pope, Alexander VI. The university of Barcelona, which specialized in medicine, received new ordinances from the city council in 1507–8. Also in this period, between 1483 and 1505, attempts were made to establish a university in Majorca, with the great theologian and mystic of the Balearics, Ramón Llull, as its spiritual patron, though it failed to gain degree-giving powers until the eighteenth century. In the meantime, Ferdinand gave official support, in 1503, to the teaching of Llullian doctrine, perhaps because its deep Christian dialogue with Islam still suited the political agenda, if only briefly. Despite this proliferation of institutions of higher education, between about 1350 and 1500, three universities remained pre-eminent at the end of Ferdinand's reign, Salamanca and Valladolid in Castile, and Lleida in Catalonia. At the beginning of the sixteenth century, they acquired a new Castilian competitor, the university of Alcalá de Henares.[4]

The new university in Alcalá was the brainchild of Cardinal Francisco Jiménez de Cisneros. It was authorized by Alexander VI in 1499, and began to function in the autumn of 1509, with theology as its main subject of study, and the training of a reforming clergy for the Catholic Church as its primary purpose. It was set up in one of the main towns over which Cisneros exercised lordship (señorío) as archbishop of Toledo, and consisted, in its original conception, of one graduate college (colegio mayor), dedicated to St Ildefonso, and eighteen undergraduate colleges, many of them run by religious orders. The project was based on an Observant Franciscan study house in the town, which had been established in 1473, in the time of Cisneros's predecessor Archbishop Carrillo. San Ildefonso College was built and opened first, and, according to the 1510 statutes, which appear to have been modelled on those of the university of Paris of the same period, it was headed by a rector, who was elected annually by the thirty-three full members of the college. There were also twelve chaplains and a domestic staff, and the rule of life of the college was closely modelled on monastic establishments. In contrast with Salamanca and Valladolid, theology was the dominant discipline and law had only a minor role, though there was one professor of canon law. The arts faculty, which acted as a preparation for the other faculties in the medieval university system, developed strongly, as did the medical faculty, a university hospital being added later. Nevertheless, the 1510 statutes make clear that theology, and the necessary ancillary disciplines for its study, were always to have priority. Among the latter, in a manner which would have contented humanists in any part of Europe at the time, priority was given to the art of rhetoric, which was taught by Hernando Alonso de Herrera, and by Antonio Nebrija, who was poached from Salamanca. To assist with biblical and classical studies, a chair of Greek was set up, and others were planned in Arabic and Syriac/Chaldaean. Although San Ildefonso always retained its original supremacy, the cluster of colleges around it grew steadily. The fame of Cisneros's new university is mainly associated, however, with the Complutensian Polyglot.

Cisneros seems to have had the idea of such a project even before the university of Alcalá began to operate. It followed in the tradition of the multilingual edition of the Old Testament by Origen (c.185–c.254), and consisted of six folio volumes, containing the complete Bible text in parallel columns. The first four volumes contained the Old Testament in Hebrew, Greek and Latin, as well as the Torah or Pentateuch, that is, the five books of Moses, in Syriac (Chaldean). The fifth volume contained the New Testament in Greek and Latin, with cross-references to the Old Testament, while the final volume consisted of study tools, such as Hebrew and Chaldean dictionaries, a Hebrew grammar and interpretations of proper names used in the Bible. The printing of the Polyglot was complete by 1517, but papal authorization was not obtained until March 1520, when Leo X finally gave his approval. The production of the Polyglot seems to have been closely connected with the development of printing, in Spain in general and in Alcalá in particular. Work seems not to have started in earnest until Arnao Guillén de Brócar set up his press in the new university city. Brócar had begun printing in Pamplona in 1490, and moved in 1502 to Logroño, where he produced a number of works by Nebrija. Indeed, it is quite possible that Nebrija, who was to be involved, controversially, in the Polyglot project, recommended the printer to Cisneros, who may have funded his acquisition of new Greek, Hebrew and Roman type for that purpose. The Cardinal Archbishop not only assembled a team of scholars, but also bought large numbers of manuscripts. According to one of his early biographers, he paid no less than 4000 ducats for seven Hebrew manuscripts. The prologue to the Polyglot states that many Greek and Latin manuscripts were personally supplied from the papal library by Leo X. Others, presumably Greek texts, were copied from the collection of Cardinal Bessarion, which was sent by the Venetian

Republic. It is not entirely certain how the work of preparing the Polyglot was distributed among the editors, but the Hebrew texts seems to have been the responsibility of two *conversos*, Pablo Coronel and Alfonso de Zamora. The Greek was probably in the care of Hernán Núñez de Guzmán and of the only non-Spaniard in the team, Demetrius Ducas, a Cretan who had worked for the famous Aldine press in Venice. The controversial work on the Vulgate Latin text was probably done by Juan de Vergara, who gained a doctorate in theology at Alcalá in 1517, and Diego López de Zúñiga, a Salamancan biblical scholar who later became involved in debates with the great humanists Jacques Lefèvre and Desiderius Erasmus. The most famous, if not notorious, scholar who worked on the project was Nebrija, whose forays into biblical work had led to the confiscation of his papers by Torquemada's successor as inquisito-general, Fray Diego de Deza. Cisneros, who took over that post in 1507, viewed Nebrija's work more favourably, even though he was not a trained theologian. As a precursor of much nineteenth- and twentieth-century biblical criticism, the Salamancan grammarian insisted on the importance of philology in establishing the text of the Bible. Variants in the Latin text (then the Vulgate translation attributed to St Jerome [c.345–420]) of the New Testament should be referred back to the Greek, while variants in the Latin and Greek manuscripts of the Old Testament should be compared with the Hebrew. Cisneros asked Nebrija to join the Polyglot team in 1513, but trouble soon broke out and he resigned, for two stated reasons. First, he disapproved of the use in the project of Remigius's etymological dictionary of names. More seriously, he objected to the Latin team's practice of collating only manuscripts in that language, without reference to the Greek. Cisneros also tried to persuade Erasmus to help with the project, but the cardinal probably had quite enough trouble dealing with Nebrija, whose criticism of the editorial methods used was, characteristically, not entirely fair. There is evidence in the published work that some comparison of manuscripts did take place across the boundaries of language traditions.

Although the Polyglot was probably his pride and joy, Cisneros's patronage of other publications perhaps indicates more about his ideas and tastes, though dedication of books in this period does not necessarily indicate his personal involvement. Members of his Complutensian editorial team, for instance, published works and editions on their own initiative. Cisneros, as archbishop of Toledo and primate of the Spanish Church, undoubtedly secured the publication of numerous liturgical texts, with two main aims. These were to reform and improve the liturgy and music of the Roman rite, in his diocese as well as his own cathedral, and in particular to preserve the so-called 'Mozarabic' rite, a liturgy which predated both the Muslim invasion of 711 and the

Roman liturgical reforms of the eleventh century. A whole new set of liturgical books for Toledo cathedral was published in 1499, while the Eucharist according to the Mozarabic rite is celebrated there to this day. Although scholastic theology still formed the basis of teaching at Alcalá, Cisneros himself seems not to have been interested in publishing works of that kind, though he lived in an Aristotelian intellectual world. He did, however, support the publication of clearly humanistic works, for example by Nebrija. He also gave patronage to Hernando Alonso de Herrera, a follower of the papal secretary Lorenzo Valla, who was famed for exposing as a forgery the 'Donation of Constantine', whereby power over the Church was supposedly given to Pope Sylvester in the early fourth century. Unsurprisingly, given his deep devotion to his own Franciscan order, especially in its Observant form, he had republished the original rules of St Francis, St Clare and the Franciscan tertiaries, but he also favoured the work of the Franciscans' great rivals, the Dominicans. Although often regarded as a precursor of the Reformation as well as a figure of the Renaissance, Cisneros's spiritual and intellectual life was in many respects typical of the age of Isabella and Ferdinand, determinedly taking the past into the future.[5]

If one thing is demonstrated by the cardinal-inquisitor's career, it is the immense and growing influence of printing, in which Spain played its part, though under strong foreign influence. The first Spanish press seems to have been set up in Segovia in about 1472, when John Parix of Heidelberg printed a *Sinodal*, a record of that see's diocesan synods. Thereafter presses were soon established in nearly every major population centre, except in Muslim Granada. Numerous native printers sought to emulate the Germans and other central Europeans who brought the craft to Spain, but few were successful, and foreigners quickly re-established their dominance. The commercial ethic, rather than intellectual concerns, governed the Spanish printing trade from the start. For instance, the first printers in Valencia were imported by a factor of the Ravensburg trading company, Jakob Vizlandt, and it is thus no surprise that the first printing houses in the crown of Aragon were set up there and in Barcelona, the major commercial centres. It is equally obvious that the early printers in Spain were not tied to the humanist movement, like Aldus in Venice. Presses were generally small and, as in other countries in the period, frequently just produced a few books and then disappeared. The market was so shaky that syndicates were formed by merchants or booksellers to share out the loss. These backers were generally the same people as operated the national and international trade in commodities such as wool and cloth, and books were treated in exactly the same way. High-minded patronage, in which category Cisneros might be placed, was rare and the profit motive predominated. Printers such as those of Barcelona were constantly harried by creditors, often went bankrupt and were under the constant threat of the debtors' prison. Spanish printing was sometimes of very high quality but total production was small in comparison with that of France, Italy and Germany. In Spain, there were rarely more than three or four printing houses in one town, while Venice alone had over two hundred by 1520. Spanish printers were thus unable to enter into the mass export market, and instead, Castile and Aragon imported books on a large scale. Foreign editions were also imported, and these were generally versions of the Classics, legal and theological works and other academic texts. When the books themselves were printed in Spain, the paper often had to be imported as well. Although paper had been manufactured in the country since the Muslim period, for example in Játiva in the kingdom of Valencia, and had been used for Castilian royal documents since the thirteenth century, production was quite inadequate in the face of the new demand which resulted from printing. Most books printed in Spanish presses in this period were intended for local markets, though some were distributed nationally. Yet, although the Catalan Benedictine abbey of Montserrat, which was reformed by Cisneros's brother Abbot García, began publishing in 1499, liturgical books for Spanish dioceses were often printed abroad. Sometimes, as in the case of Alfonso X's *Siete Partidas*, which had been printed in Seville in 1491, in two editions, was sent to Venice for the third.

It was sometimes felt that Spanish printers were technically limited compared with their foreign competitors. For example, when in 1506 Salamanca university decided to commission an edition of one of its most distinguished theologians of the fifteenth century, Alonso de Madrigal ('El Tostado'), the original Latin text was sent to Venice, although the Spanish version was entrusted to a local printer. Given the prevailing perception of Spanish printers' technical ability, Brócar's work on the Complutensian Polyglot appears all the more impressive. It should be noted that an excess of demand over Spanish ability to supply had been a feature even before the arrival of printing. Castilian scriptoria are known to have been swamped in the mid-fifteenth century, and this appetite for foreign texts helps to confirm the falsehood of the notion that Spain was closed to foreign cultural influences before the reign of Ferdinand and Isabella. As a reaction to their virtual exclusion from the elite of international publishing, Spanish craftsmen tended to settle for humbler commissions, such as the printing of indulgences and official forms, as well as routine vernacular texts such as schoolbooks, almanacs and devotional literature. It should be remembered, however, that the great bulk of Ferdinand and Isabella's subjects did not share the elitist prejudices of the small humanist minority, so that the work of the Spanish printers was generally as influential as it was widely distributed. Nevertheless, the total market for books remained small, and, even as late as the 1490s, there were, to the horror of modern book-obsessed scholars, some who believed that the very technique of printing was not indispensable. Although many early printed books merely reproduced texts which were already available in manuscript, the new technique does seem to have reduced prices. Whether these books reached a wider public, except perhaps in Valencia, is more doubtful. It is more probable that the same number of readers simply bought more books. Nevertheless, the new craft, with all its limitations, was of immense value not just to a small cultural elite but to the very government and political and social objectives of the Catholic Monarchs.[6]

Between 1499 and 1503, three inventories were made of books which belonged to Isabella of Castile. Whether or not the royal owner read all these works, they appear to reflect the tastes of the period. The authors range widely in period and geographical area, from the Classical to the contemporary and from Greece to her own domains. The Classics are present both in the original Latin, accompanied by aids for an inexperienced reader to decipher them, and in Castilian translation. Biblical and devotional texts are numerous, together with works associated with the business of government, including political treatises and collections of the laws of Castile. Also conspicuous in the list are chivalric romances, in the Arthurian tradition, such as the *Ballad of Merlin* and the *Quest for the Holy Grail*. In modern times, 'Spanish literature', in its canonical form, has not generally been held to include many of these potboilers, which, in written and oral form, entertained much of western Europe, from monarchs to peasants, for several centuries. What, then was 'high taste' in the time of Ferdinand and Isabella? To begin with, the religious, generally Christian, core of the literature of all their kingdoms must never be forgotten. Whether in literary or purely visual form, 'popular religion', like chivalric romances, effectively included everyone in the 'Old', and increasingly in the 'New' Christian population. Particularly influential were the written works which accompanied the preaching of the friars, and in particular the Observant Franciscans who were so much patronized by the Royal Court. Francis himself had no great regard for the activities of the intellectuals of his day, although, like Isabella apparently, he loved chivalric romances. The spirituality of the late medieval Franciscans entered Castile through the translation of passages of the Scriptures and of foreign works of spirituality and devotion, such as the Netherlander Thomas à Kempis's *Imitation of Christ* and Ludolph of Saxony's *Life of Christ*, the latter being translated by the Franciscan poet Ambrosio de Morales (d.1520). The *Cancionero general* (general song, or poetry, book), a selection of poetry edited by Hernando del Castillo and published in 1511, is a good example of the secular work of the period, insofar as this can be distinguished from the explicitly religious. The work of over two hundred poets, most of them from the fifteenth century, is included, much of it consisting of courtly love poetry, in which religious images are frequently used in a manner which may seem almost blasphemous to modern eyes. The finest poet of this kind in Castilian was Juan del Encina (1468–1530), whose 1496 *Cancionero* was reprinted many times. Encina was a composer, whose poetry was written to be sung, and blended courtly and 'popular' material in a manner which, again, cuts across modern conventions, which are often created as much by academic institutionalization as by the reality of the subject being studied. At the court of Isabella and Ferdinand, lyric poetry was commonly written to be sung, so that musical and literary developments in the period were tightly interlocked.

Another strong genre in Castilian poetry at this time was satire and parody. An extremely popular and successful exponent of this art, between about 1490 and 1520, was Rodrigo de Reinosa, whose work mainly survives in small chapbooks (*pliegos sueltos*), which were the main method whereby literature of all kinds, from the religious to the scurrilous, was transmitted. In the Spain of the Catholic Monarchs, the most popular literature from Italy, translated into the vernacular, was Dante and Petrarch, rather than the work of the fifteenth-century humanists, and Reinosa, too, was typical in looking back to medieval precedents. His highly popular *Coplas de las comadres* ('Verses about godmothers'; the latter seem to have played the role of the 'mother-in-law' of more recent comedy) took the side of the misogynists in the medieval debate with the defenders of women ('feminists' in that restricted sense), which had dominated much religious and secular literature in the preceding centuries. Earlier in the century, the marquis of Santillana had condemned popular ballads as fit only for the illiterate, but in Ferdinand and Isabella's time they were fully accepted by court poets and composers. The ballads were kept in their traditional form, with love and Spanish history, including the deeds of the Reconquest and life on the frontier of Granada, as their main themes. Although professional musicians brought to the composition and performance of ballad (*villancico*) settings all the skills which they applied to the elaborate liturgical music of the period, there is also evidence of a change in musical taste at the Court, in which simpler settings became more common. Once again, religious influence was paramount, in that early Christian liturgical hymns, with simple plainsong tunes, became a model for music which stressed the text, and avoided the polyphonic and mellismatic techniques which were all the rage in the great churches and courts of Europe at the time. One of the leading exponents of the new style was Juan del Encina, who acted as a bridge not only between poetry and music, but also between those arts and drama. Trained at Salamanca university, with which he retained a strong connection, Encina also worked for the local magnate, the duke of Alba. His *Eclogues*, as the Virgilian reference implies, nodded in the direction of the classics, but they also reflected the new fashion for 'rustic' and 'popular' culture. One such musical play, performed in the hall of the duke at Alba de Tormes, probably on Christmas Eve 1492, represented the Nativity in verse and song. In Spain, as elsewhere in Europe at the time, dramatic representation of the Christmas story commonly formed a part of the liturgy of the first mass of the Nativity on what was called the *Noche buena* (good night). For the entertainment of the ducal court, and no doubt his intellectual friends from Salamanca, Encina gave the shepherds the names of the four gospel-writers, Matthew, Mark, Luke and John, and made them allude, in a way remarkably prescient of modern biblical criticism, to the differing contributions which their gospels make to the story of the birth of Jesus.

Prose romance was also popular in the time of the Catholic Monarchs. Since at least the thirteenth century, European literature, again in large measure under the influence of trends in the Catholic understanding of Christianity, had increasingly tended to neglect the male violence of earlier epics, such as the *Song of Roland*. Warfare and violence certainly continued to play a large part in later medieval romance, but there was now a stress on a religious, chivalric world which, like the growing devotion to the Virgin Mary, gave greater emphasis to the feminine, and to the psychological dimension of human relationships. In late fifteenth-century Spain, Diego de San Pedro, in particular, expounded the art of what some have called, anachronistically, the 'sentimental novel'. His *Cárcel de amor* ('Prison of love'), first published in 1492, was translated into several languages and became a European bestseller. It tells the tale of the relationship between Loriano and Laureola, and explores in minute detail the painful process whereby a strict adherence to the sclerotic code of courtly love led this unfortunate couple to frustration, misery and eventually death. The story was dedicated to a Cordoban magnate, Diego Fernández de Córdoba, who held the courtly office of *alcaide de los donceles* (governor of the royal pages), and set notionally in the Sierra Morena, a land of very real banditry to the north of that city, but spacial and temporal references have little or no importance within it. Diego de San Pedro's work nevertheless displays a subtlety which was not in evidence in the chivalric characters which 'starred' among the Spanish reading, and listening, public of Isabella and Ferdinand's day, above all Amadis of Gaul, whose adventures had first appeared in the fourteenth century and continued to spawn sequels long after the arrival of printing. If there was one work, however, which placed Castile, if not Spain as a whole, in the forefront of European literature it was the prose dialogue, entitled the *Comedia de Calisto y Melibea*, which seems first to have appeared in Burgos in 1499, and after additions, by Fernando de Rojas to a text which he claimed to have been written by another, was reissued as the *Tragicomedia* of Calixtus and Melibea, and is known to history as *La Celestina*. With its exceptional depth of characterization, Rojas's work, which is set out in 'acts' like a play, consisting of dialogues and soliloquies, has come to be regarded as the first 'modern' piece of Spanish literature, and hence has spawned a huge and expanding critical industry. Grandiose claims have been made, and as vehemently rejected, for the *Celestina* as a representation of the values and attitudes of Spain's 'New Christian', or *converso*, population in Ferdinand and Isabella's Spain. The original plot concerns a young nobleman called Calixtus, who loses his senses and his moral values in an infatuation with a young lady called Melibea. When the lady rejects him, he takes the advice of his unfaithful servant Sempronio, and obtains the services of a notorious procuress and witch called Celestina, who uses her black arts to achieve the desired result. The couple's physical pleasure, which defies all conventional morality, is shortlived, and the lives of all the main characters then proceed to disintegrate. Celestina is murdered by the servants, Sempronio and Pármeno, who are hanged for their crime. Calixtus falls to his death when leaving an assignation with Melibea, who commits suicide by jumping from a tower when she hears the news. In the fuller, revised version, the couple's enjoyment lasts a month, before the final dénouement, but the moral ambiguities remain. The difficulty of fitting the *Celestina* into the conventional values of Ferdinand and Isabella's Spain has sometimes led to the book's being regarded as either 'realistic' or out of its time. Whatever its author's real motivation, it undoubtedly serves as a warning of the danger of taking official statements of values and morality, whether public or personal, at face value, in the early sixteenth century or in any other period.[7]

It is noticeable that this survey of cultural production in the monarchies of Isabella and Ferdinand has paid scant attention to the territories of the crown of Aragon, or to parts of the crown of Castile which did not have Castilian Spanish as their traditional tongue, that is, Galicia and the Basque country. Despite subsequent revivals of Catalan, Galician, and now Basque, as literary languages, the Trastamaran dynasty, especially after Fernando de Antequera's accession to the Aragonese throne, brought about a huge extension of the Castilian language. By the latter part of the fifteenth century, Castilian, and to some extent

Latin, had totally eclipsed the former literary language of Portuguese–Galician, which had been beloved of Alfonso X and his circle in the thirteenth. During Alfonso V's reign, despite his transfer to Naples, where Italian, Castilian and Latin mainly flourished at court, some of the finest Catalan writing was produced. The most famous products were the poetry of Ausias March (c.1397–1458) and the chivalric novel of Joannot Martorell (c.1413–68), *Tirant lo Blanc*, the latter providing a somewhat more naturalistic accompaniment to the Castilian chivalric prose of the same period. Thereafter, the historic Catalan language showed a tendency to decline in favour of an ever more confident, and politically favoured, Castilian.

In the visual arts, however, the balance of achievement between Ferdinand and Isabella's various kingdoms and territories was somewhat more even. If the reception of the Italian Renaissance in Spain is debatable in literature, there is no doubt that, in 1520, the overwhelming influence in Spanish painting and engraving, tapestry-weaving, sculpture and architecture was Gothic and Netherlandish. This is not to say, however, that local and historic influences did not have an important effect on these arts. In particular, the continuing dominance of the building trade by *mudéjares* resulted in the extensive use of Muslim styles in architecture, both external and internal. The king and queen themselves were energetic patrons of the arts, often with an overt political purpose, as in the case of the Observant Franciscan church of San Juan de los Reyes in Toledo, which commemorated their victory over Alfonso and Joanna. When they captured Granada in 1492, the monarchs launched a huge programme of monumental building, including a new cathedral and many other churches and convents. Nevertheless, they conserved and restored the great Nasrid palace of the Alhambra itself, which they regarded as a glory of their kingdom. That other great architectural achievement of Muslim Spain, the Mezquita of Córdoba, began in Ferdinand and Isabella's period to receive its first major intrusion of Hispano-Gothic vaulting and chapel-building, though this work pales into insignificance when compared with what was to happen from Charles V's reign onwards. Isabella's own literary tastes, as expressed in her recorded collections, have already been noted, but she also assembled, in her royal chapel, at least 225 paintings, 370 tapestries, and many books of hours and precious liturgical objects, many of which she bequeathed to the royal chapel (*capilla real*) in the precincts of Granada cathedral, where she and Ferdinand were both buried. Other regional centres which displayed the arts of the style and time of the Catholic Kings included the wealthy mercantile city of Burgos. There, Hispano-Gothic reigned, particularly in the work of John of Cologne, at the cathedral and in the nearby Carthusian monastery of Miraflores, which Isabella founded. His son Simon built, in the cathedral, the private chapel of the Velasco, constables of Castile. Both Burgos and Miraflores received many sculptures, again in the northern European rather than the Italian Renaissance style, and the new Carthusian house also became a Trastamaran mausoleum, containing the tombs of John II of Castile, his second wife, Isabella of Portugal, mother of the Catholic queen, and the short-lived Prince Alfonso. Also in Old Castile, new façades in the Hispano-Gothic style were added in this period to Santa María el Real in Aranda de Duero, and San Pablo and San Gregorio in Valladolid. To the south, in New Castile, Toledo saw a spectacular fusion of Flemish Gothic and *mudéjar* styles, in Jan Waas's San Juan de los Reyes and the Guadalupe hospital. Waas (Juan Guas) also built a new palace in Guadalajara, and rebuilt the castle of Manzanares el Real, for the dukes of the Infantado, while the chapel of San Gregorio in Valladolid was also his work. His colleague as royal architect, Enrique Egas, designed the royal hospitals of 'Los Reyes' in Santiago de Compostela and Santa Cruz in Toledo, as well as the hospital and the royal chapel in Granada. The Toledan projects also had their influence on others in the region, such as the Dominican convents of Santo Tomás in Avila, Santa Cruz and El Parral in Segovia, and San Jerónimo el Real in Madrid. In Andalusia, the building of Seville cathedral, which had begun in 1402, was completed in 1506. It had attracted craftsmen from much of western Europe, and some of the most notable works in the huge building in Ferdinand and Isabella's time were external sculptures by the Breton known in Spain as Lorenzo Mercadante, and the Frenchman Michel Perrin. The reredos behind the high altar was made by the Fleming Pyeter Dancart and the Spaniard Jorge Fernández. In the castle (*alcázares reales*) of Seville, new rooms were added in this period which combined the 'Isabelline' Gothic with the *mudéjar*. At the same time, the rampant Gothic spread to several other cathedrals, notably Plasencia, Coria, Astorga and Calahorra, as well as the new constructions at Palencia, Salamanca and Segovia. In the crown of Aragon, this was not a period of major artistic creativity, though Valencia saw the building of a new silk exchange, an extension to the *consulado*, or merchant consulate, and the creation of the Borja chapel in the cathedral. Other notable achievements, at the end of the period, were the altarpieces by Damian Forment in Huesca, Zaragoza and Poblet, while the sculptor Gil de Morlanes decorated the facade of the Jeronymite house of Santa Engracia in Zaragoza, and the chapel of the Corporales in Daroca. It is clear that artistic creation in Ferdinand and Isabella's Spain knew no national boundaries. Some of the earliest works of architecture in the Spanish Renaissance style, known as the 'plateresque', were produced by Lorenzo Vázquez de

Figueroa for the Mendoza and the dukes of Medinaceli, and by Pedro Gumiel for Cardinal Cisneros, in the university of Alcalá de Henares and the antechamber of the chapter-house of Toledo cathedral. Despite the Catholic Monarchs' strong preference for Flemish art, for example the work of their court painter, from 1496, Juan de Flandés, Renaissance classicism influenced several major commissions between 1490 and 1520. These included the tombs carved by Domenico Alessandro Fancelli for the king and queen themselves, in the royal chapel at Granada, and for their son John, in Santo Tomás, Avila. A fine example of the fusion of the two styles, Italian and Hispano-Flemish, was the early sixteenth-century work of Philippe Vagarny, which is to be found in Burgos, Avila, Toledo and Granada. Although, to later observers, the artistic works of Ferdinand and Isabella's reigns may appear to be overwhelmed by the lavish creations of the Habsburg and Bourbon eras, a more careful examination reveals the vitality and productivity of their years, in culture as well as political, military and religious matters.[8]

9

Crisis, Death and Legacy

On 26 November 1504, between eleven and twelve o'clock, Isabella of Castile died, after receiving the sacraments of the Church. In the view of many, she had been in decline since her beloved son Prince John died in 1497, but her final withdrawal from the affairs of government had taken place on 14 September 1504, the feast of the exaltation of the Holy Cross, in the castle of Medina del Campo. After that day, she signed no more state papers, and developed an unassuagable thirst, which was ascribed to dropsy (oedema), or excessive water in the body, from which she already suffered. Twelve days later, Ferdinand sent a secret message to tell Prince Philip and Princess Joanna that she was dying. On 12 October, the twefth anniversary of Columbus's 'discovery' of the New World, the queen made her will, as a normal part of a medieval Christian's preparation for death. Having declared herself, in conventional form, to be of sound mind, she pledged her soul to God with the invocation of angels and saints, ordering that she should be buried, dressed in a Franciscan habit, in the chapel of the Franciscan house of Santa Isabel, Granada, though if her husband wished to lie elsewhere she would be buried with him. In the celebration of the conquest of Granada, the original thought of San Juan de los Reyes in Toledo appeared to have been abandoned. Isabella's funeral was to be modest and the money saved was to be spent on the poor, of whom many remained in the difficult latter years of her reign. Although its primary purpose was evidently to help purge the conscience of a Christian, Isabella's will, together with the codicil which she signed on 23 November, provides a startlingly frank appraisal of the weaknesses and remaining problems of the regime which she and her husband had conducted in Castile over thirty years.

Isabella clearly had no great hopes of her daughter Joanna as queen, and her doubts appear to have spread to her son-in-law Philip, who was to reign all too briefly as king of Castile. Although she was almost certainly unaware of the significance of the discoveries which had been made by her 'Admiral of the Ocean Sea' and by others, Isabella ordered her heirs to pursue the American adventure on behalf of the Castilian crown, and to consolidate her kingdom's rule in the Canary Islands. Both her will and the subsequent codicil were entirely Castilian documents, concerned as in the beginning, back in 1469, with her 'hereditary' domain. As befitted a Christian soul preparing for a 'good death' in accordance with the prescriptions of the period, the queen attempted to draw up her own profit and loss account of her stewardship as monarch. Having been a doughty fighter, with her husband, against the popes, on many occasions in previous years, she now ordered her successors to continue as Christian monarchs, on the policy lines to which she had devoted herself ever since her throne had been finally secured in 1479. It is evident that, at the approach of death, Isabella continued to see the agenda of the government of Castile as primarily religious. Not only was the 'reformation' of the kingdom and its Church to be continued, on the lines which had been set out in the council of Seville in 1478, but the war against the 'infidel' was to be pursued on two fronts. At home, not only was the 'observance' of the highest Christian standards to be maintained and extended, but Joanna and Philip were to support the work of the Inquisition as she and Ferdinand had done. At home and abroad, not only was the victory over the Nasrid emirate of Granada to be consolidated, but the war against Islam was to be continued in North Africa and the Mediterranean. Thus the 'crusading' activities of Ferdinand and, in particular, Cardinal Cisneros, in the first two decades of the sixteenth century were prefigured. There has been much debate, both at the time and since, concerning the intended role, after her death, of her husband Ferdinand in the government of Castile. The matter had been raised in the Cortes of 1502, and in her will she claimed to have consulted further with her leading nobles on the subject. Everything in this document indicates that Isabella had little confidence in either Joanna or Philip to govern their kingdom successfully. She provided not only that they should give the fullest respect and filial obedience to Ferdinand, but that in the event of Joanna's proving incapable of ruling, he should administer Castile on her behalf, until her son Charles reached the age of twenty. It is thus evident that Isabella did not wish her son-in-law Philip to exercise authority in the kingdom, and his brief time in this role, in 1505–6, did indeed demonstrate the wisdom of this concern. Even if he was not to have legal control of the kingdom, Ferdinand was to retain some economic benefits from Castile, in addition to his hereditary rule in the crown of Aragon. In particular, he was to retain the revenues which he had previously received from the islands of the 'Ocean Sea', even though they belonged, by papal authority, to the Castilian crown. He was also to continue to enjoy the revenues which accrued to him as master of the three Castilian military orders, Santiago, Calatrava and Alcántara. These wealthy institutions, which had traditionally combined the characteristics of religious orders with those of a military force, were in a sense relics of a previous, crusading age both within Spain and elsewhere. By the beginning of the sixteenth century, they had largely lost their military function, but retained sufficient importance in the seigneurial sector to have attracted the attention of the crown. They were to provide a useful pretext for Ferdinand's continued involvement in Castilian affairs.

In her will, Isabella laid down the order of succession to the throne of Castile. Joanna was to be succeeded by her son Charles and his descendants, with preference for males in accordance with Alfonso X's *Siete Partidas* (legal code of seven parts), but if there were none, the throne should go to Princess Catherine and her descendants. In the codicil of 23 November 1504, the queen made further efforts to prepare for her approaching death by alluding more explicitly to the failings of her regime. For example, she ordered that, if the revenue from the crusading tax (*cruzada*), which had been granted by the papacy for the pursuit of war against Islam, both in Spain and abroad, had been misappropriated, the money was to be returned to the proper fund. In another aspect of policy which was dear to her heart, she admitted that the visitors whom she had appointed had sometimes exceeded their powers in the reform of monasteries. In a manner rare among rulers, in that period or any other, Isabella alluded remarkably honestly, both in her will and in its codicil, to continuing abuses in the Castilian governmental system, including royal taxation. The queen's concerns mirror very accurately those expressed in an anonymous memorandum, which may be dated to just after 1500. The author begins his criticisms at the top, expressing concern that too many petitions to the Crown were being handled by the royal secretaries, rather than members of the royal council. In addition, too many royal documents (*cédulas* and *provisiones*) were drawn up not by qualified lawyers (*letrados*) but by particular officials, such as the secretary Hernando de Zafra, the treasurer Morales, and Diego de la Muela. An Andalusian origin for the document is suggested by the writer's forceful complaint about the renewed and massive expenditure on warfare, for example in Lanjarón and the Sierra Bermeja, which resulted from Muslim rebellions in the kingdom of Granada. The memorandum conveys a strong sense of the crisis of Isabella and Ferdinand's regime at this time, which is also indicated by other sources. It urges that more responsibility, and royal support, should be given to *corregidores*, but, to avoid abuses in municipal government, their terms of office should not be extended beyond the legal limit of three years, with a possible extension of one year. The *residencia* system of inspection of their government by royal judges from outside should be maintained and strengthened, and the resulting reports should be attended to personally by members of the royal council. This writer was also concerned that *corregidores* who were *caballeros*, and not qualified in law, should have deputies (*tenientes*) who were.[1]

Isabella's will and codicil had a similar but wider agenda. The problem of excessive numbers of public offices in the royal towns (*oficios acrecentados*), which had preoccupied the regime at least since the cortes of Toledo in 1480, was recognized as having not been solved. The queen also expressed her regret at the grant to individuals of certain royal towns and fortresses, claiming that many of them had been made unwillingly. In particular, she stated that the marquisate of Villena, which had caused her so much trouble at the beginning of her reign, should never be given away again, likewise Gibraltar, which had for a while been in the hands of the duke of Medina Sidonia. Isabella also recognized, in her will, that her initial success in restoring the royal finances had been neither complete nor long-lasting. The Crown's taxes, including *alcabalas*, continued to find their way into private hands, and the queen willed that such practices should be ended, even if they had been in existence for a century or more. She also expressed continuing concern at the alienation of parts of the royal jurisdiction to members of the nobility, urged her successors to revoke such grants, and returned to the problem of the assignment of parts of the royal revenues to individuals, in the form of *juros*. Every effort was to be made to prevent such life grants from becoming permanent by means of entail (*amortización*). In the codicil to her will, Isabella returned to the question of faults in the collection and administration of the *alcabala*, which remained, at the beginning of the sixteenth century, the most important source of royal revenue in Castile. It is evident that the quality, and in some cases the honesty, of the Crown's agents, both in the centre and at the periphery, had deteriorated somewhat in the years around 1500, though it became increasingly unlikely that Isabella's wishes in this matter would be fulfilled. Of greater duration, though it was to cause controversy at the beginning of the reign of Charles V (see below), was the remedy which the queen proposed for abusive collection of the *alcabala* within the royal jurisdiction (*realengo*). This was the procedure known as *encabezamiento*, whereby a locality, such as a town, would contract to pay to the Crown a set sum annually, for a period of years, rather than being subject to the vagaries of individual tax-farmers and their agents. Clearly, the merits of such an arrangement from the point of view of the taxpayers depended on economic conditions at the time, but its very existence points to major difficulties in the administration of this vital source of royal revenue. Isabella's proposed investigation into the collection of the *alcabala* was to be paralleled by similar inquiries into the *servicio* and *montazgo* on livestock, various customs duties, and the separate *alcabala* in the recently-conquered kingdom of Granada.[2]

As well as making further provision for masses to be said for her own soul, Isabella expressed concern that Ferdinand and Joanna should not allow abuses in the evangelization of the native inhabitants of the Americas. Her admiral, Christopher Columbus, had previously been brought back to Spain in chains, accused of violence and cruelty in the governance of his domain, but he was evidently not alone in his failings of government and compassion. Isabella, in the face of death, evidently wished to put matters straight, though it was not to be until 1512, under Ferdinand's administration, that a serious attempt was made, in the so-called laws of Burgos, to improve the situation. By that time, the Dominican friar Bartolomé de las Casas's campaign on behalf of the Indians was already beginning. The queen evidently feared, not without justification, that misgovernment of the newly discovered territories, by breaking the terms of the papal grants of 1493, would jeopardize Castilian claims to rule them. Somewhat rashly, as it turned out, Columbus had not only been made hereditary admiral, viceroy and governor-general of the new and future discoveries in the 'Indies', but been granted a tenth of all their products. He proved to have little talent for administration, however, and by 1499, his titles of viceroy and governor-general had been taken away. More regular government of the Indies began in 1501, when Nicolás de Ovando was made governor of Hispaniola (now Haiti and the Dominican Republic). As Isabella was well aware, the grant of rule over the Indies, which she and her husband had received from Pope Alexander VI, entrusted to them the duty of evangelizing their new conquests for the Christian faith, and setting up the Church there. Franciscan missions began work in 1500, the year in which the Portuguese first reached what was to become Brazil. Such high ideals contrasted, though, with the temptation to enslave the 'innocent' and vulnerable native Caribbeans and Americans.

As early as 1495, Columbus himself despatched 500 slaves to Spain, and some survived as captives in the peninsula. Nevertheless, when Isabella died in 1504, the legal position, on the advice of theologians and canon lawyers, had been for four years that while 'Indians' were vassals of the Castilian crown, under the terms of the papal legislation, they might not be enslaved. Exceptions were, however, made for cannibals, those who resisted the Spanish conquerors, and those who had been acquired by purchase and were therefore regarded as goods and chattels. In 1503, under pressure both to convert the native inhabitants to Christianity and to gain the maximum possible wealth, especially in precious metals, from the Americas, Isabella accepted the principle of forced labour. The establishment of allocations (*repartimientos*), later to become *encomiendas*, was ordered, dividing the 'Indians' among the Spanish settlers. The Crown tried to link the power to exploit with a duty to convert, and the intention was that these effectively forced labourers should be paid, but the opportunities which the new system provided for exploitation and abuse were clearly massive and unlikely to be resisted. Bishop Juan Rodríguez de Fonseca, who was effectively in overall charge of the administration of the Indies from 1493 until after Ferdinand's death in 1516, seems to have attempted to preserve a balance between the colonists, who wished to exploit the native population as much as possible, and the missionaries, who wanted to protect them, if only for the purpose of converting them to the Christian faith. Exposure to previously unknown diseases quickly killed thousands, and, as early as 1501, black Africans were being imported to replace the lost labour force, but the difficulties of the colonies remained unresolved at the time of Isabella's death.[3]

Between then and his own demise, Ferdinand tended to regard the New World as of interest only for the resources which it might provide for more important enterprises elsewhere, such as Italy and North Africa. The 1512 laws of Burgos resulted from the deliberations of a committee (junta) of theologians and lawyers. They constituted the first legal code for the colonists in 'America', and although at first they mainly applied to Hispaniola, thier provisions also covered Indians who were brought there from other settlements. The new laws were a response to complaints about the Spaniards' behaviour towards their labour force, and focused on the main social and economic unit in the colonies, the *encomienda*. The Crown here attempted to set out in detail the duties and obligations of the settlers, and although it was anxious to put an end to conspicuous abuses, it betrayed, in contrast to some of the missionaries, a fairly low view of the character of native American society. According to this account, Indians were naturally idle and prone to vice, but they were nevertheless not to be abused. They should not be treated as beasts of burden, and their own social hierarchies should be respected to the extent that the sons of their chiefs should be given priority in education. Particular stress was placed on the obligations of *encomenderos* to their Indians in matters of religion, such as church attendance and instruction in, and practice of, the sacraments of the Catholic Church. In some of the code's provisions, a concern is expressed for the well-being of the native populations, though their very nature provides an insight into the conditions under which the labourers in the Caribbean *encomiendas* were living. Pregnant women, for instance, were only to be excused service in the mines after their fourth month. Subsequent observations, not least by Las Casas, who was first an *encomendero* himself and then a missionary friar, indicate that little notice was in practice taken of these royal provisions. As Ferdinand's stewardship of Castile and its overseas possessions came to an end, Las Casas appeared to be fighting a losing battle against the colonists, though Cardinal Cisneros, as regent in 1516–17, did respond by sending out, with little success, an ecclesiastical commission to transform the *encomiendas* into free mission stations. During all of this period, Ferdinand seems to have regarded the New World, of which along with his contemporaries he had only the haziest of notions, as merely a source of supplies for his renewed warfare against Islam, particularly in North Africa.[4]

Back in the Peninsula, on the day of his wife's death, Ferdinand formally renounced his title as king of Castile, which he had held since 1474, and instead became governor (*gobernador*) of the kingdom. His claim was dubious, however, as the normal regent in the case of a married queen who proved incapable of rule was her husband. Ferdinand summoned the Castilian cortes to Toro, in order to recognize his title, but there was evidently a school of thought in the kingdom which regarded Philip as the rightful ruler on behalf of Joanna, if her supposed mental instability proved to be too debilitating. In the last years of Isabella's reign, as she duly noted in her will and its codicil, there had been an undeniable decline in the efficiency of the royal administration in Castile, and a resurgence of the power of the upper nobility, which had been held more or less in check during and immediately after the Granada war. Since 1502, Philip had been conspiring from abroad with dissident magnates and, with Isabella dead, there seemed to be a danger that he would invade and seize the Castilian throne for his wife, whom he claimed to be sane and fit to rule. Ferdinand solved this problem, for the immediate future, by making an alliance with France, in July 1505. One consequence of this treaty was that Philip would have to accept a role for his father-in-law in the government of Castile. Ferdinand cemented his new alliance, which went against the long-standing tradition of Aragonese foreign policy, by means of a fairly unpopular marriage with Germaine of Foix, who continued the marital misfortune of the house of Trastámara by failing to give him an heir. Had the result been different, the crown of Aragon would inevitably have been separated from Castile. In the meantime, events moved inexorably towards a Habsburg succession in both kingdoms. The cortes of Toro recognized Joanna as 'proprietary' queen of Castile, and succeeding assemblies, later in the year, at Simancas and Valladolid, granted similar recognition to her children, in this case referring specifically to Charles of Ghent, who had been born in February 1500. Deprived of any legal rights to rule in Castile, Ferdinand left the kingdom on 13 July 1506, but on 25 September Philip was dead. At this point, the accumulating social and economic problems of Castile crystallized into a political crisis. Cardinal Cisneros was made regent, but at the local level, the upper nobility asserted itself, and the *bandos* re-emerged, while Joanna, in her bereavement, appeared less and less cap-able of ruling.[5] In Córdoba, for instance, the marquis of Priego took control by force in 1508, and was eventually defeated only by a large army under the command of Ferdinand.[6] In addition, between 1506 and 1517, Spanish politics were inextricably linked with those of the Nether-lands, as Ferdinand and the Emperor Maximilian shared the guardian-ship of Joanna and Philip's children. While Ferdinand, as king of Aragon, pursued his ambitions in the complex politics of Italy, and engineered the annexation of Navarre in 1512, old tensions re-emerged in the crown of Castile, which were to lead to the rebellion of the 'Comuneros', at the beginning of Charles's reign. In Italy, particularly after his forced depar-ture from Castile in 1506, he pursued the aims of consolidating his power in newly-conquered Naples, becoming a player in the tortured politics of Italy, and clipping the wings of his star commander, Gonzalo Fernández de Córdoba, the 'Great Captain'. As for Navarre, although the end of the independence of the small Pyrenean kingdom might appear, with hindsight, to have been inevitable, its final demise resulted from a piece of opportunism by Ferdinand. Jean d'Albret and his wife were accused of entering into a secret alliance with France, against Ferdinand and his son-in-law Henry VIII of England, and invasion soon followed, though Navarre was not incorporated legally into the crown of Castile until 1515.[7]

Some of the difficulties in Castile, which were exposed by the pol-itical crises following Isabella's death, applied equally to the crown of Aragon. In both kingdoms, for example, the inquisitors continued their work. The arrest, and sometimes the execution, of 'Judaizers' contin-ued, and was only to fall off after 1520, but forced conversions of Muslims after 1502 began to bring the growing number of *Moriscos* within the orbit of the Holy Office.[8] At the same time, 'purity of blood' statutes continued their sporadic progress through the corporations and institutions of both Castile and Aragon, although, as in the case of the Inquisition itself, their disturbing and deterrent effect was probably much greater than their specific action. The two regencies of Cardinal Cisneros, together with the governorship of Ferdinand, revealed both the strengths and weaknesses of the Catholic Monarchs' regime, which were to be tested, at the beginning of Charles's reign, by the *Comuni-dades* in Castile and the *Germanías* in Valencia. It has commonly been observed that any reform or change which took place under Isabella and Ferdinand's rule was conservative in nature. When Ferdinand finally went to his Maker, at Madrigalejo in Extremadura, on 23 January 1516, he left to Charles of Ghent, much against his will, a group of kingdoms which retained a hierarchical social structure and a deep preoccupation with religion, which was to have huge consequences under Habsburg rule, in Spain itself, in the rest of Europe, and increasingly throughout the world. Older historiography tended to regard the Comunero revolt, and to a lesser extent the *Germanías*, as early manifestations of modern 'bourgeois' revolution.[9] It may more plausibly be argued that the Spain of the Catholic Monarchs was not to be altered, in many of its essential features, until the nineteenth century.

Notes

Preface

1 Paul Preston, *Franco* (London, 1995), pp. 289, 459.

Chapter 1

1 William H. Prescott, *History of the reign of Ferdinand and Isabella the Catholic* (London, c.1880), p. 121; P. E. Russell, 'Castilian documentary sources for the history of the Portuguese expansion in Guinea in the last years of the reign of Dom Afonso V', in *Portugal, Spain and the African Atlantic, 1343–1490* (Aldershot, 1995), XII, p. 1; J. H. Elliott, *Imperial Spain, 1469–1716* (London, 1963), p. 11; Henry Kamen, *Spain, 1469–1714. A society of conflict*, second edition (London and New York, 1991), p. 2; Joseph Perez, *Isabel y Fernando. Los Reyes Católicos* (Madrid, 1988), p. 111; Tarsicio de Azcona, *Isabel la Católica. Estudio crítico de su vida y su reinado* (Madrid, 1964), pp. 229–30.

2 Perez, *Isabel y Fernando*, p. 20; P. E. Russell, *The English intervention in Spain and Portugal in the time of Edward III and Richard II* (Oxford, 1955). Antonio de la Torre and Luis Suárez Fernández, eds, *Documentos referentes a las relaciones con Portugal durante el reinado de los Reyes Católicos*, 3 vols (Valladolid, 1959–63), i, pp. 43–57, 58–9, 67–70.

3 Tarsicio de Azcona, *Juana de Castilla, mal llamada La Beltraneja* (Madrid, 1998), p. 24.

4 Fernando del Pulgar, *Claros varones de Castilla*, ed. Robert Brian Tate (Oxford, 1971, pp. 5, 6.

5 Alonso de Palencia, *Crónica de Enrique IV*, ed. and trans. A. Paz y Melia, *Biblioteca de Autores Españoles*, vol. 257 (Madrid, 1973), p. 39.

6 Adeline Rucquoi, *Valladolid en la Edad Media*, 2 vols (Valladolid, 1987), ii, *El mundo abreviado, 1367–1474*, pp. 515–19.

7 De la Torre and Suárez Fernández, *Relaciones con Portugal*, i, pp. 73–4; Palencia, *Crónica de Enrique IV*, pp. 174–6; Luis Suárez Fernández, *Política internacional de Isabel la Católica*, 5 vols (Valladolid, 1965–72), p. 89; Góis, *Crónica de Dom João*, pp. 106–9 ['pessoa que alem de sua antiga

nobreza, era muim sagaz, e bom cortesão', p. 106]; De la Torre and Suárez Fernández, *Relaciones con Portugal*, i, pp. 75–8; Azcona, *Isabel*, pp. 232–4.

8 Azcona, *Isabel*, pp. 235–43.

9 Palencia, *Crónica de Enrique IV*, pp. 174–200; Prescott, *Ferdinand and Isabella*, pp. 121–4; Perez, *Isabel y Fernando*, pp. 102–4; De la Torre and Suárez Fernández, *Relaciones con Portugal*, pp. 78–82, 84–7, 89–92.

10 Azcona, *Isabel*, pp. 243–9; Prescott, *Ferdinand and Isabella*, pp. 125–30; Edward Cooper, *Castillos señoriales en la Corona de Castilla*, 4 vols (Salamanca, 1991), ii, p. 1013; Palencia, *Crónica de Enrique IV*, pp. 267–74; Perez, *Isabel y Fernando*, p. 105.

11 Prescott, *Ferdinand and Isabella*, pp. 130–1.

12 Philippe de Commynes, *Mémoires*, ed. Joseph Calmette, 2 vols (Paris, 1965), ii, pp. 146–7 and *Memoirs. The reign of Louis XI, 1461–1483* (Harmondsworth, 1972), pp. 302–3.

13 Palencia, *Crónica de Enrique IV*, pp. 311–12.

14 P. E. Russell, *Prince Henry 'the Navigator'. A life* (New Haven and London, 2000), especially pp. 81–106, 147–8, 213–14, 264–90, 327–44; Felipe Fernández Armesto, *Before Columbus. Exploration and colonization from the Mediterranean to the Atlantic, 1229–1492* (London, 1987), pp. 185–202.

Chapter 2

1 J. N. Hillgarth, *The Spanish kingdoms, 1250–1516*, ii, *1410–1516. Castilian hegemony* (Oxford, 1978), pp. 361–2; Joseph Perez, *Isabel y Fernando. Los Reyes Católicos* (Madrid, 1988), pp. 117–18.

2 Hillgarth, *Spanish kingdoms*, ii, p. 563; Perez, *Reyes Católicos*, pp. 129–31.

3 John Edwards, 'Conversos, Judaism and the language of monarchy in fifteenth-century Castile', in Edwards, *Religion and society in Spain, c.1492* (Aldershot, 1996), XVII, pp. 207–16.

4 Hillgarth, *Spanish kingdoms*, ii, 195, 505–8; Edwards, *Christian Córdoba. The city and its region in the late Middle Ages* (Cambridge, 1982), pp. 43–5; Perez, *Reyes Católicos*, pp. 136–40; J. M. Nieto Soria, *Iglesia y génesis del estado moderno en Castilla (1369–1480)* (Madrid, 1993), pp. 180–2.

5 Nieto Soria, *Iglesia*, pp. 154, 162–4.

6 Hillgarth, *Spanish kingdoms*, ii, 46–7; Edwards, *Christian Córdoba*, pp. 54–5; Nieto Soria, *Iglesia*, pp. 179–80.

7 Edwards, *Christian Córdoba*, pp. 34–42; Teófilo F. Ruiz, *Crisis and continuity. Land and town in late medieval Castile* (Philadelphia, 1994), pp. 187–91.

8 Edwards, 'La noblesse de Cordoue et la révolte des "Comunidades" de Castille', in *Bandos y querellas dinásticas en España al final de la Edad Media* (Paris, 1991), pp. 142–3.

9 Edwards, *Christian Córdoba*, pp. 27–8; Marvin Lunenfeld, *Keepers of the city. The 'corregidores' of Isabella I of Castile (1474–1504)* (Cambridge, 1987), pp. 14–23.
10 Lunenfeld, *Keepers*, pp. 33–7.
11 Edwards, *Christian Córdoba*, pp. 31–4.
12 Edwards, *Christian Córdoba*, pp. 45–8; Lunenfeld, *Keepers*, pp. 40–3.
13 Edwards, *Christian Córdoba*, pp. 151–2; Marie-Claude Gerbet, *La noblesse dans le royaume de Castille* (Paris, 1979), pp. 447–51; Lunenfeld, *Keepers*, pp. 25–33; Miguel Angel Ladero Quesada, *Andalucía en el siglo XV. Estudios de historia política* (Madrid, 1973), pp. 105–34.
14 Hillgarth, *Spanish kingdoms*, ii, 513–28; Perez, *Reyes Católicos*, pp. 164–5; Edwards, 'Jewish testimony to the Spanish Inquisition: Teruel, 1484–87', in Edwards, *Religion and society*, XII, pp. 343–4 and 'Religion, constitutionalism and the Inquisition in Teruel, 1484–5'; in *Religion and society*, XIII, pp. 141–7; Marie-Claude Gerbet, 'Patriciat et noblesse à Barcelone à l'époque de Ferdinand le Catholique', in *Villes et sociétés urbaines au Moyen Age* (Paris, 1994), pp. 185–8; Ernest Belenguer, *Fernando el Católico* (Barcelona, 1999), pp. 130–1.
15 Hillgarth, *Spanish kingdoms*, pp. 518–26; Perez, *Reyes Católicos*, pp. 166–8; Alan Ryder, *Alfonso the Magnanimous* (Oxford, 1990), pp. 382–8; Gerbet, 'Patriciat', pp. 188–90; Belenguer, *Fernando*, pp. 129–36.
16 Hillgarth, *Spanish kingdoms*, pp. 526–8; Jacqueline Guiral-Hadziiossif, *Valence, port méditerranéen au XVe siècle* (Paris, 1986), pp. 393–7; Gerbet, 'Patriciat', pp. 136–40; Belenguer, *Fernando*, pp. 136–40.

Chapter 3

1 Tarsicio de Azcona, *Isabel la Católica* (Madrid, 1964), p. 281–2; Miguel Angel Ladero Quesada, *La España de los Reyes Católicos* (Madrid, 1999), pp. 139–48.
2 Alfredo Alvar, *La leyenda negra* (Madrid, 1997), p. 5.
3 John S. Richardson, *The Romans in Spain* (Oxford, 1996), pp. 262, 281–3; John Edwards, *The Spanish Inquisition* (Stroud, 1999), p. 33.
4 Edwards, *Spanish Inquisition*, pp. 16, 33–9.
5 Roger Collins, *Early medieval Spain. Unity in diversity, 400–1000* (Basingstoke and London, 1983), pp. 129–45; Dwayne E. Carpenter, *Alfonso X and the Jews: an edition of and commentary on 'Siete Partidas' 7:24* (Berkeley, California, 1986); Bernard F. Reilly, *The contest of Christian and Muslim Spain, 1031–1157* (Oxford, 1992), pp. 17–21; Edwards, *Spanish Inquisition*, pp. 39–44.
6 Edwards, *Spanish Inquisition*, pp. 15–16, 23–31.
7 Archivo Histórico Provincial de Córdoba, Protocolos Oficio 14 tomo 11(08) cuaderno 12 fol. 55; Azcona, *Isabel*, pp. 381–3; Alonso de Palencia, *Crónica de Enrique IV*, i (Madrid, 1973), pp. 86–7, 130–9; Edwards, *Christian Córdoba. The city and its region in the late Middle Ages* (Cambridge, 1982), pp. 151–3; Julio Valdeón Baruque, 'Los orígenes de la

Inquisición en Castilla', in *Inquisición y conversos. III Curso de Cultura Hispano-Judía y Sefardí* (Toledo, 1994), pp. 37–8; Benzion Netanyahu, *The origins of the Inquisition in fifteenth-century Spain* (New York, 1995), pp. 768–93; Edwards, 'The "massacre" of Jewish Christians in Córdoba, 1473–1474', in *The massacre in history*, ed. Mark Levene and Penny Roberts (New York and Oxford, 1999), pp. 55–68.

8   Diego Ortiz de Zúñiga, *Anales de Sevilla*, iii (Seville, 1988), pp. 152–3.
9   Azcona, *Isabel*, pp. 395–400; Hernando del Pulgar, *Crónica de los Reyes Católicos*, ed. Juan de Mata Carriazo (Madrid, 1943), ii, p. 334; Edwards, 'The popes, the Inquisition and Jewish converts in Spain, 1444–1515', in Edwards, *Religion and society in Spain, c. 1492* (Aldershot, 1996), V, pp. 75–80; Henry Kamen, *The Spanish Inquisition An historical revision* (London, 1997), pp. 46–7.
10   Haim Beinart, *Conversos on trial* (Jerusalem, 1981), pp. 91–2; Rafael Gracia Boix, *Colección de documentos para la historia de la Inquisición de Córdoba* (Córdoba, 1982), pp. 31–79; Edwards, *Spanish Inquisition*, p. 59.
11   Edwards, 'Religion, constitutionalism and the Inquisition in Teruel, 1484–85', in Edwards, *Religion and society*, XIII, pp. 133–4; Edwards, *Spanish Inquisition*, pp. 59–62.
12   Edwards, *Spanish Inquisition*, pp. 69–75.
13   Edwards, 'Religious faith and doubt in late medieval Spain: Soria *circa* 1450–1500', in *Religion and society*, III, pp. 3–25; Edwards, *Spanish Inquisition*, pp. 78–9.

Chapter 4

1   Alonso de Palencia, *Historia de la guerra de Granada* (1975), p. 85; Hernando del Pulgar, *Crónica de los Reyes Católicos*, ed. Juan de Mata Carriazo (Madrid, 1943), ii, pp. 3–5.
2   Palencia, *Granada*, p. 101.
3   Pulgar, *Crónica*, ii, pp. 75–6.
4   Pulgar, *Crónica*, ii, pp. 175–6.
5   Palencia, *Granada*, pp. 183–4.
6   Pulgar, *Crónica*, ii, p. 314.
7   Miguel Angel Ladero Quesada, *Castilla y la conquista de Granada* (Valladolid, 1967), pp. 105–8.
8   Ladero, *Castilla*, pp. 108–17.
9   Ladero, *Castilla*, pp. 132–7, 234–59, 271–3; John Edwards, *Christian Córdoba. The city and its region in the late Middle Ages* (Cambridge, 1982), pp. 144–7.
10   Ladero, *Castilla*, pp. 137–44.
11   Norman Housley, *The later Crusades, from Lyons to Alcazar, 1274–1580* (Oxford, 1992), pp. 292–302.

12 Eloy Benito Ruano, 'Extranjeros en la guerra de Granada', in *Gente del siglo XV* (Madrid, 1998), pp. 169–70; J. Goñi Gaztambide, *Historia de la bula de la Cruzada en España* (Vitoria, 1958), pp. 337, 657.

13 Ladero, *Castilla*, pp. 144–6.

14 Benito, 'Un cruzado inglés en la guerra de Granada', in *Gente del siglo XV*, pp. 149–66; Consuelo Varela, *Ingleses en España y Portugal, 1480–1515. Aristócratas, mercaderes y impostores* (Lisbon, 1998), pp. 112–30.

15 Nicholas Hooper and Matthew Bennett, *Cambridge illustrated atlas: warfare. The Middle Ages, 768–1487* (Cambridge, 1996), pp. 154–62; Bert S. Hall, *Weapons and warfare in Renaissance Europe* (Baltimore, 1997), pp. 16–20, 133.

16 John Edwards, 'War and peace in fifteenth-century Castile: Diego de Valera and the Granada war', in *Studies in medieval history presented to R. H. C. Davis*, ed. Henry Mayr-Harting and R. I. Moore (London and Ronceverte, 1985), pp. 288–93.

17 Hooper and Bennett, *Warfare*, pp. 162–3; Robert Bartlett, *The making of Europe. Conquest, colonisation, and cultural change, 950–1350* (London, 1994), pp. 65–70; Manuel Rojas Gabriel, *La frontera entre los reinos de Sevilla y Granada en el siglo XV (1390–1481)* (Cádiz, 1995), pp. 271–371.

18 José Enrique López de Coca, 'Institutions on the Castilian–Granadan frontier', in *Medieval frontier societies*, ed. Robert Bartlett and Angus MacKay (Oxford, 1989), pp. 127–35, Rojas Gabriel, *La frontera*, pp. 153–204.

19 James William Brodman, *Ransoming captives in crusading Spain. The order of Merced on the Christian Islamic frontier* (Philadelphia, 1986), p. 15; López de Coca, 'Institutions', pp. 135–50; Rojas Gabriel, *La frontera*, pp. 204–34.

20 Robert I. Burns, 'The significance of the frontier in the Middle Ages', in Bartlett and MacKay, *Medieval frontier societies*, pp. 307–30.

Chapter 5

1 Henry Kamen, *Spain, 1469–1714. A society of conflict* (London, 1991), p. 48.

2 Mary Vincent and R. A. Stradling, *Cultural atlas of Spain and Portugal* (Abingdon, 1994), pp. 12–22.

3 J. N. Hillgarth, *The Spanish kingdoms, 1250–1516*, ii, *1410-1516. Castilian hegemony* (Oxford, 1978), p. 500; Miguel Angel Ladero Quesada, *La España de los Reyes Católicos* (Madrid, 1999), pp. 19–28.

4 John Edwards, *Christian Córdoba. The city and its region in the late Middle Ages* (Cambridge, 1982), p. 5; Bartolomé Yun Casalilla, *Crisis de subsistencias y conflictividad social en Córdoba a principios del siglo XVI* (Córdoba, 1980), pp. 56–7; Kamen, *Spain*, p. 52; Máximo Diago Hernando, *Soria en la Baja Edad Media. Espacio rural y economía agraria* (Madrid, 1993), p. 83; José Rodríguez Molina, *El reino de Jaén en la Baja*

Edad Media (Granada, 1978), pp. 155–9; Rodríguez Molina, 'Instrumental agrícola bajomedieval en Andalucía', in *Andalucía entre Oriente y Occidente* (Córdoba, 1988), pp. 309–16; Isabel Montes Romero-Camacho, *El paisaje rural sevillano en la Baja Edad Media* (Seville, 1989), pp. 279–306.

5 Edwards, *Christian Córdoba*, pp. 3–6, 12, 78, 84–95, 196–7; David Vassberg, *Land and society in Golden Age Castile* (Cambridge, 1986), pp. 5–56; Tomás Quesada Quesada, *El paisaje rural de la Campiña de Jaén en la Baja Edad Media según los Libros de Dehesas* (Jaén, 1994), pp. 37–74; Julius Klein, *The Mesta* (Cambridge, MA, 1920); Hillgarth, *Spanish kingdoms*, ii, p. 495; Kamen, *Spain*, pp. 50–2.

6 Jaime Vicens Vives, 'The economies of Catalonia and Castile', in *Spain in the fifteenth century (1369–1516)*, ed. Roger Highfield (London and Basingstoke, 1972), pp. 36–41; Angus MacKay, *Spain in the Middle Ages. From frontier to empire* (London and Basingstoke, 1977), pp. 169–70; Hillgarth, *Spanish kingdoms*, ii, p. 495; Charles Julian Bishko, 'The Andalusian municipal mestas in the 14th–16th centuries: administrative and social aspects', in *Andalucía Medieval (Actas del I Congreso Historia de Andalucía)* (Córdoba, 1978), pp. 341–74; Edwards, *Christian Córdoba*, pp. 114–20; Kamen, *Spain*, p. 50; Marie-Claude Gerbet, *L'élevage dans le royaume de Castille sous les Rois catholiques* (Madrid, 1999), 57–90; Diago Hernando, *Soria*, pp. 129–43.

7 Edwards, *Christian Córdoba*, pp. 13–17, 131–3; Vassberg, *Land and society*, pp. 90–150; James Casey, *Early modern Spain. A social history* (London, 1999), pp. 87–98.

8 MacKay, *Spain*, pp. 176–8; Carlos Barros, *A mentalidade xusticieira dos Irmandiños* (Vigo, 1988); Joseph Perez, *Isabel y Fernando. Los Reyes Católicos* (Madrid, 1988), p. 106.

9 M. Mollat and P. Wolff, *The popular revolutions of the late Middle Ages* (London, 1973), pp. 239–42; MacKay, *Spain*, pp. 177–8; Hillgarth, *Spanish kingdoms*, ii, pp. 520–1; Perez, *Isabel y Fernando*, pp. 166–7; Alan Ryder, *Alfonso the Magnanimous* (Oxford, 1990), pp. 388, 392; Paul Freedman, *The origins of peasant servitude in medieval Catalonia* (Cambridge, 1991), pp. 179–223; Ernest Belenguer, *Fernando el Católico* (Barcelona, 1999), pp. 159–66.

10 Hillgarth, *Spanish kingdoms*, ii, pp. 517–18; Edwards, *Christian Córdoba*, pp. 147–8; Adeline Rucquoi, *Valladolid en la Edad Media*, ii (Valladolid, 1987), pp. 189–235; Marie-Claude Gerbet, 'Patriciat et noblesse à Barcelone à l'époque de Ferdinand le Catholique', in *Villes et sociétés urbaines au Moyen Age* (Paris, 1994), pp. 218–32; Belenguer, *Fernando*, pp. 167–73.

11 Hillgarth, *Spanish kingdoms*, ii, pp. 510–23; Belenguer, *Fernando*, pp. 176–8.

12 Belenguer, *Valencia en la crisi del segle XV* (Barcelona, 1976), and *Fernando*, pp. 173–5; Hillgarth, *Spanish kingdoms*, ii, pp. 526–8, Jacqueline

Guiral- Hadziiossif, *Valence, port méditerranéen au XVe siècle* (Paris, 1986), pp. 9–20, 249–90; MacKay, *Spain*, pp. 170–1.

13 Edwards, *Christian Córdoba*, pp. 124–7; Rucquoi, *Valladolid*, ii, pp. 403–26; Enrique Otte, *Sevilla y sus mercaderes a fines de la Edad Media* (Seville, 1996), p. 194; Edwards, '"Development" and "underdevelopment" in the Western Mediterranean: the case of Córdoba and its region in the late fifteenth and early sixteenth centuries', in *Religion and society in Spain, c.1492* (Aldershot, 1996), XVI, pp. 30–3.

14 Pierre Vilar, *A history of gold and money, 1450–1920* (London, 1976), pp. 46–9; Jacques Heers, 'Los genoveses en la sociedad andaluza del siglo XV: orígenes, grupos, solidaridades', in *Actas del II Coloquio de Historia Medieval Andaluza* (Seville, 1982), pp. 419–44.

15 Edwards, *Christian Córdoba*, pp. 102–13; Rucquoi, *Valladolid*, ii, pp. 426–50.

16 Edwards, *Christian Córdoba*, pp. 128–30.

17 Edwards, 'La noblesse de Cordoue et la révolte des "Comunidades" de Castille', in *Bandos y querellas dinásticas en España al final de la Edad Media* (Paris, 1991), pp. 141–3; Ladero, *España*, pp. 75–7.

18 Edwards, *Christian Córdoba*, pp. 202–4; Ladero, *España*, p. 96.

19 MacKay, *Spain*, pp. 170–1; Miguel Angel Ladero Quesada, *Las ferias de Castilla, siglos XIII a XV* (Madrid, 1994); Otte, *Mercaderes*, pp. 167–83.

20 Hillgarth, *Spanish kingdoms*, ii, pp. 513–14; John Edwards, 'Córdoba and Jerez de la Frontera in the reign of Ferdinand and Isabella', doctoral thesis (Oxford, 1976), pp. 157–60, and *Christian Córdoba*, pp. 58–92; Ladero, *España*, pp. 172–81.

21 Ladero, *España*, pp. 401–95.

22 Edwards, *Christian Córdoba*, p. 129.

Chapter 6

1 Tarsicio de Azcona, *Isabel la Católica* (Madrid, 1964), pp. 425–8; Demetrio Mansilla, 'Panorama histórico-geográfico de la Iglesia española en los siglos XV y XVI', in *Historia de la Iglesia en España*, vol. 3 part 1 [HIE3i] (Madrid, 1980), pp. 3–23.

2 Tarsicio de Azcona, 'Reforma del episcopado y del clero de España en tiempo de los Reyes Católicos', in HIE3i, p. 163.

3 Azcona, 'Reforma', p. 118.

4 John Edwards, *Christian Córdoba. The city and its region in the late Middle Ages* (Cambridge, 1982), p. 150.

5 Azcona, 'Reforma', pp. 122–30.

6 Azcona, 'Reforma', p. 179.

7 Balbina Martínez Caviró, *Conventos de Toledo. Toledo, castillo interior* (Madrid, 1990), pp. 255–78.

8 Fray Toribio de Motolinía, *Historia de los índios de la Nueva España* (Madrid, 1991), pp. 1–15 (introduction by Georges Baudot).

9   C. M. D. Crowder, *Unity, heresy and reform* (London, 1977), pp. 128–9, 179–81.

10 Michael Mullett, *The Catholic Reformation* (London, 1999), pp. 4–5.

11 J. N. Hillgarth, *The Spanish kingdoms, 1250–1516*, ii, *1410–1516. Castilian hegemony* (Oxford, 1978), pp. 363–4, 371–3, 571, 605–6; Jodi Bilinkoff, 'A Spanish prophetess and her patrons: the case of Maria de Santo Domingo', *Sixteenth Century Journal*, xxiii (1992), pp. 21–34.

12 Christopher Columbus, *The book of prophecies*, ed. Roberto Rusconi (Berkeley, 1997).

13 Valerie Flint, *The imaginative landscape of Christopher Columbus* (Princeton, 1992), p. 185; Columbus, *Book of prophecies*, pp. 31–3, 316–17, 390.

14 John Edwards, 'Ritual murder in the Siglo de Oro; Lope de Vega's *El niño inocente de La Guardia*', in *The Proceedings of the 10th British Conference on Judeo-Spanish Studies* (London, 1999), pp. 73–88.

15 Andrés Bernáldez, *Memorias del reinado de los Reyes Católicos*, ed. M. Gómez Moreno and Juan de Mata Carriazo (Madrid, 1962), p. 251; Elijah Capsali in David Raphael, ed., *The expulsion 1492 chronicles* (North Hollywood, CA, 1992), p. 57.

16 John Edwards, 'Jews and *conversos* in the region of Soria and Almazán: departures and returns', in Edwards, *Religion and society in Spain, c.1492* (Aldershot, 1996), VI, p. 7 and *The Spanish Inquisition* (Stroud, 1999), pp. 100–3.

17 John Edwards, 'Expulsion or indoctrination? The fate of Portugal's Jews in and after 1497', in *Portuguese, Brazilian and African Studies. Studies presented to Clive Willis*, ed. T. F. Earle and Nigel Griffin (Warminster, 1995), pp. 87–96.

18 Edwards, *Spanish Inquisition*, pp. 99–100.

19 Bernáldez, *Memorias*, p. 254; John Edwards, *The Jews in Western Europe, 1400–1600* (Manchester, 1994), pp. 53–5; Raphael, *Expulsion chronicles*, pp. 1–45, 51–4, 91–104.

20 Fritz (Yitzhak) Baer, *Die Juden im christlichen Spanien*, ii (Berlin, 1936), pp. 437, 468–72, 513–15; Edwards, 'Elijah and the Inquisition: messianic prophecy among *conversos* in Spain', in Edwards, *Religion and society*, VIII, pp. 79–94.

21 L. P. Harvey, *Islamic Spain, 1250–1500* (Chicago, 1990), pp. 324–39; John Edwards, 'Christian mission in the kingdom of Granada, 1492–1568', in Edwards, *Religion and society*, XI, pp. 20–33; Erika Rummel, *Jiménez de Cisneros* (Tempe, AZ, 1999), pp. 32–5.

Chapter 7

1 Joseph Perez, *Isabel y Fernando. Los Reyes Católicos* (Madrid, 1988), pp. 293–5; Miguel Angel Ladero Quesada, *La España de los Reyes Católicos* (Madrd, 1999), p. 426; Ernest Belenguer, *Fernando el Católico* (Barcelona, 1999), p. 191.

2 J. N. Hillgarth, *The Spanish kingdoms, 1250–1516*, ii, *1410–1516. Castilian hegemony* (Oxford, 1978), pp. 539–40, 575–6; Tarsicio de Azcona, *Juana de Castilla, mal llamada La Beltraneja* (Madrid, 1998), pp. 77–95; Perez, *Isabel y Fernando*, pp. 295–6; Belenguer, *Fernando*, pp. 213–14; Sanjay Subrahmanyam, *The career and legend of Vasco da Gama* (Cambridge, 1997), pp. 42–53.

3 Belenguer, *Fernando*, pp. 214–18, 359; Ladero, *La España*, p. 464; Luis Suárez Fernández, *Fernando el Católico y Navarra* (Madrid, 1985), pp. 107–77.

4 David Abulafia, *Western Mediterranean kingdoms, 1200–1500* (London, 1997), pp. 223–57; Christine Shaw, *Julius II. The warrior pope* (Oxford, 1993), pp. 83–115; Frederic J. Baumgartner, *Louis XII* (Basingstoke and London, 1994), pp. 39–40; Ladero, *La España*, pp. 436–48; Belenguer, *Fernando*, pp. 229–56, 275–82; Hillgarth, *Spanish kingdoms*, ii, pp. 545–59.

Chapter 8

1 Helen Nader, *The Mendoza family in the Spanish Renaissance, 1350–1550* (New Brunswick, NJ, 1979), pp. 1–16.

2 Jeremy Lawrance, 'Humanism in the Iberian peninsula', in *The impact of humanism on Western Europe*, ed. Anthony Goodman and Angus MacKay (London 1990), pp. 220–57.

3 Alfonso de Palencia, *Gesta hispaniensia ex annalibus suorum dierum collecta*, ed. Brian Tate and Jeremy Lawrence, i (Madrid, 1998), pp. xxxv–lv; John Edwards, 'Pride and prejudice: Alfonso de Palencia as historian', *Nottingham Medieval Studies*, xliii (1999), 206–11.

4 Miguel Angel Ladero Quesada *La España de los Reyes Católicos* (Madrid, 1999), pp. 342–6, 353–7.

5 Erika Rummel, *Jiménez de Cisneros: on the threshold of Spain's Golden Age* (Tempe, AZ, 1999), pp. 57–65.

6 Clive Griffin, *The Crombergers of Seville. The history of a printing and merchant dynasty* (Oxford, 1988), esp. pp. 1–7; *Monsterrat. Cinc-cents anys de publicacions, 1499–1999* (exhibition catalogue, Montserrat, 1999), pp. 11–29.

7 Francisco Javier Sánchez Cantón, *Libros, tapices y cuadros que coleccionó Isabel la Católica* (Madrid, 1950), pp. 21–38; P. E. Russell, 'Spanish literature (1474–1681)', in *Spain. A companion to Spanish studies*, ed. Russell (London, 1973), pp. 265–90; A. D. Deyermond, *A literary history of Spain: the Middle Ages* (London, 1971), pp. 136–205.

8 Sánchez Cantón, *Libros*, pp. 89–105, 151–64; Ladero, *La España*, pp. 370–8; Judith Berg Sobré, *Behind the altar table. The development of the painted retable in Spain, 1350–1500* (Columbia, MO, 1989); Ignace Vandevivere, *Juan de Flandés* (Bruges, 1985); M. Nieto Cumplido and F. Moreno Cuadro, *Córdoba 1492. Ambiente artístico y cultural* (Córdoba, 1992); Tess Knighton, 'Northern influence on cultural developments in the Iberian

peninsula during the fifteenth century', *Renaissance Studies*, i (1987), 221–37.

Chapter 9

1 'De lo que convendría hacerse para evitar algunos abusos en el gobierno – copia de otra de letra de últimos del siglo XV o principios del XVI – sin autor ni fecha', *Colección de documentos inéditos para la historia de España*, vol. lxxxviii, pp. 504–6.

2 Antonio de la Torre y del Cerro, *Testamentaria de Isabel la Católica* (Valladolid, 1968), pp. 446–85.

3 Felipe Fernández-Armesto, *Columbus* (Oxford, 1991), pp. 133–51; J. N. Hillgarth, *The Spanish kingdoms, 1250–1516*, ii, *1410–1516. Castilian hegemony* (Oxford, 1978), pp. 378–583.

4 L. B. Simpson, trans., *The laws of Burgos of 1512–1513. Royal ordinances for the good government and treatment of the Indians* (San Francisco, CA, 1960), pp. 11–47.

5 Hillgarth, *Spanish kingdoms*, ii, pp. 592–603; Ernest Belenguer, *Fernando el Católico* (Barcelona, 1999), pp. 283–315, 326–31.

6 John Edwards, 'La révolte du marquis de Priego à Cordoue en 1508. Un symptôme des tensions d'une société urbaine', *Mélanges de la Casa de Velázquez*, xii (1976), pp. 165–72.

7 Hillgarth, *Spanish kingdoms*, ii, pp. 560–9; Belenguer, *Fernando*, pp. 315–26, 355–62; Luis Suárez Fernández, *Fernando el Católico* (Madrid, 1985), pp. 209–44.

8 See, for example, Edwards, *The Spanish Inquisition* (Stroud, 1999), pp. 90–2.

9 Joseph Perez, 'Les "comunidades" de Castille: nouvel examen de la question', in *Les sociétés urbaines en France méridionale et en péninsule ibérique au Moyen Âge* (Paris, 1991), pp. 143–57.

Bibliographical Essay

The impressive scale of research and publication on the period of Ferdinand and Isabella which has been achieved in recent years, both in Spain and abroad, means inevitably that the selection which follows has to exclude many valuable works which deserve no such fate. Lack of space has required a concentration on books, and particularly those of national or regional scope, rather than articles and conference papers, though a rigid distinction has not in practice been made. Readers who wish to pursue specific matters are recommended to seek out work in journals and conference proceedings, which are referred to in the more specialized bibliographies of some of the works cited below, particularly those by Hillgarth and Ladero in the 'General' section.

General

Short surveys of the reign of Ferdinand and Isabella are to be found in books on the early modern period of Spanish history. Notable examples are those of John Lynch, *Spain 1516–1598. From nation state to world empire* (Oxford, 1991, 1994), John Elliott, *Imperial Spain, 1469–1716* (London, 1963) and Henry Kamen, *Spain, 1469–1714. A society of conflict* (1983, 1991). From the medieval perspective, there are useful sections, especially on religious and cultural matters, in Angus MacKay, *Spain in the Middle Ages. From frontier to empire, 1000–1500* (London and Basingstoke, 1977). J. N. Hillgarth's *The Spanish kingdoms, 1250–1516*, vol. 2, *1410–1516. Castilian hegemony* (Oxford, 1978), while comprehensive, is particularly valuable for its treatment of the crown of Aragon, while Ferdinand's rule is discussed briefly in T. N. Bisson, *The medieval Crown of Aragon. A short history* (Oxford, 1986). Translations of a wide range of original sources for fifteenth-century Spain and the New World are to be found in *Medieval Iberia: readings from Christian, Muslim and Jewish sources*, ed. Olivia Remie Constable (Philadelphia, 1997). Important articles by Luis Suárez Fernández and Jaime Vicens Vives, among others, are translated in *Spain in the fif-*

teenth century, 1369–1516, ed. Roger Highfield (London and Basingstoke, 1972). Stephen Haliczer, *The Comuneros of Castile: the forging of a revolution, 1475–1520* (Madison, WI 1981) concentrates mainly on the Castilian municipalities (see below).

Still of great value are the two relevant volumes of the *Historia de España*, directed by Ramón Menéndez Pidal, vol. 17, *La España de los Reyes Católicos (1474–1516)* (Madrid, 1978), part 1 edited by Luis Suárez Fernández and Juan de Mata Carriazo, and part 2 by Suárez Fernández and Manuel Fernández Alvarez. Surveys in English of Ferdinand, Isabella and their reign begin with William H. Prescott's *History of the reign of Ferdinand and Isabella the Catholic* (Boston, 1837 and numerous subsequent editions). Joseph Perez's *Isabelle et Ferdinand. Rois Catholiques d'Espagne* (Paris, 1988), translated as *Isabel y Fernando. Los Reyes Cathólicos* (Madrid, 1988), is in fact a treatment of the period as a whole. Miguel Angel Ladero Quesada's *La España de los Reyes Católicos* (Madrid, 1999) provides a comprehensive survey of the reign with a full bibliography of works in Spanish, and acts as a foil to Luis Suárez Fernández's five-volume work *Los Reyes Católicos* (Madrid, 1989–90). Various aspects of the reign are discussed in essay form in Angus MacKay, *Society, economy and religion in late medieval Castile* (London, 1987) and John Edwards, *Religion and society in Spain, c.1492* (Aldershot, 1996). A variety of aspects of the crown of Aragon are surveyed in *La Corona de Aragón y el Mediterráneo, siglos XV-XVI*, ed. Esteban Sarasa and Eliseo Serrano (Zaragoza, 1997). Biographical works on Ferdinand of Aragon include J. Vicens Vives, *Fernando el Católico, príncipe de Aragón y rey de Sicilia (1458–1478)* (Madrid, 1954), J. Angel Sesma Muñoz, *Fernando de Aragón. Hispaniarum Rex* (Zaragoza, 1992) and Ernest Belenguer, *Fernando el Católico* (Barcelona, 1999). In English, the somewhat hagiographical, but scholarly, biography by William Thomas Walsh, *Isabella of Spain* (London, 1931), has now been supplemented by Peggy K. Liss, *Isabel, the queen* (New York, 1992), while Luis Suárez Fernández's *Isabel, mujer y reina* (Madrid, 1992) focuses on the queen's difficulties as a ruler. Of very great value is the scholarly biography by Tarsicio de Azcona, *Isabel la Católica: estudio crítico de su vida y su reinado* (Madrid, 1964, 1993). For Isabella's earlier years, see María Isabel del Val Valdivieso, *Isabel la Católica princesa (1468–1474)* (Valladolid, 1974), and for this period in general, W. D. Phillips, *Enrique IV and the crisis of fifteenth-century Castile, 1425–1480* (Cambridge, MA., 1978). The main chronicles of the period are available in modern editions. They include Andrés Bernáldez's *Memorias del reinado de los Reyes Católicos*, ed. M. Gómez Moreno and Juan de Mata Carriazo (Madrid, 1962), Hernando del Pulgar's *Crónica de los Reyes Católicos*, ed. Juan de

Mata Carriazo, 2 vols (Madrid, 1943) and Diego de Valera's *Crónica de los Reyes Católicos*, ed. Juan de Mata Carriazo (Madrid, 1927). Until recently, Alfonso de Palencia's Latin history of events up to 1492 has been largely available only in the Spanish translation by A. Paz y Melia, in 5 vols (Madrid, 1904–9), as the *Crónica de Enrique IV* and *Historia de la Guerra de Granada*. This version was republished in the *Biblioteca de Autores Españoles*, vols 257–8, 267 (Madrid, 1973–5). Of the Latin original, the fourth *Decade* was edited by José López de Toro as *Cuarto década de Alonso de Palencia*, 2 vols (Madrid, 1970–4), but a much superior edition is now being published by Brian Tate and Jeremy Lawrance as *Gesta hispaniensia ex annalibus suorum dierum collecta*, vols 1–2 (Madrid, 1998–9).

The Political Regime

Apart from the sources and studies already mentioned, the issue of the Castilian succession is analysed, with sympathy for Princess Joanna, in Tarsicio de Azcona, *Juana de Castilla, mal llamada La Beltraneja* (Madrid, 1998). Two of the institutional supports of Isabella and Ferdinand's regime in Castile are studied in Marvin Lunenfeld, *The Council of the Hermandad. A study of the pacification forces of Ferdinand and Isabella* (Coral Gables, FL, 1970) and *Keepers of the city. The corregidores of Isabella I of Castile 1474–1504* (Cambridge, 1987). The most useful work on the cortes of Castile is now J. M. Carretero Zamora, *Corpus documental de las Cortes de Castilla (1475–1517)* (Madrid, 1993). The master of Castilian royal finances is Miguel Angel Ladero Quesada, whose main books on the subject are *La hacienda real de Castilla en el siglo XV* (La Laguna de Tenerife, 1973) and *El siglo xv en Castilla. Fuentes de renta y política fiscal* (Barcelona, 1982). Literature on the major towns of Castile (and some minor ones) is now so extensive that only a small selection may be offered here: Adeline Rucquoi, *Valladolid en la Edad Media*, 2 vols (Valladolid, 1987), M. Asenjo González, *Segovia. La ciudad y su tierra a fines del medioevo* (Segovia, 1986) A. Collantes de Terán, *Sevilla en al Baja Edad Media. La ciudad y sus hombres* (Seville, 1977) and John Edwards, *Christian Córdoba. The city and its region in the late Middle Ages* (Cambridge, 1982). In addition to the general works mentioned above, the political life of the crown of Aragon receives attention in J. Arrieta Alberdi, *El consejo supremo de la Corona de Aragón (1494–1707)* (Zaragoza, 1995), J. A. Sesma Muñoz, *La Diputación del reino de Aragón (1479–1516)* (Zaragoza, 1978) and J. Vicens Vives, *Política del Rey Católico en Cataluña* (Barcelona, 1940). Relations between the Crown and the major cities are treated in J. Vicens Vives, *Ferran II í la ciutat de Barcelona*, 3 vols (Barcelona, 1936–9) and Ernest Belenguer Cebriá, *Valencia en la crisi del segle XV* (Barcelona, 1976).

Economy and Society

In addition to the works cited in the previous sections, especially studies of individual towns, in recent years there has been a huge expansion in research and publication on social and economic subjects in Ferdinand and Isabella's Spain. Other useful works on Spanish towns in this period include I. Falcón Pérez, *Zaragoza en el siglo XV* (Zaragoza, 1981), J. J. Vidal, *Mallorca en tiempos del descubrimiento de América* (Majorca, 1991), H. Casado Alonso, *Señores, mercaderes y campesinos. La comarca de Burgos a fines de la Edad Media* (Valladolid, 1987), and L. R. Villegas Díaz, *Ciudad Real en la Edad Media. La ciudad y sus hombres (1200–1500)* (Ciudad Real, 1981). Valuable regional studies include, on the Basque provinces, J. A. García de Cortázar, *Vizcaya en el siglo xv: aspectos económicos* (Bilbao, 1966) and on Galicia, J. Garcia Oro, *Galicia en los siglos XIV y XV*, 2 vols (Pontevedra, 1987) and Carlos Barros, *A mentalidade xusticieira dos irmandiños* (Vigo, 1988). Equally, if not even more, immense is the output of publication on rural society. A useful overview is provided by J. A. García de Cortázar in *La sociedad rural en la España medieval* (Madrid, 1988), while David Vassberg, *Land and society in Golden Age Castile* (Cambridge, 1986), has relevant material for this period. Royal, seigneurial and ecclesiastical archives have been exploited in numerous studies of the use of the land in the realms of Isabella and Ferdinand. Examples include, for Castile, Juan Antonio Bonachia, *El señorío de Burgos durante la Baja Edad Media (1255–1508)* (Valladolid, 1988), Francisco Ruiz Gómez, *Las aldeas castellanas en la Edad Media. Oña en los siglos XIV y XV* (Madrid, 1990), and Máximo Diago Hernando, *Soria en la Baja Edad Media. Espacio rural y economía* (Madrid, 1993). Among the studies of Andalusian agriculture, the following are particularly useful: Isabel Montes Romero-Camacho, *El paisaje rural sevillano en la Baja Edad Media* (Seville, 1989) and *Propiedad y explotación de la tierra en la Sevilla de la Baja Edad Media* (Seville, 1988), Miguel Angel Ladero Quesada and Manuel González Jiménez, *Diezmo eclesiástico y producción de cereales en el reino de Sevilla, 1408–1503* (Seville, 1978), José Rodríguez Molina, *El reino de Jaén en la Baja Edad Media. Aspectos demográficos y económicos* (Granada, 1978) and Bartolomé Yun Casalilla, *Crisis de subsistencias y conflictividad social en Córdoba a principios del siglo XVI* (Córdoba, 1980). A fine study of a lordship on the northern fringe of Andalusia is Emilio Cabrera Muñoz, *El condado de Belalcázar (1444–1518)* (Córdoba,

1977). Works on Catalan rural history include Jaime Vicens Vives, *Historia de los remensas en el siglo XV* (Barcelona, 1945, 1978) and M. Golobardes Vila, *Els remences, dins el quadre de la pagesia catalana fins el segle XV*, 2 vols (Girona, 1970–3). Perhaps not surprisingly, considerable attention has been paid to stock breeding in general and sheep and the Mesta in particular. Recent studies include Marie-Claude Gerbet, *L'élevage dans le royaume de Castille sous les Rois Catholiques (1454–1516)* (Madrid, 1999), *Mesta, transhumancia y vida pastoril*, ed. G. Anes and A. Garcia Sanz (Madrid, 1994), J. C. Fernández Otal, *La Casa de Ganaderos de Zaragoza. Derecho y trashumancia a fines del siglo XV* (Zaragoza, 1993) and C. R. Phillips and W. D. Phillips, *Spain's golden fleece. Wool production and the wool trade from the Middle Ages to the nineteenth century* (Baltimore, 1997). The pioneering monograph on the textile industry in the Spain of the Catholic Monarchs is Paulino Iradiel, *Evolución de la industria textil castellana en los siglos XII-XV* (Salamanca, 1974), which concentrates mainly on Cuenca. The Valencian silk industry is studied by G. Navarro in *El despegue de la industria sedera en la Valencia del siglo XV* (Valencia, 1992). The wide range of industries and crafts in a medium-sized town is surveyed by Ricardo Córdoba de la Llave in *La industria medieval de Córdoba* (Córdoba, 1990). Perhaps even more attention has been given to trade and commerce in Ferdinand and Isabella's Spain. In Castile, trade fairs have been surveyed by Miguel Angel Ladero Quesada in *Las ferias de Castilla. Siglos XII a XV* (Madrid, 1994), while that kingdom's international trade is studied in its English aspect by Wendy R. Childs in *Anglo-Castilian trade in the later Middle Ages* (Manchester, 1978), and more generally in *Castilla y Europa. Comercio y mercaderes en los siglos XIV, XV y XVI*, ed. H. Casado Alonso (Burgos, 1995). The crucial mercantile role of Seville is the subject of studies by Enrique Otte in *Sevilla y sus mercaderes a fines de la Edad Media* (Seville, 1996), while the trade of Valencia is comprehensively surveyed in Jacqueline Guiral-Hadziiossif, *Valence. Port méditerranéen (1410–1525)* (Paris, 1986).

Given their social importance, and the consequent existence of ample documentation, it is natural that historians have paid great attention to the nobles and knights of Ferdinand and Isabella's Spain. The best recent survey is Marie-Claude Gerbet's *Les noblesses espagnoles au Moyen Age, XIe-XVe siècle* (Paris, 1994), which follows from her detailed study of the Extremaduran nobility in *La noblesse dans le royaume de Castille. Étude sur ses structures sociales en Estrémadure (1454–1516)* (Paris, 1979). The issues of lineage and political affiliation among the Castilian nobility are examined in I. Beceiro Pita and Ricardo Córdoba de la Llave, *Parentesco, poder y mentalidad. La nobleza castellana, siglos XIII-XV* (Madrid, 1990). Other useful studies by A. Franco Silva are *La fortuna y el poder. Estudios sobre las bases económicas de la aristocracia castellana (siglos XIV y XV)* (Cádiz, 1996) and *Señores y señoríos (siglos XIV-XVI)* (Jaén, 1997). As in the cases of urban and rural history, regional studies of the nobility have proliferated. They include Miguel Angel Ladero Quesada, *Los señores de Andalucía. Investigaciones sobre nobles y señores en los siglos XIII a XV* (Cádiz, 1998) and R. Sánchez Saus, *Caballería y linaje en la Sevilla medieval* (Seville, 1989). An important basis of noble power was the possession and building of castles. The standard reference work for Castile is Edward Cooper, *Castillos Señoriales en la Corona de Castilla*, 4 vols (Salamanca, 1991), but also of great value is Manuel Rojas Gabriel, *La frontera entre los reinos de Sevilla y Granada en el siglo XV (1390–1481)* (Cádiz, 1995). Other aspects of Spanish society in this period which have received special attention are poverty, in C. López Alonso, *La pobreza en la España medieval* (Madrid, 1986) and crime, in I. Bazán Díaz, *Delincuencia y criminalidad en el País Vasco en la transición de la Edad Medieval a la Moderna* (Vitoria, 1995). Slavery in different parts of the peninsula is studied in V. Cortés Alonso, *La esclavitud en Valencia durante el reinado de los Reyes Católicos* (Valencia, 1964) and A. Franco Silva, *La esclavitud en Andalucía (1450–1550)* (Granada, 1992).

Religion and the Inquisition

The Christian Church in Castile receives a thorough treatment in Azcona's *Isabel la Católica* (see 'General' section), but the best work of reference is now the multi-author *Historia de la Iglesia en España*, ed. José Luis González Novalín, vol. 3, parts 1 and 2, *La Iglesia en la España de los siglos XV y XVI* (Madrid, 1979–80). Important background to the institution and thought of Isabella and Ferdinand's Church is provided in J. M. Nieto Soria, *Iglesia y génesis del estado moderno en Castilla (1369–1480)* (Madrid, 1994). In addition to essays by these respective authors in *Historia de la Iglesia*, vol. 3, part 1, the subject of church reform is comprehensively discussed in Tarsicio de Azcona, *La elección y reforma del episcopado español en tiempo de los Reyes Católicos* (Madrid, 1960) and J. García Oro, *Cisneros y la reforma del clero español en tiempo de los Reyes Católicos* (Madrid, 1971). A good, learned survey of the life of Cardinal Cisneros is Erika Rummel, *Jiménez de Cisneros: on the threshold of Spain's Golden Age* (Tempe, AZ, 1999), though a much fuller biography is J. García Oro's *El Cardenal Cisneros. Vida y empresas*, 2 vols (Madrid, 1992–3). Examples of studies of reform in individual religious orders are the well-established work on the Dominicans by V. Beltrán de Heredia, *Historia de la reforma de la provincia de España (1450–1550)* (Rome, 1939), and on the Augustinians, I. Alvarez Gutierrez, *El movimiento 'observante' augustiniano en España y su culminación en tiempo de los Reyes Católicos* (Madrid, 1978).

The best general history of the Spanish Jewish community is Yitzhak Baer's *A history of the Jews in Christian Spain*, 2 vols, reissued with a useful introduction by Benjamin R. Gampel (Philadelphia and Jerusalem, 1992). Two valuable works by Luis Suárez Fernández are his general survey *Judíos españoles en la Edad Media* (Madrid, 1980) and *La expulsión de los judíos de España* (Madrid, 1991). Useful essays on Jewish life in Spain and the expulsion are to be found in *Spain and the Jews. The Sephardi experience 1492, and after*, ed. Elie Kedourie (London, 1992) and *Moreshet Sepharad: the Sephardi legacy*, ed. Haim Beinart, 2 vols (Jerusalem, 1992). A fine study of the Aragonese situation is J. A. Motís Dolader's *La expulsión de los judíos del reino de Aragón*, 2 vols (Zaragoza, 1990). Benjamin R. Gampel surveys effectively the Navarrese Jewish community in *The last Jews on Iberian soil. Navarrese Jewry, 1479–1498* (Berkeley, Los Angeles, Oxford, 1989), while the best study of Portuguese Jewry in this period is M. J. Pimenta Ferro, *Os judeus em Portugal no século XV*, 2 vols (Lisbon, 1982–4).

The basis for the study in English of the Spanish Inquisition is still Henry Charles Lea's *A history of the Inquisition of Spain*, 4 vols (New York, 1906–7). Other venerable and useful studies of the Inquisition and the *conversos* are Cecil Roth's *The Spanish Inquisition* (New York, London, 1937, 1996) and *A history of the Marranos* (New York, 1932, 1974). More recent general accounts are Henry Kamen, *The Spanish Inquisition. An historical revision* (London, 1997) and John Edwards, *The Spanish Inquisition* (Stroud, 1999). Some local inquisitorial tribunals, for which records survive, have benefited from systematic study. Notable examples are those of Toledo, in Jean-Pierre Dedieu, *L'administration de la Foi. L'Inquisition de Tolède (XVIe–XVIIIe siècle)* (Madrid, 1989) and Valencia, in Stephen Haliczer, *Inquisition and society in the kingdom of Valencia, 1478–1834* (Berkeley, Los Angeles, Oxford, 1990). Also of value on Valencia is R. García Carcel, *Orígenes de la Inquisición española. El tribunal de Valencia, 1478–1530* (Barcelona, 1985). The vexed question of the religious identity of the *conversos* from Judaism has inspired an enormous and growing corpus of literature, including the works concerning the Inquisition which have already been noted. Antonio Domínguez Ortiz provides a valuable guide in *Los judeoconversos en la España moderna* (Madrid, 1992), as do the useful essays by Eloy Benito Ruano in *Los orígenes del problema converso* (Barcelona, 1976). Specific studies of *converso* life, mainly based on inquisitorial evidence, include Haim Beinart, *Conversos on trial. The Inquisition in Ciudad Real* (Jerusalem, 1981) and *Trujillo. A converso community in Extremadura on the eve of the expulsion from Spain* (Jerusalem, 1980). Further evidence, from Andalusia, is provided by Luis Coronas Tejada, in *Conversos and Inquisition in Jaén* (Jerusalem, 1988) and *La Inquisición en Jaén* (Jaén, 1991). Combative works, which challenge common assumptions about the 'Jewishness' of Spanish *conversos* in this period, are Benzion Netanyahu, *The origins of the Inquisition in fifteenth-century Spain* (New York, 1995) and Norman Roth, *Conversos, Inquisition, and the expulsion of the Jews from Spain* (Madison, Wisconsin, 1995). The best study of 'purity of blood' (*limpieza de sangre*) statutes is still Albert A. Sicroff, *Los estatutos de limpieza de sangre. Controversias entre los siglos XV y XVII* (Madrid, 1985).

The outstanding survey of Muslims in Spain, and particularly the kingdom of Granada, up to 1500 is L. P. Harvey, *Islamic Spain, 1250–1500* (Chicago, 1990). On *mudéjares*, that is, Muslims in established Christian kingdoms, some of the best studies are Miguel Angel Ladero Quesada, *Los mudéjares de Castilla y otros estudios de historia medieval* (Granada, 1989) and M. L. Ledesma Rubio, *Estudios sobre los mudéjares en Aragón* (Teruel, 1996). The most comprehensive, however, is Mark D. Meyerson, *The Muslims of Valencia in the age of Fernando and Isabel. Between co-existence and Crusade* (Berkeley, Los Angeles, Oxford, 1991). The best examination of the Castilian effort in the war to conquer Granada is Miguel Angel Ladero Quesada's *Castilla y la conquista del reino de Granada* (Granada, 1987). Post-1492 Granada is examined in the same author's *Granada después de la conquista. Repobladores y mudéjares* (Granada, 1988).

Spain in Europe and America: Foreign Policy

Spain's relations with other peninsular and European states, as well as the country's first contacts with the Americas, are considered in a number of the works included above in the 'General' section. The documentary basis for the study of Ferdinand and Isabella's foreign policy is A. de la Torre y del Cerro's monumental collection, *Documentos sobre las relaciones internacionales de los Reyes Católicos*, 6 vols (Barcelona, 1949–66), based mainly on Aragonese sources, while Luis Suárez Fernández's collection, *Política internacional de Isabel la Católica*, 5 vols (Valladolid, 1965–72), contains Castilian material. Documentation for relations between Castile and Portugal may be found in A. de la Torre and Luis Suárez Fernández, *Documentos sobre las relaciones con Portugal durante el reinado de los Reyes Católicos*, 3 vols (Valladolid, 1956). Ferdinand's foreign policy is considered in a series of works by J. M. Doussinague, *La política internacional de Fernando el Católico* (Madrid, 1944), *Fernando el Católico y Germana de Foix. Un matrimonio por razón de Estado* (Madrid, 1944), and *El testamento político de Fernando el Católico* (Madrid, 1950). Spain's Mediterranean policy receives a lively overview in David Abulafia's *The Western Mediterranean kingdoms, 1200–1500. The struggle for dominion* (London, 1997). The Catholic Monarchs' relations with Navarre are well surveyed by Luis Suárez Fernández in *Fernando el Católico y Navarra. El proceso de incorporación del reino a la Corona de España* (Madrid, 1985). On Spain's politics and warfare in Italy, apart from sections of works in the 'General' section and the documentary collections noted above, useful material is to be found in Frederic J. Baumgartner, *Louis XII* (Basingstoke and London, 1996) and Christine Shaw, *Julius II. The warrior pope* (Oxford, 1993). On Princess Catherine in England, Garrett Mattingly's scholarly and lively biography, *Catherine of Aragon* (London, 1942), still holds the field.

The earlier phases of western European exploration in the Atlantic are surveyed by Felipe Fernández-Armesto in *Before Columbus: Exploration and colonisation from the Mediterranean to the Atlantic, 1229–1492* (London, 1987). The Castilian establishment in the Canary Islands is analysed by E. Aznar Vallejo in *La integración de las Islas Canarias (1478–1526)* (Las Palmas, 1992) Fernández-Armesto also offers a reliable biography of *Columbus* (Oxford, 1991), while the religious side of the 'discoverer' and his mission is discussed with more sympathy by Valerie I. J. Flint, in *The imaginative landscape of Christopher Columbus* (Princeton, 1992). The relevant documents are excellently edited by Consuelo Varela in *Cristóbal Colón, Textos y documentos completos* (Madrid, 1984), and by Juan Gil and the same editor in *Cartas de particulares a Colón y relaciones coetáneas* (Madrid, 1984). A valuable reference work is *The Cambridge History of Latin America*, ed. Leslie Bethell, vol. 1 (Cambridge, 1984).

Cultural Life

Useful surveys in English of cultural developments in Ferdinand and Isabella's Spain are to be found in essays by P. E. Russell, 'Spanish literature (1474–1681)', in *Spain. A companion to Spanish studies*, ed. P. E. Russell (London, 1973), pp. 265–90 and, more specifically on the period in question, J. N. L. Lawrance, 'Humanism in the Iberian peninsula', in *The impact of humanism on Western Europe*, ed. Anthony Goodman and Angus MacKay (London, 1990), pp. 220–58. A short introduction to the literature of the period may be found in A. D.

Deyermond, *A literary history of Spain: the Middle Ages* (London, 1971). Of much greater scope than its focus on one family may suggest is Helen Nader's *The Mendoza family in the Spanish Renaissance, 1350–1550.* Useful collections of essays on the literature of the period are to be found in *The age of the Catholic Monarchs, 1474–1516,* ed. Alan Deyermond and Ian Macpherson (Liverpool, 1989), while literature and social history are well combined in Ian Macpherson and Angus MacKay, *Love, religion and politics in fifteenth-century Spain* (Leiden, 1998). Among the most notable literary texts of the period, excellent editions are available of Diego de San Pedro's *Cárcel de amor* by Keith Whinnom (Madrid, 1971), and of Fernando de Rojas's *Comedia o tragicomedia de Calisto y Melibea (La Celestina),* by Peter E. Russell (Madrid, 1991). Other general works on Spanish humanism include O. di Camillo, *El humanismo castellano del siglo XV* (Valencia, 1976) and A. Gómez Moreno, *España y la Italia de los humanistas. Primeros ecos* (Madrid, 1994). The established history of the Spanish universities in this period is C. M. Ajo y Sainz de Zúñiga, *Historia de las universidades hispánicas,* vol. 1 (Madrid, 1957), while a more recent study of Cisneros's new university is A. Alvar Ezquerra, *La universidad de Alcalá de Henares a principios del siglo XVI* (Alcalá de Henares, 1996). As in his own day, the grammarian Nebrija continues to attract scholarly attention, notably in a fine collection of papers edited by Víctor García de la Concha, *Nebrija y la introducción del Renacimiento en España* (Salamanca, 1983, 1996). On the Renaissance in Catalonia and Valencia, see M. Peña, *Cataluña en el Renacimiento: libros y lenguas* (Lleida, 1996) and P. Berger, *Libro y lectura en la Valencia del Renacimiento (1473–1560)* (Valencia, 1986). Books and the visual arts are considered from the royal point of view in F. J. Sánchez Cantón, *Libros, tapices y cuadros que coleccionó Isabel la Católica* (Madrid, 1950). The artistic scene in the period is surveyed by J. Yarza Luaces in *Los Reyes Católicos. Paisaje artístico de una monarquía* (Madrid, 1994). The Flemish influence is thoroughly examined by E. Bermejo in *La pintura de los primitivos flamencos en España,* 2 vols (Madrid, 1980–2), while the work of one particular painter is studied and presented by Ignace Vandervivere in *Juan de Flandés* (Bruges, 1985). The art of altarpieces, of which so many were constructed in this period throughout Spain, is examined by Judith Berg Sobré, in *Behind the altar table. The development of the painted retable in Spain, 1350–1500* (Columbia, MO, 1989). A good impression of the arts and crafts of a major Andalusian town is given in M. Nieto Cumplido and F. Moreno Cuadro, *Córdoba 1492. Ambiente artístico y cultural* (Córdoba, 1992). The established work on the music at the court of Ferdinand and Isabella is H. Anglés, *La música en la Corte de los Reyes Católicos*

(Barcelona, 1940), but a new interpretation is being developed by Tess Knighton. An example of her approach is to be found in 'Northern influence on cultural developments in the Iberian peninsula during the fifteenth century', *Renaissance Studies*, vol. 1 (1987), pp. 221–37. Juan del Encina's poems, songs and music are edited by R. O. Jones and Carolyn R. Lee in his *Poesía lírica y cancionero musical* (Madrid, 1975).

The End of the Reign, 1504–1516

Apart from the relevant works in the 'General' section, there are specific studies of various aspects of the turbulent political history of Spain in the period between Isabella's death and Ferdinand's. There is a useful recent study of Isabella's eldest daughter, and her successor as queen of Castile, Princess Joanna, by Manuel Fernández Alvarez, *Juana la Loca (1479–1555)* (Palencia, 1994), while R. Pérez-Bustamante and J. M. Calderón Ortega examine the brief rule of her Habsburg husband in *Felipe I. 1506* (Palencia, 1995). Cardinal Cisneros's periods as regent of Castile are discussed in works cited in previous sections. In addition, and in preparation for the rebellions in Castile and Valencia which greeted the arrival of Charles on the thrones of Castile and Aragon, Joseph Perez offers a series of works: *La hora de Cisneros* (Madrid, 1995), *La révolution des 'Comunidades' de Castille (1520–1521)* (Bordeaux, 1970) and 'Les "Comunidades" de Castille: nouvel examen de la question', in *Les sociétés urbaines en France méridionale et en péninsule ibérique au Moyen Age* (Paris, 1991), pp. 143–57. Also of value is J. I. Gutiérrez Nieto, *La Comunidades como movimiento antiseñorial* (Barcelona, 1973). The best recent works on the Valencian 'Germanías' are R. García Cárcel, *Las Germanías de Valencia* (Barcelona, 1975) and E. Duran, *Les germanies als països catalans* (Barcelona, 1982).

Index